MAGILL INDEX
TO
MASTERPLOTS

MAGILL INDEX
TO
MASTERPLOTS

Cumulative Indexes

1963–1990

SALEM PRESS
Pasadena, California   Englewood Cliffs, New Jersey

Library of Congress Cataloging-in-Publication Data
Magill index to masterplots.
     p. cm.
   Includes indexes.
   ISBN 0-89356-592-X
   1. Literature—Stories, plots, etc.—Indexes.   2.
Authors—
Biography—Indexes. I. Magill, Frank Northen, 1907-
   . II Title: Index to masterplots. III Title: Magill
index to masterplots.
Z6511.M253 1990
[PN44]   90-9155
016.809—dc20   CIP

PUBLISHER'S NOTE

This index to the Masterplots publications combines and collates the indexes from the multivolume reference sets in this family of publications about books, plays, poems, and stories. The twelve-volume revised edition combines the contents of all editions published prior to 1976 and replaces those earlier editions. The Revised Category Editions (American, British, and European Fiction) compile in individual three-volume sets the appropriate titles selected from the twelve-volume Masterplots. Cyclopedia of World Authors and Cyclopedia of Literary Characters provide author biographies and character descriptions for the works included in the twelve-volume Revised Edition, completing the first generation of the Masterplots family.

The second generation of Masterplots publications have been published under the series name Masterplots II. They include American Fiction Series, British and Commonwealth Fiction Series, Drama Series, Nonfiction Series, Short Story Series, and World Fiction Series, adding Masterplots treatment for many additional works of literature. In the Masterplots tradition, Cyclopedia of World Authors II and Cyclopedia of Literary Characters II supplement the Masterplots II titles by providing author biographies and character descriptions for the works included in the six series.

Hence, the current index offers, in one location, a guide to discussions of books, plays, stories, poems, authors, and characters appearing in the sixty volumes of the Masterplots publications.

Entries are followed by a code indicating the series in which the discussion appears, which in turn is followed by the page or pages locating the discussion:

CLC	Cyclopedia of Literary Characters
CLCII	Cyclopedia of Literary Characters II
CWA	Cyclopedia of World Authors
CWAII	Cyclopedia of World Authors II
MP	Masterplots, revised edition
MP:AF	Masterplots, Revised Category Edition: American Fiction Series
MP:BF	Masterplots, Revised Category Edition: British Fiction Series
MP:EF	Masterplots, Revised Category Edition: European Fiction Series
MPII:AF	Masterplots II: American Fiction Series
MPII:BCF	Masterplots II: British and Commonwealth Fiction Series
MPII:D	Masterplots II: Drama Series
MPII:NF	Masterplots II: Nonfiction Series
MPII:SS	Masterplots II: Short Story Series
MPII:WP	Masterplots II: World Fiction Series

Alphabetization is by word rather than letter, and transposed elements are disregarded; hence, "Circle, The" precedes "Circle of Chalk." Hyphenated compounds are treated as two separate words if the two elements could stand

independently (as in "fifty-five") but are treated as one word if one of the elements could not stand alone (as in "non-being"). Numerals are alphabetized as though they were spelled out ("*1919*" under "nineteen-nineteen"), as are common abbreviations: "Mr." as "mister"; "Mrs." as "mistress"; "St." as "saint"; "Dr." as "doctor." The *Mc* particle in names such as McPherson is alphabetized as though it were spelled *Mac*.

There are two prominent exceptions to the alpha-by-word rule: First, surnames composed of more than one element are alphabetized as though one word; hence, "Le Carré, John" is preceded by "Leavitt, David." Second, series of enumerated titles by the same author (such as the plays *Henry IV, Part I, Henry IV, Part II*, and *Henry V*, all by William Shakespeare) appear in numerical order rather than alphabetical order, for the sake of logical consistency.

Titles of books, plays, stories, essays, and poems are followed, in parentheses, by the author's surname; in an index of this size and scope, the editors found that further identification, by means of a first initial or a first name, was sometimes necessary to avoid confusion with another author.

Code System

CLC   *Cyclopedia of Literary Characters.* 4 vols.   Salem Press, Englewood Cliffs, N.J. 1963.

CWA   *Cyclopedia of World Authors.* 3 vols. Salem Press, Englewood Cliffs, N.J. 1974.

MP   *Masterplots, revised edition.* 12 vols. Salem Press, Englewood Cliffs, N.J. 1976.

MP:AF   *Masterplots, Revised Category Edition: American Fiction Series.* 3 vols. Salem Press, Englewood Cliffs, N.J. 1985.

MP:BF   *Masterplots, Revised Category Edition: British Fiction Series.* 3 vols. Salem Press, Englewood Cliffs, N.J. 1985.

MP:EF   *Masterplots, Revised Category Edition: European Fiction Series.* 3 vols. Salem Press, Englewood Cliffs, N.J. 1985.

MPII:AF   *Masterplots II: American Fiction Series.* 4 vols.   Salem Press, Englewood Cliffs, N.J. 1986.

MPII:SS   *Masterplots II: Short Story Series.* 6 vols.   Salem Press, Englewood Cliffs, N.J. 1986.

MPII:BCF   *Masterplots II: British and Commonwealth Fiction Series.* 4 vols. Salem Press, Englewood Cliffs, N.J., and Pasadena, Calif. 1987.

MPII:WF   *Masterplots II: World Fiction Series.* 4 vols.   Salem Press, Englewood Cliffs, N.J., and Pasadena, Calif. 1987.

CWAII   *Cyclopedia of World Authors II.* 4 vols.   Salem Press, Englewood Cliffs, N.J., and Pasadena, Calif. 1989.

MPII:NF   *Masterplots II: Nonfiction Series.* 4 vols.   Salem Press, Englewood Cliffs, N.J., and Pasadena, Calif. 1989.

CLCII   *Cyclopedia of Literary Characters II.* 2 vols.   Salem Press, Englewood Cliffs, N.J., and Pasadena, Calif. 1990.

MPII:D   *Masterplots II: Drama Series.* 4 vols. Salem Press, Englewood Cliffs, N.J., and Pasadena, Calif. 1990.

TITLE INDEX

A

"A & P" (Updike) MPII:SS I-1

A ciascuno il suo. *See* Man's Blessing, A

À combien l'amour revient aux vieillards. *See* Splendors and Miseries of Courtesans, The

A maçã no escuro. *See* Apple in the Dark, The

"A menor mulher do mundo." *See* "Smallest Woman in the World, The"

"A terceira margem do rio." *See* "Third Bank of the River, The"

Aaron's Rod (Lawrence) CLCII I-1; MPII:BCF I-1

Abbé Constantin, The (Halévy) CLC I-1; MP I-1; MP:EF I-1

Abbess of Crewe, The (Spark) CLCII I-1; MPII:BCF I-6

ABC of Reading (Pound) MPII:NF I-1

Abe Lincoln in Illinois (Sherwood) CLC I-1; MP I-4

Abel Sánchez (Unamuno) CLCII I-3; MPII:WF I-1

"Abenteuer der Sylvester Nacht, Die." *See* "New Year's Eve Adventure, A"

Abraham and Isaac (Unknown) CLC I-2; MP I-8

Abraham Lincoln (Sandburg) MP I-11

Absalom, Absalom! (Faulkner) CLC I-3; MP I-14; MP:AF I-1

Absalom and Achitophel (Dryden) CLC I-4; MP I-19

Absentee, The (Edgeworth) CLC I-5; MP I-21; MP:BF I-1

"Absolution" (Fitzgerald) MPII:SS I-5

Absurd Person Singular (Ayckbourn) CLCII I-4; MPII:D I-1

Abyss, The (Yourcenar) CLCII I-5; MPII:WF I-6

Acceptance World, The. *See* Dance to the Music of Time, A

Accident, The (Wiesel) CLCII I-7; MPII:WF I-12

Accidental Death of an Anarchist (Fo) CLCII I-8; MPII:D I-6

"Ace in the Hole" (Updike) MPII:SS I-9

Acharnians, The (Aristophanes) CLC I-6; MP I-26

Acolyte, The (Astley) CLCII I-9; MPII:BCF I-12

Acoso, El. *See* Manhunt

Acquainted with Grief (Gadda) CLCII I-10; MPII:WF I-16

Across (Handke) CLCII I-11; MPII:WF I-20

Across the River and into the Trees (Hemingway) CLCII I-11; MPII:AF I-1

Ada or Ardor (Nabokov) CLCII I-12; MPII:AF I-6

Adam Bede (Eliot, G.) CLC I-7; MP I-29; MP:BF I-7

Adding Machine, The (Rice) CLCII I-14; MPII:D I-11

Addresses (Lincoln) MP I-32

Admirable Crichton, The (Barrie) CLC I-9; MP I-35

"Admiral and the Nuns, The" (Tuohy) MPII:SS I-12

"Admirer, The" (Singer) MPII:SS I-16

Adolphe (Constant) CLC I-10; MP I-39; MP:EF I-5

"Adulterous Woman, The" (Camus) MPII:SS I-19

"Adventure of the Dancing Men, The" (Doyle) MPII:SS I-23

"Adventure of the German Student" (Irving) MPII:SS I-27

"Adventure of the Speckled Band, The" (Doyle) MPII:SS I-31

Adventures of Augie March, The (Bellow) MP I-43; MP:AF I-7

Adventures of Gil Blas of Santillane. *See* Gil Blas

Adventures of Hajji Baba of Ispahan, The. *See* Hajji Baba of Ispahan

Adventures of Huckleberry Finn, The (Twain) CLC I-495; MP V-2755; MP:AF I-11

Adventures of Roderick Random, The. *See* Roderick Random

1

Adventures of Simplicissimus, The. *See* Simplicissimus the Vagabond

Adventures of Tom Sawyer, The (Twain) CLC II-1145; MP XI-6604; MP:AF I-17

Aeneid, The (Vergil) CLC I-11; MP I-46

Aerodrome, The (Warner) CLCII I-16; MPII:BCF I-16

"Aeroplanes at Brescia, The" (Davenport) MPII:SS I-34

Aesop's Fables (Aesop) MP I-51; MP:EF I-10

Aesthetic (Croce) MP I-53

Af Borgslaegtens Historie. *See* Guest the One-Eyed

Affair, The (Snow) MP I-56; MP:BF I-11. *See also* Strangers and Brothers

After Babel (Steiner) MPII:NF I-7

After Many a Summer Dies the Swan (Huxley) CLCII I-17; MPII:BCF I-22

"After Saturday Nite Comes Sunday" (Sanchez) MPII:SS I-38

After Strange Gods (Eliot, T. S.) MP I-60

After the Banquet (Mishima) CLCII I-19; MPII:WF I-24

"After the Fair" (Thomas) MPII:SS I-43

After the Fall (Miller, A.) CLCII I-20; MPII:D I-17

"After the Storm" (Hemingway) MPII:SS I-46

After Virtue (MacIntyre) MPII:NF I-12

Afternoon Men (Powell) CLCII I-21; MPII:BCF I-27

Against Interpretation and Other Essays (Sontag) MPII:NF I-19

Against the Grain (Huysmans) CLC I-13; MP I-62; MP:EF I-13

Âge de raison, L'. *See* Roads to Freedom, The

Age of Innocence, The (Wharton) CLC I-14; MP I-65; MP:AF I-23

Age of Reason, The (Paine) MP I-70

Age of Reason, The (Sartre). *See* Roads to Freedom, The

Age of Wonders, The (Appelfeld) CLCII I-22; MPII:WF I-29

Agents and Patients (Powell) CLCII I-23; MPII:BCF I-32

Agneau, L'. *See* Lamb, The

Agnes Grey (Brontë, A.) CLC I-15; MP I-73; MP:BF I-16

Agony and the Ecstasy, The (Stone, I.) CLCII I-24; MPII:AF I-12

Aguila y la serpiente, El. *See* Eagle and the Serpent, The

Ah Q cheng-chuan. *See* True Story of Ah Q, The

Ahasverus död. *See* Tobias Trilogy, The

"Ahogado más hermoso del mundo." *See* "Handsomest Drowned Man in the World, The"

Aiglon, L' (Rostand) CLC I-590; MP VI-3222

Ajax (Sophocles) CLC I-16; MP I-77

Akatsuki no tera. *See* Sea of Fertility, The

Aké (Soyinka) MPII:NF I-24

Al filo del agua (Yáñez) CLC I-17; MP I-81

Albany Cycle, The (Kennedy) MPII:AF I-18

"Albatross, The" (Hill) MPII:SS I-49

Alcestis (Euripides) CLC I-18; MP I-84

Alchemist, The (Jonson) CLC I-19; MP I-88

Aleck Maury, Sportsman (Gordon) CLC I-20; MP I-93; MP:AF I-28

"Aleph, The" (Borges) MPII:SS I-52

Alexanderplatz, Berlin. *See* Berlin Alexanderplatz

Alexandria Quartet, The (Durrell) MP I-96; MP:BF I-20

Alice Adams (Tarkington) CLC I-21; MP I-104; MP:AF I-32

Alice's Adventures in Wonderland (Carroll) CLC I-22; MP I-107; MP:BF I-30

"Alien Corn, The" (Maugham) MPII:SS I-56

"Alienista, O." *See* "Psychiatrist, The"

All Creatures Great and Small (Herriot) MPII:NF I-29

All Fall Down (Herlihy) MP I-112; MP:AF I-35

All Fools (Chapman) CLC I-24; MP I-114

All for Love (Dryden) CLC I-24; MP I-117

All God's Children Need Traveling Shoes (Angelou) MPII:NF I-34

All God's Chillun Got Wings (O'Neill) CLCII I-26; MPII:D I-22

All Green Shall Perish (Mallea) CLCII I-26; MPII:AF I-25

All Hallows' Eve (Williams, C.) MP I-122; MP:BF I-36

All Men Are Brothers (Shih Nai-an) CLC I-26; MP I-125; MP:EF I-17

All Men Are Enemies (Aldington) CLCII I-28; MPII:BCF I-37

All My Sons (Miller, A.) CLCII I-29; MPII:D I-27

All Our Yesterdays (Ginzburg) CLCII I-31; MPII:WF I-34

All Quiet on the Western Front (Remarque) CLC I-27; MP I-130; MP:EF I-23

All That Fall (Beckett) CLCII I-32; MPII:D I-33

All the King's Men (Warren) CLC I-28; MP I-133; MP:AF I-38

"All the Years of Her Life" (Callaghan) MPII:SS I-60

"All You Zombies--" (Heinlein) MPII:SS I-63

All's Well That Ends Well (Shakespeare) CLC I-29; MP I-143

Allegory of Love, The (Lewis, C. S.) MP I-138

Almanac for Moderns, An (Peattie) MP I-146

Almayer's Folly (Conrad) CLC I-30; MP I-149; MP:BF I-40

"Almos' a Man." See "Man Who Was Almost a Man, The"

"Alpine Idyll, An" (Hemingway) MPII:SS I-66

"Altar of the Dead, The" (James, H.) MPII:SS I-70

"Alyosha the Pot" (Tolstoy) MPII:SS I-74

Amadeus (Shaffer, P.) CLCII I-33; MPII:D I-37

Amadís de Gaul (Lobeira) CLCII I-31; MP I-152; MP:EF I-26

Amant, L'. See Lover, The

Ambassadors, The (James, H.) CLC I-32; MP I-156; MP:AF I-44

Ambiguous Adventure (Kane) CLCII I-34; MPII:WF I-39

"Ambitious Guest, The" (Hawthorne) MPII:SS I-78

Ambrosio. See Monk, The

Amelia (Fielding) CLC I-33; MP I-161; MP:BF I-44

"America! America!" (Schwartz) MPII:SS I-81

America Hurrah (van Itallie) CLCII I-36; MPII:D I-44

American, The (James, H.) CLC I-34; MP I-166; MP:AF I-49

American Buffalo (Mamet) CLCII I-37; MPII:D I-49

American Childhood, An (Dillard) MPII:NF I-39

American Commonwealth, The (Bryce) MP I-169

American Dream, The (Albee) CLCII I-39; MPII:D I-55

American Dream, An (Mailer) CLCII I-38; MPII:AF I-29

American Notebooks, The (Hawthorne) MP I-172

American Scene, The (James) MPII:NF I-44

American Tragedy, An (Dreiser) CLC I-35; MP I-175; MP:AF I-53

America's Coming-of-Age (Brooks) MP I-179

Amerika (Kafka) CLCII I-40; MPII:WF I-45

Amigo Manso, El. See Our Friend Manso

Among the Believers (Naipaul) MPII:NF I-50

"Among the Dangs" (Elliott) MPII:SS I-85

Among Women Only (Pavese) CLCII I-41; MPII:WF I-50

Amores (Ovid) MP I-183

Amorosa Fiammetta, L' (Boccaccio) CLC I-591; MP VI-3240; MP:EF II-746

Amortajada, La. See Shrouded Woman, The

Amphitryon (Plautus) CLC I-37; MP I-185

Amphitryon 38 (Giraudoux) CLC I-37; MP I-189

Anabasis (Perse) MP I-192

Anabasis, The (Xenophon) MP I-196

Anamnesis (Voegelin) MPII:NF I-56

Anatomy Lesson, The (Roth, P.) CLCII I-42. See also Zuckerman Bound

Anatomy of Criticism (Frye) MPII:NF I-61

Anatomy of Melancholy, The (Burton) MP I-200

And Quiet Flows the Don (Sholokhov) CLC I-38; MP I-202; MP:EF I-31

". . . and the earth did not part" (Rivera) MPII:SS I-89

Andersen's Fairy Tales (Andersen) MP:EF I-34; MP I-205

Andorra (Frisch) CLCII I-43; MPII:D I-60

Andria (Terence) CLC I-38; MP I-212

Andromache (Euripides) CLC I-40; MP I-216

Andromache (Racine) CLC I-41; MP I-219

Andromeda Strain, The (Crichton) CLCII I-44; MPII:AF I-34

Ángel Guerra (Pérez Galdós) CLC I-42; MP I-223; MP:EF I-43

"Angel Levine" (Malamud) MPII:SS I-92

"Angel of the Bridge, The" (Cheever) MPII:SS I-95

Ángel Pavement (Priestley) CLCII I-45; MPII:BCF I-43

Angels Fall (Wilson, L.) CLCII I-47; MPII:D I-66

Angle of Repose (Stegner) CLCII I-48; MPII:AF I-38

Anglo-Saxon Attitudes (Wilson, Angus) CLCII I-49; MPII:BCF I-48

Angst des Tormanns beim Elfmeter, Die. See Goalie's Anxiety at the Penalty Kick, The

Animal Farm (Orwell) CLCII I-51; MPII:BCF I-53

Anna Christie (O'Neill) CLC I-43; MP I-226

Anna Karénina (Tolstoy) CLC I-44; MP I-229; MP:EF I-47

Anna of the Five Towns (Bennett) CLC I-46; MP I-233; MP:BF I-50

Annals of Tacitus, The (Tacitus) MP I-236

Annals of the Parish (Galt) CLC I-47; MP I-240; MP:BF I-54

Annals of the Roman People (Livy) MP I-243

Anne of the Thousand Days (Anderson, M.) CLCII I-52; MPII:D I-71

Anniversaries (Johnson, U.) CLCII I-53; MPII:WF I-55

Annonce faite à Marie, L'. See Tidings Brought to Mary, The

Another Country (Baldwin) CLCII I-55; MPII:AF I-43

Another Life (Trifonov) CLCII I-57; MPII:WF I-60

Ansichten eines Clowns. See Clown, The

Anthony Adverse (Allen) CLC I-47; MP I-246; MP:AF I-58

Antigone (Anouilh) CLCII I-58; MPII:D I-77

Antigone (Sophocles) CLC I-48; MP I-250

Anti-Memoirs (Malraux) MPII:NF I-68

Antiquary, The (Scott, Sir W.) CLC I-49; MP I-254; MP:BF I-58

Antony and Cleopatra (Shakespeare) CLC I-50; MP I-258

Anxiety of Influence, The (Bloom, H.) MPII:NF I-75

Apalache (Metcalf) MPII:NF I-79

Apes of God, The (Lewis, W.) CLCII I-59; MPII:BCF I-58

Apocalypse (Lawrence) MPII:NF I-85

"Apocalypse at Solentiname" (Cortázar) MPII:SS I-99

4

Apologia pro Vita Sua (Newman) MP I-263

Apology for the Life of Colley Cibber, Comedian, An (Cibber) MP I-266

Apostle, The (Asch) CLC I-53; MP I-269; MP:AF I-62

Apple in the Dark, The (Lispector) CLCII I-62; MPII:AF I-48

Apple of the Eye, The (Wescott) CLC I-54; MP I-273; MP:AF I-66

Appointment in Samarra (O'Hara) CLC I-55; MP I-276; MP:AF I-70

Apprenticeship of Duddy Kravitz, The (Richler) CLCII I-63; MPII:BCF I-63

"April Witch, The" (Bradbury) MPII:SS I-103

"Aptekarsha." See "Chemist's Wife, The"

Arabian Nights' Entertainments, The (Unknown) CLC I-55; MP I-281; MP:EF I-52

"Araby" (Joyce) MPII:SS I-106

Arbitration, The (Menander) CLC I-56; MP I-288

Árbol de la ciencia, El. See Tree of Knowledge, The

Arcadia (Sidney) CLC I-57; MP I-293; MP:BF I-62

Architect and the Emperor of Assyria, The (Arrabal) CLCII I-65; MPII:D I-82

Architecte et l'Empereur d'Assyrie, L'. See Architect and the Emperor of Assyria, The

Arco y la lira, El. See Bow and the Lyre, The

Areopagitica (Milton) MP I-299

Argenis (Barclay) CLC I-59; MP I-302; MP:BF I-69

"Ark of Bones" (Dumas) MPII:SS I-110

"Arkhierey." See "Bishop, The"

Arkhipelag GULag, 1918-1956. See Gulag Archipelago, 1918-1956, The

Arme Heinrich, Der (Hartmann von Aue) CLC I-60; MP I-307

Armies of the Night, The (Mailer) CLCII I-65; MPII:AF I-51

Arms and the Man (Shaw, G.) CLCII I-67; MPII:D I-88

Arne (Björnson) CLC I-61; MP I-310; MP:EF I-61

Around the World in Eighty Days (Verne) CLCII I-68; MPII:WF I-66

Arrow of God (Achebe) CLCII I-69; MPII:BCF I-67

Arrowsmith (Lewis, S.) CLC I-61; MP I-313; MP:AF I-75

Ars amatoria (Ovid) MP I-317

Ars Poetica (Horace) MP I-319

Art and Illusion (Gombrich) MPII:NF I-90

"Art of Living, The" (Gardner) MPII:SS I-114

Artamène (Scudéry) CLC I-63; MP I-322; MP:EF I-64

Artamonov Business, The (Gorky) CLC I-64; MP I-326; MP:EF I-68

"Artificial Nigger, The" (O'Connor, Flannery) MPII:SS I-118

"Artist of the Beautiful, The" (Hawthorne) MPII:SS I-122

Arturo's Island (Morante) CLCII I-70; MPII:WF I-71

As a Man Grows Older (Svevo) CLCII I-71; MPII:WF I-75

As for Me and My House (Ross) CLCII I-72; MPII:BCF I-72

As I Lay Dying (Faulkner) CLC I-64; MP I-330; MP:AF I-80

As the Crow Flies (Clarke, Austin) CLCII I-74; MPII:D I-94

As You Like It (Shakespeare) CLC I-66; MP I-334

Ash Wednesday (Eliot, T. S.) MP I-339

Ashes (Żeromski) CLC I-67; MP I-341; MP:EF I-73

Ashes and Diamonds (Andrzejewski) CLCII I-75; MPII:WF I-80

Asiatics, The (Prokosch) CLCII I-76; MPII:AF I-56

Asmodeus. See Diable Boiteux, Le

"Aspern Papers, The" (James, H.) CLCII I-77; MPII:SS I-125

Assault on Mount Helicon (Barnard) MPII:NF I-97

Assistant, The (Malamud) CLCII I-78; MPII:AF I-61

Astillero, El. *See* Shipyard, The

"Astrologer's Day, An" (Narayan) MPII:SS I-129

Asya (Turgenev) CLCII I-80; MPII:WF I-85

At Lady Molly's. *See* Dance to the Music of Time, A, *and* Dance to the Music of Time: Second Movement, A

At Play in the Fields of the Lord (Matthiessen) CLCII I-81; MPII:AF I-65

At Swim-Two-Birds (O'Brien, F.) CLCII I-82; MPII:BCF I-77

"At the Bay" (Mansfield) MPII:SS I-132

"At the Bottom of the River" (Kincaid) MPII:SS I-135

At the Sign of the Reine Pédauque (France) CLC I-68; MP I-345; MP:EF I-77

Atala (Chateaubriand) CLC I-69; MP I-349; MP:EF I-81

Atalanta in Calydon (Swinburne) CLC I-69; MP I-353

Atem, Der. *See* Gathering Evidence

Aucassin and Nicolette (Unknown) CLC I-70; MP I-356; MP:EF I-85

Aufstieg und Fall der Stadt Mahagonny. *See* Rise and Fall of the City of Mahagonny

Augenspiel, Das. *See* Play of The Eyes, The

August 1914 (Solzhenitsyn) CLCII I-84; MPII:WF I-90

Aunt Dan and Lemon (Shawn) CLCII I-86; MPII:D I-99

Aunt Julia and the Scriptwriter (Vargas Llosa) CLCII I-87; MPII:AF I-71

Aunt's Story, The (White) CLCII I-88; MPII:BCF I-81

Aura (Fuentes) CLCII I-90; MPII:AF I-76

Australia Felix. *See* Fortunes of Richard Mahony, The

Auto-da-Fé (Canetti) CLCII I-91; MPII:WF I-95

Autobiographical Novel, An (Rexroth) MPII:NF I-104

Autobiographies. *See* Autobiography of William Butler Yeats, The

Autobiography (Chesterton) MPII:NF I-109

Autobiography, An (Trollope) MP I-359

Autobiography of an Ex-Coloured Man, The (Johnson, J.) CLCII I-92; MPII:AF I-81

Autobiography of Benjamin Franklin, The (Franklin) MP I-362

Autobiography of Benjamin Robert Haydon, The (Haydon) MP I-365

Autobiography of Benvenuto Cellini, The (Cellini) MP I-368

Autobiography of Leigh Hunt, The (Hunt) MP I-373

Autobiography of Lincoln Steffens, The (Steffens) MPII:NF I-115

Autobiography of Malcolm X, The (Malcolm X) MPII:NF I-121

Autobiography of Miss Jane Pittman, The (Gaines) CLCII I-93; MPII:AF I-87

Autobiography of William Butler Yeats, The (Yeats) MP I-376

Autobiography of William Carlos Williams, The (Williams) MPII:NF I-127

Autocrat of the Breakfast-Table, The (Holmes) MP I-379

"Autopista del sur, La." *See* "Southern Thruway, The"

Autumn of the Patriarch, The (García Márquez) CLCII I-95; MPII:AF I-92

Avalovara (Lins) CLCII I-97; MPII:AF I-97

Aventure ambiguë, L'. *See* Ambiguous Adventure

Avgust chetyrnadtsatogo. *See* August 1914

Awake and Sing! (Odets) CLCII I-98; MPII:D I-104

Awakening of Spring, The (Wedekind) CLC I-71; MP I-383

B

Baal (Brecht) MP I-397

"Babas del Diablo, Las." *See* "Blow-Up"

Babbitt (Lewis, S.) CLC I-72; MP I-400; MP:AF I-90

Babel-17 (Delany) CLCII I-99; MPII:AF I-102

"Babylon Revisited" (Fitzgerald) MPII:SS I-140

Bacchae, The (Euripides) CLC I-74; MP I-405

Bachelors, The (Spark) MP I-409; MP:BF I-75

Back to Methuselah (Shaw) CLC I-75; MP I-412

Backwater. *See* Pilgrimage

"Bad Characters" (Stafford) MPII:SS I-144

Badenheim, 'ir nofesh. *See* Badenheim 1939

Badenheim 1939 (Appelfeld) CLCII I-101; MPII:WF I-101

Baga (Pinget) CLCII I-102; MPII:WF I-107

Bahía de silencio, La. *See* Bay of Silence, A

Balcon, Le. *See* Balcony, The

Balcony, The (Genet) CLCII I-103; MPII:D I-109

Bald Soprano, The (Ionesco) CLCII I-105; MPII:D I-116

Balkan trilogy, The (Manning, O.) CLCII I-106; MPII:BCF I-86

Ballad of Peckham Rye, The (Spark) CLCII I-108; MPII:BCF I-91

"Ballad of the Sad Café, The" (McCullers) CLCII I-109; MPII:SS I-147

Balthazar (Balzac). *See* Quest of the Absolute, The

Balthazar (Durrell). *See* Alexandria Quartet, The

Bambi (Salten) CLC I-78; MP I-415; MP:EF I-92

"Bambino, The" (Sinclair) MPII:SS I-151

Banana Bottom (McKay) CLCII I-110; MPII:AF I-106

Bang the Drum Slowly (Harris, M.) CLCII I-112; MPII:AF I-111

Bangüê. *See* Plantation Boy

Banjo (McKay) CLCII I-113; MPII:AF I-116

Banya. *See* Bathhouse, The

Barabbas (Lagerkvist) CLC I-78; MP I-419; MP:EF I-96

"Barbados" (Marshall) MPII:SS I-154

Barbarian in the Garden (Herbert) MPII:NF I-138

Barbarzyńca w ogrodzie. *See* Barbarian in the Garden

Barber of Seville, The (Beaumarchais) CLC I-79; MP I-423

Barchester Towers (Trollope) CLC I-80; MP I-426; MP:BF I-79

Barefoot in the Head (Aldiss) CLCII I-114; MPII:BCF I-98

Barefoot in the Park (Simon, N.) CLCII I-115; MPII:D I-122

Bark Tree, The (Queneau) CLCII I-116; MPII:WF I-111

"Barn Burning" (Faulkner) MPII:SS I-158

Bàrnabo delle montagne. *See* Bàrnabo of the Mountains

Bàrnabo of the Mountains (Buzzati) CLCII I-177; MPII:WF I-116

Barnaby Rudge (Dickens) CLC I-81; MP I-431; MP:BF I-85

Barometer Rising (MacLennan) CLCII I-118; MPII:BCF I-103

Baron in the Trees, The (Calvino) CLCII I-119; MPII:WF I-121

Baron Münchausen's Narrative (Raspe) CLC I-84; MP I-435; MP:EF I-101

Barone rampante, Il. *See* Baron in the Trees, The

Barracks, The (McGahern) CLCII I-121; MPII:BCF I-108

Barrage contre la Pacifique, Un. *See* Sea Wall, The

Barren Ground (Glasgow) CLC I-84; MP I-438; MP:AF I-96

Barry Lyndon (Thackeray) CLC I-85; MP I-443; MP:BF I-91

Barsetshire series. *See* Barchester Towers; Doctor Thorne; Framley Parsonage; Last Chronicle of Barset; Small House at Allington, The; *and* Warden, The

Bartholomew Fair (Jonson) CLC I-86; MP I-446

"Bartleby the Scrivener" (Melville) MPII:SS I-162

"Basement Room, The" (Greene) MPII:SS I-166

Basic Training of Pavlo Hummel, The (Rabe) CLCII I-122; MPII:D I-127

Bass Saxophone, The (Škvorecký) CLCII I-123; MPII:WF I-126

Bassaxofon. *See* Bass Saxophone, The

Bašta, pepeo. *See* Garden, Ashes

Bataille de Pharsale, La. *See* Battle of Pharsalus, The

Bathazar. *See* Alexandria Quartet, The

Bathhouse, The (Mayakovsky) CLCII I-124; MPII:D I-133

Batouala (Maran) CLC I-88; MP I-451; MP:EF I-105

Battle of Pharsalus, The (Simon, C.) CLCII I-125; MPII:WF I-131

"Bau, Der." *See* "Burrow, The"

Bay of Silence, The (Mallea) CLC I-89; MP I-454; MP:AF I-101

Beach of Falesá, The (Stevenson) CLC I-89; MP I-456; MP:BF I-95

Beachmasters (Astley) CLCII I-126; MPII:BCF I-114

"Beast in the Jungle, The" (James, H.) MPII:SS I-169

Beat to Quarters. *See* Captain Horatio Hornblower

Beauchamp's Career (Meredith) CLC I-90; MP I-460; MP:BF I-99

Beautiful and Damned, The (Fitzgerald, F. S.) CLCII I-127; MPII:AF I-122

Beauty and Sadness (Kawabata) CLCII I-128; MPII:WF I-136

Beautyful Ones Are Not Yet Born, The (Armah) CLCII I-129; MPII:BCF I-118

Beaux' Stratagem, The (Farquhar) CLC I-91; MP I-464

Beaver Coat, The (Hauptmann) CLC I-92; MP I-469

Becket (Anouilh) CLCII I-130; MPII:D I-139

"Beckoning Fair One, The" (Onions) MPII:SS I-173

Bedbug, The (Mayakovsky) CLCII I-132; MPII:D I-146

"Beet Queen, The" (Erdrich) MPII:SS I-177

Beetlecreek (Demby) CLCII I-133; MPII:AF I-126

Beggar in Jerusalem, A (Wiesel) CLCII I-135; MPII:WF I-141

"Beggar My Neighbor" (Jacobson) MPII:SS I-181

Beggar on Horseback (Connelly) CLCII I-136; MPII:D I-153

Beggars' Bush, The (Fletcher *and* Massinger) CLC I-92; MP I-472

Beggar's Opera, The (Gay) CLC I-94; MP I-476

"Beggarwoman of Locarno, The" (Kleist) MPII:SS I-184

Beginnings of Architecture, The. *See* Eternal Present, The

Beginnings of Art, The. *See* Eternal Present, The

Beichte eines Toren, Die. *See* Confession of a Fool, The

"Beim Bau der chinesischen Mauer." *See* "Great Wall of China, The"

Bel-Ami (Maupassant) CLC I-95; MP I-481; MP:EF I-108

Bell, The (Murdoch) MP I-485; MP:BF I-104

Bell for Adano, A (Hersey) CLC I-96; MP I-488; MP:AF I-104

Bell Jar, The (Plath) CLCII I-137; MPII:AF I-131

Bellefleur (Oates) CLCII I-138; MPII:AF I-136

"Belye nochi." *See* "White Nights"

Ben Hur (Wallace) CLC I-96; MP I-491; MP:AF I-107

Bend in the River, A (Naipaul, V. S.) CLCII I-139; MPII:BCF I-124

Bend Sinister (Nabokov) CLCII I-141; MPII:AF I-142

Benefactors (Frayn) CLCII I-142; MPII:D I-158

"Benito Cereno" (Melville) CLC I-97; MP I-495; MP:AF I-111; MPII:SS I-188

Beowulf (Unknown) CLC I-98; MP I-500

Bérénice (Racine) CLC I-99; MP I-504

"Bericht für eine Akademie, Ein." See "Report to an Academy, A"

Berlin Alexanderplatz (Döblin) CLCII I-143; MPII:WF I-146

Beso de la mujer araña, El. See Kiss of the Spider Woman

Bespokoynaya yunost. See Story of a Life, The

Besuch der alten Dame, Der. See Visit, The

"Bet, The" (Chekhov) MPII:SS I-192

Beton. See Concrete

Betrayal (Pinter) CLCII I-145; MPII:D I-163

Betrayed by Rita Hayworth (Puig) CLCII I-146; MPII:AF I-146

Betrothed, The (Manzoni) CLC I-100; MP I-507; MP:EF I-113

Better Class of Person, A (Osborne) MPII:NF I-144

Between the Acts (Woolf) CLC I-101; MP I-512; MP:BF I-108

Beulah Quintet, The (Settle) MPII:AF I-151

Bevis of Hampton (Unknown) CLC I-101; MP I-516

Beyond Dark Hills (Stuart) MPII:NF I-150

Beyond Good and Evil (Nietzsche) MP I-520

Beyond Human Power, II (Björnson) CLC I-102; MP I-523

Beyond the Bedroom Wall (Woiwode) CLCII I-147; MPII:AF I-161

"Beyond the Glass Mountain" (Stegner) MPII:SS I-196

"Bezhin Meadow" (Turgenev) MPII:SS I-200

Bible in Spain, The (Borrow) MP I-528

"Biblioteca de Babel, La." See "Library of Babel, The"

Biedermann und die Brandstifter. See Firebugs, The

"Big Blonde" (Parker) MPII:SS I-203

Big Knife, The (Odets) CLCII I-150; MPII:D I-169

Big Sea, The (Hughes) MPII:NF I-156

Big Sky, The (Guthrie) CLC I-102; MP I-531; MP:AF I-116

Big Sleep, The (Chandler) CLCII I-151; MPII:AF I-166

"Big Two-Hearted River" (Hemingway) MPII:SS I-206

Biglow Papers, The (Lowell, J.) MP I-535

Billard um halbzehn. See Billiards at Half-Past Nine

Billiards at Half-Past Nine (Böll) CLCII I-153; MPII:WF I-152

Billy Budd, Foretopman (Melville) CLC I-104; MP I-538; MP:AF I-121

Billy Phelan's Greatest Game (Kennedy, W.) CLCII I-154. See also Albany Cycle, The

Biloxi Blues (Simon, N.) CLCII I-155; MPII:D I-175

Bilvar yamim. See In the Heart of the Seas

Bilvav yamim. See In the Heart of the Seas

Biodlares död, En. See Death of a Beekeeper, The

Biographia Literaria (Coleridge) MP I-544

Birds, The (Aristophanes) CLC I-105; MP I-547

Birds Fall Down, The (West, R.) CLCII I-157; MPII:BCF I-129

Birthday King, The (Fielding) CLCII I-158; MPII:BCF I-134

Birthday Party, The (Pinter) CLCII I-159; MPII:D I-180

"Birthmark, The" (Hawthorne) MPII:SS I-210

"Bishop, The" (Chekhov) MPII:SS I-214

"Bit of a Smash in Madras, A" (Maclaren-Ross) MPII:SS I-218

"Bitter Honeymoon" (Moravia) MPII:SS I-222

"Blacáman the Good, Vendor of Miracles" (García Márquez) MPII:SS I-227

Black Arrow, The (Stevenson) CLC I-106; MP I-552; MP:BF I-113

Black Boy (Wright) MPII:NF I-162

"Black Cat, The" (Poe) MPII:SS I-231

Black Hermit, The (Ngugi) CLCII I-160; MPII:D I-185

Black Lamb and Grey Falcon (West, R.) MP I-556

Black Mischief (Waugh) CLCII I-161; MPII:BCF I-139

"Black Prince, The" (Grau) MPII:SS I-235

Black Prince, The (Murdoch) CLCII I-162; MPII:BCF I-145

Black Robe (Moore) CLCII I-163; MPII:BCF I-150

Black Swan, The (Mann) MP I-559; MP:EF I-119

Black Thunder (Bontemps) CLCII I-164; MPII:AF I-171

"Black Tickets" (Phillips) MPII:SS I-239

Black Valley (Wast) CLC I-107; MP I-562; MP:AF I-127

"Blackberry Winter" (Warren) MPII:SS I-242

Blacker the Berry, The (Thurman) CLCII I-166; MPII:AF I-175

Blacks, The (Genet) CLCII I-167; MPII:D I-190

"Blank Page, The" (Dinesen) MPII:SS I-246

Blasting and Bombardiering (Lewis, W.) MPII:NF I-168

Blaubart. See Bluebeard

Blé en herbe, Le. See Ripening Seed, The

Bleak House (Dickens) CLC I-107; MP I-566; MP:BF I-118

Blendung, Die. See Auto-da-Fé

Blindfold Games (Ross) MPII:NF I-172

"Bliss" (Mansfield) MPII:SS I-250

Blithe Spirit (Coward) CLCII I-169; MPII:D I-195

Blithedale Romance, The (Hawthorne) CLC I-110; MP I-571; MP:AF I-131

"Blizzard, The" (Pushkin) MPII:SS I-254

"Blood-Burning Moon" (Toomer) MPII:SS I-258

Blood Knot, The (Fugard) CLCII I-169; MPII:D I-200

Blood of the Lamb, The (De Vries) CLCII I-170; MPII:AF I-181

Blood Wedding (García Lorca) CLC I-112; MP I-574

Bloodsmoor Romance, A (Oates) CLCII I-171; MPII:AF I-186

Bloody Poetry (Brenton) CLCII I-172; MPII:D I-207

Blooming (Toth) MPII:NF I-178

Blossoming World, The (Bates) MPII:NF IV-1628

Blot in the 'Scutcheon, A (Browning, R.) CLC I-112; MP I-578

"Blow-Up" (Cortázar) MPII:SS I-262

Blue Bird, The (Maeterlinck) CLCII I-173; MPII:D I-213

Blue Boy (Giono) CLCII I-175; MPII:WF I-158

Blue Highways (Heat-Moon) MPII:NF I-184

"Blue Hotel, The" (Crane) MPII:SS I-266

Blue Mountains of China, The (Wiebe) CLCII I-176; MPII:BCF I-154

Blue Room, The (Simenon) CLCII I-177; MPII:WF I-164

Bluebeard (Frisch) CLCII I-178; MPII:WF I-169

Blues for Mister Charlie (Baldwin) CLCII I-179; MPII:D I-219

Bluest Eye, The (Morrison) CLCII I-180; MPII:AF I-191

"Boarding House, The" (Joyce) MPII:SS I-270

Boarding-House, The (Trevor) CLCII I-182; MPII:BCF I-158

"Bobok" (Dostoevski) MPII:SS I-273

Bodalsia telenok s dubom. *See* Oak and the Calf, The

Boesman and Lena (Fugard) CLCII I-183; MPII:D I-225

Bogmail (McGinley) CLCII I-184; MPII:BCF I-163

Bohemians of the Latin Quarter, The (Murger) CLC I-113; MP I-581; MP:EF I-122

Bondman, The (Massinger) CLC I-113; MP I-585

Bonds of Interest, The (Benavente) CLC I-115; MP I-589

Bone People, The (Hulme) CLCII I-185; MPII:BCF I-168

Bonecrack (Francis) CLCII I-186; MPII:BCF I-172

Bonnes, Les. *See* Maids, The

"Bontche Shveig." *See* "Bontsha the Silent"

"Bontsha the Silent" (Peretz) MPII:SS I-277

Book of Bebb, The (Buechner) CLCII I-187; MPII:AF I-196

Book of Laughter and Forgetting, The (Kundera) CLCII I-190; MPII:WF I-174

Book of Lights, The (Potok) CLCII I-192; MPII:AF I-202

Book of Songs (Heine) MP I-593

Book of the Courtier, The (Castiglione) MP I-596

Book of the Thousand and One Nights, The. *See* Arabian Nights' Entertainment, The

Books Do Furnish a Room. *See* Dance to the Music of Time, A

Books of the Small Souls, The. *See* Small Souls

Boquitas pintadas. *See* Heartbreak Tango

Borderline (Hospital) CLCII I-193; MPII:BCF I-177

Boris Godunov (Pushkin) CLC I-115; MP I-599

Born in Captivity (Wain) CLCII I-194; MPII:BCF I-181

Borough: A Poem in Twenty-Four Letters, The (Crabbe) MP I-602

Borstal Boy (Behan) MPII:NF I-190

Bosnian Chronicle (Andrić) CLCII I-195; MPII:WF I-182

Bostonians, The (James, H.) MP I-605; MP:AF I-135

Boswell's London Journal: 1762-1763 (Boswell) MP I-608

Botchan (Natsume) CLCII I-196; MPII:WF I-188

"Bottle Imp, The" (Stevenson) MPII:SS I-281

"Bottle of Milk for Mother, A" (Algren) MPII:SS I-285

Bouc émissaire, Le. *See* Scapegoat, The

"Boule de Suif" (Maupassant) MPII:SS I-289

Bourgeois Gentleman, The (Molière) CLC I-116; MP II-611

Bouts de bois de Dieu, Les. *See* God's Bits of Wood

Bouvard and Pécuchet (Flaubert) CLC I-117; MP II-615; MP:EF I-127

Bow and the Lyre, The (Paz) MPII:NF I-196

Bowen's Court (Bowen) MPII:NF I-201

"Bowmen of Shu, The" (Davenport) MPII:SS I-293

"Boxcar of Chrysanthemums" (Enchi) MPII:SS I-297

Boys in the Band, The (Crowley) CLCII I-197; MPII:D I-230

Boys of Summer, The (Kahn) MPII:NF I-206

Bracknels, The (Reid) CLC I-119; MP II-619; MP:BF I-124

Braggart Soldier, The (Plautus) CLC I-119; MP II-623

Brand (Ibsen) CLC I-120; MP II-627

Brave New World (Huxley, A.) CLC I-121; MP II-631; MP:BF I-128

Bread and Wine (Silone) CLC I-122; MP II-636; MP:EF I-131

Bread Givers (Yezierska) CLCII I-198; MPII:AF I-207

Break of Noon (Claudel) CLCII I-199; MPII:D I-237

Bridal Canopy, The (Agnon) CLCII I-200; MPII:WF I-194

"Bride Comes to Yellow Sky, The" (Crane) MPII:SS I-300

Bride of Lammermoor (Scott, Sir W.) CLC I-122; MP II-640; MP:BF I-134

Brideshead Revisited (Waugh) CLC I-123; MP II-645; MP:BF I-139

Bridge, The (Crane, H.) MP II-649

"Bridge of Dreams, The" (Tanizaki) MPII:SS I-304

Bridge of San Luis Rey, The (Wilder) CLC I-124; MP II-651; MP:AF I-139

Bridge on the Drina, The (Andrić) MP II-656; MP:EF I-136

Brief an Lord Liszt. *See* Letter to Lord Liszt

Brief Life, A (Onetti) CLCII I-201; MPII:AF I-212

Brief Lives (Aubrey) MP II-659

Briefe an Felice. *See* Letters to Felice

Briefe über Cézanne. *See* Letters on Cézanne

"Brigadier and the Golf Widow, The" (Cheever) MPII:SS I-308

Brighter Sun, A (Selvon) CLCII I-203; MPII:BCF I-185

Brighton Beach Memoirs (Simon, N.) CLCII I-205; MPII:D I-243

Brighton Rock (Greene) CLCII I-206; MPII:BCF I-191

Britannicus (Racine) CLC I-125; MP II-662

Broad and Alien Is the World (Alegría) CLC I-126; MP II-666; MP:AF I-144

Broken Jug, The (Kleist) CLC I-127; MP II-671

Bronze Horseman, The (Pushkin) MP II-674

Brosok na yug. *See* Story of a Life, The

Brother Ass (Barrios) MP II-677; MP:AF I-149

Brothers, The (Terence) CLC I-127; MP II-681

Brothers and Keepers (Wideman) MPII:NF I-212

Brothers Ashkenazi, The (Singer) CLC I-128; MP II-684; MP:EF I-140

Brothers Karamazov, The (Dostoevski) CLC I-129; MP II-688; MP:EF I-144

Brown Decades, The (Mumford) MP II-693

Browning Version, The (Rattigan) CLCII I-207; MPII:D I-250

Bruno's Dream (Murdoch) CLCII I-208; MPII:BCF I-196

Brushwood Boy, The (Kipling) CLC I-130; MP II-696; MP:BF I-143

Brut, The (Layamon) CLC I-131; MP II-699

Buchanan Dying (Updike) CLCII I-209; MPII:D I-255

Büchse der Pandora, Die. *See* Pandora's Box

Buddenbrooks (Mann) CLC I-133; MP II-702; MP:EF I-150

Buenas conciencias, Las. *See* Good Conscience, The

Bull from the Sea, The (Renault) CLCII II-831; MPII:BCF II-920

Bullet Park (Cheever) CLCII I-210; MPII:AF I-216

Bullivant and the Lambs (Compton-Burnett) MP:BF I-147

Bulwark, The (Dreiser) CLC I-135; MP II-707; MP:AF I-154

Burger's Daughter (Gordimer) CLCII I-212; MPII:BCF I-201

Buried Alive. *See* House of the Dead, The

Buried Child (Shepard) CLCII I-213; MPII:D I-260

Burmese Days (Orwell) CLCII I-214; MPII:BCF I-206

Burn, The (Aksyonov) CLCII I-215; MPII:WF I-200

Burning Brand, The (Pavese) MPII:NF I-218

Burning Water (Bowering) CLCII I-217; MPII:BCF I-211

Burnt-Out Case, A (Greene, G.) MP II-711; MP:BF I-150

Burr (Vidal) CLCII I-219; MPII:AF I-221

"Burrow, The" (Kafka) MPII:SS I-312

Bus Stop (Inge) CLCII I-221; MPII:D I-267

Bushūkō hiwa. *See* Secret History of the Lord of Musashi, The

Bussy d'Ambois (Chapman) CLC I-136; MP II-714

"But at the Stroke of Midnight" (Warner) MPII:SS I-316

Butley (Gray, S.) CLCII I-222; MPII:D I-273

Butt, Der. *See* Flounder, The

Buyer's Market, A. *See* Dance to the Music of Time, A

By Love Possessed (Cozzens) CLCII I-223; MPII:AF I-226

C

Cab at the Door, A (Pritchett) MPII:NF I-223

Cabala, The (Wilder) CLC I-136; MP II-719; MP:AF I-159

Cabin, The (Blasco Ibáñez) CLC I-137; MP II-722; MP:EF I-156

Cadmus (Unknown) CLC I-138; MP II-725; MP:EF I-160

Caesar and Cleopatra (Shaw) CLC I-138; MP II-728

Caesar or Nothing (Baroja) CLC I-139; MP II-731; MP:EF I-163

Cain (Byron) CLC I-140; MP II-734

Caine Mutiny, The (Wouk) CLCII I-224; MPII:AF I-231

Cakes and Ale (Maugham) CLC I-140; MP II-737; MP:BF I-154

Caleb Williams (Godwin) CLC I-141; MP II-740; MP:BF I-158

Caliban's Filibuster (West, P.) CLCII I-225; MPII:BCF I-215

Caligula (Camus) CLCII I-226; MPII:D I-278

Call, The (Hersey) CLCII I-227; MPII:AF I-237

Call It Sleep (Roth) MP II-744; MP:AF I-162

Call of the Wild, The (London) CLC I-142; MP II-748; MP:AF I-167

"Camberwell Beauty, The" (Pritchett) MPII:SS I-320

Cambio de piel. See Change of Skin, A

Camera Lucida (Barthes) MPII:NF I-227

Camera Obscura. See Laughter in the Dark

Camille (Dumas, *fils*) CLC I-142; MP II-751

Campaspe (Lyly) CLC I-143; MP II-754

"Canary for One, A" (Hemingway) MPII:SS I-323

Cancer Ward (Solzhenitsyn) CLCII I-228; MPII:WF I-205

Candida (Shaw) CLC I-143; MP II-757

Candide (Voltaire) CLC I-144; MP II-759; MP:EF I-167

Candle in the Wind, The. *See* Once and Future King, The

Cannery Row (Steinbeck) CLCII I-231; MPII:AF I-242

Cannibal, The (Hawkes) MP II-763; MP:AF I-171

Cantatrice chauve, La. *See* Bald Soprano, The

Canterbury Tales, The (Chaucer) CLC I-146; MP II-769

Canticle for Leibowitz, A (Miller, W.) CLCII I-233; MPII:AF I-247

Cantos (Pound) MP II-776

"Cap for Steve, A" (Callaghan) MPII:SS I-326

Capricornia (Herbert, X.) CLCII I-234; MPII:BCF I-220

Captain Blackman (Williams, J.) CLCII I-236; MPII:AF I-252

Captain Digby Grand. *See* Digby Grand

Captain Horatio Hornblower (Forester) CLC I-148; MP II-779; MP:BF I-163

Captain Singleton (Defoe) CLC I-149; MP II-783; MP:BF I-168

Captain with the Whiskers, The (Kiely) CLCII I-237; MPII:BCF I-225

Captains Courageous (Kipling) CLC I-150; MP II-787; MP:BF I-173

Captain's Daughter, The (Pushkin) CLC I-150; MP II-792; MP:EF I-172

Captive Mind, The (Miłosz) MPII:NF I-232

Captives, The (Plautus) CLC I-151; MP II-797

"Careful" (Carver) MPII:SS I-330

Caretaker, The (Pinter) MP II-800

Carmen (Mérimée) CLC I-152; MP II-803; MP:EF I-178

Carmina (Catullus) MP II-806

Casa in collina, La. *See* House on the Hill, The

Casa verde, La. *See* Green House, The

Casamiento, El. *See* Marriage, The

Casanova's Chinese Restaurant. *See* Dance to the Music of Time, A, *and*

Dance to the Music of Time: Second Movement, A

Case of Sergeant Grischa, The (Zweig) CLC I-152; MP II-809; MP:EF I-181

"Cask of Amontillado, The" (Poe) MPII:SS I-334

Cass Timberlane (Lewis, S.) CLC I-153; MP II-813; MP:AF I-178

Cassandra (Wolf) CLCII I-239; MPII:WF I-210

Caste (Robertson) CLC I-154; MP II-816

Castello dei destini incrociati, Il. *See* Castle of Crossed Destinies, The

Castle, The (Kafka) CLC I-154; MP II-820; MP:EF I-185

Castle of Crossed Destinies, The (Calvino) CLCII I-240; MPII:WF I-216

Castle of Fratta, The (Nievo) CLC I-155; MP II-823; MP:EF I-189

Castle of Otranto, The (Walpole, Horace) CLC I-156; MP II-829; MP:BF I-178

Castle Rackrent (Edgeworth) CLC I-157; MP II-834; MP:BF I-183

Castle to Castle (Céline) CLCII I-241; MPII:WF I-221

Casuals of the Sea (McFee) CLC I-158; MP II-839; MP:BF I-189

Cat, The (Colette) CLCII I-243; MPII:WF I-229

Cat and Mouse (Grass) MP II-842; MP:EF I-195

Cat on a Hot Tin Roof (Williams, T.) MP II-845

"Catbird Seat, The" (Thurber) MPII:SS I-337

"Catch, The" (Ōe) MPII:SS I-340

Catch-22 (Heller) MP II-848; MP:AF I-181

Catcher in the Rye, The (Salinger) CLCII I-244; MPII:AF I-259

Cathleen ni Houlihan (Yeats) CLCII I-245; MPII:D I-284

Catiline (Jonson) CLC I-159; MP II-852

Cat's Cradle (Vonnegut) CLCII I-246; MPII:AF I-264

Caucasian Chalk Circle, The (Brecht) CLCII I-247; MPII:D I-288

Caught (Green, Henry) CLCII I-248; MPII:BCF I-230

Cavalier, The. *See* Woodstock

Cavaliere inesistente, Il. *See* Non-existent Knight, The

"Cavalleria Rusticana" (Verga) CLC I-160; MP II-855; MP:EF I-198

Caves du Vatican, Les. *See* Lafcadio's Adventures

Cawdor (Jeffers) CLC I-161; MP II-858

Cecilia (Burney) CLC I-162; MP II-861; MP:BF I-193

"Celebrated Jumping Frog of Calaveras County, The" (Twain) MPII:SS I-344

"Celestial Omnibus, The" (Forster) MPII:SS I-348

Celestina (Rojas) CLC I-163; MP II-865; MP:EF I-201

Cenci, The (Artaud) CLCII I-249; MPII:D I-293

Cenci, The (Shelley, P.) CLC I-164; MP II-869

Centaur, The (Updike) CLCII I-250; MPII:AF I-269

Century of the Wind. *See* Memory of Fire

Ceremony in Lone Tree (Morris, Wright) MP II-872; MP:AF I-186

Ceremony of Innocence, The (Ribman) CLCII I-252; MPII:D I-299

César Birotteau (Balzac) CLC I-165; MP II-876; MP:EF I-206

Cesarz. *See* Emperor, The

Cette voix. *See* That Voice

Chain of Chance, The (Lem) CLCII I-253; MPII:WF I-234

"Chain of Love, A" (Price) MPII:SS I-351

Chain of Voices, A (Brink) CLCII I-254; MPII:BCF I-235

Chainbearer, The (Cooper) CLC I-166; MP II-880; MP:AF I-191

Chairs, The (Ionesco) CLCII I-255; MPII:D I-305

Chaises, Les. *See* Chairs, The

Chambre bleue, La. *See* Blue Room, The

Chambre claire, La. *See* Camera Lucida

Chaneysville Incident, The (Bradley) CLCII I-256; MPII:AF I-274

"Change" (Woiwode) MPII:SS I-355

Change of Heart, A (Butor) CLCII I-257; MPII:WF I-239

Change of Skin, A (Fuentes) CLCII I-259; MPII:AF I-279

Changeling, The (Middleton *and* Rowley) CLC I-167; MP II-885

Changing Places (Lodge) CLCII I-260; MPII:BCF I-241

Changing Room, The (Storey) CLCII I-261; MPII:D I-312

Chant of Jimmie Blacksmith, The (Keneally) CLCII I-262; MPII:BCF I-247

"Charles" (Jackson) MPII:SS I-359

Charles Demailly (Goncourt *and* Goncourt) CLC I-168; MP I-888; MP:EF I-210

Charles O'Malley (Lever) CLC I-169; MP II-892; MP:BF I-198

Charterhouse of Parma, The (Stendhal) CLC I-169; MP II-895; MP:EF I-214

Chaste Maid in Cheapside, A (Middleton) CLC I-171; MP II-900

Chatte, La. *See* Cat, The

"Cheap in August" (Greene) MPII:SS I-361

"Chef-d'œuvre inconnu, Le." *See* "Unknown Masterpiece, The"

"Chelovek v futlyare." *See* "Man in a Case, The"

Chemins de la liberté, Les. *See* Roads to Freedom, The

"Chemist's Wife, The" (Chekhov) MPII:SS I-364

Chéri (Colette) CLC I-172; CLCII I-264; MP II-905; MP:EF I-219; MPII:WF I-243

Cherokee (Echenoz) CLCII I-265; MPII:WF I-248

Cherry Orchard, The (Chekhov) CLC I-173; MP II-908

Chevalier de Maison Rouge, The. *See* Chevalier of the Maison Rouge, The

Chevalier of the Maison Rouge, The (Dumas, *père*) CLC I-174; MP II-912; MP:EF I-223

Chevengur (Platonov) CLCII I-266; MPII:WF I-252

Cheyenne Autumn (Sandoz) CLCII I-267; MPII:AF I-285

Chiave a stella, La. *See* Monkey's Wrench, The

Chicago Poems (Sandburg) MP II-918

"Chickamauga" (Bierce) MPII:SS I-368

Chicken Soup with Barley (Wesker) CLCII I-269; MPII:D I-317

Chickencoop Chinaman, The (Chin) CLCII I-270; MPII:D I-323

Chiendent, Le. *See* Bark Tree, The

Chijin no ai. *See* Naomi

Child Story. *See* Slow Homecoming

Childe Byron (Linney) CLCII I-271; MPII:D I-329

Childe Harold's Pilgrimage (Byron) MP II-921

Childermass, The. *See* Human Age, The

Childhood and Schooldays. *See* Story of a Life, The

Childhood, Boyhood, Youth (Tolstoy) MP II-924; MP:EF I-229

"Childhood of Luvers, The" (Pasternak) MPII:SS I-372

Childhood's End (Clarke, Arthur C.) CLCII I-272; MPII:AF I-290

Children of a Lesser God (Medoff) CLCII I-274; MPII:D I-335

Children of Crisis (Coles) MPII:NF I-237

Children of Dune. *See* Dune Trilogy, The

Children of God (Fisher) CLC I-175; MP II-927; MP:AF I-196

Children of Heracles, The (Euripides) CLC I-176; MP II-930

Children of Kaywana. *See* Kaywana trilogy, The

Children of the Games. *See* Holy Terrors, The

Children of the Ghetto (Zangwill) CLC I-177; MP II-933; MP:BF I-202

Children of Violence (Lessing) CLCII I-275; MPII:BCF I-252

"Children on Their Birthdays" (Capote) MPII:SS I-376

"Children's Campaign, The" (Lagerkvist) MPII:SS I-380

Children's Hour, The (Hellman) CLCII I-279; MPII:D I-341

"Child's Drawings, A" (Shalamov) MPII:SS I-384

Chimmoku. See Silence

China Men (Kingston) MPII:NF I-244

Chinese des Schmerzes, Der. See Across

Chinese Wall, The (Frisch) CLCII I-280; MPII:D I-347

Chinesische Mauer, Die. See Chinese Wall, The

Chips with Everything (Wesker) MP II-937

Chita (Hearn) CLC I-178; MP II-940; MP:AF I-200

Chosen, The (Potok) CLCII I-281; MPII:AF I-295

Chouans, The (Balzac) CLC I-178; MP II-943; MP:EF I-232

Christ Recrucified. See Greek Passion, The

Christ Stopped at Eboli (Levi, C.) CLCII I-283; MPII:WF I-257

Christmas Carol, A (Dickens) CLC I-179; MP II-947; MP:BF I-207

"Christmas Morning" (O'Connor, Frank) MPII:SS I-388

Chronicle of a Death Foretold (García Márquez) CLCII I-284; MPII:AF I-300

Chronicle of the Conquest of Granada, A (Irving) MP II-950

Chronicle of the Fortunes of Richard Mahony, The. See Fortunes of Richard Mahony, The

Chronicles of Froissart (Froissart) MP II-953

Chronique (Perse) MP II-956

"Chrysanthemums, The" (Steinbeck) MPII:SS I-392

Ciascuno a suo modo. See Each in His Own Way

Cicero's Orations (Cicero) MP II-959

Cid, The (Corneille) CLC I-180; MP II-961

Cien años de soledad. See One Hundred Years of Solitude

Cinkos, A. See Loser, The

Cinna (Corneille) CLC I-180; MP II-966

"Cinnamon Shops" (Schulz) MPII:SS I-396

Cinq-Mars (Vigny) CLC I-181; MP II-969; MP:EF I-236

Cinquième Fils, Le. See Fifth Son, The

Circle, The (Maugham) CLCII I-286; MPII:D I-353

Circle of Chalk, The (Unknown) CLC I-182; MP II-973

"Circular Ruins, The" (Borges) MPII:SS I-399

Citadel, The (Cronin) CLCII I-287; MPII:BCF I-262

Cities of Salt (Munif) CLCII I-287. See also Mudun al-milh

Città e la casa, La. See City and the House, The

Città invisibili, Le. See Invisible Cities

City and the House, The (Ginzburg) CLCII I-289; MPII:WF I-262

City and the Pillar, The (Vidal) CLCII I-291; MPII:AF I-306

City Builder, The (Konrád) CLCII I-292; MPII:WF I-267

Ciudad y los perros, La. See Time of the Hero, The

CIVIL warS, the (Wilson, R.) CLCII I-293; MPII:D I-358

Clarissa (Richardson, S.) CLC I-183; MP II-976; MP:BF I-211

Claudius the God and His Wife Messalina (Graves) CLC I-184; MP II-981; MP:BF I-216

"Clay" (Joyce) MPII:SS I-403

Clayhanger Trilogy, The (Bennett) CLC I-185; MP II-984; MP:BF I-220

Clea. See Alexandria Quartet, The

"Clean, Well-Lighted Place, A" (Hemingway) MPII:SS I-406

Clear Horizon. See Pilgrimage

Clear Light of Day (Desai) CLCII I-294; MPII:BCF I-267

Cligés (Chrétien de Troyes) CLC I-187; MP II-989

Clinging to the Wreckage (Mortimer) MPII:NF I-249

Cloak of Light, A (Morris) MPII:NF IV-1696

Clockwork Orange, A (Burgess) CLCII I-295; MPII:BCF I-271

Cloister and the Hearth, The (Reade) CLC I-188; MP II-993; MP:BF I-225

Closed Garden, The (Green, J.) CLC I-189; MP II-998; MP:EF I-240

Closely Watched Trains (Hrabal) CLCII I-296; MPII:WF I-272

Closing of the American Mind, The (Bloom, A.) MPII:NF I-255

"Cloud, Castle, Lake" (Nabokov) MPII:SS I-409

Cloud Forest, The (Matthiessen) MP II-1003

Cloud Howe. See Scots Quair, A

Cloud Nine (Churchill) CLCII I-297; MPII:D I-365

Clouds, The (Aristophanes) CLC I-189; MP II-1006

Cloven Viscount, The (Calvino) CLCII I-299; MPII:WF I-277

Clown, The (Böll) CLCII I-300; MPII:WF I-281

Cock-a-Doodle Dandy (O'Casey) CLCII I-301; MPII:D I-370

Cocktail Party, The (Eliot, T. S.) CLC I-190; MP II-1010

"Cœur simple, Un." See "Simple Heart, A"

Coffin for Dimitrios, A (Ambler) CLCII I-303; MPII:BCF I-276

Cognizione del dolore, La. See Acquainted with Grief

Coin in Nine Hands, A (Yourcenar) CLCII I-304; MPII:WF I-286

Cold Comfort Farm (Gibbons) MP II-1016; MP:BF I-230

Cold Storage (Ribman) CLCII I-306; MPII:D I-377

Collected Letters of D. H. Lawrence, The (Lawrence, D. H.) MP II-1019

Collected Poems (de la Mare) MP II-1022

Collected Poems, 1934-1952 (Thomas) MP II-1025

Collector, The (Fowles) CLCII I-307; MPII:BCF I-281

"Collector of Treasures, The" (Head) MPII:SS I-413

Collegians, The (Griffin) CLC I-191; MP II-1028; MP:BF I-234

Colomba (Mérimée) CLC I-192; MP II-1031; MP:EF I-245

Colonel Jacque. See History of Colonel Jacque, The

"Color of Darkness" (Purdy) MP II-1034; MP:AF I-203; MPII:SS I-418

Color Purple, The (Walker, A.) CLCII I-308; MPII:AF I-311

Colours in the Dark (Reaney) CLCII I-309; MPII:D I-382

Come Back, Little Sheba (Inge) CLCII I-310; MPII:D I-387

Comedians, The (Greene) CLCII I-311; MPII:BCF I-288

Comedy of Calisto and Melibea," "The. See Celestina

Comedy of Errors, The (Shakespeare) CLC I-192; MP II-1037

"Comendadora, La." See "Nun, The"

Comforters, The (Spark) CLCII I-312; MPII:BCF I-293

"Coming, Aphrodite" (Cather) MPII:SS I-422

Coming into the Country (McPhee) MPII:NF I-260

Coming Up for Air (Orwell) CLCII I-314; MPII:BCF I-297

Comment aiment les filles. See Splendors and Miseries of Courtesans, The

Comment c'est. See How It Is

Commentaries (Caesar) MP II-1040

Common Reader, The. See Literary Essays of Virginia Woolf, The

Como en la guerra. *See* He Who Searches

Compagnie. *See* Company

Company (Beckett) CLCII I-314; MPII:BCF I-303; MPII:WF I-291

Company of Women, The (Gordon) CLCII I-316; MPII:AF I-315

Complaint, The (Young, E.) MP II-1042

Compleat Angler, The (Walton) MP II-1044

Compromise, The (Dovlatov) CLCII I-317; MPII:WF I-295

Comrades (Strindberg) CLC I-194; MP II-1047

Comus (Milton) CLC I-194; MP II-1051

Concerning Illustrious Men (Suetonius) MP II-1054

Concluding (Green, Henry) CLCII I-318; MPII:BCF I-307

Conclusive Evidence. *See* Speak, Memory

Concrete (Bernhard) CLCII I-319; MPII:WF I-300

Confederacy of Dunces, A (Toole) CLCII I-320; MPII:AF I-319

Confederate General from Big Sur, A (Brautigan) CLCII I-321; MPII:AF I-325

Confederates (Keneally) CLCII I-322; MPII:BCF I-312

Confession of a Fool, The (Strindberg) CLCII I-324; MPII:WF I-304

Confessions (Augustine) MP II-1057

Confessions (Rousseau) MP II-1060

Confessions of a Mask (Mishima) CLCII I-325; MPII:WF I-310

Confessions of an English Opium Eater (De Quincey) MP II-1063

Confessions of Felix Krull, Confidence Man (Mann) CLC I-195; MP II-1067; MP:EF I-249

Confessions of Nat Turner, The (Styron) CLCII I-326; MPII:AF I-330

Confessions of Zeno (Svevo) CLCII I-328; MPII:WF I-315

Confidence Man, The (Melville) CLC I-196; MP II-1071; MP:AF I-207

Confidential Clerk, The (Eliot, T. S.) MP II-1074

Confieso que he vivido. *See* Memoirs

Conformist, The (Moravia) CLCII I-329; MPII:WF I-319

Conformista, Il. *See* Conformist, The

"Conforti." *See* "Consolation"

Coningsby (Disraeli) CLC I-196; MP II-1077; MP:BF I-238

Conjectures of a Guilty Bystander (Merton) MPII:NF I-265

Conjure Woman, The (Chesnutt) CLC I-197; MP II-1080; MP:AF I-211

Connecticut Yankee in King Arthur's Court, A (Twain) CLC I-198; MP II-1083; MP:AF I-215

Connection, The (Gelber) CLCII I-330; MPII:D I-391

Conquistador (MacLeish) MP II-1088

Conscience of the Rich, The (Snow) MP II-1091; MP:BF I-242. *See also* Strangers and Brothers

Conscious Lovers, The (Steele) CLC I-198; MP II-1094

Conservationist, The (Gordimer) CLCII I-331; MPII:BCF I-318

Considerations on the Principal Events of the French Revolution (Staël) MP II-1100

"Consolation" (Verga) MPII:SS I-425

Consolations of Philosophy, The (Boethius) MP II-1104

Consuelo (Sand) CLC I-199; MP II-1106; MP:EF I-253

Contesto, Il. *See* Equal Danger

Contractor, The (Storey) CLCII I-333; MPII:D I-397

Conversation About Dante (Mandelstam, O.) MPII:NF I-270

Conversation in the Cathedral (Vargas Llosa) CLCII I-334; MPII:AF I-335

Conversations of Goethe with Eckermann and Soret (Eckermann) MP II-1109

Conversazione in Sicilia. *See* In Sicily

"Conversion of the Jews, The" (Roth) MPII:SS I-429

Coonardoo (Prichard) CLCII I-335; MPII:BCF I-322

Copperhead, The (Frederic) CLC I-200; MP II-1113; MP:AF I-220

Coriolanus (Shakespeare) CLC I-201; MP II-1116

Corn Is Green, The (Williams, E.) CLCII I-336; MPII:D I-402

Cornerstone, The (Oldenbourg) MP II-1121; MP:EF I-257

Coronation (Donoso) CLCII I-337; MPII:AF I-340

Coronel no tiene quien le escriba, El. See No One Writes to the Colonel

Correction (Bernhard) CLCII I-338; MPII:WF I-323

Corregidora (Jones, G.) CLCII I-339; MPII:AF I-346

Corridors of Power. See Strangers and Brothers

Corsican Brothers, The (Dumas, père) CLC I-202; MP II-1124; MP:EF I-260

Coscienza di Zeno, La. See Confessions of Zeno

Cosmos (Gombrowicz) CLCII I-340; MPII:WF I-328

Cossacks, The (Tolstoy) CLC I-203; MP II-1128; MP:EF I-264

Count Frontenac and New France Under Louis XIV (Parkman) MP II-1133

Count Julian (Goytisolo) CLCII III-974; MPII:WF III-958

Count of Monte-Cristo, The (Dumas, père) CLC I-204; MP II-1136; MP:EF I-281

Counterfeiters, The (Gide) CLC I-206; MP II-1140; MP:EF I-274

Counterfeiters, The (Kenner) MPII:NF I-275

"Counterparts" (Joyce) MPII:SS I-433

Counterpoints (Needham) MPII:NF I-281

Countess de Charny (Dumas, père) CLC I-207; MP II-1146; MP:EF I-281

Country Doctor, The (Balzac) CLC I-209; MP II-1152; MP:EF I-285

Country Doctor, A (Jewett) CLC I-208; MP II-1149; MP:AF I-224

"Country Doctor, A" (Kafka) MPII:SS I-437

Country Girls, The. See Country Girls Trilogy, The

Country Girls Trilogy, The (O'Brien, E.) CLCII I-341; MPII:BCF I-327

Country House, The (Galsworthy) CLC I-210; MP II-1155; MP:BF I-246

"Country Husband, The" (Cheever) MPII:SS I-440

"Country Love Story, A" (Stafford) MPII:SS I-444

Country of the Pointed Firs, The (Jewett) CLC I-211; MP II-1158; MP:AF I-227

Country Wife, The (Wycherley) CLC I-211; MP II-1162

"Count's Wife, The" (Buzzati) MPII:SS I-448

Coup, The (Updike) CLCII I-342; MPII:AF I-351

Coup de Grâce (Yourcenar) CLCII I-344; MPII:WF I-332

Couples (Updike) CLCII I-345; MPII:AF I-356

Cours de linguistique générale. See Course in General Linguistics

Course in General Linguistics (Saussure) MPII:NF I-288

Courtesan, The (Aretino) CLC I-212; MP II-1168

Courtship of Miles Standish, The (Longfellow) CLC I-213; MP II-1172

Cousin Bazilio (Eça de Queiróz) CLCII I-348; MPII:WF I-337

Cousin Bette (Balzac) CLC I-213; MP II-1175; MP:EF I-289

Cousin Pons (Balzac) CLC I-215; MP II-1180; MP:EF I-294

Cowards, The (Škvorecký) CLCII I-349; MPII:WF I-341

Coxcomb, The (Beaumont and Fletcher) CLC I-218; MP II-1185

Crack-Up, The (Fitzgerald) MPII:NF I-293

MASTERPLOTS

Cradle Song, The (Martínez Sierra) CLC I-218; MP II-1188
Cranford (Gaskell) CLC I-219; MP II-1191; MP:BF I-250
"Crazy Sunday" (Fitzgerald) MPII:SS I-452
Cream of the Jest, The (Cabell) CLC I-220; MP II-1194; MP:AF I-231
Crime and Punishment (Dostoevski) CLC I-221; MP II-1197; MP:EF I-299
Crime of Sylvestre Bonnard, The (France) CLC I-222; MP II-1202; MP:EF I-304
Crimes of the Heart (Henley) CLCII I-350; MPII:D I-407
Crisis, The (Churchill, W.) CLC I-223; MP II-1207; MP:AF I-235
Crisis, The (Paine) MP II-1211
Cristo si è fermato a Eboli. See Christ Stopped at Eboli
Critic, The (Sheridan) CLC I-224; MP II-1214
Critical Essays of William Hazlitt, The (Hazlitt) MP II-1217
"Critical Introduction to The Best of S. J. Perelman by Sidney Namlerep, A" (Perelman) MPII:SS I-456
Critical Path (Fuller) MPII:NF I-299
"Critique de la Vie Quotidienne" (Barthelme, D.) MPII:SS I-459
Critique of Pure Reason (Kant) MP II-1220
Crock of Gold, The (Stephens) CLC I-224; MP III-1223; MP:BF I-254
Crome Yellow (Huxley, A.) CLC I-225; MP III-1226; MP:BF I-258
Crónica de una muerte anunciada. See Chronicle of a Death Foretold
"Crossing into Poland" (Babel) MPII:SS II-463
Crotchet Castle (Peacock) CLC I-226; MP III-1229; MP:BF I-261
Crowds and Power (Canetti) MPII:NF I-304
Crucible, The (Miller, A.) CLCII I-351; MPII:D I-414

"Cruel and Barbarous Treatment" (McCarthy) MPII:SS II-467
"Cruise of The Breadwinner, The" (Bates) MPII:SS II-471
Cruise of the Cachalot, The (Bullen) CLC I-227; MP III-1232; MP:BF I-265
Cruising Speed (Buckley) MPII:NF I-310
Crusoe's Daughter (Gardam) CLCII I-352; MPII:BCF I-333
Cry, the Beloved Country (Paton) CLC I-227; MP III-1235; MP:EF I-310
Crying of Lot 49, The (Pynchon) CLCII I-354; MPII:AF I-361
Crystal World, The (Ballard) CLCII I-355; MPII:BCF I-339
Cudjo's Cave (Trowbridge) CLC I-228; MP III-1238; MP:AF I-239
Cultural Literacy (Hirsch) MPII:NF I-316
Culture and Anarchy (Arnold) MP III-1242
Culture and Value (Wittgenstein) MPII:NF I-321
Cupid and Psyche (Unknown) CLC I-229; MP III-1245; MP:EF I-314
Curse of the Starving Class (Shepard) CLCII I-356; MPII:D I-420
Custom House, The (King, F.) CLCII I-357; MPII:BCF I-344
Custom of the Country, The (Wharton) CLC I-229; MP III-1249; MP:AF I-244
Cuttlefish, The (Witkiewicz) CLCII I-359; MPII:D I-425
Cyclone, The. See Strong Wind
Cyclops, The (Euripides) CLC I-230; MP III-1252
Cymbeline (Shakespeare) CLC I-231; MP III-1255
Cypresses Believe in God, The (Gironella) MP III-1259; MP:EF I-319
Cyrano de Bergerac (Rostand) CLC I-233; MP III-1262
Cyropaedia (Xenophon) MP III-1267; MP:EF I-322

22

D

Da (Leonard) CLCII I-360; MPII:D II-431
"Daddy Wolf" (Purdy) MPII:SS II-474
Dagbok för Selma Lagerlöf. *See* Diary of
Selma Lagerlöf, The
Daisy Miller (James, H.) CLC I-234; MP
III-1270; MP:AF I-248
Daiyon kampyōki. *See* Inter Ice Age 4
Dalyokie gody. *See* Story of a Life, The
"Dama s sobachkoi." *See* "Lady with the
Dog"
Damaged Souls (Bradford, G.) MP III-
1273
Damballah. *See* Homewood Trilogy, The
"Damballah" (Wideman) MPII:SS II-476
Dame Care (Sudermann) CLC I-234; MP
III-1275; MP:EF I-326
"Damma s sobachkoi." *See* Lady with the
Dog, The
Damnation of Theron Ware, The
(Frederic) CLC I-235; MP III-1279;
MP:AF I-251
Damned, The. *See* Wretched of the Earth,
The
Damnés de la terre, Les. *See* Wretched
of the Earth, The
Dämonen, Die. *See* Demons, The
Damskii master. *See* Ladies' Hairdresser
Dance in the Sun, A (Jacobson) CLCII I-
361; MPII:BCF I-350
Dance of Death, The (Strindberg) CLC I-
236; MP III-1283
Dance of the Forests, A (Soyinka) CLCII
I-362; MPII:D II-437
Dance to the Music of Time, A (Powell)
MP III-1288; MP:BF I-269
Dance to the Music of Time: Second
Movement, A (Powell) MP III-1293
Dangerous Acquaintances (Laclos) CLC I-
236; MP III-1299; MP:EF I-330
Dangerous Connections. *See* Dangerous
Acquaintances
"Dangers de l'inconduite, Les." *See*
"Gobseck"
Dangling Man (Bellow) CLCII I-363;
MPII:AF I-366

Daniel Deronda (Eliot, G.) CLC I-237;
MP III-1304; MP:BF I-278
Daniel Martin (Fowles) CLCII I-364;
MPII:BCF I-354
Dans le labyrinthe. *See* In the Labyrinth
Danse Macabre (King) MPII:NF I-327
Dante (Eliot, T. S.) MP III-1308
"Dante and the Lobster" (Beckett) MPII:SS
II-480
Daphnis and Chloë (Longus) CLC I-239;
MP III-1310; MP:EF I-335
Dar. *See* Gift, The
"Daring Young Man on the Flying
Trapeze, The" (Saroyan) MPII:SS II-
484
Dark Child, The (Laye) CLCII I-366;
MPII:WF I-345
"Dark City, The" (Aiken) MPII:SS II-488
Dark Journey, The (Green, J.) CLC I-240;
MP III-1313; MP:EF I-338
Dark Laughter (Anderson, S.) CLC I-241;
MP III-1317; MP:AF I-255
Darkness at Noon (Koestler) CLC I-242;
MP III-1321; MP:EF I-342
Darkness Visible (Golding) CLCII I-367;
MPII:BCF I-360
"Darling, The" (Chekhov) MPII:SS I-492
Daughter of Earth (Smedley) CLCII I-368;
MPII:AF I-373
"Daughters of the Late Colonel, The"
(Mansfield) MPII:SS II-495
David Copperfield (Dickens) CLC I-242;
MP III-1324; MP:BF I-283
David Harum (Westcott) CLC I-247; MP
III-1331; MP:AF I-260
"Dawn of Remembered Spring" (Stuart)
MPII:SS II-499
Dawn's Left Hand. *See* Pilgrimage
Day in the Death of Joe Egg, A (Nichols)
CLCII I-370; MPII:D II-443
Day of the Scorpion, The. *See* Raj
Quartet, The
"Day Stalin Died, The" (Lessing) MPII:SS
II-502

"Day the Flowers Came, The" (Madden) MPII:SS II-507

Days of Hope. *See* Man's Hope

Days of the Turbins (Bulgakov) CLCII I-371; MPII:D II-449

De abajo, Los. *See* Underdogs, The

"De Daumier-Smith's Blue Period" (Salinger) MPII:SS II-546

De dónde son los cantantes. *See* From Cuba with a Song

De la grammatologie. *See* Of Grammatology

De Profundis (Wilde) MP III-1334

De quelques formes primitives de classification. *See* Primitive Classification

De Rerum Natura (Lucretius) MP III-1337

"Dead, The" (Joyce) CLCII I-372; MPII:SS II-510

Dead Class, The (Kantor) CLCII I-373; MPII:D II-456

Dead Fires (Lins do Rêgo) CLC I-247; MP III-1339

Dead Man Leading (Pritchett) CLCII I-374; MPII:BCF I-364

Dead Souls (Gogol) CLC I-248; MP III-1342; MP:EF I-345

Dead Yesterdays. *See* All Our Yesterdays

Deadlock. *See* Pilgrimage

"Deal in Wheat, A" (Norris) MPII:SS II-516

Dean's December, The (Bellow) CLCII I-375; MPII:AF I-378

Dear Brutus (Barrie) CLC I-249; MP III-1345

Dear Shadows (Wain) MPII:NF I-331

"Death and the Child" (Crane) MPII:SS II-520

Death and the King's Horseman (Soyinka) CLCII I-377; MPII:D II-463

Death and the Lover. *See* Narcissus and Goldmund

Death Comes for the Archbishop (Cather) CLC I-251; MP III-1349; MP:AF I-264

"Death in Midsummer" (Mishima) MPII:SS II-524

Death in the Afternoon (Hemingway) MPII:NF I-337

Death in the Family, A (Agee) MP III-1354; MP:AF I-269

"Death in the Woods" (Anderson) MPII:SS II-528

"Death in Venice" (Mann) CLC I-253; MP III-1357; MP:EF I-349; MPII:SS II-532

Death of a Beekeeper, The (Gustafsson) CLCII I-378; MPII:WF I-349

Death of a Hero (Aldington) CLC I-254; MP III-1362; MP:BF I-291

"Death of a Huntsman" (Bates) MPII:SS II-535

Death of a Salesman (Miller, A.) CLC I-255; MP III-1365

"Death of a Traveling Salesman" (Welty) MPII:SS II-539

Death of Ahasuerus, The. *See* Tobias Trilogy, The

Death of Artemio Cruz, The (Fuentes) MP III-1369; MP:AF I-273

"Death of Ivan Ilyich, The" (Tolstoy) CLC I-256; MP III-1373; MP:EF I-354; MPII:SS II-542

Death of Synge and Other Passages from an Old Diary, The. *See* Autobiography of William Butler Yeats, The

Death of the Fox (Garrett) CLCII I-379; MPII:AF I-384

Death of the Gods, The (Merezhkowsky) CLC I-256; MP III-1377; MP:EF I-359

Death of the Heart, The (Bowen) CLC I-257; MP III-1381; MP:BF I-295

Death of Virgil, The (Broch) CLC I-257; MP III-1385; MP:EF I-363

Death on the Installment Plan (Céline) CLCII I-380; MPII:WF I-353

Death Ship, The (Traven) MP III-1388; MP:AF I-278

Death's Duell (Donne) MP III-1391

Deathwatch (Genet) CLCII I-382; MPII:D II-471

Debit and Credit (Freytag) CLC I-258; MP III-1393; MP:EF I-367

Debut, The (Brookner) CLCII I-383; MPII:BCF I-370

Decadence. *See* Artamonov Business, The

Decameron, The (Boccaccio) MP III-1397; MP:EF I-371

Decay of the Angel, The. *See* Sea of Fertility, The

Decline and Fall (Waugh) CLC I-259; MP III-1404; MP:BF I-299

Deephaven (Jewett) CLC I-260; MP III-1409; MP:AF I-282

Deerslayer, The (Cooper) CLC I-260; MP III-1413; MP:AF I-286

Defence of Guenevere and Other Poems, The (Morris, William) MP III-1417

Defence of Poesie (Sidney) MP III-1420

Defence of Poetry, A (Shelley, P.) MP III-1423

"Defender of the Faith" (Roth) MPII:SS II-550

Defense, The (Nabokov) CLCII I-384; MPII:WF I-359

Defense of the Constitutions of Government of the United States of America, A (Adams, J.) MP III-1426

Deirdre (Stephens) CLC I-262; MP III-1428; MP:BF I-305

Deirdre of the Sorrows (Synge) CLC I-263; MP III-1432

Delicate Balance, A (Albee) CLCII I-385; MPII:D II-475

"Delicate Prey, The" (Bowles, P.) MPII:SS II-553

Delphine (Staël) CLC I-263; MP III-1436; MP:EF I-380

"Delta Autumn" (Faulkner) MPII:SS II-557

Delta Wedding (Welty) CLC I-264; MP III-1439; MP:AF I-290

"Deluge at Norderney, The" (Dinesen) MPII:SS II-561

Demian (Hesse) CLCII I-386; MPII:WF I-364

Democracy (Didion) CLCII I-387; MPII:AF I-389

Democracy in America (Tocqueville) MP III-1443

Democratic Vistas (Whitman) MP III-1446

Demon: An Eastern Tale, The (Lermontov) MP III-1449

"Demon Lover, The" (Bowen) MPII:SS II-565

Demons, The (Doderer) CLCII I-389; MPII:WF I-369

Denier du rêve. *See* Coin in Nine Hands, A

Deptford Trilogy, The (Davies) CLCII I-390; MPII:BCF I-375

Deputy, The (Hochhuth) CLCII I-393; MPII:D II-481

Dernier des Justes, Le. *See* Last of the Just, The

Dernière Incarnation de Vautrin, La. *See* Splendors and Miseries of Courtesans, The

Descent into Hell (Williams, C.) MP III-1452; MP:BF I-310

"Descent into the Maelström, A" (Poe) MPII:SS II-568

Descent of Man, and Selection in Relation to Sex (Darwin) MP III-1455

Desert Solitaire (Abbey) MPII:NF I-342

Deserto dei Tartari, Il. *See* Tartar Steppe, The

Desierta de piedra. *See* Stone Desert

Design for Living (Coward) CLCII I-394; MPII:D II-486

Desire Under the Elms (O'Neill) CLC I-265; MP III-1458

"Désirée's Baby" (Chopin) MPII:SS II-572

Destiny Bay (Byrne) CLC I-266; MP III-1463; MP:BF I-314

Det heliga landet. *See* Tobias Trilogy, The

Detained (Ngugi) MPII:NF I-348

"Detskie kartinki." *See* "Child's Drawings, A"

"Detstvo Lyuvers." *See* "Childhood of Luvers, The"

Deuxième Sexe, Le. *See* Second Sex, The

"Devil and Daniel Webster, The" (Benét) MPII:SS II-575

"Devil and Tom Walker, The" (Irving) MPII:SS II-579

Devil upon Two Sticks. *See* Diable boiteux, Le

Devils, The (Dostoevski). *See* Possessed, The

Devils, The (Whiting) CLCII I-395; MPII:D II-492

Devil's Elixir, The (Hoffman) CLC I-267; MP III-1467; MP:EF I-384

Devotion (Strauss) CLCII I-396; MPII:WF I-376

Devotion of the Cross, The (Calderón de la Barca) CLC I-267; MP III-1471

Dharma Bums, The (Kerouac) CLCII I-397; MPII:AF I-394

"Di Grasso" (Babel) MPII:SS II-600

Diable boiteux, Le (Lesage) CLC I-268; MP III-1474; MP:EF I-388

Dialogic Imagination, The (Bakhtin) MPII:NF I-355

Dialogue des héros de roman (Boileau-Despréaux) MP III-1479

Dialogues of Plato, The (Plato) MP III-1482

"Diamond as Big as the Ritz, The" (Fitzgerald) MPII:SS II-582

"Diamond Lens, The" (O'Brien, F.) MPII:SS II-587

Diana of the Crossways (Meredith) CLC I-269; MP III-1486; MP:BF I-318

Diaries of Kafka: 1910-1923, The (Kafka) MP III-1491

Diaries of Paul Klee, The (Klee) MPII:NF I-361

Diario de la guerra del cerdo. *See* Diary of the War of the Pig

Diary (Evelyn) MP III-1494

Diary (Gombrowicz) MPII:NF I-367

Diary (Pepys) MP III-1497

Diary and Letters of Mme. D'Arblay, The (Burney) MP III-1499

Diary of a Country Priest, The (Bernanos) CLC I-270; MP III-1503; MP:EF I-394

Diary of a Mad Old Man (Tanizaki) CLCII I-398; MPII:WF I-381

"Diary of a Madman, The" (Gogol) MPII:SS II-591

Diary of a Writer (Dostoevski) MP III-1506

Diary of Anaïs Nin, The (Nin) MPII:NF I-373

Diary of Henry Crabb Robinson, The (Robinson, H.) MP III-1509

Diary of Selma Lagerlöf, The (Lagerlöf) MPII:NF I-380

Diary of the War of the Pig (Bioy Casares) CLCII I-399; MPII:AF I-400

Diary of Virginia Woolf, The (Woolf) MPII:NF I-386

"Dichter, Der." *See* "Poet, The"

"Difference, The" (Glasgow) MPII:SS II-595

Different Drummer, A (Kelley, W.) CLCII I-400; MPII:AF I-404

Digby Grand (Whyte-Melville) CLC I-270; MP III-1512; MP:BF I-324

Dimanche de la vie, Le. *See* Sunday of Life, The

Dimitri Roudine. *See* Rudin

Dimple Hill. *See* Pilgrimage

Dining Room, The (Gurney) CLCII I-402; MPII:D II-497

Dinner at the Homesick Restaurant (Tyler) CLCII I-403; MPII:AF I-409

Dinner Party, The (Mauriac, C.) MP III-1516; MP:EF I-398

Dirty Linen (Stoppard) CLCII I-404; MPII:D II-502

Disciple, The (Bourget) CLC I-271; MP III-1519; MP:EF I-402

Discourse on the Origin of Inequality (Rousseau) MP III-1522

Discourses (Aretino) MP III-1524

"Disent les imbéciles." *See* "Fools Say"

Disinherited Mind, The (Heller) MPII:NF I-393

"Disorder and Early Sorrow" (Mann) MPII:SS II-604

Dispatches (Herr) MPII:NF I-398

"Displaced Person, The" (O'Connor, Flannery) MPII:SS II-607

Dispossessed, The (Le Guin) CLCII I-405; MPII:AF I-413

Disprezzo, Il. *See* Ghost at Noon, A

"Distant Episode, A" (Bowles, P.) MPII:SS II-610

Distant Relations (Fuentes) CLCII I-406; MPII:AF I-418

"District Doctor, The" (Turgenev) MPII:SS II-614

Divan, The (Hāfiz) MP III-1527

Divine Comedy, The (Dante Alighieri) CLC I-272; MP III-1529

Divine Fire, The (Sinclair, M.) CLC I-275; MP III-1534; MP:BF I-329

Divine Love and Wisdom (Swedenborg) MP III-1537

Diviners, The (Laurence) CLCII I-407; MPII:BCF I-383

Division of the Spoils, A. *See* Raj Quartet, The

Dni Turbinykh. *See* Day of the Turbins

Doctor Copernicus (Banville) CLCII II-409; MPII:BCF I-388

Doctor Faustus (Mann) CLC I-276; MP III-1539; MP:EF I-406

Doctor Faustus (Marlowe) CLC I-278; MP III-1543

"Dr. Heidegger's Experiment" (Hawthorne) MPII:SS II-617

Doctor in Spite of Himself, The (Molière) CLC I-279; MP III-1546

Dr. Jekyll and Mr. Hyde (Stevenson) CLC I-280; MP III-1550; MP:BF I-333

Doctor Pascal (Zola) CLC I-280; MP III-1553; MP:EF I-411

Doctor Thorne (Trollope) CLC I-281; MP III-1558; MP:BF I-337

Doctor Zhivago (Pasternak) MP III-1561; MP:EF I-417

"Doctor's Son, The" (O'Hara) MPII:SS II-621

Dodsworth (Lewis, S.) CLC I-283; MP III-1565; MP:AF I-294

Dog Beneath the Skin, The (Auden *and* Isherwood) CLCII II-410; MPII:D II-507

Dog Soldiers (Stone, R.) CLCII II-411; MPII:AF I-423

Dog Years (Grass) CLCII II-412; MPII:WF I-386

Doidinho. *See* Plantation Boy

"Doktor Murkes gesammeltes Schweigen." *See* "Murke's Collected Silences"

Dolina Issy. *See* Issa Valley, The

Dollmaker, The (Arnow) CLCII II-414; MPII:AF I-428

Doll's House, A (Ibsen) CLC I-284; MP III-1570

Dom na naberezhnoi. *See* House on the Embankment, The

Dombey and Son (Dickens) CLC I-286; MP III-1574; MP:BF I-341

Dominique (Fromentin) CLC I-288; MP III-1579; MP:EF I-422

Don Carlos (Schiller) CLC I-289; MP III-1582

Don Flows Home to the Sea, The (Sholokhov) CLC I-290; MP III-1585; MP:EF I-426

Don Goyo (Aguilera Malta) CLCII II-416; MPII:AF I-434

Don Juan (Byron) CLC I-291; MP III-1590

Don Juan (Molière) CLC I-293; MP III-1595

Don Juan Tenorio (Zorrilla) CLC I-294; MP III-1599

Don Quixote de la Mancha (Cervantes Saavedra) CLC I-294; MP III-1603; MP:EF I-431

Don Segundo Sombra (Güiraldes) CLC I-296; MP III-1609; MP:AF I-299

Doña Bárbara (Gallegos) CLC I-296; MP III-1614; MP:AF I-304

Dona Flor and Her Two Husbands (Amado) CLCII II-416; MPII:AF I-439

Doña Perfecta (Pérez Galdós) CLC I-298; MP III-1618; MP:EF I-438

"Donagh, The" (Carleton) MPII:SS II-624

Donne di Messina, Le. *See* Women of Messina

Dopisy Olze. *See* Letters to Olga

Dôra, Doralina (Queiroz) CLCII II-418; MPII:AF I-445

"Dos Elenas, Las." *See* "Two Elenas, The"

Dostoevsky (Berdyaev) MP III-1621

Dotazník, aneb modlitba za jedno město a přítele. *See* Questionnaire, The

Double, The (Dostoevski) CLCII II-419; MPII:WF I-390

Double-Dealer, The (Congreve) CLC I-298; MP III-1624

Double Helix, The (Watson) MPII:NF I-404

Down and Out in Paris and London (Orwell) MPII:NF I-409

Down from the Hill (Sillitoe) CLCII II-420; MPII:BCF I-393

Down There (Huysmans) CLC I-300; MP III-1627; MP:EF I-441

Downfall, The (Zola) CLC I-300; MP III-1629; MP:EF I-444

Dracula (Stoker) CLC I-301; MP III-1633; MP:BF I-347

Dragon Can't Dance, The (Lovelace) CLCII II-421; MPII:BCF I-398

Dragon Seed (Buck) CLC I-302; MP III-1638; MP:AF I-309

Dragon's Teeth. *See* Cousin Bazilio

Dram-shop, The. *See* Drink

Dramatic Lyrics. *See* Dramatic Monologues and Lyrics of Browning

Dramatic Monologues and Lyrics of Browning (Browning, R.) MP III-1641

Dramatic Romances and Lyrics. *See* Dramatic Monologues and Lyrics of Browning

Dramatis Personae (Browning, R.) MP III-1644

Dramatis Personae (Yeats). *See* Autobiography of William Butler Yeats, The

Dream Journey, A (Hanley) CLCII II-423; MPII:BCF I-403

"Dream of a Ridiculous Man, The" (Dostoevski) MPII:SS II-628

Dream of the Golden Mountains, The (Cowley) MPII:NF I-414

Dream of the Red Chamber (Tsao Hsüeh-ch'in) CLC I-302; MP III-1648; MP:EF I-448

Dream on Monkey Mountain (Walcott) CLCII II-424; MPII:D II-513

Dream Play, A (Strindberg) CLCII II-425; MPII:D II-518

Dreambook for Our Time, A (Konwicki) CLCII II-426; MPII:WF I-395

"Dreamers in a Dead Language" (Paley) MPII:SS II-632

Dreigroschenoper, Die. *See* Threepenny Opera, The

Drink (Zola) CLC I-306; MP III-1653; MP:EF I-454

"Drive in the Country, A" (Greene) MPII:SS II-636

Drömspel, Ett. *See* Dream Play, A

"Drover's Wife, The" (Lawson) MPII:SS II-639

Drowned and the Saved, The (Levi) MPII:NF I-420

Drugaya zhizn'. *See* Another Life

Drugie Berega. *See* Speak, Memory

Drums (Boyd) CLC I-307; MP III-1656; MP:AF I-313

Drums Along the Mohawk (Edmonds) CLC I-307; MP III-1659; MP:AF I-317

Drums Under the Window. *See* Mirror in My House

"Drunkard, The" (O'Connor, Frank) MPII:SS II-643

"Dry September" (Faulkner) MPII:SS II-646

Duchess of Malfi, The (Webster) CLC I-308; MP III-1664

"Duel, The" (Chekhov) CLCII II-428;
    MPII:SS II-650
"Duel" (Matheson) MPII:SS II-653
Duino Elegies (Rilke) MP III-1669
Dumb Waiter, The (Pinter) CLCII II-429;
    MPII:D II-524
D'un château l'autre. *See* Castle to Castle
Dunciad, The (Pope) MP III-1672
Dune. *See* Dune trilogy, The
Dune Messiah. *See* Dune trilogy, The
Dune trilogy, The (Herbert, F.) CLCII
    II-430; MPII:AF I-451
"Dunwich Horror, The" (Lovecraft)
    MPII:SS II-657

"Dushechka." *See* "Darling, The"
Dusty Answer (Lehmann) CLCII II-433;
    MPII:BCF I-408
Dutchman (Baraka) CLCII II-434; MPII:D
    II-529
"Dvadtsat'shest' i odna." *See* "Twenty-six
    Men and a Girl"
Dvärgen. *See* Dwarf, The
Dvoynik. *See* Double, The
Dwarf, The (Lagerkvist) CLCII II-435;
    MPII:WF I-399
Dynasts, The (Hardy) CLC I-310; MP III-
    1675
Dziennik. *See* Diary

E

Each in His Own Way (Pirandello) CLCII
II-436; MPII:D II-534

Eagle and the Serpent, The (Guzmán) MP
III-1679; MP:AF I-322

Early Diary of Anaïs Nin, The. *See*
Diary of Anaïs Nin, The

Earth (Zola) CLC I-311; MP III-1682;
MP:EF I-458

Earthly Paradise, The (Morris, William)
MP III-1687

Earthly Powers (Burgess) CLCII II-437;
MPII:BCF I-413

"Earthquake in Chile, The" (Kleist)
MPII:SS II-661

East of Eden (Steinbeck) CLC I-313; MP
III-1689; MP:AF I-326

Eastward Ho! (Chapman, Jonson, *and*
Marston) CLC I-313; MP III-1693

Eating People Is Wrong (Bradbury, M.)
CLCII II-439; MPII:BCF I-418

Ebony and Ivory (Powys, L.) MP III-
1697; MP:BF I-352

Ebony Tower, The (Fowles) CLCII II-440;
MPII:BCF I-422

Ecclesiazusae, The (Aristophanes) CLC I-
314; MP III-1699

Echoing Grove, The (Lehmann) CLCII II-
442; MPII:BCF I-427

Eclogues (Vergil) MP III-1702

Écrits (Lacan) MPII:NF I-425

Écriture et la différence, L'. *See* Writing
and Difference

Ecstasy of Rita Joe, The (Ryga) CLCII II-
443; MPII:D II-540

Eden End (Priestley) CLCII II-444;
MPII:D II-546

Edge of the Storm, The (Yáñez) MP:AF
I-331

Edible Woman, The (Atwood) CLCII II-
445; MPII:BCF I-432

Edmund Campion (Waugh) MP III-1705

Educated Cat, The. *See* Life and Opinions
of Kater Murr, The

Education of Henry Adams, The (Adams,
H.) MP III-1708

"Edward and God" (Kundera) MPII:SS II-
664

Edward the Second (Marlowe) CLC I-315;
MP III-1711

Effi Briest (Fontane) CLC I-317; MP III-
1716; MP:EF I-464

"Egg, The" (Anderson) MPII:SS II-668

Egmont (Goethe) CLC I-317; MP III-1719

Egoist, The (Meredith) CLC I-318; MP
III-1723; MP:BF I-355

Eichmann in Jerusalem (Arendt) MPII:NF
I-431

"Eight Views of Tokyo" (Dazai) MPII:SS
II-672

1876 (Vidal) CLCII II-446; MPII:AF I-457

Eighth Day, The (Wilder) CLCII II-447;
MPII:AF I-462

"Eighty-Yard Run, The" (Shaw) MPII:SS
II-677

Einstein on the Beach (Wilson, R., *and*
Glass) CLCII II-449; MPII:D II-551

El Señor Presidente (Asturias) MP III-1726

Elder Statesman, The (Eliot, T. S.) MP
III-1728

Elective Affinities (Goethe) CLC I-319;
MP III-1731; MP:EF I-468

Electra (Euripides) CLC I-320; MP III-
1735

Electric Kool-Aid Acid Test, The (Wolfe)
MPII:NF II-437

Elegia di Madonna Fiametta. *See*
L'Amorosa Fiammetta

Elegies of Propertius, The (Propertius) MP
III-1739

Elegy of Madonna Fiametta. *See*
L'Amorosa Fiammetta

Elementary Forms of the Religious Life,
The (Durkheim) MPII:NF II-443

Elmer Gantry (Lewis, S.) MP III-1742;
MP:AF I-335

Èloges and Other Poems (Perse) MP III-
1746

Eloise. *See* New Héloïse, The

Elsewhere, Perhaps (Oz) CLCII II-450;
MPII:WF I-403

Embers (Beckett) CLCII II-451; MPII:D II-557

Embezzler, The (Auchincloss) CLCII II-452; MPII:AF II-467

Emigrants, The (Bojer) CLC I-321; MP III-1749; MP:EF I-473

Emigrants of Ahadarra, The (Carleton) CLC I-322; MP III-1752; MP:BF I-359

Émile (Rousseau) CLC I-322; MP III-1755; MP:EF I-476

Emilia Galotti (Lessing) CLC I-323; MP III-1758

Eminent Victorians (Strachey) MP III-1760

Emma (Austen) CLC I-324; MP III-1763; MP:BF I-363

Emperor, The (Kapuściński) MPII:NF II-449

Emperor Jones, The (O'Neill) CLC I-325; MP III-1769

Empire of the Sun (Ballard) CLCII II-453; MPII:BCF I-437

Emploi du temps, L'. See Passing Time

"Empress's Ring, The" (Hale) MPII:SS II-680

"Enchanted Doll, The" (Gallico) MPII:SS II-683

"End, The" (Beckett) MPII:SS II-686

End of Bad Roads, The. See Splendors and Miseries of Courtesans, The

End of the Affair, The (Greene) CLCII II-454; MPII:BCF I-442

End of the Battle, The. See Sword of Honour

"End of the Game" (Cortázar) MPII:SS II-689

End of the Road, The (Barth) MP III-1772; MP:AF I-339

End of the World News, The (Burgess) CLCII II-455; MPII:BCF I-447

End to Torment (H. D.) MPII:NF II-454

End Zone (DeLillo) CLCII II-457; MPII:AF II-472

"Ende einer Welt, Das." See "World Ends, A"

Endgame (Beckett) CLCII II-458; MPII:D II-563

"Enduring Chill, The" (O'Connor, Flannery) MPII:SS II-692

Endymion (Lyly) CLC I-325; MP III-1774

Enemies (Singer) CLCII II-458; MPII:AF II-476; MPII:WF I-409

"Enemies, The" (Thomas) MPII:SS II-695

Enemy of the People, An (Ibsen) CLC I-326; MP III-1777

"Enfant malade, L'." See "Sick Child, The"

Enfant noir, L'. See Dark Child, The

"Engagement in Santo Domingo, The" (Kleist) MPII:SS II-698

Engineer of Human Souls, The (Škvorecký) CLCII II-460; MPII:WF I-414

England Under the Stuarts (Trevelyan) MP III-1781

English Notebooks, The (Hawthorne) MP III-1784

English Teacher, The. See Grateful to Life and Death

Enoch Arden (Tennyson) CLC I-328; MP III-1787

"Enoch Soames" (Beerbohm) MPII:SS II-702

"Enormous Radio, The" (Cheever) MPII:SS II-706

Enormous Room, The (Cummings) CLC I-328; MP III-1789; MP:AF I-342

Enquiry Concerning Human Understanding, An (Hume) MP III-1793

Enrico IV. See Henry IV

Entertainer, The (Osborne) CLCII II-461; MPII:D II-569

Entertaining Mr. Sloane (Orton) CLCII II-462; MPII:D II-574

"Entropy" (Pynchon) MPII:SS II-709

Envy (Olesha) CLCII II-463; MPII:WF I-421

"Envy" (Ozick) MPII:SS II-712

Epic of Gilgamesh, The (Unknown) CLC I-329; MP III-1796

Epigrams of Martial (Martial) MP III-1800

Epigrams of Meleager, The (Meleager) MP III-1802

Epilogue. *See* Country Girls Trilogy, The

Epilogue: The Prague Orgy. *See* Zuckerman Bound

Epinicia (Pindar) MP III-1805

Epistles of Horace, The (Horace) MP III-1808

Epitaph of a Small Winner (Machado de Assís) CLC I-330; MP:AF I-346; MP III-1811

Equal Danger (Sciascia) CLCII II-464; MPII:WF I-425

Equations of Love, The (Wilson, E.) CLCII II-465; MPII:BCF I-452

Equus (Shaffer, P.) CLCII II-466; MPII:D II-579

Erasers, The (Robbe-Grillet) CLCII II-467; MPII:WF I-430

"Erdbeben in Chili." *See* "Earthquake in Chile, The"

Erde und Feuer. *See* Silesian Tetralogy, The

Erec and Enide (Chrétien de Troyes) CLC I-331; MP III-1816

Erewhon (Butler) CLC I-331; MP III-1822; MP:BF I-370

Erinnerungen, Träume, Gedanken von C. G. Jung. *See* Memories, Dreams, Reflections

Erste Polka, Die. *See* Silesian Tetralogy, The

Erwählte, Der. *See* Holy Sinner, The

"Erzähler, Der." *See* Storyteller, The

Eskimos, Chicanos, Indians. *See* Children of Crisis

Esmond in India (Jhabvala) CLCII II-468; MPII:BCF I-456

Espoir, L'. *See* Man's Hope

Essais (Montaigne) MP III-1825

Essay Concerning Human Understanding, An (Locke) MP III-1828

Essay of Dramatic Poesy, An (Dryden) MP III-1831

Essay on Criticism (Pope) MP III-1834

Essay on Man (Pope) MP IV-1837

Essay Towards a New Theory of Vision, An (Berkeley) MP IV-1840

Essays (Bacon) MP IV-1842

Essays: First and Second Series (Emerson) MP IV-1845

Essays of a Biologist (Huxley, J.) MP IV-1848

Essays of Aldous Huxley, The (Huxley, A.) MP IV-1851

Essays of Edgar Allan Poe, The (Poe) MP IV-1854

Essays of Elia and Last Essays of Elia (Lamb) MP IV-1857

Essays of G. K. Chesterton, The (Chesterton) MP IV-1859

Essays of Henry David Thoreau, The (Thoreau) MP IV-1863

Essays of Max Beerbohm, The (Beerbohm) MP IV-1866

Este domingo. *See* This Sunday

"Esther" (Toomer) MPII:SS II-716

Esther Waters (Moore, G.) CLC I-332; MP IV-1870; MP:BF I-374

Estrangement. *See* Autobiography of William Butler Yeats, The

Eternal Present, The (Giedion) MPII:NF II-460

"Ethan Brand" (Hawthorne) MPII:SS II-720

Ethan Frome (Wharton) CLC I-333; MP IV-1873; MP:AF I-351

Ethics (Bonhoeffer) MPII:NF II-466

Ethics (Spinoza) MP IV-1876

Ethik. *See* Ethics (Bonhoeffer)

Eugene Aram (Bulwer-Lytton) CLC I-334; MP IV-1879; MP:BF I-378

Eugene Onegin (Pushkin) CLC I-334; MP IV-1883

Eugénie Grandet (Balzac) CLC I-335; MP IV-1886; MP:EF I-480

Eunuch, The (Terence) CLC I-336; MP IV-1891

Euphues and His England (Lyly) CLC I-338; MP IV-1894; MP:BF I-382

Euphues, the Anatomy of Wit (Lyly) CLC I-338; MP IV-1898; MP:BF I-387

Eva Trout (Bowen) CLCII II-470; MPII:BCF I-461

Evan Harrington (Meredith) CLC I-339;
MP IV-1902; MP:BF I-391
Evangeline (Longfellow) CLC I-340; MP
IV-1906
"Evangelio según Marco, El." *See*
"Gospel According to Mark, The"
Eva's Man (Jones, G.) CLCII II-471;
MPII:AF II-481
Eve of St. Agnes, The (Keats) CLC I-
340; MP IV-1909
Evelina (Burney) CLC I-341; MP IV-
1913; MP:BF I-395
"Eveline" (Joyce) MPII:SS II-724
"Evening Performance, An" (Garrett)
MPII:SS II-727
Everlasting Man, The (Chesterton)
MPII:NF II-471
Every Man in His Humour (Jonson) CLC
I-343; MP IV-1918
Every Man out of His Humour (Jonson)
CLC I-344; MP IV-1924
"Everyday Use" (Walker) MPII:SS II-731
Everyman (Unknown) CLC I-345; MP IV-
1928
"Everything That Rises Must Converge"
(O'Connor, Flannery) MPII:SS II-735
Excellent Women (Pym) CLCII II-473;
MPII:BCF I-466

Except the Lord. *See* Second Trilogy
Executioner's Song, The (Mailer) CLCII
II-474; MPII:AF II-486
Exemplary Novels (Cervantes Saavedra)
MP IV-1933; MP:EF II-485
Exile and the Kingdom (Camus) MP IV-
1936; MP:EF II-489
Exiles (Arlen) MPII:NF II-476
Exiles (Joyce) CLC I-345; MP IV-1939
Exile's Return (Cowley) MPII:NF II-481
Exit the King (Ionesco) CLCII II-475;
MPII:D II-585
Exodus (Uris) CLCII II-475; MPII:AF II-
491
Expedition of Humphry Clinker, The. *See*
Humphry Clinker
"Expérience de la vie d'usine." *See*
Factory Journal
"Experiment in Misery, An" (Crane)
MPII:SS II-739
Explosion in a Cathedral (Carpentier)
CLCII II-477; MPII:AF II-496
Eye of the Storm, The (White) CLCII II-
478; MPII:BCF I-472
Eyeless in Gaza (Huxley) CLCII II-480;
MPII:BCF I-478
Ezra (Kops) CLCII II-481; MPII:D II-590

F

Fable, A (Faulkner) CLC I-346; MP IV-1942; MP:AF I-354

Fable for Critics, A (Lowell, J.) MP IV-1948

Fables (La Fontaine) MP IV-1951

Faces and Masks. *See* Memory of Fire

Faces in My Time. *See* To Keep the Ball Rolling

"Faces of Blood Kindred, The" (Goyen) MPII:SS II-743

Fackel im Ohr, Die. *See* Torch in My Ear, The

Factory Journal (Weil) MPII:NF II-487

Facts, The (Roth) MPII:NF II-492

Faerie Queene, The (Spenser) CLC I-347; MP IV-1953

Fahrenheit 451 (Bradbury, R.) CLCII II-482; MPII:AF II-501

Fair, The (Arreola) CLCII II-483; MPII:AF II-505

Fair Maid of Perth, The (Scott, Sir W.) CLC I-351; MP IV-1958; MP:BF I-400

Fairly Honourable Defeat, A (Murdoch) CLCII II-485; MPII:BCF I-483

Faith and the Good Thing (Johnson, C.) CLCII II-487; MPII:AF II-510

"Faith in a Tree" (Paley) MPII:SS II-747

Faith, Sex, Mystery (Gilman) MPII:NF II-497

Faithful Shepherdess, The (Fletcher) CLC I-352; MP IV-1962

Falconer (Cheever) CLCII II-488; MPII:AF II-515

"Falešný autostop." *See* "Hitchhiking Game, The"

Fall, The (Camus) MP IV-1965; MP:EF II-493

"Fall of the House of Usher, The" (Poe) CLC I-353; MP IV-1968; MP:AF I-360; MPII:SS II-751

Familia lejana, Una. *See* Distant Relations

Familiar Essays of William Hazlitt, The (Hazlitt) MP IV-1974

"Family Affair, A" (Maupassant) MPII:SS II-755

Family at Gilje, The (Lie) CLC I-354; MP IV-1977; MP:EF II-497

Family Happiness (Tolstoy) CLCII II-489; MPII:WF I-435

Family of Pascual Duarte, The (Cela) MP IV-1980; MP:EF II-501

Family Reunion, The (Eliot, T. S.) CLC I-355; MP IV-1983

Family Voices (Pinter) CLCII II-490; MPII:D II-595

"Fancy Woman, The" (Taylor) MPII:SS II-759

Far Away and Long Ago (Hudson) MP IV-1986

Far from the Madding Crowd (Hardy) CLC I-356; MP IV-1990; MP:BF I-405

Far Journey of Oudin, The. *See* Guyana Quartet, The

Far Tortuga (Matthiessen) CLCII II-491; MPII:AF II-521

Farewell from Nowhere (Maximov) CLCII II-492; MPII:WF I-440

Farewell, My Lovely (Chandler) CLCII II-493; MPII:AF II-527

Farewell Party, The (Kundera) CLCII II-494; MPII:WF I-446

Farewell to Arms, A (Hemingway) CLC I-357; MP IV-1995; MP:AF I-366

"Fat of the Land, The" (Yezierska) MPII:SS II-763

Fate of the Earth, The (Schell) MPII:NF II-502

Father, The (Strindberg) CLC I-358; MP IV-2000

Father Goriot (Balzac) CLC I-359; MP IV-2007; MP:EF II-505

Fathers, The (Tate) MP IV-2012; MP:AF I-371

Fathers and Sons (Turgenev) CLC I-361; MP IV-2015; MP:EF II-510

"Father's Daughters, The" (Spark) MPII:SS II-767

Faust (Goethe) CLC I-362; MP IV-2020

Federalist, The (Hamilton, Madison, *and* Jay) MP IV-2025

Felix Holt, the Radical (Eliot, G.) CLC I-364; MP IV-2029; MP:BF I-410

Fellowship of the Ring, The (Tolkien) MP IV-2033; MP:BF I-414

Female Friends (Weldon) CLCII II-495; MPII:BCF I-488

Female Man, The (Russ) CLCII II-496; MPII:AF II-532

Feminine Mystique, The (Friedan) MPII:NF II-507

"Femme adultère, La." *See* "Adulterous Woman, The"

Fences (Wilson, August) CLCII II-498; MPII:D II-600

Fenian Cycle. *See* Finn Cycle, The

Ferdydurke (Gombrowicz) CLCII II-499; MPII:WF II-451

Feria, La. *See* Fair, The

Fermo e Lucia. *See* Betrothed, The

Fêtes Galantes and Other Poems (Verlaine) MP IV-2038

Fiasco (Lem) CLCII II-500; MPII:WF II-456

Ficciones (Borges) MP IV-2040; MP:AF I-375

"Ficelle, La." *See* "Piece of String, The"

Fiddler's House, The (Colum) CLCII II-501; MPII:D II-605

"Field of Mustard, The" (Coppard) MPII:SS II-771

Field of Vision, The (Morris, Wright) MP IV-2042; MP:AF I-378

Fields, The (Richter) CLC I-366; MP IV-2046; MP:AF I-382

Fiesta en noviembre. *See* Fiesta in November

Fiesta in November (Mallea) MP IV-2050; MP:AF I-386

Fifth Business. *See* Deptford Trilogy, The

Fifth Queen, The (Ford, F.) MP IV-2055; MP:BF I-420

Fifth Queen Crowned, The. *See* Fifth Queen, The

Fifth Son, The (Wiesel) CLCII II-502; MPII:WF II-461

Fifties, The (Wilson) MPII:NF IV-1500

"Fight, The" (Thomas) MPII:SS II-774

"Figure in the Carpet, The" (James, H.) MPII:SS II-777

File No. 113 (Gaboriau) CLC I-366; MP IV-2058; MP:EF II-515

Filo del agua, Al. *See* Edge of the Storm, The

Filostrato, Il (Boccaccio) MP IV-2062

"Fin, La." *See* "End, The"

Fin de Chéri, La. *See* Last of Chéri, The

Fin de partie. *See* Endgame

"Final del juego." *See* "End of the Game"

Final Mist, The (Bombal) CLCII II-503; MPII:AF II-537

Final Payments (Gordon) CLCII II-504; MPII:AF II-542

Financial Expert, The (Narayan) CLCII II-505; MPII:BCF II-493

Financier, The (Dreiser) CLC I-367; MP IV-2067; MP:AF I-391

Finn Cycle, The (Unknown) CLC I-369; MP IV-2071; MP:BF I-424

Finnegans Wake (Joyce) CLC I-370; MP IV-2076; MP:BF I-430

Fire-Dwellers, The (Laurence) CLCII II-506; MPII:BCF II-509

Fire from Heaven (Renault) CLCII II-508; MPII:BCF II-498

Fire Next Time, The (Baldwin) MPII:NF II-512

Fire on the Mountain (Desai) CLCII II-509; MPII:BCF II-504

Fire Raisers, The. *See* Firebugs, The

Firebugs, The (Frisch) CLCII II-510; MPII:D II-610

Fireflies (Naipaul, S.) CLCII II-511; MPII:BCF II-514

First Circle, The (Solzhenitsyn) CLCII II-512; MPII:WF II-465

First Love (Turgenev) CLCII II-516; MPII:WF II-470

First Mondays. *See* Monday Conversations

First Polka, The. *See* Silesian Tetralogy, The

"Firstborn" (Woiwode) CLCII II-517;
MPII:SS II-781
Fisher King, The (Powell) CLCII II-518;
MPII:BCF II-520
Fisher Maiden, The (Björnson) CLC I-371;
MP IV-2079; MP:EF II-519
"Five-Forty-Eight, The" (Cheever)
MPII:SS II-785
"Five-Twenty" (White) MPII:SS II-788
Five Women Who Loved Love (Ibara
Saikaku) CLC I-372; MP IV-2082;
MP:EF II-522
Fixer, The (Malamud) CLCII II-519;
MPII:AF II-548
Flanders Road, The (Simon, C.) CLCII II-
520; MPII:WF II-475
Flaubert's Parrot (Barnes, J.) CLCII II-
521; MPII:BCF II-526
Flaws in the Glass (White) MPII:NF II-
517
"Flea, The." See "Lefty"
Fliehendes Pferd, Ein. See Runaway
Horse
Flies, The (Azuela) MP IV-2085; MP:AF
I-395
Flies, The (Sartre) MP IV-2089
"Flight" (Steinbeck) MPII:SS II-792
Flight to Canada (Reed) CLCII II-522;
MPII:AF II-551
Floating Opera, The (Barth) CLCII II-524;
MPII:AF II-557
Flounder, The (Grass) CLCII II-525;
MPII:WF II-481
"Flowering Judas" (Porter) MPII:SS II-795
Flowering Peach, The (Odets) CLCII II-
527; MPII:D II-616
Flowers of Evil (Baudelaire) MP IV-2092
"Fly, The" (Mansfield) MPII:SS II-799
Flying Colours. See Captain Horatio
Hornblower
"Flying Home" (Ellison) MPII:SS II-803
Fogo morto (Lins do Rêgo) MP:AF I-400
Folie et déraison. See Madness and
Civilization
Folks, The (Suckow) MP IV-2094;
MP:AF I-404

Folkways (Sumner) MP IV-2097
Foma Gordeyev (Gorky) CLC I-373; MP
IV-2100; MP:EF II-526
Fontamara (Silone) MP IV-2104; MP:EF
II-530
Fool for Love (Shepard) CLCII II-529;
MPII:D II-622
Fool of Quality, The (Brooke, H.) CLC I-
374; MP IV-2107; MP:BF I-434
Fool's Errand, A (Tourgée) MP IV-2110;
MP:AF I-408
"Fools Say" (Sarraute) CLCII II-530;
MPII:WF II-486
for colored girls who have considered
suicide/when the rainbow is enuf
(Shange) CLCII II-531; MPII:D II-627
"For Esmé--with Love and Squalor"
(Salinger) MPII:SS II-809
For Whom the Bell Tolls (Hemingway)
CLC I-374; MP IV-2114; MP:AF I-413
Forbidden Forest, The (Eliade) CLCII II-
532; MPII:WF II-491
Force de l'âge, La. See Prime of Life,
The
Forerunner, The. See Romance of
Leonardo da Vinci, The
Forêt interdite, La. See Forbidden Forest,
The
Fork River Space Project, The (Morris)
CLCII II-534; MPII:AF II-561
Formes élémentaires de la vie religieuse,
Les. See Elementary Forms of the
Religious Life, The
Forsyte Saga, The (Galsworthy) CLC I-
376; MP IV-2119; MP:BF I-438
Forties, The (Wilson) MPII:NF IV-1500
Fortitude (Walpole, Hugh) CLC I-377; MP
IV-2124; MP:BF I-443
Fortress, The (Walpole, Hugh) CLC I-378;
MP IV-2128; MP:BF I-447
Fortunata and Jacinta (Pérez Galdós)
CLC I-379; MP IV-2132; MP:EF II-534
Fortunate Man, A (Berger) MPII:NF II-
521
Fortunate Mistress, The. See Roxana

Fortunes and Misfortunes of the Famous Moll Flanders. *See* Moll Flanders

Fortunes of Nigel, The (Scott, W.) CLC I-380; MP IV-2137; MP:BF I-452

Fortunes of Richard Mahony, The (Richardson, H.) CLC I-382; MP IV-2142; MP:BF I-458

Forty Days of Musa Dagh, The (Werfel) CLC I-382; MP IV-2145; MP:EF II-539

Foundation. *See* Foundation trilogy, The

Foundation and Empire. *See* Foundation trilogy, The

Foundation Pit, The (Platonov) CLCII II-534; MPII:WF II-497

Foundation trilogy, The (Asimov) CLCII II-536; MPII:AF II-565

Fountain Overflows, The (West, R.) CLCII II-540; MPII:BCF II-532

Four-Gated City, The. *See* Children of Violence

Four Quartets (Eliot, T. S.) MP IV-2148

Four Years. *See* Autobiography of William Butler Yeats, The

Fox, The (Lawrence) CLCII II-541; MPII:BCF II-538

Fragmented Life of Don Jacobo Lerner, The (Goldemberg) CLCII II-542; MPII:AF II-572

Framley Parsonage (Trollope) CLC I-383; MP IV-2151; MP:BF I-462

Franchiser, The (Elkin) CLCII II-543; MPII:AF II-576

Frankenstein (Shelley, M.) CLC I-385; MP IV-2154; MP:BF I-466

Frankenstein Unbound (Aldiss) CLCII II-544; MPII:BCF II-542

Franny and Zooey (Salinger) MP IV-2157; MP:AF I-418

Fraternity (Galsworthy) CLC I-386; MP IV-2159; MP:BF I-470

Free Fall (Golding) MP IV-2163; MP:BF I-475

Freedom of the City, The (Friel) CLCII II-545; MPII:D II-633

Freedom or Death (Kazantzakis) MP IV-2166; MP:EF II-543

French Lieutenant's Woman, The (Fowles) CLCII II-546; MPII:BCF II-549

French Revolution, The (Carlyle) MP IV-2169

French Without Tears (Rattigan) CLCII II-547; MPII:D II-639

"Freshest Boy, The" (Fitzgerald) MPII:SS II-813

Friar Bacon and Friar Bungay (Greene, R.) CLC I-386; MP IV-2172

Friday (Tournier) CLCII II-548; MPII:WF II-502

"Friend of Kafka, A" (Singer) MPII:SS II-817

Friends and Heroes. *See* Balkan trilogy, The

Frithiof's Saga (Tegnér) CLC I-387; MP IV-2175

Frogs, The (Aristophanes) CLC I-388; MP IV-2178

From Bauhaus to Our House (Wolfe) MPII:NF II-527

From Berlin to Jerusalem (Scholem) MPII:NF II-534

From Cuba with a Song (Sarduy) CLCII II-550; MPII:AF II-581

From Here to Eternity (Jones, J.) CLCII II-551; MPII:AF II-586

From the Terrace (O'Hara) CLCII II-552; MPII:AF II-591

Frontier in American History, The (Turner) MP IV-2182

Fruit of the Tree, The (Wharton) CLC I-389; MP IV-2185; MP:AF I-421

Fruits of the Earth (Grove) CLCII II-554; MPII:BCF II-553

Full Moon (Wodehouse) CLCII II-555; MPII:BCF II-557

Funeral, The (Steele) CLC I-390; MP IV-2188

Funeral Games (Renault) CLCII II-557; MPII:BCF II-561

"Funes, the Memorious" (Borges) MPII:SS II-820

Funnyhouse of a Negro (Kennedy, A.) CLCII II-558; MPII:D II-645

Fürsorgliche Belagerung. *See* Safety Net, The

Füten rōjin nikki. *See* Diary of a Mad Old Man

Futile Life of Pito Pérez, The (Romero) CLCII II-559; MPII:AF II-597

G

G. (Berger, J.) CLCII II-560; MPII:BCF II-567

Gabriela, Clove and Cinnamon (Amado) MP IV-2192; MP:AF I-425

Gabriela, cravo e canela. *See* Gabriela, Clove and Cinnamon

Galileo (Brecht) CLCII II-562; MPII:D II-650

Gambler, The (Dostoevski) CLC I-390; MP IV-2195; MP:EF II-547

Games Were Coming, The (Anthony) CLCII II-563; MPII:BCF II-572

"Gamlet Shchigrovskogo uezda." *See* "Hamlet of the Shchigrovsky District"

Garden, The (Strong) CLC I-392; MP IV-2200; MP:BF I-479

Garden, Ashes (Kiš) CLCII II-564; MPII:WF II-507

Garden of Earthly Delights, The (Clarke, M.) CLCII II-565; MPII:D II-654

"Garden of Forking Paths, The" (Borges) MPII:SS II-824

Garden of the Finzi-Continis, The (Bassani) CLCII II-566; MPII:WF II-511

Garden Party, The (Havel) CLCII II-567; MPII:D II-660

"Gardener, The" (Kipling) MPII:SS II-828

Gardener's Dog, The (Vega) CLC I-392; MP IV-2203

Gargantua and Pantagruel (Rabelais) CLC I-393; MP IV-2208; MP:EF II-553

Gargoyles (Bernhard) CLCII II-568; MPII:WF II-516

Gates of the Forest, The (Wiesel) CLCII II-570; MPII:WF II-520

Gathering Evidence (Bernhard) MPII:NF II-539

Gaucho: Martín Fierro, The (Hernández) CLC I-394; MP IV-2213

Gaudier-Brzeska (Pound) MPII:NF II-544

Gaudy Night (Sayers) CLCII II-571; MPII:BCF II-577

Gazapo (Sainz) CLCII II-572; MPII:AF II-602

Gemini (Giovanni) MPII:NF II-549

Gemini (Tournier) CLCII II-573; MPII:WF II-524

General Introduction to Psychoanalysis, A (Freud) MP IV-2218

Generous Man, A (Price) CLCII II-574; MPII:AF II-607

Genesis. *See* Memory of Fire

"Genius," The (Dreiser) CLC I-395; MP IV-2221; MP:AF I-428

Gentleman Dancing Master, The (Wycherley) CLC I-396; MP IV-2226

"Gentleman from Cracow, The" (Singer) MPII:SS II-831

"Gentleman from San Francisco, The" (Bunin) MPII:SS II-835

Gentleman Usher, The (Chapman) CLC I-396; MP IV-2230

Gentlemen in England (Wilson, A. N.) CLCII II-575; MPII:BCF II-582

Geography of a Horse Dreamer (Shepard) CLCII II-577; MPII:D II-666

George Passant. *See* Strangers and Brothers

Georgia Scenes (Longstreet) MP IV-2233; MP:AF I-433

Georgics (Vergil) MP IV-2236

Gerettete Zunge, Die. *See* Tongue Set Free, The

Germinal (Zola) CLC I-397; MP IV-2238; MP:EF II-558

Germinie Lacerteux (Goncourt *and* Goncourt) CLC I-398; MP IV-2242; MP:EF II-563

Geschichten Jaakobs, Die. *See* Joseph and His Brothers

Getting Out (Norman) CLCII II-577; MPII:D II-672

Gettysburg (Singmaster) MP IV-2246; MP:AF I-436

Gewicht der Welt, Das. *See* Weight of the World, The

"Ghost and Flesh, Water and Dirt" (Goyen) MPII:SS II-839

Ghost at Noon, A (Moravia) CLCII II-578; MPII:WF II-529

Ghost Sonata, The (Strindberg) CLCII II-579; MPII:D II-678

Ghost Writer, The (Roth, P.) CLCII II-580. *See also* Zuckerman Bound

Ghosts (Ibsen) CLC I-399; MP IV-2250

Giants in the Earth (Rölvaag) CLC I-400; MP IV-2255; MP:AF I-440

Giardino dei Finzi-Contini, Il. *See* Garden of the Finzi-Continis, The

Gift, The (Nabokov) CLCII II-581; MPII:WF II-534

"Gift, The" (Steinbeck) MPII:SS II-843

Gift of Good Land, The (Berry) MPII:NF II-555

"Gift of the Magi, The" (O. Henry) MPII:SS II-847

Gigi (Colette) CLCII II-582; MPII:WF II-539

Gil Blas (Lesage) CLC I-401; MP IV-2260; MP:EF II-567

Gil Blas of Santillane. *See* Gil Blas

Gilded Age, The (Twain *and* Warner) CLC I-402; MP IV-2263; MP:AF I-445

Giles Goat-Boy (Barth) CLCII II-584; MPII:AF II-613

"Gimpel the Fool" (Singer) MPII:SS II-850

Ginger Man, The (Donleavy) CLCII II-585; MPII:AF II-618; MPII:BCF II-586

"Giornata d'uno scrutatore, La." *See* "Watcher, The"

Giovanni's Room (Baldwin) CLCII II-586; MPII:AF II-623

Girl Green as Elderflower, The (Stow) CLCII II-587; MPII:BCF II-590

Girl in Winter, A (Larkin) CLCII II-589; MPII:BCF II-597

Girl, 20 (Amis) CLCII II-590; MPII:BCF II-602

Girls in Their Married Bliss. *See* Country Girls Trilogy, The

"Girls in Their Summer Dresses, The" (Shaw) MPII:SS II-853

"Giui de Mopassan." *See* "Guy de Maupassant"

"Gladius Dei" (Mann) MPII:SS II-857

Glance Away, A (Wideman) CLCII II-591; MPII:AF II-628

Glasperlenspiel, Das. *See* Glass Bead Game, The

Glass Bead Game, The (Hesse) CLCII II-592; MPII:WF II-543

Glass Key, The (Hammett) CLC I-403; MP IV-2267; MP:AF I-449

Glass Menagerie, The (Williams, T.) CLC I-403; MP IV-2270

Glass of Blessings, A (Pym) CLCII II-594; MPII:BCF II-607

"Gleaner, The" (Bates) MPII:SS II-860

Glengarry Glen Ross (Mamet) CLCII II-595; MPII:D II-684

Gli sposi promesi. *See* Betrothed, The

"Glimpse into Another Country" (Morris) MPII:SS II-863

Głos pana. *See* His Master's Voice

Go-Between, The (Hartley) CLCII II-597; MPII:BCF II-612

Go Down, Moses (Faulkner) MP IV-2272; MP:AF I-453

Go Tell It on the Mountain (Baldwin) MP IV-2276; MP:AF I-458

Goalie's Anxiety at the Penalty Kick, The (Handke) CLCII II-598; MPII:WF II-549

Goat Song (Werfel) CLC I-404; MP IV-2279

"Gobseck" (Balzac) MPII:SS II-867

God Bless You, Mr. Rosewater (Vonnegut) CLCII II-599; MPII:AF II-634

God on the Rocks (Gardam) CLCII II-600; MPII:BCF II-617

Gödel, Escher, Bach (Hofstadter) MPII:NF II-561

Gods Are Athirst, The (France) CLC I-405; MP IV-2282; MP:EF II-571

God's Bits of Wood (Sembène) CLCII II-601; MPII:WF II-553

God's Little Acre (Caldwell) CLCII II-603; MPII:AF II-639

Gogo no eikō. *See* Sailor Who Fell from Grace with the Sea, The

"Gogol's Wife" (Landolfi) MPII:SS II-871

"Going Home" (Trevor) MPII:SS II-876

"Going to Meet the Man" (Baldwin) MPII:SS II-880

"Gold Bug, The" (Poe) CLC I-406; MP IV-2286; MP:AF I-462; MPII:SS II-889

"Gold Coast" (McPherson) MPII:SS II-885

Gold-Rimmed Eyeglasses, The (Bassani) CLCII II-604; MPII:WF II-557

Golden Apples, The (Welty) MP IV-2289; MP:AF I-465

Golden Ass of Lucius Apuleius, The (Apuleius) CLC I-406; MP IV-2292; MP:EF II-575

Golden Bough, The (Frazer) MP IV-2296

Golden Bowl, The (James, H.) CLC I-407; MP IV-2299; MP:AF I-469

Golden Boy (Odets) CLC I-409; MP IV-2304

"Golden Honeymoon, The" (Lardner) MPII:SS II-893

Golden Notebook, The (Lessing) CLCII II-605; MPII:BCF II-621

Golden Serpent, The (Alegría) CLCII II-607; MPII:AF II-645

"Goloeditsa." See "Icicle, The"

Gommes, Les. See Erasers, The

Goncourt Journals, The (Goncourt and Goncourt) MP IV-2307

Gondoliers, The (Gilbert) CLC I-409; MP IV-2310

Gone with the Wind (Mitchell, M.) CLC I-410; MP IV-2313; MP:AF I-474

"Gonzaga Manuscripts, The" (Bellow) MPII:SS II-896

Good Apprentice, The (Murdoch) CLCII II-608; MPII:BCF II-627

Good Companions, The (Priestley) CLC I-410; MP IV-2316; MP:BF I-483

Good Conscience, The (Fuentes) CLCII II-610; MPII:AF II-650

"Good Country People" (O'Connor, Flannery) MPII:SS II-900

Good Earth, The (Buck) CLC I-411; MP IV-2319; MP:AF I-478

"Good Man Is Hard to Find, A" (O'Connor, Flannery) MPII:SS II-903

Good Morning, Midnight (Rhys) CLCII II-612; MPII:BCF II-632

Good Person of Setzuan, The. See Good Woman of Setzuan, The

Good Soldier, The (Ford) CLCII II-613; MPII:BCF II-637

Good Soldier: Schweik, The (Hašek) MP IV-2324; MP:EF II-580

Good Terrorist, The (Lessing) CLCII II-614; MPII:BCF II-643

Good Woman of Setzuan, The (Brecht) CLCII II-615; MPII:D II-689

Goodbye Look, The (Macdonald) CLCII II-616; MPII:AF II-655

Goodbye, Mr. Chips (Hilton) CLC I-412; MP IV-2328; MP:BF I-487

"Goodbye, My Brother" (Cheever) MPII:SS II-907

Good-bye to All That (Graves) MPII:NF II-567

Goodnight! (Tertz) CLCII II-617

"Gooseberries" (Chekhov) MPII:SS II-911

Gorboduc (Norton and Sackville) CLC I-412; MP IV-2332

Gormenghast. See Gormenghast trilogy, The

Gormenghast trilogy, The (Peake) CLCII II-618; MPII:BCF II-648

"Gospel According to Mark, The" (Borges) MPII:SS II-915

"Gospel Singers" (Hughes) MPII:SS II-918

"Gospodin iz San Frantsisko." See "Gentleman from San Francisco, The"

Gospodjica. See Woman from Sarajevo, The

Gossip from the Forest (Keneally) CLCII II-621; MPII:BCF II-655

Grammar of Motives. A (Burke) MPII:NF II-573

Grand Hotel (Baum) CLC I-414; MP IV-2335; MP:EF II-585

Grand Voyage, Le. See Long Voyage, The

Grandissimes, The (Cable) CLC I-414; MP IV-2338; MP:AF I-483

Grandmothers, The (Wescott) CLC I-416; MP IV-2341; MP:AF I-487

Grania (Gregory) CLCII II-622; MPII:D II-696

Grapes of Wrath, The (Steinbeck) CLC I-417; MP IV-2344; MP:AF I-491

"Graphomaniacs" (Sinyavsky) MPII:SS II-922

Grateful to Life and Death (Narayan) CLCII II-623; MPII:BCF II-660

Gravity and Grace (Weil) MPII:NF II-578

Gravity's Rainbow (Pynchon) CLCII II-624; MPII:AF II-661

"Greasy Lake" (Boyle, T.) MPII:SS III-925

Great American Novel, The (Roth, P.) CLCII II-626; MPII:AF II-666

Great Dune trilogy, The. See Dune trilogy, The

Great Expectations (Dickens) CLC I-418; MP IV-2349; MP:BF I-491

Great Fortune, The. See Balkan trilogy, The

Great Galeoto, The (Echegaray) CLC I-420; MP IV-2355

Great Gatsby, The (Fitzgerald, F.) CLC I-421; MP IV-2358; MP:AF I-496

Great God Brown, The (O'Neill) CLCII II-628; MPII:D II-701

"Great Good Place, The" (James, H.) MPII:SS III-929

Great Meadow, The (Roberts, E.) CLC I-422; MP IV-2363; MP:AF I-501

Great Plains, The (Webb, W.) MP IV-2367

Great Ponds, The (Amadi) CLCII II-629; MPII:BCF II-665

Great River (Horgan) MPII:NF II-584

Great Testament, The (Villon) MP IV-2370

Great Valley, The (Johnston) CLC I-423; MP IV-2372; MP:AF I-505

"Great Wall of China, The" (Kafka) MPII:SS III-932

Great White Hope, The (Sackler) CLCII II-630; MPII:D II-706

"Greek Interpreter, The" (Doyle) MPII:SS III-936

Greek Passion, The (Kazantzakis) MP IV-2375; MP:EF II-589

Green Bay Tree, The (Bromfield) CLC I-424; MP IV-2378; MP:AF II-509

Green Card (Akalaitis) CLCII II-631; MPII:D II-711

Green Fool, The (Kavanagh) MPII:NF II-589

Green Grow the Lilacs (Riggs) CLC I-425; MP IV-2382

Green Hills of Africa (Hemingway) MPII:NF II-595

Green House, The (Vargas Llosa) CLCII II-632; MPII:AF II-672

Green Huntsman, The. See Lucien Leuwen

Green Man, The (Amis) CLCII II-633; MPII:BCF II-670

Green Mansions (Hudson) CLC I-425; MP IV-2386; MP:BF I-497

Green Mountain Boys, The (Thompson, D.) CLC I-426; MP IV-2389; MP:AF II-514

Green Pastures, The (Connelly) CLCII II-634; MPII:D II-717

"Green Tea" (Le Fanu) MPII:SS III-940

Greene's Groatsworth of Wit Bought with a Million of Repentance (Greene, R.) MP IV-2394

"Greenleaf" (O'Connor, Flannery) MPII:SS III-944

Grendel (Gardner) CLCII II-637; MPII:AF II-677

Grettir the Outlaw. See Grettir the Strong

Grettir the Strong (Unknown) CLC I-427; MP IV-2396; MP:EF II-593

Grey Granite. See Scots Quair, A

"Greyhound People" (Adams) MPII:SS III-948

Grief Observed, A (Lewis, C. S.) MPII:NF II-601

Gringa, La (Sánchez) CLC I-429; MP IV-2401

Grobnica za Borisa Davidoviča. *See* Tomb for Boris Davidovich, A

Group, The (McCarthy, M.) CLCII II-638; MPII:AF II-682

Group Portrait with Lady (Böll) CLCII II-641; MPII:WF II-562

Growing Up (Baker) MPII:NF II-606

Growth of the Soil (Hamsun) CLC I-429; MP IV-2404; MP:EF II-599

Grüne Heinrich, Der (Keller) CLC I-430; MP IV-2408; MP:EF II-603

Gruppenbild mit Dame. *See* Group Portrait with Lady

Guard of Honor (Cozzens) CLC I-431; MP IV-2412; MP:AF II-520

Guardian of the Word, The (Laye) CLCII II-643; MPII:WF II-567

Guerra del fin del mundo, La. *See* War of the End of the World, The

Guerrillas (Naipaul, V. S.) CLCII II-644; MPII:BCF II-675

"Guest, The" (Camus) MPII:SS III-952

Guest for the Night, A (Agnon) CLCII II-645; MPII:WF I-194

Guest the One-Eyed (Gunnarsson) CLC I-432; MP IV-2416; MP:EF II-607

"Guests of the Nation" (O'Connor, Frank) MPII:SS III-956

Guide, The (Narayan) MP IV-2418; MP:EF II-610

Guide to Kulchur (Pound) MPII:NF II-611

Gulag Archipelago, 1918-1956, The (Solzhenitsyn) MPII:NF II-617

Gulliver's Travels (Swift) CLC I-432; MP IV-2421; MP:BF I-501

Gull's Hornbook, The (Dekker) MP IV-2426

"Gun Shop, The" (Updike) MPII:SS III-959

"Gusev" (Chekhov) MPII:SS III-962

Gute Mensch von Sezuan, Der. *See* Good Woman of Setzuan, The

Gutenberg Galaxy, The (McLuhan) MPII:NF II-624

"Guy de Maupassant" (Babel) MPII:SS III-966

Guy Mannering (Scott, Sir W.) CLC I-433; MP IV-2429; MP:BF I-507

Guy of Warwick (Unknown) CLC I-434; MP IV-2433

Guyana Quartet, The (Harris, W.) CLCII II-646; MPII:BCF II-679

Guzmán de Alfarache (Alemán) CLC I-435; MP IV-2437; MP:EF II-613

H

Habana para un infante difunto, La. *See* Infante's Inferno

Habit of Being, The (O'Connor) MPII:NF II-630

Hadji Murad (Tolstoy) CLCII II-649; MPII:WF II-571

Hadrian's Memoirs (Yourcenar) MP V-2443; MP:EF II-620

"Haircut" (Lardner) MPII:SS III-970

Hairy Ape, The (O'Neill) CLCII II-651; MPII:D II-723

Hajji Baba of Ispahan (Morier) CLC I-436; MP V-2446; MP:BF I-511

Hakhnasat kala. *See* Bridal Canopy, The

Hakluyt's Voyages (Hakluyt) MP V-2450

Ham Funeral, The (White) CLCII II-652; MPII:D II-727

"Ha-mitpahat." *See* "Kerchief, The"

Hamlet, The (Faulkner) CLC I-436; MP V-2454; MP:AF II-525

Hamlet of Stepney Green, The (Kops) CLCII II-653; MPII:D II-732

"Hamlet of the Shchigrovsky District" (Turgenev) MPII:SS III-973

Hamlet, Prince of Denmark (Shakespeare) CLC I-437; MP V-2457

Hampshire Days (Hudson) MP V-2462

Handful of Dust, A (Waugh) CLC I-440; MP V-2464; MP:BF I-516

Handley Cross (Surtees) CLC I-440; MP V-2467; MP:BF I-520

Handmaid's Tale, The (Atwood) CLCII II-654; MPII:BCF II-690

Hands Around. *See* Ronde, La

"Handsomest Drowned Man in the World, The" (García Márquez) MPII:SS III-977

Handy Andy (Lover) CLC I-441; MP V-2470; MP:BF I-524

Hangman's House (Byrne) CLC I-442; MP V-2473; MP:BF I-528

Hapgood (Stoppard) CLCII II-656; MPII:D II-737

"Happy August the Tenth" (Williams, T.) MPII:SS III-981

"Happy Autumn Fields, The" (Bowen) MPII:SS III-985

Happy Days (Beckett) CLCII II-657; MPII:D II-742

Hard Times (Dickens) CLC I-443; MP V-2477; MP:BF I-532

Harland's Half Acre (Malouf) CLCII II-658; MPII:BCF II-695

Harmonium (Stevens, W.) MP V-2480

"Harmony" (Lardner) MPII:SS III-989

Harp of a Thousand Strings (Davis) CLC I-445; MP V-2484; MP:AF II-529

Harp-Weaver and Other Poems, The (Millay) MP V-2489

Harriet Said (Bainbridge) CLCII II-658; MPII:BCF II-700

Harrowing of Hubertus, The. *See* Kaywana trilogy, The

Haru no yuki. *See* Sea of Fertility, The

Hasty Heart, The (Patrick) CLCII II-660; MPII:D II-747

Haute Surveillance. *See* Deathwatch

Havelok the Dane (Unknown) CLC I-445; MP V-2492

Hawaii (Michener) CLCII II-661; MPII:AF II-688

Hazard of New Fortunes, A (Howells) CLC I-446; MP V-2495; MP:AF II-535

He Who Searches (Valenzuela) CLCII II-663; MPII:AF II-696

Headbirths (Grass) CLCII II-665; MPII:WF II-578

"Headless Hawk, The" (Capote) MPII:SS III-993

Headlong Hall (Peacock) CLC I-447; MP V-2498; MP:BF I-536

Healers, The (Armah) CLCII II-666; MPII:BCF II-705

Hearing Secret Harmonies. *See* Dance to the Music of Time, A

Heart is a Lonely Hunter, The (McCullers) CLC I-447; MP V-2501; MP:AF II-539

Heart of a Dog, The (Bulgakov) CLCII II-667; MPII:WF II-583

Heart of Darkness (Conrad) CLC I-448; MP V-2505; MP:BF I-539

Heart of Midlothian, The (Scott, Sir W.) CLC I-449; MP V-2510; MP:BF I-544

Heart of the Matter, The (Greene, G.) CLC I-450; MP V-2515; MP:BF I-550

Heartbreak House (Shaw, G.) CLC I-451; CLCII II-669; MP V-2520; MPII:D II-752

Heartbreak Tango (Puig) CLCII II-670; MPII:AF II-701

Heat and Dust (Jhabvala) CLCII II-671; MPII:BCF II-710

Heat of the Day, The (Bowen) CLC I-453; MP V-2523; MP:BF I-555

Heaven's My Destination (Wilder) CLC I-453; MP V-2528; MP:AF II-543

Hedda Gabler (Ibsen) CLC I-454; MP V-2532

Heidi Chronicles, The (Wasserstein) CLCII II-673; MPII:D II-758

Heimkehr der Fronttruppen. See November 1918

Heimskringla (Snorri Sturluson) CLC I-456; MP V-2537; MP:EF II-623

Helen (Euripides) CLC I-458; MP V-2544

Heliga Landet, Det. See Tobias Trilogy, The

Hemsöborna. See Natives of Hemsö, The

Henderson the Rain King (Bellow) MP V-2547; MP:AF II-547

Henry Esmond (Thackeray) CLC I-459; MP V-2550; MP:BF I-560

Henry IV (Pirandello) CLCII II-674; MPII:D II-764

Henry the Fourth, Part One (Shakespeare) CLC I-464; MP V-2562

Henry the Fourth, Part Two (Shakespeare) CLC I-464; MP V-2567

Henry the Fourth, Parts One and Two (Shakespeare) CLC I-464

Henry the Fifth (Shakespeare) CLC I-462; MP V-2558

Henry the Sixth, Part One (Shakespeare) CLC I-466; MP V-2572

Henry the Sixth, Part Two (Shakespeare) CLC I-466; MP V-2576

Henry the Sixth, Part Three (Shakespeare) CLC I-466; MP V-2580

Henry the Sixth, Parts One, Two, and Three (Shakespeare) CLC I-466

Henry the Eighth (Shakespeare) CLC I-460; MP V-2555

"Her First Ball" (Mansfield) MPII:SS III-997

Her Privates, We (Manning, F.) CLCII II-675; MPII:BCF II-717

"Her Table Spread" (Bowen) MPII:SS III-1000

"Herakleitos" (Davenport) MPII:SS III-1003

Herakles Mad (Euripides) CLC I-468; MP V-2584

Hercules and His Twelve Labors (Unknown) CLC I-470; MP V-2587; MP:EF II-631

Hereward the Wake (Kingsley, C.) CLC I-470; MP V-2591; MP:BF I-566

Heritage and Its History, A (Compton-Burnett) MP V-2594; MP:BF I-570

Herland (Gilman) CLCII II-676; MPII:AF II-706

Hermano asno, El. See Brother Ass

Hero of Our Time, A (Lermontov) CLC I-471; MP V-2597; MP:EF II-636

Hero with a Thousand Faces, The (Campbell) MPII:NF II-636

"Herodias" (Flaubert) MPII:SS III-1007

"Heroes in the Dark House, The" (Kiely) MPII:SS III-1011

Heroides (Ovid) MP V-2601

Herries chronicle, The. See Fortress, Judith Paris, Rogue Herries, and Vanessa

Herself Surprised (Cary) CLC I-472; MP V-2603; MP:BF I-574

Herzog (Bellow) CLCII II-677; MPII:AF II-712

Hesperides (Herrick) MP V-2606

Hiding Place. See Homewood trilogy, The

"Higgler, The" (Coppard) MPII:SS III-1014

High Wind in Jamaica, A. *See* Innocent Voyage, The

High Wind Rising, A (Singmaster) CLC I-472; MP V-2609; MP:AF II-551

Hijo de hombre. *See* Son of Man

Hill of Dreams, The (Machen) CLC I-473; MP V-2613; MP:BF I-578

Hillingdon Hall (Surtees) CLC I-474; MP V-2616; MP:BF I-582

"Hills Like White Elephants" (Hemingway) MPII:SS III-1018

Hiob. *See* Job

Hippolytus (Euripides) CLC I-474; MP V-2620

Hiroshima (Hersey) MPII:NF II-641

His Master's Voice (Lem) CLCII II-678; MPII:WF II-588

"His Son, in His Arms, in Light, Aloft" (Brodkey) MPII:SS III-1022

Historia Calamitatum (Abélard) MP V-2624

History (Morante) CLCII II-679; MPII:WF II-593

History and Remarkable Life of the Truly Honourable Colonel Jacque, The. *See* History of Colonel Jacque, The

History Man, The (Bradbury, M.) CLCII II-680; MPII:BCF II-721

History of a Scoundrel, The. *See* Bel-Ami

History of Amelia, The. *See* Amelia

History of Colonel Jacque, The (Defoe) CLC I-475; MP V-2627; MP:BF I-586

History of England, The (Macaulay) MP V-2631

History of Frederick II of Prussia (Carlyle) MP V-2634

History of Henry Esmond, Esq., The. *See* Henry Esmond

History of King Richard III (More, Sir T.) MP V-2637

History of Mr. Polly, The (Wells) CLC I-476; MP V-2640; MP:BF I-590

History of New York, by Diedrich Knickerbocker, A (Irving) MP V-2643

History of Pendennis, The. *See* Pendennis

History of Rasselas, The. *See* Rasselas

History of Sandford and Merton, The. *See* Sandford and Merton

History of the Adventures of Joseph Andrews, The. *See* Joseph Andrews

History of the Conquest of Mexico (Prescott) MP V-2646

History of the Decline and Fall of the Roman Empire, The (Gibbon) MP V-2649

History of the Peloponnesian War (Thucydides) MP V-2652

History of the Persian Wars, The (Herodotus) MP V-2655

History of the Rebellion and Civil Wars in England (Hyde) MP V-2658

History of the Reign of King Henry VII (Bacon) MP V-2660

History of Tom Jones, a Foundling, The. *See* Tom Jones

"Hitchhiking Game, The" (Kundera) MPII:SS III-1026

Hive, The (Cela) MP V-2663; MP:EF II-641

Hizakurige (Jippensha Ikku) CLC I-478; MP V-2667; MP:EF II-646

H.M.S. Pinafore (Gilbert) CLC I-478; MP V-2669

Ho teleutaios peirasmos. *See* Last Temptation of Christ, The

Hobbit, The (Tolkien) CLCII II-681; MPII:BCF II-727

"Hodel" (Aleichem) MPII:SS III-1029

Hojarasca, La. *See* Leaf Storm

Hōjō no umi. *See* Sea of Fertility, The

Holy Ghosts (Linney) CLCII II-683; MPII:D II-769

Holy Land, The. *See* Tobias trilogy, The

Holy Place (Fuentes) CLCII II-684; MPII:AF II-717

Holy Sinner, The (Mann) CLCII II-685; MPII:WF II-599

Holy State and the Profane State, The (Fuller) MP V-2672

Holy Terrors, The (Cocteau) CLC I-479; MP V-2675; MP:EF II-648

Holzfällen (Bernhard) MPII:WF II-603. *See also* Woodcutters

Homage to Catalonia (Orwell) MPII:NF II-645

Homage to Mistress Bradstreet (Berryman) MP V-2678

Homba. *See* Sea of Fertility, The

Hombres de maíz. *See* Men of Maize

"Home" (Phillips) MPII:SS III-1033

Home (Rybczynski) MPII:NF II-651

Home-maker, The (Fisher) CLCII II-686; MPII:AF II-728

Home to Harlem (McKay) CLCII II-687; MPII:AF II-722

Homecoming, The (Pinter) CLCII II-688; MPII:D II-774

Homecomings. *See* Strangers and Brothers

Homewood trilogy, The (Wideman) CLCII II-689; MPII:AF II-732

Homme qui regardait passer les trains, L'. *See* Man Who Watched the Trains Go By, The

Homme révolté, L'. *See* Rebel, The

Homo Faber (Frisch) CLCII II-692; MPII:WF II-608

Honest Whore, Part One, The (Dekker *and* Middleton) CLC I-479; MP V-2680

Honest Whore, Part Two, The (Dekker) CLC I-479; MP V-2684

Honey in the Horn (Davis) CLC I-480; MP V-2688; MP:AF II-555

Honeycomb. *See* Pilgrimage

Honorary Consul, The (Greene) CLCII II-693; MPII:BCF II-732

Honourable Schoolboy, The (le Carré) CLCII II-694; MPII:BCF II-737

Hoosier Schoolmaster, The (Eggleston) CLC I-481; MP V-2691; MP:AF II-559

Hope Abandoned (Mandelstam, N.) MPII:NF II-656

Hope Against Hope (Mandelstam, N.) MPII:NF II-662

Hopscotch (Cortázar) CLCII II-695; MPII:AF II-739

Horace (Corneille) CLC I-482; MP V-2695

Horacker (Raabe) CLCII II-697; MPII:WF II-612

Horloger d'Everton, L'. *See* Watchmaker of Everton, The

"Horse and Two Goats, A" (Narayan) MPII:SS III-1037

"Horse Dealer's Daughter, The" (Lawrence) MPII:SS III-1041

Horseman on the Roof, The (Giono) CLCII II-699; MPII:WF II-618

Horse's Mouth, The (Cary) CLC I-482; MP V-2699; MP:BF I-593

Horseshoe Robinson (Kennedy) CLC I-483; MP V-2702; MP:AF II-563

Hostage, The (Behan) CLCII II-700; MPII:D II-778

Hot l Baltimore, The (Wilson, L.) CLCII II-701; MPII:D II-783

"Hôte, L'." *See* "Guest, The"

Hotel du Lac (Brookner) CLCII II-702; MPII:BCF II-743

Hotel New Hampshire, The (Irving) CLCII II-703; MPII:AF II-743

House Behind the Cedars, The (Chesnutt) CLCII II-705; MPII:AF II-748

House by the Churchyard, The (Le Fanu) CLC I-484; MP V-2705; MP:BF II-597

House by the Medlar Tree, The (Verga) CLC I-485; MP V-2709; MP:EF II-652

House for Mr. Biswas, A (Naipaul, V. S.) CLCII II-706; MPII:BCF II-748

House in Paris, The (Bowen) CLC I-486; MP V-2714; MP:BF II-602

"House in Turk Street, The" (Hammett) MPII:SS III-1045

House Made of Dawn (Momaday) CLCII II-707; MPII:AF II-754

House of All Nations (Stead) CLCII II-708; MPII:BCF II-753

House of Atreus, The (Aeschylus) CLC I-486; MP V-2719

House of Blue Leaves, The (Guare) CLCII II-710; MPII:D II-789

House of Gentlefolk, A (Turgenev) CLC I-487; MP V-2724; MP:EF II-657

House of Mirth, The (Wharton) CLC I-489; MP V-2729; MP:AF II-567

House of the Dead, The (Dostoevski) CLCII II-711; MPII:WF II-623

House of the Seven Gables, The (Hawthorne) CLC I-491; MP V-2734; MP:AF II-572

House of the Sleeping Beauties, The (Kawabata) CLCII II-712; MPII:WF II-629

House on the Embankment, The (Trifonov) CLCII II-713; MPII:WF II-633

House on the Hill, The (Pavese) CLCII II-715; MPII:WF II-639

"House with the Grape-vine, The" (Bates) MPII:SS III-1049

House with the Green Shutters, The (Douglas, G.) CLC I-492; MP V-2739; MP:BF II-608

"Housebreaker of Shady Hill, The" (Cheever) MPII:SS III-1052

Householder, The (Jhabvala) CLCII II-716; MPII:BCF II-758

"How Claeys Died" (Sansom) MPII:SS III-1056

How Far Can You Go? See Souls and Bodies

How Green Was My Valley (Llewellyn) CLC I-493; MP V-2742; MP:BF II-612

"How I contemplated the world from the Detroit House of Correction and began my life over again" (Oates) MPII:SS III-1060

"How I Finally Lost My Heart" (Lessing) MPII:SS III-1064

How It Is (Beckett) CLCII II-717; MPII:WF II-644

"How It Was Done in Odessa" (Babel) MPII:SS III-1067

"How Mr. Rabbit Was Too Sharp for Mr. Fox." See "Wonderful Tar-Baby Story, The"

"How Much Land Does a Man Need?" (Tolstoy) MPII:SS III-1070

How Much Love Costs Old Men. See Splendors and Miseries of Courtesans, The

"How the Devil Came Down Division Street" (Algren) MPII:SS III-1073

Howards End (Forster) CLC I-493; MP V-2745; MP:BF II-616

Huasipungo (Icaza) CLC I-494; MP V-2750. See also Villagers, The

Hubertus. See Kaywana trilogy, The

Huckleberry Finn. See Adventures of Huckleberry Finn, The

Hudibras (Butler) CLC I-497; MP V-2760

Hugh Wynne, Free Quaker (Mitchell, S.) CLC I-497; MP V-2763; MP:AF II-577

Huis clos. See No Exit

Human Age, The (Lewis, W.) CLCII II-718; MPII:BCF II-764

Human Comedy, The (Saroyan) CLC I-498; MP V-2766; MP:AF II-581

Humboldt's Gift (Bellow) CLCII II-721; MPII:AF II-759

Humphry Clinker (Smollett) CLC I-499; MP V-2769; MP:BF II-621

Hunchback of Notre Dame, The (Hugo) CLC I-500; MP V-2774; MP:EF II-663

Hundejahre. See Dog Years

Hunger (Hamsun) CLC I-502; MP V-2780; MP:EF II-670

"Hunger Artist, A" (Kafka) MPII:SS III-1077

Hunger of Memory (Rodriguez) MPII:NF II-668

"Hunter Gracchus, The" (Kafka) MPII:SS III-1081

"Hunting Season" (Greenberg) MPII:SS III-1085

Huon de Bordeaux (Unknown) CLC I-502; MP V-2784; MP:EF II-674

Hurlyburly (Rabe) CLCII II-723; MPII:D II-794

Hurry Home (Wideman) CLCII II-724; MPII:AF II-764

Hurry on Down. See Born in Captivity

Hussar on the Roof, The. See Horseman on the Roof, The

Hussard sur le toit, Le. *See* Horseman on the Roof, The

Hyde Park (Shirley) CLC I-503; MP V-2787

Hydriotaphia: Urn-Burial (Browne) MP V-2791

Hypatia (Kingsley, C.) CLC I-504; MP V-2794; MP:BF II-627

Hypochondriac, The (Molière) CLC I-505; MP V-2798

I

I Am a Cat (Natsume) CLCII II-724; MPII:WF II-648

I, Claudius (Graves) CLC I-507; MP V-2803; MP:BF II-632

I de dage. *See* Giants in the Earth

"I Don't Have to Show You No Stinking Badges!" (Valdez) CLCII II-726; MPII:D II-799

I for One . . . (Sargeson) CLCII II-726; MPII:BCF II-772

I Knock at the Door. *See* Mirror in My House

I Know Why the Caged Bird Sings (Angelou) MPII:NF II-673

I Like It Here (Amis) CLCII II-728; MPII:BCF II-777

"I Look Out for Ed Wolfe" (Elkin) MPII:SS III-1088

I Never Promised You a Rose Garden (Green, Hannah) CLCII II-728; MPII:AF II-769

I Speak for Thaddeus Stevens (Singmaster) MP V-2806

"I Stand Here Ironing" (Olsen) MPII:SS III-1091

"I Want to Know Why" (Anderson) MPII:SS III-1095

I Will Marry When I Want (Ngugi *and* Ngugi) CLCII II-729; MPII:D II-804

"Iber a Hitl." *See* "On Account of a Hat"

Ice (Kavan) CLCII II-730; MPII:BCF II-782

Ice Age, The (Drabble) CLCII II-731; MPII:BCF II-787

"Ice House, The" (Gordon) MPII:SS III-1099

"Ice Wagon Going Down the Street, The" (Gallant) MPII:SS III-1103

Iceland Fisherman, An (Loti) CLC I-508; MP V-2810; MP:EF II-678

Iceman Cometh, The (O'Neill) CLCII II-732; MPII:D II-809

"Icicle, The" (Sinyavsky) MPII:SS III-1106

Ides of March, The (Wilder) CLC I-509; MP V-2814; MP:AF II-584

Idiot, The (Dostoevski) CLC I-510; MP V-2817; MP:EF II-682

"Idiots First" (Malamud) MPII:SS III-1109

"Idle Days on the Yann" (Dunsany) MPII:SS III-1112

Idler, The (Johnson, S.) MP V-2822

Idylls of the King, The (Tennyson) CLC I-511; MP V-2825

If Beale Street Could Talk (Baldwin) CLCII II-733; MPII:AF II-774

If He Hollers Let Him Go (Himes) CLCII II-734; MPII:AF II-778

If Not Now, When? (Levi, P.) CLCII II-735; MPII:WF II-653

If on a Winter's Night a Traveler (Calvino) CLCII II-736; MPII:WF II-659

If This Is a Man (Levi) MPII:NF II-678

If Winter Comes (Hutchinson) CLC I-513; MP V-2831; MP:BF II-636

Ignatius His Conclave (Donne) MP V-2834

Iliad, The (Homer) CLC I-513; MP V-2837

Iliad, The (Weil) MPII:NF II-684

Iliade, L'. See Iliad, The

Ill-Made Knight, The. *See* Once and Future King, The

Ill Seen Ill Said (Beckett) CLCII II-738; MPII:WF II-664

Illness as Metaphor (Sontag) MPII:NF II-689

Illywhacker (Carey) CLCII II-739; MPII:BCF II-794

"I'm a Fool" (Anderson) MPII:SS III-1116

I'm Not Stiller (Frisch) CLCII II-740; MPII:WF II-669

Images and Shadows (Origo) MPII:NF II-694

Imaginary Conversations (Landor) MP V-2842

Imaginary Life, An (Malouf) CLCII II-742; MPII:BCF II-799

"Imagination Dead Imagine" (Beckett) MPII:SS III-1119

"Imagined Scenes" (Beattie) MPII:SS III-1122

Imitation of Christ, The (Thomas à Kempis) MP V-2845

Immense Journey, The (Eiseley) MPII:NF II-699

Immoralist, The (Gide) CLCII II-743; MPII:WF II-673

Immoraliste, L'. *See* Immoralist, The

Importance of Being Earnest, The (Wilde) CLC I-517; MP V-2847

"Impulse" (Aiken) MPII:SS III-1126

In a Free State (Naipaul, V. S.) CLCII II-744; MPII:BCF II-804

"In Another Country" (Hemingway) MPII:SS III-1130

In Chancery. *See* Forsyte Saga, The

In Cold Blood (Capote) MPII:NF II-704

"In der Strafkolonie." *See* "In the Penal Colony"

"In Dreams Begin Responsibilities" (Schwartz) MPII:SS III-1134

In Dubious Battle (Steinbeck) CLC I-518; MP V-2850; MP:AF II-588

"In Greenwich There Are Many Gravelled Walks" (Calisher) MPII:SS III-1137

In Joy Still Felt (Asimov) MPII:NF II-709

In Memoriam (Tennyson) MP V-2853

In Memory Yet Green (Asimov) MPII:NF II-714

In My Father's Court (Singer) MPII:NF II-719

In Patagonia (Chatwin) MPII:NF II-725

In Praise of Shadows (Tanizaki) MPII:NF II-731

In Sicily (Vittorini) CLCII II-745; MPII:WF II-681

In That Dawn. *See* Story of a Life, The

In the American Grain (Williams, W.) MP V-2856

In the Beginning (Potok) CLCII II-746; MPII:AF II-782

"In the Cage" (James, H.) MPII:SS III-1141

In the Castle of My Skin (Lamming) CLCII II-747; MPII:BCF II-809

"In the Garden of the North American Martyrs" (Wolff) MPII:SS III-1146

"In the Heart of the Heart of the Country" (Gass) MPII:SS III-1150

In the Heart of the Seas (Agnon) CLCII II-749; MPII:WF I-194

In the Labyrinth (Robbe-Grillet) CLCII II-750; MPII:WF II-686

"In the Penal Colony" (Kafka) MPII:SS III-1154

In the Shadow of the Glen (Synge) CLCII II-750; MPII:D II-815

In the Time of Greenbloom (Fielding) CLCII II-751; MPII:BCF II-814

"In the White Night" (Beattie) MPII:SS III-1158

In the Wilderness (Undset) CLC I-519; MP V-2861; MP:EF II-687

In the Wine Time (Bullins) CLCII II-753; MPII:D II-820

In Watermelon Sugar (Brautigan) CLCII II-754; MPII:AF II-787

Inadmissible Evidence (Osborne) CLCII II-755; MPII:D II-826

Inazuma-byōshi (Santō Kyōden) CLC I-520; MP V-2864; MP:EF II-691

İnce Memed. *See* Memed, My Hawk

Incident at Vichy (Miller, A.) CLCII II-756; MPII:D II-831

Incognito (Dumitriu) MP V-2868; MP:EF II-696

Increased Difficulty of Concentration, The (Havel) CLCII II-757; MPII:D II-835

Independent People (Laxness) CLC I-521; MP V-2872; MP:EF II-701

"Indian Camp" (Hemingway) MPII:SS III-1162

Indian Summer (Howells) CLC I-522; MP V-2877; MP:AF II-591

Indian Summer (Stifter) CLCII II-757; MPII:WF II-691

"Indian Uprising, The" (Barthelme, D.) MPII:SS III-1165

Indiana (Sand) CLC I-523; MP V-2880; MP:EF II-707

Indians (Kopit) CLCII II-759; MPII:D II-840

Indifferenti, Gli. *See* Time of Indifference, The

"Indissoluble Matrimony" (West, R.) MPII:SS III-1169

In'ei raisan. *See* In Praise of Shadows

Inês de Castro (Ferreira) CLC I-524; MP V-2883

"Infant Prodigy, The" (Mann) MPII:SS III-1173

Infante's Inferno (Cabrera Infante) CLCII II-760; MPII:AF II-792

Infants of the Spring. *See* To Keep the Ball Rolling

Infernal Machine, The (Cocteau) CLCII II-761; MPII:D II-846

Inferno (Strindberg) CLCII II-762; MPII:WF II-697

Informer, The (O'Flaherty) CLC I-524; MP V-2886; MP:BF II-640

Ingoldsby Legends, The (Ingoldsby) MP V-2891

Inhabitants, The (Morris) MPII:NF II-736

Inheritors, The (Golding) MP V-2894; MP:BF II-645

Inimitable Jeeves, The (Wodehouse) CLCII II-763; MPII:BCF II-820

Inishfallen, Fare Thee Well. *See* Mirror in My House

Injury and Insult. *See* Insulted and the Injured, The

"Innen und Aussen." *See* "Within and Without"

"Innocence" (O'Faoláin) MPII:SS III-1176

Innocent Voyage, The (Hughes, R.) CLC I-525; MP V-2897; MP:BF II-649

Innommable, L'. *See* Trilogy, The, *and* Unnamable, The

Inquiry Concerning Political Justice, An (Godwin)

Inquisitoire, L'. *See* Inquisitory, The

Inquisitory, The (Pinget) CLCII II-764; MPII:WF II-701

Inspector Calls, An (Priestley) CLCII II-765; MPII:D II-852

Inspector General, The (Gogol) CLC I-526; MP V-2904

"Instructions for John Howell" (Cortázar) MPII:SS III-1180

Insular Possession, An (Mo) CLCII II-766; MPII:BCF II-825

Insulted and the Injured, The (Dostoevski) CLCII II-767; MPII:WF II-706

Intellectual Follies, The (Abel) MPII:NF II-742

Intensive Care (Frame) CLCII II-769; MPII:BCF II-831

Inter Ice Age 4 (Abe) CLCII II-770; MPII:WF II-711

"Interest in Life, An" (Paley) MPII:SS III-1184

Interim. *See* Pilgrimage

"Interlopers, The" (Saki) MPII:SS III-1187

Interpretation of Cultures, The (Geertz) MPII:NF II-747

Interpretation of Dreams, The (Freud) MP V-2908

Interpreters, The (Soyinka) CLCII II-770; MPII:BCF II-836

Interrupted Life, An (Hillesum) MPII:NF II-751

Intruder in the Dust (Faulkner) CLC I-527; MP V-2911; MP:AF II-595

Invention of Morel, The (Bioy Casares) CLCII II-772; MPII:AF II-798

Investigation, The (Lem) CLCII II-773; MPII:WF II-717

Invincible, The (Lem) CLCII II-774; MPII:WF II-722

Invisible Cities (Calvino) CLCII II-774; MPII:WF II-727

"Invisible Man, The" (Chesterton) MPII:SS III-1191

Invisible Man (Ellison) MP V-2915; MP:AF II-599

Invisible Man, The (Wells) CLC I-528; MP V-2918; MP:BF II-653

Invitation to a Beheading (Nabokov) CLCII II-775; MPII:WF II-732

Iolanthe (Gilbert) CLC I-528; MP V-2922

Ion (Euripides) CLC I-529; MP V-2925

Iphigenia in Aulis (Euripides) CLC I-530; MP V-2928

Iphigenia in Tauris (Euripides) CLC I-532; MP V-2931

Irish Melodies (Moore, T.) MP V-2935

Iron Earth, Copper Sky (Kemal) CLCII IV-1718; MPII:WF IV-1754

Iron in the Soul. *See* Roads to Freedom, The

Ironweed (Kennedy, W.) CLCII II-776. *See also* Albany Cycle, The

Island of Crimea, The (Aksyonov) CLCII II-778; MPII:WF II-737

Islands in the Stream (Hemingway) CLCII II-780; MPII:AF II-803

"Islas nuevas, Las." *See* "New Islands"

Isola di Arturo, L'. *See* Arturo's Island

Israel Potter (Melville) CLC I-533; MP V-2938; MP:AF II-603

Issa Valley, The (Miłosz) CLCII II-781; MPII:WF II-743

"Istoriia moei golubiatni." *See* "Story of My Dovecot, The"

It Is Better than It Was (Calderón de la Barca) CLC I-534; MP V-2942

It Is Worse than It Was (Calderón de la Barca) CLC I-534; MP V-2945

"It May Never Happen" (Pritchett) MPII:SS III-1194

Italian, The (Radcliffe) CLC I-535; MP V-2948; MP:BF II-657

Itching Parrot, The (Fernández de Lizardi) CLC I-536; MP V-2955; MP:AF II-607

Ivanhoe (Scott, Sir W.) CLC I-536; MP V-2959; MP:BF II-665

Ivona, Princess of Burgundia (Gombrowicz) CLCII II-782; MPII:D II-857

Ivory Swing, The (Hospital) CLCII II-784; MPII:BCF II-843

"Ivy Day in the Committee Room" (Joyce) MPII:SS III-1197

"Ivy Gripped the Steps" (Bowen) MPII:SS III-1201

Iwona, księżniczka Burgunda. *See* Ivona, Princess of Burgundia

J

Jack of Newberry (Deloney) CLC I-538;
MP V-2964; MP:BF II-671
Jack Sheppard (Ainsworth) CLC I-538;
MP V-2969; MP:BF II-676
"Jackals and Arabs" (Kafka) MPII:SS III-
1205
"Jacklighting" (Beattie) MPII:SS III-1208
Jacob's Room (Woolf) CLCII II-785;
MPII:BCF II-848
Jacques le fataliste et son maître. See
Jacques the Fatalist and His Master
Jacques the Fatalist and His Master
(Diderot) CLCII II-785; MPII:WF II-
748
"Jäger Gracchus, Der." See "Hunter
Gracchus, The"
Jahrestage. See Anniversaries
Jailbird (Vonnegut) CLCII II-786;
MPII:AF II-809
Jake's Thing (Amis) CLCII II-787;
MPII:BCF II-852
Jalna (de la Roche) CLC I-539; MP V-
2973; MP:AF II-611
Jalousie, La. See Jealousy
Jane Eyre (Brontë, C.) CLC I-540; MP V-
2976; MP:BF II-681
"Japanese Quince, The" (Galsworthy)
MPII:SS III-1211
"Jardín de senderos que se bifurcan, El."
See "Garden of Forking Paths, The"
Jason and the Golden Fleece (Unknown)
CLC I-542; MP V-2981; MP:EF II-710
Java Head (Hergesheimer) CLC I-543; MP
V-2985; MP:AF II-615
J. B. (MacLeish) CLCII II-788; MPII:D
III-861
Jealousy (Robbe-Grillet) CLCII II-790;
MPII:WF II-755
"Jean-ah Poquelin" (Cable) MPII:SS III-
1214
Jean-Christophe (Rolland) CLC I-543; MP
V-2988; MP:EF II-714
Jean le bleu. See Blue Boy

Jefferson and Hamilton: The Struggle for
Democracy in America (Bowers) MP V-
2993
Jennie Gerhardt (Dreiser) CLC I-544; MP
V-2996; MP:AF II-619
Jerusalem Delivered (Tasso) CLC I-545;
MP V-3000
Jeu Süss. See Power
Jew of Malta, The (Marlowe) CLC I-546;
MP V-3004
"Jewbird, The" (Malamud) MPII:SS III-
1218
Jewel in the Crown, The. See Raj
Quartet, The
Jewess of Toledo, The (Grillparzer) CLC
I-547; MP V-3008
Jill (Larkin) CLCII II-790; MPII:BCF II-
857
"Jim Baker's Bluejay Yarn" (Twain)
MPII:SS III-1222
Joanna Godden (Kaye-Smith) CLC I-548;
MP V-3012; MP:BF II-687
Job (Roth, J.) CLCII II-792; MPII:WF II-
760
Joe Turner's Come and Gone (Wilson,
August) CLCII II-793; MPII:D III-866
John Brown's Body (Benét) CLC I-549;
MP V-3016
John Bull's Other Island (Shaw, G.) CLCII
II-794; MPII:D III-871
John-Christopher. See Jean-Christophe
John Dryden: The Poet, The Dramatist,
The Critic (Eliot, T. S.) MP V-3020
John Halifax, Gentleman (Mulock) CLC I-
550; MP V-3023; MP:BF II-691
John Inglesant (Shorthouse) CLC I-551;
MP V-3026; MP:BF II-695
"John Napper Sailing Through the
Universe" (Gardner) MPII:SS III-1226
Joke, The (Kundera) CLCII II-795;
MPII:WF II-766
"Jolly Corner, The" (James, H.) MPII:SS
III-1230
Jonathan Wild (Fielding) CLC I-551; MP
V-3030; MP:BF II-699

"Jordan's End" (Glasgow) MPII:SS III-1234

"Jorinda and Jorindel" (Gallant) MPII:SS III-1237

Jorrocks' Jaunts and Jollities (Surtees) CLC I-552; MP V-3033; MP:BF II-703

Joseph and His Brothers (Mann) CLCII II-797; MPII:WF II-772

Joseph Andrews (Fielding) CLC I-552; MP V-3036; MP:BF II-707

Joseph Balsamo. *See* Memoirs of a Physician

Joseph, der Ernährer. *See* Joseph and His Brothers

Joseph in Egypt. *See* Joseph and His Brothers

Joseph the Provider. *See* Joseph and His Brothers

Joseph und seine Brüder. *See* Joseph and His Brothers

Joseph Vance (De Morgan) CLC I-554; MP V-3041; MP:BF II-713

"Josephine the Singer" (Kafka) MPII:SS III-1241

Jour, Le. *See* Accident, The

Journal of a Solitude (Sarton) MPII:NF II-756

Journal of a Tour to the Hebrides (Boswell) MP V-3044

Journal of the Fictive Life (Nemerov) MPII:NF II-762

Journal of the Plague Year, A (Defoe) MP V-3047; MP:BF II-717

Journal of Thoreau, The (Thoreau) MP V-3050

Journal to Eliza (Sterne) MP V-3053

Journal to Stella (Swift) MP V-3056

Journals, 1939-1983 (Spender) MPII:NF II-767

Journals of André Gide, The (Gide) MP VI-3059

Journals of Denton Welch, The (Welch) MPII:NF II-773

Journals of Dorothy Wordsworth (Wordsworth, D.) MP VI-3062

Journals of Lewis and Clark, The (Lewis, M. *and* Clark, William) MP VI-3065

Journey into Fear (Ambler) CLCII II-799; MPII:BCF II-862

Journey to Armenia (Mandelstam, O.) MPII:NF II-779

Journey to the Center of the Earth (Verne) CLCII II-800; MPII:WF II-781

Journey to the End of the Night (Céline) CLC I-555; MP VI-3068; MP:EF II-720

Journey to the Sky (Highwater) CLCII II-801; MPII:AF II-814

Journey to the West, The. *See* Monkey

Journeyman Years. *See* Wilhelm Meister's Travels

Journey's End (Sherriff) CLC I-556; MP VI-3071

Jovial Crew, A (Brome) CLC I-556; MP VI-3075

Joy of Man's Desiring (Giono) CLCII II-802; MPII:WF II-786

Joy of the Worm (Sargeson) CLCII II-803; MPII:BCF II-866

Juan sin tierra. *See* Juan the Landless

Juan the Landless (Goytisolo) CLCII III-974; MPII:WF III-958

Jubiabá (Amado) CLCII II-804; MPII:AF II-819

Jubilee (Walker, M.) CLCII II-806; MPII:AF II-825

Jude the Obscure (Hardy) CLC I-557; MP VI-3079; MP:BF II-721

Judgment Day. *See* Studs Lonigan

Judith Hearne. *See* Lonely Passion of Judith Hearne, The

Judith Paris (Walpole, Hugh) CLC I-558; MP VI-3084; MP:BF II-726

"Julia and the Bazooka" (Kavan) MPII:SS III-1245

Julius Caesar (Shakespeare) CLC I-559; MP VI-3089

July's People (Gordimer) CLCII II-807; MPII:BCF II-872

Jumpers (Stoppard) CLCII II-808; MPII:D III-877

Junge Joseph, Der. *See* Joseph and His Brothers

Jungle, The (Sinclair, U.) CLC I-560; MP VI-3094; MP:AF II-623

Jungle Books, The (Kipling) CLC I-561; MP VI-3097; MP:BF II-731

Juno and the Paycock (O'Casey) CLC I-562; MP VI-3100

Jurgen (Cabell) CLC I-563; MP VI-3105; MP:AF II-626

Just Above My Head (Baldwin) CLCII II-809; MPII:AF II-830

Justice (Galsworthy) CLC I-564; MP VI-3108

Justine. *See* Alexandria Quartet, The

K

"Kak eto delalos v Odesse." *See* "How It Was Done in Odessa"

Kalevala, The (Lönnrot) CLC I-565; MP VI-3111

Kalkwerk, Das. *See* Lime Works, The

Kälte, Die. *See* Gathering Evidence

Kamen no kokuhaku. *See* Confessions of a Mask

Kamera obskura. *See* Laughter in the Dark

"Kamienny świat." *See* "World of Stone, The"

Kamongo (Smith, H.) MP VI-3115; MP:AF II-630

Kangaroo (Aleshkovsky) CLCII II-811; MPII:WF II-790

Kangaroo (Lawrence) CLCII II-812; MPII:BCF II-877

Kanthapura (Rao) CLCII II-813; MPII:BCF II-882

Kapital, Das (Marx) MP VI-3117

Karl and Rosa. *See* November 1918

Karl Marx Play, The (Owens) CLCII II-815; MPII:D III-883

Kaspar (Handke) CLCII II-816; MPII:D III-890

Katar. *See* Chain of Chance, The

Kate Fennigate (Tarkington) CLC I-565; MP VI-3120; MP:AF II-632

Kaukasische Kreidekreis, Der. *See* Caucasian Chalk Circle, The

Kaywana Blood. *See* Kaywana trilogy, The

Kaywana trilogy, The (Mittelholzer) CLCII II-817; MPII:BCF II-887

"Keela, the Outcast Indian Maiden" (Welty) MPII:SS III-1248

Keep the Aspidistra Flying (Orwell) CLCII II-820; MPII:BCF II-894

Keep Tightly Closed in a Cool Dry Place (Terry) CLCII II-821; MPII:D III-895

Keepers of the House, The (Grau) CLCII II-822; MPII:AF II-835

Kein Ort. *See* No Place on Earth

Keller, Der. *See* Gathering Evidence

Kenguru. *See* Kangaroo (Aleshkovsky)

Kenilworth (Scott, Sir W.) CLC I-566; MP VI-3123; MP:BF II-735

"Kepi, The" (Colette) MPII:SS III-1252

Kepler (Banville) CLCII II-823; MPII:BCF II-899

"Kerchief, The" (Agnon) MPII:SS III-1255

Keys of the Kingdom, The (Cronin) CLCII II-824; MPII:BCF II-904

Khadzi-Murat. *See* Hadji Murad

"Khozyain i rabotnik." *See* "Master and Man"

Kidnapped (Stevenson) CLC I-568; MP VI-3127; MP:BF II-739

"Kikuguruma." *See* "Boxcar of Chrysanthemums"

Killdeer, The (Reaney) CLCII II-825; MPII:D III-900

Killer, The (Ionesco) CLCII II-827; MPII:D III-905

"Killers, The" (Hemingway) MPII:SS III-1259

Killing Ground, The (Settle) CLCII II-827. *See also* Beulah Quintet, The

Kim (Kipling) CLC I-568; MP VI-3130; MP:BF II-743

Kind, Ein. *See* Gathering Evidence

Kind of Alaska, A (Pinter) CLCII II-829; MPII:D III-910

Kindergarten (Rushforth) CLCII II-829; MPII:BCF II-909

Kindergeschichte. *See* Slow Homecoming

Kindheitsmuster. *See* Patterns of Childhood

Kindly Ones, The. *See* Dance to the Music of Time, A, *and* Dance to the Music of Time: Second Movement, A

King and No King, A (Beaumont *and* Fletcher) CLC I-569; MP VI-3133

King Horn (Unknown) MP VI-3137

King Jesus (Graves) CLCII II-830; MPII:BCF II-915

King John (Bale) CLC I-569; MP VI-3140

King John (Shakespeare) CLC I-570; MP VI-3144

King Lear (Shakespeare) CLC I-572; MP VI-3148

King Must Die, The (Renault) CLCII II-831; MPII:BCF II-920

King of the Golden River, The (Ruskin) CLC I-574; MP VI-3153; MP:BF II-747

King of the Mountains, The (About) CLC I-575; MP VI-3156; MP:EF II-724

King Paradox (Baroja) CLC I-575; MP VI-3159; MP:EF II-728

"King Solomon" (Rosenfeld) MPII:SS III-1262

King Solomon's Mines (Haggard) CLC I-576; MP VI-3163; MP:BF II-751

King, the Greatest Alcalde, The (Vega) CLC I-577; MP VI-3168

Kingdom of God, The (Martínez Sierra) CLC I-578; MP VI-3173

Kingdom of This World, The (Carpentier) CLCII II-834; MPII:AF II-840

Kings in Exile (Daudet) CLC I-578; MP VI-3176; MP:EF II-733

"King's Indian, The" (Gardner) CLCII II-835; MPII:SS III-1265

King's Row (Bellamann) CLC I-579; MP VI-3179; MP:AF II-636

Kinkakuji. See Temple of the Golden Pavilion, The

Kipps (Wells) CLC I-580; MP VI-3182; MP:BF II-757

"Kiss, The" (Chekhov) MPII:SS III-1270

Kiss of the Spider Woman (Puig) CLCII II-837; MPII:AF II-845

Kitchen, The (Wesker) CLCII II-837; MPII:D III-915

"Kleine Herr Friedemann, Der." See "Little Herr Friedemann"

"Kleist in Thun" (Walser) MPII:SS III-1273

Klingsor's Last Summer (Hesse) CLCII II-839; MPII:WF II-797

Klingsors letzter Sommer. See Klingsor's Last Summer

Klop. See Bedbug, The

Knekht, Der. See Slave, The

Kniga skitany. See Story of a Life, The

Knight of the Burning Pestle, The (Beaumont and Fletcher) CLC I-581; MP VI-3185

Knights, The (Aristophanes) CLC I-582; MP VI-3189

Know Nothing (Settle) CLCII II-839. See also Beulah Quintet, The

Knowledge of Language (Chomsky) MPII:NF II-786

Kojinteki na taiken. See Personal Matter, A

Kompleks polski. See Polish Complex, The

Kompromiss. See Compromise, The

Konerne ved vandposten. See Women at the Pump, The

Kopfgeburten. See Headbirths

Korrektur. See Correction

Kōshoku ichidai otoko. See Life of an Amorous Man, The

Kosmos. See Cosmos

Kotlovan. See Foundation Pit, The

Krapp's Last Tape (Beckett) CLCII II-841; MPII:D III-920

Kreutzer Sonata, The (Tolstoy) CLC I-583; MP VI-3192; MP:EF II-736

Kristin Lavransdatter (Undset) CLC I-584; MP VI-3195; MP:EF II-740

"Kryzhovnik." See "Gooseberries"

Kuchibue o fuku toki. See When I Whistle

"Kugelmass Episode, The" (Allen) MPII:SS III-1276

"Kunstwerk im Zeitalter seiner technischen Reproduzierbarkeit, Das." See Work of Art in the Age of Mechanical Reproduction, The

Kuntsnmakher fun Lublin, Der. See Magician of Lublin, The

Kurka Wodna. See Water Hen, The

"Kurtser Fraytik, Der." See "Short Friday"

Kurze Brief zum langen Abschied, Der. See Short Letter, Long Farewell

Kusamakura. See Three-Cornered World, The

Kutonet veha-Pasim. See Tzili

L

Labyrinth of Solitude, The (Paz) MP VI-3200

Ladies' Hairdresser (Grekova) CLCII II-841; MPII:WF II-802

Lady Chatterley's Lover (Lawrence) CLCII II-842; MPII:BCF II-927

Lady for Ransom, The (Duggan) MP VI-3203; MP:BF II-761

Lady From the Sea, The (Ibsen) CLC I-586; MP VI-3206

Lady into Fox (Garnett) CLC I-587; MP VI-3210; MP:BF II-765

"Lady Macbeth of the Mtsensk District" (Leskov) CLCII II-844; MPII:SS III-1280

Lady of the Lake, The (Scott, Sir W.) CLC I-588; MP VI-3213

"Lady or the Tiger?, The" (Stockton) MPII:SS III-1284

Lady Windermere's Fan (Wilde) CLC I-588; MP VI-3216

"Lady with the Dog, The" (Chekhov) CLCII II-846; MPII:SS III-1288

Lady's Not for Burning, The (Fry) CLC I-589; MP VI-3219

Lafcadio's Adventures (Gide) CLCII II-847; MPII:WF II-806

"Lagoon, The" (Conrad) MPII:SS III-1292

Lais, Le (Villon) MP VI-3226

Lais of Marie de France, The (Marie de France) MP VI-3230

Lalla Rookh (Moore, T.) CLC I-590; MP VI-3237

Lamb, The (Mauriac) CLCII II-848; MPII:WF II-811

"Lamb to the Slaughter" (Dahl) MPII:SS III-1295

Lanark (Gray, A.) CLCII II-850; MPII:BCF II-934

Land of Ulro, The (Miłosz) MPII:NF II-792

"Landarzt, Ein." See "Country Doctor, A"

Landlocked. See Children of Violence

Langsame Heimkehr. See Slow Homecoming

Language, Thought, and Reality (Whorf) MPII:NF II-798

Lao Ts'an youji. See Travels of Lao Ts'an, The

Largo Desolato (Havel) CLCII II-851; MPII:D III-926

Last and First Men (Stapledon) MPII:BCF II-939

Last Athenian, The (Rydberg) CLC I-592; MP VI-3243; MP:EF II-750

Last Chronicle of Barset, The (Trollope) CLC I-592; MP VI-3246; MP:BF II-768

"Last Class, The" (Daudet) MPII:SS III-1298

Last Days of Pompeii, The (Bulwer-Lytton) CLC I-594; MP VI-3249; MP:BF II-772

Last Gentleman, The (Percy) CLCII II-853; MPII:AF II-850

Last Incarnation of Vautrin, The. See Splendors and Miseries of Courtesans, The

Last Meeting of the Knights of the White Magnolia, The (Jones, P.) CLCII II-854; MPII:D III-932

"Last Mohican, The" (Malamud) MPII:SS III-1302

Last of Chéri, The (Colette) CLCII I-264; MPII:WF I-243

Last of Summer, The (O'Brien) CLC I-595; MP VI-3253; MP:BF II-776

Last of the Barons, The (Bulwer-Lytton) CLC I-595; MP VI-3257; MP:BF II-780

Last of the Just, The (Schwarz-Bart) CLCII II-856; MPII:WF II-816

Last of the Mohicans, The (Cooper) CLC I-596; MP VI-3261; MP:AF II-639

Last of the Red-Hot Lovers (Simon, N.) CLCII II-857; MPII:D III-938

Last of the Vikings, The (Bojer) CLC I-597; MP VI-3266; MP:EF II-754

Last of the Wine, The (Renault) MP VI-3271; MP:BF II-784

Last Picture Show, The (McMurtry) CLCII II-858; MPII:AF II-854

Last Post, The. *See* Parade's End

Last Puritan, The (Santayana) CLC I-598; MP VI-3274; MP:AF II-645

Last Temptation of Christ, The (Kazantzakis) CLCII II-859; MPII:WF II-820

Last Things. *See* Strangers and Brothers

Last Tycoon, The (Fitzgerald, F.) CLC I-599; MP VI-3277; MP:AF II-649

Late George Apley, The (Marquand) CLC I-599; MP VI-3280; MP:AF II-653

Late Mattia Pascal, The (Pirandello) CLC I-600; MP VI-3285; MP:EF II-759

Laughing Boy (La Farge) CLCII II-860; MPII:AF II-860

Laughter (Bergson) MP VI-3289

Laughter in the Dark (Nabokov) CLCII II-861; MPII:WF II-825

Laundromat, The. *See* Third and Oak: The Laundromat

"Laura" (Saki) MPII:SS III-1305

Lavengro (Borrow) CLC I-601; MP VI-3292; MP:BF II-787

Lawd Today (Wright) CLCII II-862; MPII:AF II-864

Lay of Igor's Campaign, The (Unknown) MP VI-3296

Lay of the Last Minstrel, The (Scott, W.) CLC I-603; MP VI-3299

Lazarillo de Tormes (Unknown) CLC I-604; MP VI-3302; MP:EF II-763

Lazarus Laughed (O'Neill) CLCII II-863; MPII:D III-944

Leaf Storm (García Márquez) CLCII II-864; MPII:AF II-868

Lean Lands, The (Yáñez) CLCII II-865; MPII:AF II-873

"Leaning Tower, The" (Porter) MPII:SS III-1309

Lear (Bond) CLCII II-866; MPII:D III-949

Leatherstocking Tales, The. *See* Deerslayer, The; Last of the Mohicans, The; Pathfinder, The; Pioneers, The; *and* Prairie, The

Leave It to Psmith (Wodehouse) CLCII II-868; MPII:BCF II-944

"Leaves" (Updike) MPII:SS III-1313

Leaves of Grass (Whitman) MP VI-3307

"Leaving the Yellow House" (Bellow) MPII:SS III-1317

Leben des Galilei. *See* Galileo

Lebensansichten des Katers Murr. *See* Life and Opinions of Kater Murr, The

Leçon, La. *See* Lesson, The

"Ledi Makbet Mtsenskogo uyez da." *See* "Lady Macbeth of the Mtsensk District"

Left Hand of Darkness, The (Le Guin) CLCII II-869; MPII:AF II-878

Left-Handed Woman, The (Handke) CLCII II-870; MPII:WF II-830

"Lefty" (Leskov) MPII:SS III-1320

"Legal Aid" (O'Connor, Frank) MPII:SS III-1325

Legend of Good Women, The (Chaucer) CLC I-605; MP VI-3311

"Legend of St. Julian, Hospitaler, The" (Flaubert) MPII:SS III-1328

"Legend of Sleepy Hollow, The" (Irving) CLC I-606; MP VI-3314; MP:AF II-659; MPII:SS III-1331

Legend of the Moor's Legacy (Irving) CLC I-607; MP VI-3317; MP:AF II-663

Legend of Tyl Ulenspiegel, The (Coster) CLC I-607; MP VI-3321; MP:EF II-768

Legs (Kennedy, W.) CLCII II-871. *See also* Albany Cycle, The

Lehre der Sainte-Victoire, Die. *See* Slow Homecoming

"Lenz" (Büchner) CLCII II-872; MPII:SS III-1335

Leopard, The (Tomasi di Lampedusa) MP VI-3324; MP:EF II-772

Leopards and Lilies (Duggan) MP VI-3327; MP:BF II-792

Less than Angels (Pym) CLCII II-873; MPII:BCF II-949

Less Than One (Brodsky) MPII:NF II-802

Lesson, The (Ionesco) CLCII II-875; MPII:D III-954

Lesson from Aloes, A (Fugard) CLCII II-875; MPII:D III-959

Lesson of Mont-Sainte-Victoire, The. *See* Slow Homecoming

"Lesson of the Master, The" (James, H.) MPII:SS III-1339

Let Us Now Praise Famous Men (Agee) MP VI-3330

Letter to Lord Liszt (Walser) CLCII II-876; MPII:WF II-836

Letters and Papers from Prison (Bonhoeffer) MPII:NF II-807

Letters from an American Farmer (Crèvecœur) MP VI-3333

Letters from the Underworld (Dostoevski) CLC I-608; MP VI-3336; MP:EF II-776

Letters of Charles Lamb, The (Lamb) MP VI-3341

Letters of D. H. Lawrence, The. *See* Collected Letters of D. H. Lawrence, The

Letters of Emily Dickinson, The (Dickinson) MP VI-3344

Letters of F. Scott Fitzgerald, The (Fitzgerald, F.) MP VI-3347

Letters of John Keats, The (Keats) MP VI-3350

Letters of Madame de Sévigné, The (Sévigné) MP VI-3353

Letters of Pliny the Younger, The (Pliny) MP VI-3355

Letters of Robert Frost, The (Frost) MP VI-3358

Letters of Thomas Gray, The (Gray) MP VI-3361

Letters of Thomas Wolfe, The (Wolfe) MP VI-3364

Letters of Walpole, The (Walpole, Horace) MP VI-3368

Letters of William Cowper, The (Cowper) MP VI-3371

Letters on Cézanne (Rilke) MPII:NF II-812

Letters to Felice (Kafka) MPII:NF II-819

Letters to His Son (Chesterfield) MP VI-3374

Letters to Olga (Havel) MPII:NF II-825

Letting Go (Roth, P.) CLCII II-878; MPII:AF II-883

Leviathan (Hobbes) MP VI-3376

"Levsha." *See* "Lefty"

"Leyenda de la Tatuana." *See* "Tatuana's Tale"

Liber Amoris (Hazlitt) CLC I-609; MP VI-3379

Liberal Imagination, The (Trilling) MPII:NF II-830

"Library of Babel, The" (Borges) MPII:SS III-1342

Libro de Manuel. *See* Manual for Manuel, A

Lie Down in Darkness (Styron) MP VI-3382; MP:AF II-667

Lie of the Mind, A (Shepard) CLCII II-879; MPII:D III-964

Lieh-kuo chih (Fêng) MP VI-3385; MP:EF II-782

Life, A (Leonard) CLCII II-880; MPII:D III-970

Life, Adventures, and Piracies of the Famous Captain Singleton, The. *See* Captain Singleton

Life and Adventures of Martin Chuzzlewit, The. *See* Martin Chuzzlewit

Life and Death of Cardinal Wolsey, The (Cavendish) MP VI-3389

Life and Death of Mr. Badman, The (Bunyan) CLC I-610; MP VI-3392; MP:BF II-796

Life and Extraordinary Adventures of Private Ivan Chonkin, The (Voinovich) CLCII II-881; MPII:WF II-841

Life and Opinions of Kater Murr, The (Hoffmann) CLCII II-883; MPII:WF II-849

Life and Opinions of Tristram Shandy, Gentleman, The. *See* Tristram Shandy

Life and Strange Surprising Adventures of Robinson Crusoe, The. *See* Robinson Crusoe

Life & Times of Michael K (Coetzee) CLCII II-884; MPII:BCF II-954

Life Before Man (Atwood) CLCII II-885;
MPII:BCF II-959
Life in London (Egan) CLC I-610; MP VI-
3394; MP:BF II-799
Life is a Dream (Calderón de la Barca)
CLC I-611; MP VI-3398
Life Is Elsewhere (Kundera) CLCII II-886;
MPII:WF II-855
Life of an Amorous Man, The (Ihara)
CLCII II-888; MPII:WF II-860
Life of Cardinal Wolsey and Metrical
Versions from the Original Autograph
Manuscript. *See* Life and Death of
Cardinal Wolsey, The
Life of Dr. Robert Sanderson, The. *See*
Lives
Life of John Donne, The. *See* Lives
Life of Man, The (Andreyev) CLCII II-
889; MPII:D III-975
Life of Mr. George Herbert, The. *See*
Lives
Life of Mr. Jonathan Wild the Great, The.
See Jonathan Wild
Life of Mr. Richard Hooker, The. *See*
Lives
Life of Nelson (Southey) MP VI-3403
Life of Richard Savage (Johnson, S.) MP
VI-3406
Life of Samuel Johnson, LL.D., The
(Boswell) MP VI-3409
Life of Sir Henry Wotton, The. *See* Lives
Life on the Mississippi (Twain) MP VI-
3412
"Life-Story" (Barth) MPII:SS III-1348
Life with Father (Day, C.) CLC I-612;
MP VI-3415; MP:AF II-670
"Lifeguard" (Updike) MPII:SS III-1345
"Ligeia" (Poe) CLC I-613; MP VI-3418;
MP:AF II-674; MPII:SS III-1352
Light (Figes) CLCII II-890; MPII:BCF II-
965
Light and the Dark, The. *See* Strangers
and Brothers
Light in August (Faulkner) CLC I-613;
MP VI-3423; MP:AF II-679

"Lightning" (Barthelme, D.) MPII:SS III-
1355
"Like the Night" (Carpentier) MPII:SS III-
1359
Liliom (Molnár) CLC I-615; MP VI-3428
"Lilla fälttåget, Det." *See* "Children's
Campaign, The"
Lime Twig, The (Hawkes) MP VI-3431;
MP:AF II-684
Lime Works, The (Bernhard) CLCII II-
891; MPII:WF II-866
Lincoln (Vidal) CLCII II-892; MPII:AF II-
887
Link, The (Strindberg) CLC I-615; MP
VI-3434
Linkshändige Frau, Die. *See* Left-Handed
Woman, The
Lion and the Jewel, The (Soyinka) CLCII
III-893; MPII:D III-981
Lion Country. *See* Book of Bebb, The
Lion of Flanders, The (Conscience) CLC
I-616; MP VI-3438; MP:EF II-787
"Lions, Harts, Leaping Does" (Powers)
MPII:SS III-1363
"Lispeth" (Kipling) MPII:SS III-1367
Literary Essays of Virginia Woolf, The
(Woolf) MP VI-3442
Little Big Man (Berger, T.) CLCII III-893;
MPII:AF II-891
Little Boy in Search of God, A (Singer)
MPII:NF II-835
Little Clay Cart, The (Shudraka) CLC I-
617; MP VI-3444
"Little Cloud, A" (Joyce) MPII:SS III-
1371
Little Dorrit (Dickens) CLC I-617; MP VI-
3448; MP:BF II-803
Little Foxes, The (Hellman) CLC I-620;
MP VI-3451
Little Girls, The (Bowen) CLCII III-895;
MPII:BCF II-971
"Little Herr Friedemann" (Mann) MPII:SS
III-1375
Little Hotel, The (Stead) CLCII III-896;
MPII:BCF II-975

Little Minister, The (Barrie) CLC I-621; MP VI-3454; MP:BF II-807

Little Wilson and Big God (Burgess) MPII:NF II-841

Little Women (Alcott) CLC I-622; MP VI-3458; MP:AF II-687

Littlepage Manuscripts, The. See Chainbearer, The; Redskins, The; and Satanstoe

Lives (Walton) MP VI-3461

Lives of a Cell, The (Thomas) MPII:NF II-846

Lives of Girls and Women (Munro) CLCII III-898; MPII:BCF II-980

Lives of the Caesars (Suetonius) MP VI-3464

Lives of the Kings of Norway, The. See Heimskringla

Lives of the Poets (Johnson, S.) MP VI-3468

Living (Green, Henry) CLCII III-899; MPII:BCF II-984

Living Principle, The (Leavis) MPII:NF II-850

"Living Relic, A" (Turgenev) MPII:SS III-1379

"Livingstone's Companions" (Gordimer) MPII:SS III-1383

Livre du rire et de l'oubli, Le. See Book of Laughter and Forgetting, The

Liza of Lambeth (Maugham) CLC I-622; MP VI-3471; MP:BF II-812

Lizard's Tail, The (Valenzuela) CLCII III-900; MPII:AF II-896

Local Anaesthetic (Grass) CLCII III-902; MPII:WF II-872

"Lodging for the Night, A" (Stevenson) MPII:SS III-1387

Loitering with Intent (Spark) CLCII III-903; MPII:BCF III-989

Lolita (Nabokov) CLCII III-904; MPII:AF II-901

"Loneliness of the Long-Distance Runner, The" (Sillitoe) MPII:SS IV-1391

Lonely Crowd, The (Riesman) MPII:NF II-856

Lonely Girl, The. See Country Girls Trilogy, The

Lonely Londoners, The (Selvon) CLCII III-905; MPII:BCF III-993

Lonely Passion of Judith Hearne, The (Moore) CLCII III-907; MPII:BCF III-998

Long and Happy Life, A (Price) MP VI-3474; MP:AF II-691

Long Day's Journey into Night (O'Neill) CLCII III-908; MPII:D III-986

Long Dream, The (Wright) CLCII III-909; MPII:AF II-906

Long Goodbye, The (Chandler) CLCII III-910; MPII:AF II-911

Long Journey, The (Jensen) CLC I-623; MP VI-3477; MP:EF II-791

Long Loneliness, The (Day) MPII:NF II-861

Long Night, The (Lytle) CLC I-624; MP VI-3483; MP:AF II-694

Long Voyage, The (Semprun) CLCII III-911; MPII:WF II-878

Long Way Around, The. See Slow Homecoming

Longest Journey, The (Forster) CLC I-625; MP VI-3487; MP:BF II-816

Look at Me (Brookner) CLCII III-912; MPII:BCF III-1003

Look Back in Anger (Osborne) MP VI-3490

Look Homeward, Angel (Wolfe) CLC I-625; MP VI-3494; MP:AF II-698

Looking Backward (Bellamy) CLC I-626; MP VI-3497; MP:AF II-702

"Looking for Mr. Green" (Bellow) MPII:SS IV-1395

Lookout Cartridge (McElroy) CLCII III-914; MPII:AF II-916

"Loons, The" (Laurence) MPII:SS IV-1399

Loot (Orton) CLCII III-915; MPII:D III-992

Lord Jim (Conrad) CLC I-627; MP VI-3500; MP:BF II-820

Lord of the Flies (Golding) MP VI-3505; MP:BF II-825

Lord of the Rings, The. *See* Fellowship of the Ring, The; Return of the King, The; *and* Two Towers, The

Lorna Doone (Blackmore) CLC I-628; MP VI-3508; MP:BF II-829

Loser, The (Konrád) CLCII III-915; MPII:WF II-884

Losing Battles (Welty) CLCII III-917; MPII:AF II-922

Lost Flying Boat, The (Sillitoe) CLCII III-918; MPII:BCF III-1008

Lost Honor of Katharina Blum, The (Böll) CLCII III-919; MPII:WF II-890

Lost Horizon (Hilton) CLC I-629; MP VI-3512; MP:BF II-833

Lost Illusions (Balzac) CLC I-630; MP VI-3518; MP:EF II-798

Lost in America (Singer) MPII:NF II-835

"Lost in the Funhouse" (Barth) MPII:SS IV-1403

Lost Lady, A (Cather) CLC I-631; MP VI-3521; MP:AF II-706

Lost Steps, The (Carpentier) CLCII III-921; MPII:AF II-927

Lost Weekend, The (Jackson) CLC I-632; MP VI-3524; MP:AF II-710

Lo-t'o Hsiang-tzu. *See* Rickshaw

"Lottery, The" (Jackson) MPII:SS IV-1406

Louis Lambert (Balzac) CLCII III-922; MPII:WF II-896

Love and Salt Water (Wilson, E.) CLCII III-923; MPII:BCF III-1013

"Love Decoy, The" (Perelman) MPII:SS IV-1409

Love Feast. *See* Book of Bebb, The

Love for Love (Congreve) CLC I-633; MP VI-3527

Love for Lydia (Bates) CLCII III-924; MPII:BCF III-1017

Love in a Wood (Wycherley) CLC I-634; MP VI-3530

Love in the Ruins (Percy) CLCII III-925; MPII:AF III-933

Love Medicine (Erdrich) CLCII III-927; MPII:AF III-938

Loved and the Lost, The (Callaghan) CLCII III-928; MPII:BCF III-1022

Loved One, The (Waugh) CLCII III-929; MPII:BCF III-1027

Lover, The (Duras) CLCII III-931; MPII:WF II-901

Love's Labour's Lost (Shakespeare) CLC I-634; MP VI-3534

Loving (Green, H.) CLC I-636; MP VI-3537; MP:BF II-839

Lower Depths, The (Gorky) CLC I-636; MP VI-3540

Loyalties (Galsworthy) CLC I-638; MP VI-3544

Lu Ann Hampton Laverty Oberlander (Jones, P.) CLCII III-932; MPII:D III-997

Lubimow. *See* Makepeace Experiment, The

Lucien Leuwen (Stendhal) CLC I-639; MP VI-3547; MP:EF II-802

Lucinda Brayford (Boyd) CLCII III-933; MPII:BCF III-1033

Luck of Barry Lyndon, The. *See* Barry Lyndon

Luck of Ginger Coffey, The (Moore) CLCII III-935; MPII:BCF III-1039

"Luck of Roaring Camp, The" (Harte) MPII:SS IV-1412

Luck of Roaring Camp and Other Sketches, The (Harte) MP VI-3551; MP:AF II-713

Lucky Jim (Amis) MP VI-3554; MP:BF II-843

Lucy Gayheart (Cather) CLCII III-936; MPII:AF III-943

"Lullaby" (Silko) MPII:SS IV-1416

"Luna di miele, sole di fiele." *See* "Bitter Honeymoon"

Luna e i falò, La. *See* Moon and the Bonfires, The

"Lune de pluie, La." *See* "Rainy Moon, The"

"Lupa, La." *See* "She-Wolf, The"

Lusiads, The (Camoëns) CLC I-639; MP
  VI-3557
Luther (Osborne) CLCII III-937; MPII:D
  III-1002
Lydie Breeze (Guare) CLCII III-938;
  MPII:D III-1007
Lyric Poetry of Byron, The (Byron) MP
  VI-3562
Lyric Poetry of Lowell, The (Lowell, J.)
  MP VI-3565

Lyric Poetry of Milton, The (Milton) MP
  VI-3569
Lyric Poetry of Spenser, The (Spenser)
  MP VI-3573
Lysistrata (Aristophanes) CLC I-640; MP
  VI-3578
"Lyubka the Cossack" (Babel) MPII:SS
  IV-1420

M

Ma Rainey's Black Bottom (Wilson, August) CLCII III-939; MPII:D III-1012

Mabinogion, The (Unknown) CLC I-641; MP VI-3582; MP:BF II-847

Macbeth (Shakespeare) CLC I-642; MP VI-3589

Machine infernale, La. *See* Infernal Machine, The

Macunaíma (Andrade) CLCII III-940; MPII:AF III-948

Madame Bovary (Flaubert) CLC I-645; MP VI-3599; MP:EF II-806

"Madame Tellier's Establishment" (Maupassant) MPII:SS IV-1424

"Madame Zilensky and the King of Finland" (McCullers) MPII:SS IV-1427

Mademoiselle de Maupin (Gautier) CLC I-647; MP VI-3604; MP:EF II-812

Madman and the Nun, The (Witkiewicz) CLCII III-941; MPII:D III-1017

Madman's Defense, A. *See* Confession of a Fool, The

Madman's Manifesto, A. *See* Confession of a Fool, The

Madmen and Specialists (Soyinka) CLCII III-942; MPII:D III-1023

Madness and Civilization (Foucault) MPII:NF II-866

Madras House, The (Granville-Barker) CLC I-648; MP VI-3607

Madwoman in the Attic, The (Gilbert *and* Gubar) MPII:NF II-872

Madwoman of Chaillot, The (Giraudoux) CLC I-649; MP VI-3611

Maggie: A Girl of the Streets (Crane, S.) CLC I-649; MP VI-3614; MP:AF II-722

"Magic Barrel, The" (Malamud) MPII:SS IV-1431

Magic Mountain, The (Mann) CLC I-650; MP VI-3618; MP:EF II-816

Magic Skin, The. *See* Wild Ass's Skin, The

Magician of Lublin, The (Singer) CLCII III-944; MPII:AF III-954; MPII:WF III-905

Magister Ludi. *See* Glass Bead Game, The

Magnalia Christi Americana (Mather) MP VI-3623

Magnificent Obsession, The (Douglas, L.) CLC I-652; MP VI-3626; MP:AF II-726

Magus, The (Fowles) CLCII III-945; MPII:BCF III-1044

Mahabharata, The (Unknown) CLC I-652; MP VI-3629

Maid of Honour, The (Massinger) CLC I-653; MP VI-3634

Maids, The (Genet) CLCII III-946; MPII:D III-1031

Maid's Tragedy, The (Beaumont *and* Fletcher) CLC I-654; MP VI-3638

Main Currents in American Thought (Parrington) MP VI-3642

Main Street (Lewis, S.) CLC I-655; MP VI-3645; MP:AF II-730

Main-Travelled Roads (Garland) MP VI-3650; MP:AF II-735

"Maison Tellier, La." *See* "Madame Tellier's Establishment"

Maître de la parole, Le. *See* Guardian of the Word, The

Major Barbara (Shaw) CLC I-656; MP VI-3652

Makepeace Experiment, The (Sinyavsky) CLCII III-947; MPII:WF III-909

Making It (Podhoretz) MPII:NF II-878

Making of Americans, The (Stein) CLCII III-948; MPII:AF III-958

Making of Mind, The (Luria) MPII:NF II-884

Makioka Sisters, The (Tanizaki) CLCII III-950; MPII:WF III-915

Ma'kom a'her. *See* Elsewhere, Perhaps

Mal vu mal dit. *See* Ill Seen Ill Said

Maƚa apokalipsa. *See* Minor Apocalypse, A

Malcolm (Purdy) MP VI-3655; MP:AF II-737

Malcontent, The (Marston) CLC I-657; MP VI-3658

Malign Fiesta. *See* Human Age, The

Malone Dies (Beckett) CLCII III-951. *See also* Trilogy, The

Malone meurt. *See* Malone Dies *and* Trilogy, The

Maltese Falcon, The (Hammett) CLC I-658; MP VI-3661; MP:AF II-740

Man Against the Sky, The (Robinson, E.) MP VI-3664

Man and Superman (Shaw) CLC I-658; MP VI-3667

Man Could Stand Up, A. *See* Parade's End

Man Died, The (Soyinka) MPII:NF III-889

Man for All Seasons, A (Bolt) CLCII III-952; MPII:D III-1037

Man fun Notseres, Der. *See* Nazarene, The

"Man in a Case, The" (Chekhov) MPII:SS IV-1434

Man in the Holocene (Frisch) CLCII III-954; MPII:WF III-920

Man of Feeling, The (Mackenzie) CLC I-660; MP VII-3669; MP:BF II-855

Man of Mode, The (Etherege) CLC I-660; MP VII-3672

Man of Property, The. *See* Forsyte Saga, The

"Man That Corrupted Hadleyburg, The" (Twain) MPII:SS IV-1437

Man Who Came to Dinner, The (Kaufman *and* Hart) CLCII III-954; MPII:D III-1043

Man Who Cried I Am, The (Williams, J.) CLCII III-956; MPII:AF III-962

"Man Who Invented Sin, The" (O'Faoláin) MPII:SS IV-1440

Man Who Killed the Deer, The (Waters) CLCII III-957; MPII:AF III-966

Man Who Loved Children, The (Stead) CLCII III-958; MPII:BCF III-1050

"Man Who Was Almost a Man, The" (Wright) MPII:SS IV-1444

Man Who Was Thursday, The (Chesterton) CLC I-661; MP VII-3676; MP:BF II-859

Man Who Watched the Trains Go By, The (Simenon) CLCII III-959; MPII:WF III-925

"Man Who Would Be King, The" (Kipling) CLCII III-960; MPII:SS IV-1447

Man with a Bull-Tongue Plow (Stuart) MP VII-3680

Man with the Golden Arm, The (Algren) CLCII III-961; MPII:AF III-971

Man Without a Country, The (Hale) CLC I-662; MP VII-3683; MP:AF II-744

Man Without Qualities, The (Musil) CLCII III-962; MPII:WF III-930

"Manatsu no Shi." *See* "Death in Midsummer"

Mandelbaum Gate, The (Spark) CLCII III-964; MPII:BCF III-1057

Man'en san'nen no futtoboru. *See* Silent Cry, The

Manette Salomon (Goncourt *and* Goncourt) CLC I-662; MP VII-3686; MP:EF II-821

Manfred (Byron) CLC I-663; MP VII-3690

Manhattan Transfer (Dos Passos) CLC I-663; MP VII-3693; MP:AF II-748

Manhunt (Carpentier) CLCII III-965; MPII:AF III-977

Mann Moses und die monotheistiche Religion, Der. *See* Moses and Monotheism

Mann ohne Eigenschaften, Der. *See* Man Without Qualities, The

Manon Lescaut (Prévost) CLC I-664; MP VII-3696; MP:EF II-826

Man's Blessing, A (Sciascia) CLCII III-966; MPII:WF III-939

Man's Fate (Malraux) CLC I-665; MP VII-3700; MP:EF II-830

Man's Hope (Malraux) CLCII III-967; MPII:WF III-945

Man's Search for Meaning (Frankl) MPII:NF III-896

Manservant and Maidservant. *See* Bullivant and the Lambs

Mansfield Park (Austen) CLC I-666; MP VII-3704; MP:BF II-864

Mansion, The (Faulkner) MP VII-3707; MP:AF II-752

Manticore, The. *See* Deptford Trilogy, The

Manual for Manuel, A (Cortázar) CLCII III-969; MPII:AF III-981

"Many Are Disappointed" (Pritchett) MPII:SS IV-1455

Marat/Sade (Weiss) CLCII III-971; MPII:D III-1049

Marble Faun, The (Hawthorne) CLC I-667; MP VII-3710; MP:AF II-756

Marbot (Hildesheimer) CLCII III-973; MPII:WF III-952

Marching On (Boyd) CLC I-668; MP VII-3714; MP:AF II-761

Mardi, and a Voyage Thither (Melville) CLC I-669; MP VII-3717; MP:AF II-765

Margin of Hope, A (Howe) MPII:NF III-901

Maria Chapdelaine (Hémon) CLC I-669; MP VII-3721; MP:AF II-769

Maria Magdalena (Hebbel) CLC I-670; MP VII-3725

Mariage d'amour, Un. *See* Thérèse Raquin

Marianne (Marivaux) CLC I-671; MP VII-3728; MP:EF II-834

Marie Antoinette: Or, The Chevalier of the Red House. *See* Chevalier de Maison Rouge, The

Marilyn (Mailer) MPII:NF III-907

"Mario and the Magician" (Mann) MPII:SS IV-1458

Marius the Epicurean (Pater) CLC I-671; MP VII-3732; MP:BF II-868

"Mark on the Wall, The" (Woolf) MPII:SS IV-1462

Market Harborough (Whyte-Melville) CLC I-672; MP VII-3736; MP:BF II-873

Marks of Identity (Goytisolo) CLCII III-974; MPII:WF III-958

Marmion (Scott, Sir W.) CLC I-672; MP VII-3739

"Marquise of O----, The" (Kleist) CLCII III-976; MPII:SS IV-1466

Marquise von O----, Die. *See* "Marquise of O----, The"

Marriage, The (Gombrowicz) CLCII III-977; MPII:D III-1054

Marriage à la Mode (Dryden) CLC I-673; MP VII-3742

Marriage of Figaro, The (Beaumarchais) CLC I-674; MP VII-3745

Marse Chan (Page) CLC I-674; MP VII-3748; MP:AF II-773

Martha Quest. *See* Children of Violence

Martian Chronicles, The (Bradbury, R.) CLCII III-979; MPII:AF III-986

Martin Chuzzlewit (Dickens) CLC I-675; MP VII-3751; MP:BF II-877

Maru (Head) CLCII III-980; MPII:BCF III-1062

Mary (Nabokov) CLCII III-981; MPII:WF III-965

Mary Barton (Gaskell) MP VII-3756; MP:BF II-883

Mary Olivier (Sinclair) CLCII III-982; MPII:BCF III-1067

Mashenka. *See* Mary

Mask of Dimitrios, The. *See* Coffin for Dimitrios, A

Masks (Enchi) CLCII III-983; MPII:WF III-970

"Masque of the Red Death, The" (Poe) MPII:SS IV-1471

Masse und Macht. *See* Crowds and Power

"Master and Man" (Tolstoy) MPII:SS IV-1475

Master and Margarita, The (Bulgakov) CLCII III-984; MPII:WF III-976

Master Builder, The (Ibsen) CLC I-679; MP VII-3759

"MASTER HAROLD" . . . and the boys (Fugard) CLCII III-986; MPII:D III-1059

Master i Margarita. *See* Master and Margarita, The

Master of Ballantrae, The (Stevenson) CLC I-680; MP VII-3764; MP:BF II-887

Master of Go, The (Kawabata) CLCII III-986; MPII:WF III-983

Master of the Mill, The (Grove) CLCII III-987; MPII:BCF III-1072

Masters, The (Snow) MP VII-3768; MP:BF II-892. *See also* Strangers and Brothers

Mastro-don Gesualdo (Berga) CLC I-681; MP VII-3771; MP:EF II-838

Matchmaker, The (Wilder) CLCII III-988; MPII:D III-1065

"Matrenin dvor." *See* "Matryona's House"

"Matryona's House" (Solzhenitsyn) MPII:SS IV-1480

Matter and Memory (Bergson) MP VII-3776

Mątwe. *See* Cuttlefish, The

Mauerspringer, Der. *See* Wall Jumper, The

Maurice (Forster) CLCII III-989; MPII:BCF III-1076

Max Havelaar (Multatuli) CLC I-682; MP VII-3778; MP:EF II-844

Maxims, The (La Rochefoucauld) MP VII-3782

"May Day" (Fitzgerald) MPII:SS IV-1485

Mayn Tatn's Bes-din Shtub. *See* In My Father's Court

Mayor of Casterbridge, The (Hardy) CLC I-683; MP VII-3784; MP:BF II-896

Mayor of Zalamea, The (Calderón de la Barca) CLC I-684; MP VII-3788

McTeague (Norris) CLC I-644; MP VI-3594; MP:AF II-717

Measure for Measure (Shakespeare) CLC I-685; MP VII-3793

Medea (Euripides) CLC I-686; MP VII-3798

Meditación, Una. *See* Meditation, A

Meditation, A (Benet) CLCII III-990; MPII:WF III-988

Meditations (Aurelius) MP VII-3802

Meek Heritage (Sillanpää) CLC I-687; MP VII-3804; MP:EF II-849

Meeting at Telgte, The (Grass) CLCII III-991; MPII:WF III-994

Meijin. *See* Master of Go, The

Mellstock Quire, The. *See* Under the Greenwood Tree

Melmoth the Wanderer (Maturin) CLC I-689; MP VII-3809; MP:BF II-901

Member of the Wedding, The (McCullers) CLC I-690; CLCII III-992; MP VII-3815; MP:AF II-776; MPII:D III-1071

Memed, My Hawk (Kemal) CLCII III-993; MPII:WF III-999

Memento Mori (Spark) MP VII-3820; MP:BF II-908

Memnon. *See* Zadig

Mémoires. *See* Autobiography of Benjamin Franklin, The

Memoirs (Casanova de Seingalt) MP VII-3823

Memoirs (Neruda) MPII:NF III-912

Mémoirs d'une jeune fille rangée. *See* Memoirs of a Dutiful Daughter

Memoirs of a Cavalier, The (Defoe) CLC I-691; MP VII-3826; MP:BF II-912

Memoirs of a Dutiful Daughter (de Beauvoir) MPII:NF III-917

Memoirs of a Fox-Hunting Man (Sassoon) CLC I-691; MP VII-3830; MP:BF II-916

Memoirs of a Midget (de la Mare) CLC I-692; MP VII-3833; MP:BF II-920

Memoirs of a Physician (Dumas, *père*) CLC I-692; MP VII-3836; MP:EF II-854

Memoirs of an Infantry Officer (Sassoon) CLC I-693; MP VII-3842; MP:BF II-924

Memoirs of Hadrian. *See* Hadrian's Memoirs

Memoirs of the Forties (Maclaren-Ross) MPII:NF III-923

Memorandum, The (Havel) CLCII III-995; MPII:D III-1077

Memoria del fuego. *See* Memory of Fire

Memórias pósthumas de Bráz Cubas. *See* Epitaph of a Small Winner

Memories, Dreams, Reflections (Jung) MPII:NF III-928

Memories of a Catholic Girlhood (McCarthy) MPII:NF III-933

Memory of Fire (Galeano) MPII:NF III-937

Men and Women (Browning, R.) MP VII-3846. *See also* Dramatic Monologues and Lyrics of Browning

Men at Arms. *See* Sword of Honour

Men of Maize (Asturias) CLCII III-996; MPII:AF III-991

Menaechmi, The (Plautus) CLC I-694; MP VII-3849

Mendiant de Jérusalem, Le. *See* Beggar in Jerusalem, A

Menindo engenho. *See* Plantation Boy

Menino de engenho. *See* Plantation Boy

Mensch erscheint im Holozän, Der. *See* Man in the Holocene

Menteur, Le (Corneille) CLC I-695; MP VII-3852

Menuhah nekhonah. *See* Perfect Peace, A

Merchant of Venice, The (Shakespeare) CLC I-695; MP VII-3855

Meridian (Walker, A.) CLCII III-997; MPII:AF III-997

Merry-Go-Round in the Sea, The (Stow) CLCII III-998; MPII:BCF III-1081

Merry Wives of Windsor, The (Shakespeare) CLC I-697; MP VII-3860

Message in the Bottle, The (Percy) MPII:NF III-944

Messengers of Day. *See* To Keep the Ball Rolling

Messer Marco Polo (Byrne) CLC I-698; MP VII-3863; MP:BF II-928

Mestiere di vivere, Il. *See* Burning Brand, The

Metafizyka dwugłowego cielęcia. *See* Metaphysics of a Two-Headed Calf

"Metamorphoses" (Cheever) MPII:SS IV-1489

Metamorphoses, The (Ovid) MP VII-3866

"Metamorphosis, The" (Kafka) CLCII III-999; MPII:SS IV-1493

Metaphysics of a Two-Headed Calf (Witkiewicz) CLCII III-1000; MPII:D III-1082

"Metel" (Pushkin). *See* "Blizzard, The"

"Metel" (Tolstoy). *See* "Snow-Storm, The"

Météores, Les. *See* Gemini

Micah Clarke (Doyle) CLC II-699; MP VII-3869; MP:BF II-931

Michael and His Lost Angel (Jones) CLC II-699; MP VII-3873

Mickelsson's Ghosts (Gardner) CLCII III-1001; MPII:AF III-1002

Mid-Channel (Pinero) CLC II-700; MP VII-3877

Middle Age of Mrs. Eliot, The (Wilson, Angus) CLCII III-1004; MPII:BCF III-1086

Middle Ground, The (Drabble) CLCII III-1005; MPII:BCF III-1091

Middle of the Journey, The (Trilling) CLCII III-1006; MPII:AF III-1007

Middle Parts of Fortune, The. *See* Her Privates, We

Middle Passage, The (Naipaul) MPII:NF III-950

Middlemarch (Eliot, G.) CLC II-700; MP VII-3879; MP:BF II-935

Midnight Oil (Pritchett) MPII:NF III-955

Midnight's Children (Rushdie) CLCII III-1007; MPII:BCF III-1097

"Midsummer Night Madness" (O'Faoláin) MPII:SS IV-1497

Midsummer Night's Dream, A (Shakespeare) CLC II-703; MP VII-3885

Mighty and Their Fall, The (Compton-Burnett) MP VII-3890; MP:BF II-942

Migrants, Sharecroppers, Mountaineers. *See* Children of Crisis

Miguel Street (Naipaul, V. S.) CLCII III-1008; MPII:BCF III-1102

Mikado, The (Gilbert) CLC II-704; MP VII-3893

Mikha'el sheli. *See* My Michael

Military Philosophers, The. *See* Dance to the Music of Time, A

Mill on the Floss, The (Eliot, G.) CLC II-705; MP VII-3896; MP:BF II-945

Mill on the Po, The (Bacchelli) CLC II-707; MP VII-3901; MP:EF II-861

Mimesis (Auerbach) MPII:NF III-960

Mimic Men, The (Naipaul, V. S.) CLCII III-1010; MPII:BCF III-1106

Mind of Primitive Man, The (Boas) MP VII-3906

Minds, Brains, and Science (Searle) MPII:NF III-965

"Minister's Black Veil, The" (Hawthorne) MPII:SS IV-1501

Ministry of Fear, The (Greene, G.) CLC II-708; MP VII-3909; MP:BF II-951

Minna von Barnhelm (Lessing) CLC II-709; MP VII-3912

Minor Apocalypse, A (Konwicki) CLCII III-1011; MPII:WF III-1006

Minty Alley (James, C. L. R.) CLCII III-1012; MPII:BCF III-1109

Miracle of the Rose (Genet) CLCII III-1013; MPII:WF III-1011

Miracle Worker, The (Gibson) CLCII III-1015; MPII:D III-1089

Mirror for Witches, A (Forbes) CLC II-710; MP VII-3917; MP:AF II-782

Mirror in My House (O'Casey) MPII:NF III-971

Misanthrope, The (Molière) CLC II-711; MP VII-3921

Miscellanies (Cowley) MP VII-3926

Miser, The (Molière) CLC II-712; MP VII-3928

Misérables, Les (Hugo) CLC II-713; MP VII-3931; MP:EF II-866

"Miss Brill" (Mansfield) MPII:SS IV-1505

Miss Julie (Strindberg) CLC II-715; MP VII-3936

Miss Lonelyhearts (West, N.) CLC II-716; MP VII-3941; MP:AF II-787

"Miss Ogilvy Finds Herself" (Hall) MPII:SS IV-1509

Miss Peabody's Inheritance (Jolley) CLCII III-1016; MPII:BCF III-1116

Miss Ravenel's Conversion from Secession to Loyalty (De Forest) CLC II-717; MP VII-3945; MP:AF II-792

"Miss Tempy's Watchers" (Jewett) MPII:SS IV-1513

Missolonghi Manuscript, The (Prokosch) CLCII III-1018; MPII:AF III-1012

Mr. Beluncle (Pritchett) CLCII III-1018; MPII:BCF III-1121

Mr. Britling Sees It Through (Wells) CLC II-717; MP VII-3949; MP:BF II-955

Mr. Bullivant and His Lambs (Compton-Burnett) MP VII-3952

Mr. Facey Romford's Hounds (Surtees) CLC II-718; MP VII-3954; MP:BF II-959

Mr. Midshipman Easy (Marryat) CLC II-719; MP VII-3960; MP:BF II-966

Mr. Palomar (Calvino) CLCII III-1020; MPII:WF III-1015

Mister Roberts (Heggen) CLC II-720; MP VII-3964; MP:AF II-796

Mr. Sammler's Planet (Bellow) CLCII III-1020; MPII:AF III-1017

Mr. Sampath. *See* Printer of Malgudi, The

Mr. Sponge's Sporting Tour (Surtees) CLC II-721; MP VII-3967; MP:BF II-970

Mr. Stone and the Knights Companion (Naipaul, V. S.) CLCII III-1022; MPII:BCF III-1126

Mr. Weston's Good Wine (Powys, T.) CLC II-721; MP VII-3970; MP:BF II-974

Mrs. Bridge (Connell) CLCII III-1023; MPII:AF III-1022

Mrs. Caliban (Ingalls) CLCII III-1024; MPII:BCF III-1131

Mrs. Dalloway (Woolf) CLC II-722; MP
VII-3973; MP:BF II-978

Mrs. Dane's Defence (Jones) CLC II-724;
MP VII-3978

"Mrs. Fortescue" (Lessing) MPII:SS IV-
1515

Mistress of the Inn, The (Goldoni) CLC II-
724; MP VII-3982

Mrs. Stevens Hears the Mermaids Singing
(Sarton) CLCII III-1025; MPII:AF III-
1028

Mrs. Warren's Profession (Shaw, G.)
CLCII III-1026; MPII:D III-1095

Mithridate (Racine) CLC II-725; MP VII-
3987

"Mnogo li cheloveku zemli nuzhno?" See
"How Much Land Does a Man Need?"

Mobile (Butor) CLCII III-1027; MPII:WF
III-1021

Moby Dick (Melville) CLC II-725; MP
VII-3992; MP:AF II-800

Mock Astrologer, The (Calderón de la
Barca) CLC II-728; MP VII-3998

Model Childhood, A. See Patterns of
Childhood

Modern Chivalry (Brackenridge) CLC II-
728; MP VII-4001; MP:AF II-806

Modern Comedy, A (Galsworthy) CLC II-
729; MP VII-4005; MP:BF II-983

Modern Instance, A (Howells) CLC II-
730; MP VII-4010; MP:AF II-811

Modern Midas, A (Jókai) CLC II-731;
MP VII-4015; MP:EF II-872

Modification, La. See Change of Heart, A

Moetsukita chizu. See Ruined Map, The

"Moglie con le ali, La." See "Count's
Wife, The"

"Moglie di Gogol, La." See "Gogol's
Wife"

"Moi pervyi gus." See "My First Goose"

Moll Flanders (Defoe) CLC II-732; MP
VII-4020; MP:BF II-988

Molloy (Beckett) CLCII III-1028. See also
Trilogy, The

Moment of True Feeling, A (Handke)
CLCII III-1029; MPII:WF III-1026

Monday Conversations (Sainte-Beuve) MP
VII-4025

Monk, The (Lewis, M.) CLC II-733; MP
VII-4027; MP:BF II-993

"Monkey, The" (Dinesen) MPII:SS IV-
1519

Monkey (Wu Ch'eng-en) CLC II-733; MP
VII-4030; MP:EF II-878

Monkey Grip (Garner) CLCII III-1030;
MPII:BCF III-1137

Monkey's Wrench, The (Levi, P.) CLCII
III-1032; MPII:WF III-1031

Monsieur Beaucaire (Tarkington) CLC II-
735; MP VII-4034; MP:AF II-816

Monsieur D'Olive (Chapman) CLC II-736;
MP VII-4037

Monsieur Lecoq (Gaboriau) CLC II-736;
MP VII-4040; MP:EF II-883

"Monster, The" (Crane) MPII:SS IV-1523

Monstre Gai. See Human Age, The

Mont-Oriol (Maupassant) CLC II-737; MP
VII-4045; MP:EF II-889

Mont-Saint-Michel and Chartres (Adams,
H.) MP VII-4049

Month in the Country, A (Turgenev) CLC
II-738; MP VII-4052

Month of Sundays, A (Updike) CLCII III-
1033; MPII:AF III-1032

"Moon and Madness" (Singer) MPII:SS
IV-1528

Moon and Sixpence, The (Maugham) CLC
II-739; MP VII-4056; MP:BF II-997

Moon and the Bonfires, The (Pavese)
CLCII III-1034; MPII:WF III-1036

"Moon Deluxe" (Barthelme, F.) MPII:SS
IV-1532

Moon for the Misbegotten, A (O'Neill)
CLCII III-1035; MPII:D III-1100

Moon Is a Harsh Mistress, The (Heinlein)
CLCII III-1036; MPII:AF III-1037

Moon Story, The. See Bracknels, The

Moonrise, Moonset (Konwicki) CLCII III-
1037; MPII:WF III-1041

Moonstone, The (Collins, Wilke) CLC II-
740; MP VII-4059; MP:BF II-1001

Morning, Noon, and Night (Cozzens) CLCII III-1037; MPII:AF III-1042

Morning Watch, The (Agee) CLCII III-1039; MPII:AF III-1050

Mornings in Mexico (Lawrence) MPII:NF III-976

Mort à crédit. See Death on the Installment Plan

Morte accidentale di un anarchico. See Accidental Death of an Anarchist

Morte dans l'âme, La. See Roads to Freedom, The

Morte d'Arthur, Le (Malory) CLC II-742; MP VII-4063; MP:BF II-1006

Morte d'Urban (Powers) CLCII III-1040; MPII:AF III-1055

Moscas, Los. See Flies, The

Moses (Hurston) CLCII III-1041; MPII:AF III-1061

Moses and Monotheism (Freud) MPII:NF III-982

Mosquitoes (Faulkner) CLCII III-1042; MPII:AF III-1066

"Most Dangerous Game, The" (Connell, R.) MPII:SS IV-1535

"Mote in the Middle Distance, H*nry J*m*s, The" (Beerbohm) MPII:SS IV-1538

Mother, The (Deledda) CLC II-744; MP VII-4068; MP:EF II-894

Mother (Gorky) CLC II-744; MP VII-4072; MP:EF II-899

Mother and Son (Compton-Burnett) MP VII-4076; MP:BF II-1012

Mother and Two Daughters, A (Godwin) CLCII III-1043; MPII:AF III-1072

Mother Courage and Her Children (Brecht) CLCII III-1046; MPII:D III-1105

Mother Hubberd's Tale (Spenser) MP VII-4078

Mother Ireland (O'Brien) MPII:NF III-987

Mother Night (Vonnegut) CLCII III-1047; MPII:AF III-1078

Mots, Les. See Words, The

Mots et les choses, Les. See Order of Things, The

Mouchette (Bernanos) CLCII III-1048; MPII:WF III-1045

Mound Builders, The (Wilson, L.) CLCII III-1049; MPII:D III-1110

Mountain and the Valley, The (Buckler) CLCII III-1051; MPII:BCF III-1143

"Mountain Tavern, The" (O'Flaherty) MPII:SS IV-1541

Mountolive. See Alexandria Quartet, The

Mourning Becomes Electra (O'Neill) CLC II-745; MP VII-4081

Mousetrap, The (Christie) CLCII III-1052; MPII:D III-1116

Moveable Feast, A (Hemingway) MP VII-4087

Moviegoer, The (Percy) CLCII III-1053; MPII:AF III-1083

"Ms. Found in a Bottle" (Poe) MPII:SS IV-1451

Much Ado About Nothing (Shakespeare) CLC II-746; MP VII-4090

Mudun al-milh (Munīf) MPII:WF III-1049. See also Cities of Salt

Muerta de Artemio Cruz, La. See Death of Artemio Cruz, The

Mulata (Asturias) CLCII III-1054; MPII:AF III-1087

Mumbo Jumbo (Reed) CLCII III-1055; MPII:AF III-1094

Mundo es ancho y ajena, El. See Broad and Alien Is the World

"Mur, Le." See "Wall, The"

Murder in the Cathedral (Eliot, T. S.) CLC II-748; MP VII-4094

Murder of Roger Ackroyd, The (Christie) CLCII III-1056; MPII:BCF III-1148

Murderer, The (Heath) CLCII III-1057; MPII:BCF III-1153

"Murders in the Rue Morgue, The" (Poe) MPII:SS IV-1544

"Murke's Collected Silences" (Böll) MPII:SS IV-1548

Murphy (Beckett) CLCII III-1059; MPII:BCF III-1157

Mutiny on the Bounty (Nordhoff *and* Hall, J.) CLC II-749; MP VII-4099; MP:AF II-819

Mutter Courage und ihre Kinder. *See* Mother Courage and Her Children

"Muzhik Marey." *See* "Peasant Marey, The"

My. *See* We

My Ántonia (Cather) CLC II-749; MP VII-4103; MP:AF II-823

My Brilliant Career (Franklin) CLCII III-1060; MPII:BCF III-1161

My Dinner with André (Shawn *and* Gregory) CLCII III-1061; MPII:D III-1121

"My First Goose" (Babel) MPII:SS IV-1552

My Heart and My Flesh (Roberts) CLCII III-1062; MPII:AF III-1100

"My Kinsman, Major Molineux" (Hawthorne) MPII:SS IV-1556

My Life and Hard Times (Thurber) MP VII-4108

My Life in the Bush of Ghosts (Tutuola) CLCII III-1063; MPII:BCF III-1167

"My Man Bovanne" (Bambara) MPII:SS IV-1560

My Michael (Oz) CLCII III-1065; MPII:WF III-1054

My Name Is Asher Lev (Potok) CLCII III-1067; MPII:AF III-1105

"My Oedipus Complex" (O'Connor, Frank) MPII:SS IV-1564

"My Side of the Matter" (Capote) MPII:SS IV-1567

"My Warszawa" (Oates) MPII:SS IV-1571

Myshlenie i rech. *See* Thought and Language

Mysterier. *See* Mysteries

Mysteries (Hamsun) CLCII III-1068; MPII:WF III-1059

Mysteries of Paris, The (Sue) CLC II-752; MP VII-4111; MP:EF II-904

Mysteries of Udolpho, The (Radcliffe) CLC II-753; MP VII-4115; MP:BF II-1015

Mysterious Island, The (Verne) CLC II-754; MP VII-4121; MP:EF II-909

"Mysterious Kôr" (Bowen) MPII:SS IV-1575

"Mysterious Stranger, The" (Twain) CLCII III-1069; MPII:SS IV-1578

Mystery of Edwin Drood, The (Dickens) CLC II-755; MP VII-4125; MP:BF II-1022

Myth of Sisyphus, The (Camus) MP VII-4128

N

"Nabeg." *See* "Raid, The"

Nachalo nevedomogo veka. *See* Story of a Life, The

Nachdenken über Christa T. *See* Quest for Christa T., The

Nachsommer, Der. *See* Indian Summer

"Nairobi" (Oates) MPII:SS IV-1582

Nakanune. *See* On the Eve

Naked and the Dead, The (Mailer) CLCII III-1070; MPII:AF III-1110

Naked Lunch (Burroughs) CLCII III-1071; MPII:AF III-1114

Naked Year, The (Pilnyak) CLC II-755; MP VII-4131; MP:EF II-913

Name of the Rose, The (Eco) CLCII III-1072; MPII:WF III-1065

Names, The (Momaday) MPII:NF III-991

Nana (Zola) CLC II-756; MP VII-4135; MP:EF II-918

Naomi (Tanizaki) CLCII III-1074; MPII:WF III-1070

Napoleon of Notting Hill, The (Chesterton) CLC II-757; MP VII-4140; MP:BF II-1026

Napoleon Symphony (Burgess) CLCII III-1075; MPII:BCF III-1171

Narcissus and Goldmund (Hesse) CLCII III-1077; MPII:WF III-1074

Narrative of Arthur Gordon Pym, The (Poe) CLC II-758; MP VII-4143; MP:AF II-828

Narrative of the Life of David Crockett, A (Crockett) MP VII-4146

Narziss und Goldmund. *See* Narcissus and Goldmund

"Nasty Story, A" (Dostoevski) MPII:SS IV-1586

Nathan the Wise (Lessing) CLC II-759; MP VII-4149

"National Honeymoon" (Horgan) MPII:SS IV-1590

"Native of Winby, A" (Jewett) MPII:SS IV-1594

Native Realm (Miłosz) MPII:NF III-997

Native Son (Wright) CLC II-760; MP VII-4152; MP:AF II-832

Natives of Hemsö, The (Strindberg) CLCII III-1077; MPII:WF III-1079

Natives of My Person (Lamming) CLCII III-1078; MPII:BCF III-1176

Natural, The (Malamud) CLCII III-1080; MPII:AF III-1119

Natural Symbols (Douglas) MPII:NF III-1003

Nausea (Sartre) CLC II-761; MP VII-4157; MP:EF II-924

Nazarene, The (Asch) CLC II-761; CLCII III-1081; MP VII-4161; MP:AF II-837; MPII:WF III-1085

"Necklace, The" (Maupassant) MPII:SS IV-1597

Nectar in a Sieve (Markandaya) CLCII III-1082; MPII:BCF III-1182

Needle's Eye, The (Drabble) CLCII III-1083; MPII:BCF III-1188

Negotiations of Thomas Woolsey, the Great Cardinall of England, The. *See* Life and Death of Cardinal Wolsey, The

Nègres, Les. *See* Blacks, The

Neige était sale, La. *See* Snow Was Black, The

"Neighbor Rosicky" (Cather) MPII:SS IV-1602

"Neighbors" (Oliver) MPII:SS IV-1605

Nemureru bijo. *See* House of the Sleeping Beauties, The

Neshome Ekspeditsyes. *See* Shosha

Nesnesitelná lehkost bytí. *See* Unbearable Lightness of Being, The

Nest of Simple Folk, A (O'Faoláin) CLC II-762; MP VII-4165; MP:BF II-1030

Netochka Nezvanova (Dostoevski) CLCII III-1084; MPII:WF III-1089

"Nevada Gas" (Chandler) MPII:SS IV-1608

Never Come Morning (Algren) CLCII III-1085; MPII:AF III-1124

New Atlantis (Bacon) MP VII-4168

New Criticism, The (Ransom) MP VII-4171

New Day (Reid) CLCII III-1087; MPII:BCF III-1193

New Don Quixote, The. *See* Tartarin of Tarascon

New-Found-Land (Stoppard) CLCII I-404; MPII:D II-502

New Grub Street, The (Gissing) CLC II-763; MP VII-4174; MP:BF II-1034

New Héloïse, The (Rousseau) CLC II-764; MP VII-4177; MP:EF II-928

"New Islands" (Bombal) MPII:SS IV-1612

New Life, A (Malamud) CLCII III-1088; MPII:AF III-1129

New Men, The. *See* Strangers and Brothers

New Mondays. *See* Monday Conversations

New Way to Pay Old Debts, A (Massinger) CLC II-765; MP VII-4180

"New Year's Eve Adventure, A" (Hoffmann) MPII:SS IV-1616

New York Diary of Ned Rorem, The. *See* Paris and New York Diaries of Ned Rorem, The

Newcomes, The (Thackeray) CLC II-766; MP VII-4185; MP:BF II-1038

Ngaahika Ndeenda. *See* I Will Marry When I Want

Niagara (Butor) CLCII III-1089; MPII:WF III-1093

Nibelungenlied, The (Unknown) CLC II-770; MP VII-4190; MP:EF II-932

Nicholas Nickleby (Dickens) CLC II-771; MP VII-4195; MP:BF II-1044

Nick of the Woods (Bird) CLC II-775; MP VII-4199; MP:AF II-841

Nickel Mountain (Gardner) CLCII III-1091; MPII:AF III-1134

Niels Lyhne (Jacobsen) CLC II-776; MP VII-4205; MP:EF II-938

Niezwyciężóny i inne opowiadania. *See* Invincible, The

Nigger of the "Narcissus," The (Conrad) CLC II-776; MP VII-4209; MP:BF II-1049

Night (O'Brien, E.) CLCII III-1092; MPII:BCF III-1198

Night (Wiesel) MPII:NF III-1008

Night and Day (Stoppard) CLCII III-1093; MPII:D III-1128

Night and Day (Woolf) CLCII III-1094; MPII:BCF III-1203

Night Flight (Saint-Exupéry) CLC II-777; MP VII-4212; MP:EF II-942

Night in the Luxembourg, A (Gourmont) CLC II-778; MP VII-4215; MP:EF II-946

'night, Mother (Norman) CLCII III-1095; MPII:D III-1133

Night Must Fall (Williams, E.) CLCII III-1096; MPII:D III-1138

Night of the Iguana, The (Williams, T.) CLCII III-1097; MPII:D III-1143

Night Rider (Warren) MP VII-4218; MP:AF II-848

"Night-Sea Journey" (Barth) MPII:SS IV-1624

"Nightfall" (Asimov) MPII:SS IV-1620

Nightmare Abbey (Peacock) CLC II-778; MP VII-4221; MP:BF II-1053

Nightwood (Barnes, D.) CLCII III-1099; MPII:AF III-1139

Nine Tailors, The (Sayers) CLCII III-1100; MPII:BCF III-1208

Nineteen Eighty-Four (Orwell) CLC II-779; MP VII-4224; MP:BF II-1057

1934 (Moravia) CLCII III-1101; MPII:WF III-1098

Ninety-two in the Shade (McGuane) CLCII III-1102; MPII:AF III-1145

Ningen shikkaku. *See* No Longer Human

No Exit (Sartre) CLCII III-1103; MPII:D III-1148

No Laughing Matter (Wilson, Angus) CLCII III-1104; MPII:BCF III-1213

No Longer at Ease (Achebe) CLCII III-1105; MPII:BCF III-1219

No Longer Human (Dazai) CLCII III-1107; MPII:WF III-1103

No More Parades. *See* Parade's End

No Name (Collins, Wilkie) CLC II-780; MP VII-4227; MP:BF III-1061

No One Writes to the Colonel (García Márquez) CLCII III-1108; MPII:AF III-1151

No Place on Earth (Wolf) CLCII III-1109; MPII:WF III-1108

No Trifling with Love (Musset) CLC II-781; MP VII-4231

Nobleman's Nest, A. *See* House of Gentlefolk, A

Nocturne (Swinnerton) CLC II-781; MP VII-4235; MP:BF II-1065

Nœud de vipères, Le. *See* Vipers' Tangle

Noise of Time, The (Mandelstam, O.) MPII:NF III-1013

Nome della rosa, Il. *See* Name of the Rose, The

Non-existent Knight, The (Calvino) CLCII III-1110; MPII:WF III-1113

"Noon Wine" (Porter) MPII:SS IV-1628. *See also* Pale Horse, Pale Rider

Nord. *See* North

Norman Conquests, The (Ayckbourn) CLCII III-1111; MPII:D III-1153

North (Céline) CLCII I-241; MPII:WF I-121

Northanger Abbey (Austen) CLC II-782; MP VII-4238; MP:BF II-1068

Northern Lass, The (Brome) CLC II-783; MP VII-4243

Northwest Passage (Roberts, K.) MP VII-4247; MP:AF II-852

"Nose, The" (Gogol) MPII:SS IV-1633

Nostromo (Conrad) CLC II-783; MP VII-4250; MP:BF II-1074

Not Honour More. *See* Second Trilogy

Not Without Laughter (Hughes) CLCII III-1113; MPII:AF III-1155

Notebooks, 1960-1977 (Fugard) MPII:NF III-1019

Notebooks of Leonardo da Vinci, The (Vinci) MP VII-4255

Notes from a Bottle Found on the Beach at Carmel (Connell) MP VII-4258

Notes from the Century Before (Hoagland) MPII:NF III-1023

Notes from the Underground. *See* Letters from the Underworld

Notes of a Native Son (Baldwin) MPII:NF III-1029

Notes on the State of Virginia (Jefferson) MP VII-4260

Notes Towards the Definition of Culture (Eliot) MPII:NF III-1034

Nothing (Green, Henry) CLCII III-1114; MPII:BCF III-1224

Nothing Happens in Carmincross (Kiely) CLCII III-1115; MPII:BCF III-1228

Nothing Like the Sun (Burgess) CLCII III-1116; MPII:BCF III-1233

Notre-Dame des Fleurs. *See* Our Lady of the Flowers

Nouvelle Héloïse, La. *See* New Héloïse, The

Nouvelle Histoire de Mouchette. *See* Mouchette

November 1918 (Döblin) CLCII III-1117; MPII:WF III-1118

Novice, The (Lermontov) MP VII-4263

Now and Then (Buechner) MPII:NF III-1041

Nuit, La. *See* Night (Wiesel)

"Nun, The" (Alarcón) MPII:SS IV-1637

Nuns and Soldiers (Murdoch) CLCII III-1120; MPII:BCF III-1238

"Nun's Mother, The" (Lavin) MPII:SS IV-1640

O

O Beulah Land (Settle) CLCII III-1122. *See also* Beulah Quintet, The

O, How the Wheel Becomes It! (Powell) CLCII III-1123; MPII:BCF III-1243

O Pioneers! (Cather) CLC II-785; MP VII-4265; MP:AF II-856

Oak and the Calf, The (Solzhenitsyn) MPII:NF III-1046

Oath, The (Wiesel) CLCII III-1124; MPII:WF III-1125

Obaka san. *See* Wonderful Fool

Oberland. *See* Pilgrimage

"Oblako, ozero, bashnya." *See* "Cloud, Castle, Lake"

Oblomov (Goncharov) CLC II-787; MP VII-4270; MP:EF II-949

Obscene Bird of Night, The (Donoso) CLCII III-1125; MPII:AF III-1160

Obsceno pájaro de la noche, El. *See* Obscene Bird of Night, The

Occasion for Loving (Gordimer) CLCII III-1126; MPII:BCF III-1248

Occhiali d'oro, Gli. *See* Gold-Rimmed Eyeglasses, The

"Occurrence at Owl Creek Bridge, An" (Bierce) MPII:SS IV-1643

October Light (Gardner) CLCII III-1127; MPII:AF III-1165

Octopus, The (Norris) CLCII III-1129; MPII:AF III-1171

Odd Couple, The (Simon, N.) CLCII III-1130; MPII:D III-1158

Odd Woman, The (Godwin) CLCII III-1131; MPII:AF III-1176

Ode to Aphrodite (Sappho) MP VII-4273

Odin den Ivana Denisovicha. *See* One Day in the Life of Ivan Denisovich

"Odour of Chrysanthemums" (Lawrence) MPII:SS IV-1648

Odyssey, The (Homer) CLC II-788; MP VII-4275

Oedipus at Colonus (Sophocles) CLC II-792; MP VII-4280

Oedipus Tyrannus (Sophocles) CLC II-793; MP VII-4284

Œuvre au noir, L'. *See* Abyss, The

Of a Fire on the Moon (Mailer) MPII:NF III-1052

Of Grammatology (Derrida) MPII:NF III-1057

Of Human Bondage (Maugham) CLC II-794; MP VII-4288; MP:BF II-1080

Of Mice and Men (Steinbeck) CLC II-795; MP VII-4294; MP:AF II-861

Of Plimouth Plantation (Bradford, W.) MP VIII-4297

"Of This Time, Of That Place" (Trilling) MPII:SS IV-1652

Of Time and the River (Wolfe) CLC II-796; MP VIII-4300; MP:AF II-865

Offending the Audience (Handke) CLCII III-1132; MPII:D III-1164

Officers and Gentlemen. *See* Sword of Honour

"Official Position, An" (Maugham) MPII:SS IV-1656

Ogre, The (Tournier) CLCII III-1133; MPII:WF III-1129

Oh What a Paradise It Seems (Cheever) CLCII III-1134; MPII:AF III-1180

"Oh, Whistle, and I'll Come to You, My Lad" (James, M.) MPII:SS IV-1660

Oiseau bleu, L'. *See* Blue Bird, The

Okhrannaya gramota. *See* Safe-Conduct, A

Oktiabr shestnadtsatogo (Solzhenitsyn) CLCII III-1135; MPII:WF III-1134

Old and the Young, The (Pirandello) CLC II-797; MP VIII-4305; MP:EF II-953

Old Bachelor, The (Congreve) CLC II-798; MP VIII-4309

"Old Bird, The" (Powers) MPII:SS IV-1664

Old Blood, The. *See* Kaywana trilogy, The

Old Calabria (Douglas, N.) MP VIII-4313

Old Curiosity Shop, The (Dickens) CLC II-799; MP VIII-4316; MP:BF II-1087

Old Devils, The (Amis) CLCII III-1136; MPII:BCF III-1253

"Old Forest, The" (Taylor) MPII:SS IV-1668

Old Fortunatus (Dekker) CLC II-802; MP VIII-4319

Old Maid, The (Wharton) CLC II-803; MP VIII-4322; MP:AF II-870

Old Man, The (Trifonov) CLCII III-1138; MPII:WF III-1141

Old Man and the Sea, The (Hemingway) CLC II-804; MP VIII-4325; MP:AF II-874

Old Mortality (Porter, K.) CLC II-804; MP VIII-4330; MP:AF II-879; MPII:SS IV-1672. See also Pale Horse, Pale Rider

Old Mortality (Scott, Sir W.) CLC II-805; MP VIII-4334; MP:BF II-1091

"Old Red" (Gordon) MPII:SS IV-1676

Old Regime in Canada, The (Parkman) MP VIII-4338

Old St. Paul's (Ainsworth) CLC II-807; MP VIII-4341; MP:BF II-1096

"Old Vemish" (Targan) MPII:SS IV-1680

Old Wives' Tale, The (Bennett) CLC II-808; MP VIII-4344; MP:BF II-1100

Old Wives' Tale, The (Peele) CLC II-809; MP VIII-4349

"Old Woman Magoun" (Freeman) MPII:SS IV-1684

"Old-World Landowners" (Gogol) MPII:SS IV-1688

Oldest Living Graduate, The (Jones, J.) CLCII III-1139; MPII:D III-1169

Oldtown Folks (Stowe) CLC II-810; MP VIII-4353; MP:AF II-883

Oliver Twist (Dickens) CLC II-812; MP VIII-4358; MP:BF II-1105

Ölmez otu. See Undying Grass, The

Omensetter's Luck (Gass) CLCII III-1140; MPII:AF III-1184

Omoo (Melville) CLC II-813; MP VIII-4364; MP:AF II-888

"On Account of a Hat" (Aleichem) MPII:SS IV-1692

On Growth and Form (Thompson) MPII:NF III-1063

On Heroes and Tombs (Sábato) CLCII III-1142; MPII:AF III-1188

On Heroes, Hero-Worship and the Heroic in History (Carlyle) MP VIII-4368

On Human Conduct (Oakeshott) MPII:NF III-1071

On Liberty (Mill) MP VIII-4370

On Moral Fiction (Gardner) MPII:NF III-1077

On Overgrown Paths (Hamsun) MPII:NF III-1082

On the Eve (Turgenev) CLCII III-1143; MPII:WF III-1146

On the Law of War and Peace (Grotius) MP VIII-4373

On the Origin of Species (Darwin) MP VIII-4376

On the Road (Kerouac) CLCII III-1145; MPII:AF III-1193

On the Sublime (Unknown) MP VIII-4378

Once and Future King, The (White, T. H.) MP VIII-4381; MP:BF II-1112

Once in a Lifetime (Kaufman and Hart) CLCII III-1145; MPII:D III-1174

One Day in the Life of Ivan Denisovich (Solzhenitsyn) CLCII III-1147; MPII:WF III-1152

One Day of Life (Argueta) CLCII III-1148; MPII:AF III-1198

One Flew over the Cuckoo's Nest (Kesey) CLCII III-1149; MPII:AF III-1203

One Hundred Years of Solitude (García Márquez) CLCII III-1150; MPII:AF III-1207

"£1,000,000 Bank Note, The" (Twain) MPII:SS IV-1697

One of Ours (Cather) CLCII III-1154; MPII:AF III-1213

"One of the Missing" (Bierce) MPII:SS IV-1701

"One Ordinary Day, with Peanuts" (Jackson) MPII:SS IV-1705

One Way to Heaven (Cullen) CLCII III-1155; MPII:AF III-1217

One Writer's Beginnings (Welty) MPII:NF III-1087

Onnamen. *See* Masks

"Open Boat, The" (Crane) MPII:SS IV-1709

Open Heart. *See* Book of Bebb, The

"Open House" (Gordimer) MPII:SS IV-1712

"Open Window, The" (Saki) MPII:SS IV-1716

Operetka. *See* Operetta

Operetta (Gombrowicz) CLCII III-1156; MPII:D III-1180

Optimist's Daughter, The (Welty) CLCII III-1157; MPII:AF III-1222

Or, L'. *See* Sutter's Gold

Oration on the Dignity of Man (Pico della Mirandola) MP VIII-4385

Orb of the World, The. *See* Heimskringla

Ordeal of Civility, The (Cuddihy) MPII:NF III-1092

Ordeal of Gilbert Pinfold, The (Waugh) MP VIII-4387; MP:BF II-1117

Ordeal of Richard Feverel, The (Meredith) CLC II-814; MP VIII-4390; MP:BF II-1121

Order of Things, The (Foucault) MPII:NF III-1098

Oreach nata lalun. *See* Guest for the Night, A

Oregon Trail, The (Parkman) MP VIII-4394

Orfeo (Politian) CLC II-814; MP VIII-4398

Orientalism (Said) MPII:NF III-1102

Origins of Totalitarianism, The (Arendt) MPII:NF III-1107

Orlando (Woolf) CLC II-815; MP VIII-4400; MP:BF II-1126

Orlando Furioso (Ariosto) CLC II-816; MP VIII-4404

Orlando Innamorato (Boiardo) CLC II-819; MP VIII-4410

Orley Farm (Trollope) CLC II-821; MP VIII-4415; MP:BF II-1130

Oroonoko (Behn) CLC II-823; MP VIII-4421; MP:BF II-1137

Orphan, The (Otway) CLC II-823; MP VIII-4425

Orphée. *See* Orpheus

Orpheus (Cocteau) CLCII III-1159; MPII:D III-1185

Orpheus and Eurydice (Unknown) CLC II-824; MP VIII-4428; MP:EF II-957

Ortadirek. *See* Wind from the Plain, The

Örtlich betäubt. *See* Local Anaesthetic

Osaka san. *See* Wonderful Fool

Ostře sledované vlaky. *See* Closely Watched Trains

Ostrov Krym. *See* Island of Crimea, The

Othello (Shakespeare) CLC II-825; MP VIII-4431

Other Leopards (Williams, D.) CLCII III-1160; MPII:BCF III-1258

Other One, The (Colette) CLC II-826; MP VIII-4436; MP:EF II-961

"Other Paris, The" (Gallant) MPII:SS IV-1719

Other People's Worlds (Trevor) CLCII III-1161; MPII:BCF III-1262

"Other Two, The" (Wharton) MPII:SS IV-1723

Otherwise Engaged (Gray, S.) CLCII III-1161; MPII:D III-1191

Otoño del patriarca, El. *See* Autumn of the Patriarch, The

Ottepel. *See* Thaw, The

Où mènent les mauvais chemins. *See* Splendors and Miseries of Courtesans, The

Our Friend Manso (Pérez Galdós) CLCII III-1163; MPII:WF III-1157

Our Lady of the Flowers (Genet) CLCII III-1164; MPII:WF III-1163

Our Mutual Friend (Dickens) CLC II-827; MP VIII-4440; MP:BF II-1141

Our Town (Wilder) CLC II-829; MP VIII-4443

Our Village (Mitford) CLC II-830; MP VIII-4446; MP:BF II-1145

Out of My Life and Thought (Schweitzer) MP VIII-4449

Out of the Silent Planet. *See* Space Trilogy, The

"Outcasts of Poker Flat, The" (Harte) MPII:SS IV-1727

Outer Dark (McCarthy, C.) CLCII III-1166; MPII:AF III-1227

"Outpost of Progress, An" (Conrad) MPII:SS IV-1732

"Outside the Machine" (Rhys) MPII:SS IV-1737

Outsider, The (Sábato) CLCII III-1167; MPII:AF III-1232

Outsider, The (Wright) CLCII III-1168; MPII:AF III-1238

"Outstation, The" (Maugham) MPII:SS IV-1741

Oväder. *See* Stormy Weather

"Overcoat, The" (Gogol) CLC II-830; MP VIII-4452; MP:EF III-965; MPII:SS IV-1745

"Overcoat II, The" (Boyle, T.) MPII:SS IV-1749

Overdrive (Buckley) MPII:NF III-1113

Ox-Bow Incident (Clark, Walter) CLC II-831; MP VIII-4457; MP:AF II-892

Ozhog. *See* Burn, The

P

"Pacing Goose, The" (West, J.) MPII:SS IV-1753

Pack My Bag (Green) MPII:NF III-1118

Pagan Place, A (O'Brien, E.) CLCII III-1169; MPII:BCF III-1267

Painted Bird, The (Kosinski) CLCII III-1170; MPII:AF III-1243

Painter of Our Time, A (Berger, J.) CLCII III-1171; MPII:BCF III-1272

Palace of the Peacock. *See* Guyana Quartet, The

"Palata No. 6." *See* "Ward No. 6"

Pale Fire (Nabokov) MP VIII-4462; MP:AF II-897

Pale Horse, Pale Rider (Porter, K.) MP VIII-4465; MP:AF II-901

"Pale Horse, Pale Rider" (Porter) MPII:SS IV-1756

Palm-Wine Drinkard, The (Tutuola) MP VIII-4469; MP:EF III-970

Palomar. *See* Mr. Palomar

Pamela (Richardson, S.) CLC II-832; MP VIII-4472; MP:BF II-1149

Pan (Hamsun) CLCII III-1172; MPII:WF III-1168

Pandora's Box (Wedekind) CLCII III-1173; MPII:D III-1197

Panegyricus. *See* Letters of Pliny the Younger, The

Pantomime (Walcott) CLCII III-1174; MPII:D III-1202

Paper Men, The (Golding) CLCII III-1175; MPII:BCF III-1277

Parade's End (Ford, F.) CLC II-833; MP VIII-4477; MP:BF II-1155

"Paradise" (O'Brien, E.) MPII:SS IV-1759

Paradise Lost (Milton) CLC II-835; MP VIII-4482

Paradise Regained (Milton) CLC II-836; MP VIII-4487

Paradiso (Lezama Lima) CLCII III-1176; MPII:AF III-1248

Paradox, King. *See* King Paradox

"Paraguay" (Barthelme, D.) MPII:SS IV-1764

Parallel Lives (Plutarch) MP VIII-4490

Paravents, Les. *See* Screens, The

Pardoner's Tale, The (Wain) CLCII III-1178; MPII:BCF III-1282

"Pari." *See* "Bet, The"

Paris and New York Diaries of Ned Rorem, The (Rorem) MPII:NF III-1124

Paris Diary of Ned Rorem, The. *See* Paris and New York Diaries of Ned Rorem, The

"Parker's Back" (O'Connor, Flannery) MPII:SS IV-1768

Parliament of Fowls, The (Chaucer) MP VIII-4493

"Parsley Garden, The" (Saroyan) MPII:SS IV-1771

Partage de Midi. *See* Break of Noon

Party Going (Green, Henry) CLCII III-1179; MPII:BCF III-1288

"Parure, La." *See* "Necklace, The"

Parzival (Wolfram von Eschenbach) CLC II-837; MP VIII-4495

Pasos perdidos, Los. *See* Lost Steps, The

Passage, The (Palmer) CLCII III-1180; MPII:BCF III-1293

Passage to India, A (Forster) CLC II-838; MP VIII-4500; MP:BF II-1161

Passing (Larsen) CLCII III-1182; MPII:AF III-1253

Passing Time (Butor) CLCII III-1183; MPII:WF III-1173

Passion Flower, The (Benavente) CLC II-840; MP VIII-4505

Passion in Rome, A (Callaghan) CLCII III-1184; MPII:BCF III-1298

Passion Play (Nichols) CLCII III-1185; MPII:D III-1209

Passions of the Soul, The (Descartes) MP VIII-4510

Paston Letters A. D. 1422-1509, The (Paston Family) MP VIII-4513

Pastors and Masters (Compton-Burnett) MP VIII-4516; MP:BF II-1167

"Pat Shelema." *See* "Whole Loaf, A"

Patagoni (Metcalf) MPII:NF III-1129

Paterson (Williams, W.) MP VIII-4519
Path to Rome, The (Belloc) MP VIII-4521
Path to the Nest of Spiders, The (Calvino) CLCII III-1186; MPII:WF III-1178
Pathfinder, The (Cooper) CLC II-840; MP VIII-4524; MP:AF II-906
Patience (Gilbert) CLC II-842; MP VIII-4528
Patrician, The (Galsworthy) CLC II-842; MP VIII-4531; MP:BF II-1171
Patriot, The (Fogazzaro) CLC II-843; MP VIII-4534; MP:EF III-973
"Patriotism" (Mishima) MPII:SS IV-1775
Patterns of Childhood (Wolf) CLCII III-1187; MPII:WF III-1183
Paul Bunyan (Stevens, J.) CLC II-843; MP VIII-4537; MP:AF II-910
"Paul's Case" (Cather) MPII:SS IV-1779
Pauvre Christ de Bomba, Le. See Poor Christ of Bomba, The
Pea gjengrodde stier. See On Overgrown Paths
Peace, The (Aristophanes) CLC II-844; MP VIII-4541
"Peach Stone, The" (Horgan) MPII:SS IV-1782
"Pearl, The" (Steinbeck) CLCII III-1188; MPII:SS IV-1785
"Pearl of the World, The." See Pearl, The
"Peasant Marey, The" (Dostoevski) MPII:SS IV-1789
Peasants, The (Reymont) CLC II-845; MP VIII-4544; MP:EF III-977
Peder Seier. See Peder Victorious
Peder Victorious (Rölvaag) CLC II-847; MP VIII-4549; MP:AF II-914
"Pedersen Kid, The" (Gass) MPII:SS IV-1793
"Pedestrian Accident, A" (Coover) MPII:SS IV-1796
Pedro Páramo (Rulfo) MP VIII-4552; MP:AF II-918
Pedro Sánchez (Pereda) CLC II-847; MP VIII-4556; MP:EF III-983
Peer Gynt (Ibsen) CLC II-848; MP VIII-4559

Peg Woffington (Reade) CLC II-850; MP VIII-4562; MP:BF II-1175
Pelican, The (Strindberg) CLCII III-1189; MPII:D III-1214
Pelikanen. See Pelican, The
Pelle the Conqueror (Nexö) CLC II-851; MP VIII-4566; MP:EF III-987
Pélléas and Mélisande (Maeterlinck) CLC II-852; MP VIII-4569
Pendennis (Thackeray) CLC II-853; MP VIII-4575; MP:BF II-1179
Penguin Island (France) CLC II-855; MP VIII-4579; MP:EF III-994
Penny for a Song, A (Whiting) CLCII III-1190; MPII:D III-1220
Peñas arriba (Pereda) CLC II-852; MP VIII-4572; MP:EF III-991
Pensées (Pascal) MP VIII-4584
Pentimento (Hellman) MPII:NF III-1135
People Betrayed, A. See November 1918
People of Hemsö, The. See Natives of Hemsö, The
People of Juvik, The (Duun) CLC II-857; MP VIII-4587; MP:EF III-999
People of the City (Ekwensi) CLCII III-1192; MPII:BCF III-1302
People, Yes, The (Sandburg) MP VIII-4593
Pepita Jiménez (Valera) CLC II-858; MP VIII-4595; MP:EF III-1006
Peregrine Pickle (Smollett) CLC II-859; MP VIII-4599; MP:BF II-1185
"Perekhod cherez Zbruch." See "Crossing into Poland"
Perelandra. See Space Trilogy, The
"Perfect Day for Bananafish, A" (Salinger) MPII:SS IV-1800
Perfect Peace, A (Oz) CLCII III-1193; MPII:WF III-1190
Perfect Spy, A (le Carré) CLCII III-1194; MPII:BCF III-1306
Pericles, Prince of Tyre (Shakespeare) CLC II-861; MP VIII-4603
Periodic Table, The (Levi) MPII:NF III-1141
Periquillo, El. See Itching Parrot, The

Persecution and Assassination of Jean-Paul Marat as Performed by the Inmates of the Asylum of Charenton Under the Direction of the Marquis de Sade, The. *See* Marat/Sade

Persian Boy, The (Renault) CLCII III-1195; MPII:BCF III-1313

Persian Letters (Montesquieu) MP VIII-4607

Persians, The (Aeschylus) CLC II-862; MP VIII-4609

Personae (Pound) MP VIII-4612

Personal Knowledge (Polanyi) MPII:NF III-1146

Personal Matter, A (Ōe) CLCII III-1197; MPII:WF III-1195

Persuasion (Austen) CLC II-863; MP VIII-4615; MP:BF II-1190

Pervaya lyubov. *See* First Love

Pesanteur et la grâce, La. *See* Gravity and Grace

Peščanik (Kiš) CLCII III-1197; MPII:WF III-1199

Petals of Blood (Ngugi) CLCII III-1198; MPII:BCF III-1320

Peter Ibbetson (du Maurier, G.) CLC II-864; MP VIII-4618; MP:BF II-1194

Peter Pan (Barrie) CLC II-865; MP VIII-4622

Peter Simple (Marryat) CLC II-866; MP VIII-4626; MP:BF II-1199

Peter Whiffle (Van Vechten) CLC II-867; MP VIII-4629; MP:AF II-923

Petersburg (Bely) CLCII III-1199; MPII:WF IV-1442

"Petit Soldat." *See* "Two Little Soldiers"

Petrified Forest, The (Sherwood) CLCII III-1200; MPII:D III-1225

"Petrified Man" (Welty) MPII:SS IV-1804

Pharisienne, La. *See* Woman of the Pharisees, A

Phèdre (Racine) CLC II-867; MP VIII-4632

Phenomenon of Man, The (Teilhard de Chardin) MP VIII-4636

Philadelphia, Here I Come! (Friel) CLCII III-1202; MPII:D III-1230

Philadelphia Story, The (Barry) CLCII III-1203; MPII:D III-1235

Philaster (Beaumont *and* Fletcher) CLC II-868; MP VIII-4639

Philippics, The (Demosthenes) MP VIII-4644

Philoctetes (Sophocles) CLC II-870; MP VIII-4647

Philosopher or Dog? (Machado de Assis) MP VIII-4650; MP:AF II-927

Philosophiae Naturalis Principia Mathematica (Newton) MP VIII-4653

Philosophical Explanations (Nozick) MPII:NF III-1153

Philosophical Treatises and Moral Reflections of Seneca (Seneca) MP VIII-4656

Philosophy and the Mirror of Nature (Rorty) MPII:NF III-1158

Philosophy of Art (Taine) MP VIII-4659

Phineas Finn (Trollope) CLC II-871; MP VIII-4662; MP:BF III-1203

Phineas Redux (Trollope) CLC II-871; MP VIII-4666; MP:BF III-1207

Phoenician Women, The (Euripides) CLC II-872; MP VIII-4670

Phormio (Terence) CLC II-873; MP VIII-4673

Photograph: Lovers in Motion, A (Shange) CLCII III-1204; MPII:D III-1241

Physical Basis of Life, The (Huxley, T.) MP VIII-4677

Physicists, The (Dürrenmatt) CLCII III-1206; MPII:D III-1246

Physiker, Die. *See* Physicists, The

Pickwick Papers (Dickens) CLC II-874; MP VIII-4680; MP:BF III-1212

Picnic (Inge) CLCII III-1207; MPII:D III-1252

Picture of Dorian Gray, The (Wilde) CLC II-878; MP VIII-4686; MP:BF III-1218

Pictures in the Hallway. *See* Mirror in My House

"Piece of Steak, A" (London) MPII:SS IV-1807

"Piece of String, The" (Maupassant) MPII:SS IV-1810

Pierre (Melville) CLC II-879; MP VIII-4690; MP:AF II-930

"Pierre Menard, Author of the *Quixote*" (Borges) MPII:SS IV-1814

"Pigeon Feathers" (Updike) MPII:SS IV-1817

Piknik na obochine. *See* Roadside Picnic

"Pikovaya dama." *See* "Queen of Spades, The"

Pilgrim at Sea. *See* Tobias Trilogy, The

Pilgrim at Tinker Creek (Dillard) MPII:NF III-1163

Pilgrim Hawk, The (Wescott) MP VIII-4693; MP:AF II-934

Pilgrim på havet. *See* Tobias Trilogy, The

Pilgrimage (Richardson, D.) CLC II-880; MP VIII-4696; MP:BF III-1222

Pilgrimage of Charlemagne, The (Unknown) CLC II-881; MP VIII-4700

Pilgrimen. *See* Tobias Trilogy, The

Pilgrim's Progress, The (Bunyan) CLC II-882; MP VIII-4705; MP:BF III-1227

Pillars of Society, The (Ibsen) CLC II-883; MP VIII-4710

Pilot, The (Cooper) CLC II-884; MP VIII-4714; MP:AF II-938

Pincher Martin (Golding) CLCII III-1208; MPII:BCF III-1325

Pine Barrens, The (McPhee) MPII:NF III-1168

Ping-Pong (Adamov) MP VIII-4719

Pioneers, The (Cooper) CLC II-886; MP VIII-4722; MP:AF II-944

Pirates of Penzance, The (Gilbert) CLC II-888; MP VIII-4726

Pit, The (Norris) CLC II-889; MP VIII-4729; MP:AF II-949

"Pit and the Pendulum, The" (Poe) MPII:SS IV-1821

Pitch Dark (Adler) CLCII III-1209; MPII:AF III-1258

"Pkhentz" (Sinyavsky) MPII:SS IV-1824

Plague, The (Camus) CLC II-889; MP VIII-4734; MP:EF III-1010

Plaideurs, Les (Racine) CLC II-891; MP VIII-4740

Plaidoyer d'un fou, Le. *See* Confession of a Fool, The

Plain Dealer, The (Wycherley) CLC II-892; MP VIII-4743

Plains Song, for Female Voices (Morris) CLCII III-1210; MPII:AF III-1262

Planetarium, The (Sarraute) CLCII III-1211; MPII:WF III-1203

Plantation Boy (Lins do Rêgo) MP VIII-4748; MP:AF II-954

Platero and I (Jiménez) MP VIII-4752; MP:EF III-1017

Play It As It Lays (Didion) CLCII III-1212; MPII:AF III-1266

Play of the Eyes, The (Canetti) MPII:NF IV-1546

Playboy of the Western World, The (Synge) CLC II-893; MP VIII-4755

Plays of Cocteau, The (Cocteau) MP VIII-4758

Pleasant Historie of John Winchcomb, in His Younger Yeares Called Jack of Newberry, The. *See* Jack of Newberry

Plenty (Hare) CLCII III-1213; MPII:D III-1258

Plough and the Stars, The (O'Casey) CLC II-894; MP VIII-4761

Plum Bun (Fauset) CLCII III-1215; MPII:AF III-1271

Plumed Serpent, The (Lawrence, D. H.) CLC II-895; MP VIII-4765; MP:BF III-1232

Plutus (Aristophanes) CLC II-896; MP VIII-4770

Pnin (Nabokov) CLCII III-1216; MPII:AF III-1277

Podrostok. *See* Raw Youth, A

Poem of the Cid (Unknown) CLC II-897; MP VIII-4773

Poems (Tennyson) MP VIII-4777

Poems and Ballads (Swinburne) MP VIII-4780

Poems, Chiefly in the Scottish Dialect (Burns) MP VIII-4783

"Poet, The" (Hesse) MPII:SS IV-1828

Poetical Works of Edward Taylor, The (Taylor, E.) MP VIII-4786

Poetics, The (Aristotle) MP VIII-4789

Poetry and Truth from My Own Life (Goethe) MP VIII-4792

Poetry of "A. E." (Russell, G.) MP VIII-4795

Poetry of Aiken, The (Aiken) MP VIII-4798

Poetry of Anacreon, The (Anacreon) MP VIII-4801

Poetry of André Breton, The (Breton) MP VIII-4802

Poetry of Apollinaire, the (Apollinaire) MP VIII-4805

Poetry of Arnold, The (Arnold) MP VIII-4808

Poetry of Auden, The (Auden) MP VIII-4811

Poetry of Barker, The (Barker) MP VIII-4814

Poetry of Bashô, The (Bashô) MP VIII-4816

Poetry of Beddoes, The (Beddoes) MP VIII-4819

Poetry of Betjeman, The (Betjeman) MP VIII-4822

Poetry of Bion, The (Bion) MP VIII-4825

Poetry of Blake, The (Blake) MP VIII-4827

Poetry of Blok, The (Blok) MP VIII-4830

Poetry of Blunden, The (Blunden) MP VIII-4833

Poetry of Booth, The (Booth) MP VIII-4835

Poetry of Brooke, The (Brooke, R.) MP VIII-4838

Poetry of Bryant, The (Bryant) MP VIII-4841

Poetry of Campion, The (Campion) MP VIII-4844

Poetry of Carducci, The (Carducci) MP VIII-4847

Poetry of Carew, The (Carew) MP VIII-4850

Poetry of Cavafy, The (Cavafy) MP VIII-4854

Poetry of Chatterton, The (Chatterton) MP VIII-4857

Poetry of Christina Rossetti, The (Rossetti, C.) MP VIII-4860

Poetry of Clare, The (Clare) MP VIII-4863

Poetry of Claudel, The (Claudel) MP VIII-4866

Poetry of Coleridge, The (Coleridge) MP VIII-4869

Poetry of Collins, The (Collins, William) MP VIII-4873

Poetry of Corbière, The (Corbière) MP VIII-4876

Poetry of Cowper, The (Cowper) MP VIII-4880

Poetry of Crashaw, The (Crashaw) MP VIII-4883

Poetry of Cummings, The (Cummings) MP VIII-4887

Poetry of Daniel, The (Daniel) MP VIII-4889

Poetry of Dante Gabriel Rossetti, The (Rossetti, D.) MP VIII-4893

Poetry of Dickey, The (Dickey) MP VIII-4896

Poetry of Donne, The (Donne) MP VIII-4900

Poetry of Dowson, The (Dowson) MP VIII-4903

Poetry of Drayton, The (Drayton) MP VIII-4906

Poetry of Dryden, The (Dryden) MP IX-4909

Poetry of Du Bellay, The (Du Bellay) MP IX-4914

Poetry of Eberhart, The (Eberhart) MP IX-4918

Poetry of Edith Sitwell, The (Sitwell) MP IX-4920

Poetry of Eichendorff, The (Eichendorff) MP IX-4922

Poetry of Elinor Wylie, The (Wylie) MP IX-4925

Poetry of Emerson, The (Emerson) MP IX-4928

Poetry of Emily Brontë (Brontë, E.) MP IX-4932

Poetry of Emily Dickinson (Dickinson) MP IX-4935

Poetry of Esenin, The (Esenin) MP IX-4938

Poetry of Flecker, The (Flecker) MP IX-4941

Poetry of Freneau, The (Freneau) MP IX-4943

Poetry of Frost, The (Frost) MP IX-4946

Poetry of Gabriela Mistral, The (Mistral) MP IX-4949

Poetry of Garrett, The (Garrett) MP IX-4952

Poetry of Gascoigne, The (Gascoigne) MP IX-4955

Poetry of Gautier, The (Gautier) MP IX-4961

Poetry of Goldsmith, The (Goldsmith) MP IX-4964

Poetry of Graves, The (Graves) MP IX-4968

Poetry of Gray, The (Gray) MP IX-4971

Poetry of H. D., The (H. D.) MP IX-4979

Poetry of Hall, The (Hall, D.) MP IX-4973

Poetry of Hardy, The (Hardy) MP IX-4976

Poetry of Henley, The (Henley) MP IX-4982

Poetry of Heredia, The (Heredia) MP IX-4984

Poetry of Hodgson, The (Hodgson) MP IX-4986

Poetry of Hofmannsthal, The (Hofmannsthal) MP IX-4988

Poetry of Hölderlin, The (Hölderlin) MP IX-4991

Poetry of Hopkins, The (Hopkins) MP IX-4994

Poetry of Horace, The (Horace) MP IX-4997

Poetry of Hugo, The (Hugo) MP IX-5000

Poetry of Jarrell, The (Jarrell) MP IX-5003

Poetry of Jeffers, The (Jeffers) MP IX-5006

Poetry of Jiménez, The (Jiménez) MP IX-5009

Poetry of Johnson, The (Johnson, S.) MP IX-5011

Poetry of Jonson, The (Jonson) MP IX-5014

Poetry of Kipling, The (Kipling) MP IX-5019

Poetry of Laforgue, The (Laforgue) MP IX-5022

Poetry of Lamartine, The (Lamartine) MP IX-5025

Poetry of Landor, The (Landor) MP IX-5028

Poetry of Lanier, The (Lanier) MP IX-5032

Poetry of Larkin, The (Larkin) MP IX-5035

Poetry of Lawrence, The (Lawrence, D. H.) MP IX-5037

Poetry of Leopardi, The (Leopardi) MP IX-5040

Poetry of Lewis, The (Lewis, C. D.) MP IX-5043

Poetry of Lindsay, The (Lindsay) MP IX-5046

Poetry of Lovelace, The (Lovelace) MP IX-5048

Poetry of Machado, The (Machado) MP IX-5051

Poetry of MacLeish, The (MacLeish) MP IX-5054

Poetry of MacNeice, The (MacNeice) MP IX-5057

Poetry of Mallarmé, The (Mallarmé) MP IX-5059

Poetry of Marianne Moore, The (Moore, M.) MP IX-5062

Poetry of Marot, The (Marot) MP IX-5064

Poetry of Marvell, The (Marvell) MP IX-5067

Poetry of Mayakovsky, The (Mayakovsky) MP IX-5070

Poetry of Melville, The (Melville) MP IX-5073

Poetry of Meredith, The (Meredith) MP IX-5077

Poetry of Michelangelo, The (Michelangelo Buonarroti) MP IX-5080

Poetry of Mörike, The (Mörike) MP IX-5084

Poetry of Moschus, The (Moschus) MP IX-5087

Poetry of Musset, The (Musset) MP IX-5089

Poetry of Nekrasov, The (Nekrasov) MP IX-5092

Poetry of Neruda, The (Neruda) MP IX-5095

Poetry of Nerval, The (Nerval) MP IX-5098

Poetry of Nicholas Breton, The (Breton) MP IX-5103

Poetry of Owen, The (Owen) MP IX-5105

Poetry of Pasternak, The (Pasternak) MP IX-5107

Poetry of Paz, The (Paz) MP IX-5109

Poetry of Péguy, The (Péguy) MP IX-5112

Poetry of Prior, The (Prior) MP IX-5115

Poetry of Raleigh, The (Raleigh) MP IX-5118

Poetry of Robert Lowell, The (Lowell, R.) MP IX-5121

Poetry of Roethke, The (Roethke) MP IX-5126

Poetry of Ronsard, The (Ronsard) MP IX-5131

Poetry of Shapiro, The (Shapiro) MP IX-5133

Poetry of Sidney, The (Sidney) MP IX-5136

Poetry of Skelton, The (Skelton) MP IX-5141

Poetry of Smart, The (Smart) MP IX-5146

Poetry of Sor Juana Inés de la Cruz, The (Cruz) MP IX-5149

Poetry of Spender, The (Spender) MP IX-5152

Poetry of Stefan George, The (George) MP IX-5155

Poetry of Stephen Vincent Benét, The (Benét) MP IX-5159

Poetry of Stevens, The (Stevens, W.) MP IX-5161

Poetry of Suckling, The (Suckling) MP IX-5164

Poetry of Swift, The (Swift) MP IX-5167

Poetry of Tate, The (Tate) MP IX-5172

Poetry of Theocritus, The (Theocritus) MP IX-5175

Poetry of Thompson, The (Thompson, F.) MP IX-5177

Poetry of Thoreau, The (Thoreau) MP IX-5179

Poetry of Traherne, The (Traherne) MP IX-5181

Poetry of Valéry, The (Valéry) MP IX-5184

Poetry of Vaughan, The (Vaughan) MP IX-5187

Poetry of Vigny, The (Vigny) MP IX-5191

Poetry of Waller, The (Waller) MP IX-5194

Poetry of Warren, The (Warren) MP IX-5197

Poetry of Whittier, The (Whittier) MP IX-5200

Poetry of Wilbur, The (Wilbur) MP IX-5203

Poetry of Wilde, The (Wilde) MP IX-5206

Poetry of Williams, The (Williams, W.) MP IX-5209

Poetry of Wither, The (Wither) MP IX-5212

Poetry of Wordsworth, The (Wordsworth, W.) MP IX-5215

Poetry of Wyatt and Surrey, The (Wyatt *and* Surrey) MP IX-5219

Poetry of Yeats, The (Yeats) MP IX-5224

Point Counter Point (Huxley, A.) CLC II-898; MP IX-5227; MP:BF III-1237

Pointed Roofs. *See* Pilgrimage

Points for a Compass Rose (Connell) MPII:NF III-1173

Pokoušení. *See* Temptation

Police, The (Mrożek) CLCII III-1217; MPII:D III-1264

Policja. *See* Police, The

Polish Complex, The (Konwicki) CLCII III-1218; MPII:WF III-1207

Polyeucte (Corneille) CLC II-899; MP IX-5231

Ponder Heart, The (Welty) MP IX-5234; MP:AF II-958

Poor Christ of Bomba, The (Beti) CLCII III-1219; MPII:WF III-1214

Poor Folk. *See* Poor People

Poor People (Dostoevski) CLC II-900; MP IX-5237; MP:EF III-1020

Poor White (Anderson, S.) CLC II-901; MP IX-5241; MP:AF II-961

Poorhouse Fair, The (Updike) MP IX-5244; MP:AF II-965

Popiół i diamant. *See* Ashes and Diamonds

Porgy (Heyward) CLC II-902; MP IX-5247; MP:AF II-968

Pornografia (Gombrowicz) CLCII III-1221; MPII:WF III-1221

Pornographer, The (McGahern) CLCII III-1222; MPII:BCF III-1330

Portage to San Cristóbal of A. H., The (Steiner) CLCII III-1223; MPII:BCF III-1335

Porte étroite, La. *See* Strait Is the Gate

Portes de la forêt, Les. *See* Gates of the Forest, The

Portnoy's Complaint (Roth, P.) CLCII III-1224; MPII:AF III-1281

"Portobello Road, The" (Spark) MPII:SS IV-1831

Portrait d'un inconnu. *See* Portrait of a Man Unknown

Portrait of a Lady, The (James, H.) CLC II-903; MP IX-5250; MP:AF II-971

Portrait of a Man Unknown (Sarraute) CLCII III-1226; MPII:WF III-1225

Portrait of the Artist as a Young Dog (Thomas) MP IX-5256; MP:BF III-1241

Portrait of the Artist as a Young Man, A (Joyce) CLC II-904; MP IX-5259; MP:BF III-1245

Possédés, Les. *See* Possessed, The

Possessed, The (Camus) CLCII III-1227; MPII:D III-1269

Possessed, The (Dostoevski) CLC II-905; MP IX-5264; MP:EF III-1024

"Post Office, The" (O'Flaherty) MPII:SS IV-1835

Posthumas Memoirs of Bráz Cubas. *See* Epitaph of a Small Winner

Postman Always Rings Twice, The (Cain) MP IX-5270; MP:AF II-978

Pot of Gold, The (Plautus) CLC II-908; MP IX-5273

Potting Shed, The (Greene) CLCII III-1228; MPII:D III-1274

Povest o zhizni. *See* Story of a Life, The

Power (Feuchtwanger) CLC II-909; MP IX-5277; MP:EF III-1030

Power and the Glory, The (Greene, G.) CLC II-910; MP IX-5280; MP:BF III-1250

Power of Darkness, The (Tolstoy) CLC II-911; MP IX-5283

"Powerhouse" (Welty) MPII:SS IV-1839

Pragmatism (James, W.) MP IX-5287

Prague Orgy, The (Roth, P.) CLCII III-1229

Prairie, The (Cooper) CLC II-912; MP IX-5290; MP:AF II-982

Prairie Years, The. *See* Abraham Lincoln

Praise of Folly, The (Erasmus) MP IX-5294

Praisesong for the Widow (Marshall) CLCII III-1230; MPII:AF III-1286

Pravda (Brenton *and* Hare) CLCII III-1232; MPII:D III-1278

Precious Bane (Webb, M.) CLC II-913; MP IX-5296; ; MP:BF III-1254

Preface to Shakespeare (Johnson, S.) MP IX-5299

Prejudices: Six Series (Mencken) MP IX-5302

"Prelude" (Mansfield) MPII:SS IV-1843

Prelude, The (Wordsworth, W.) MP IX-5304

Premios, Los. *See* Winners, The

Presence of the Word, The (Ong) MPII:NF III-1179

Pretendent na prestol. *See* Pretender to the Throne

Pretender to the Throne (Voinovich) CLCII II-881; MPII:WF II-841

Příběh inženýra lidských duší. *See* Engineer of Human Souls, The

Price, The (Miller, A.) CLCII III-1233; MPII:D III-1283

Pride and Prejudice (Austen) CLC II-914; MP IX-5307; MP:BF III-1258

Priglashenie na kazn'. *See* Invitation to a Beheading

Prime of Life, The (de Beauvoir) MPII:NF III-1184

Prime of Miss Jean Brodie, The (Spark) CLCII III-1235; MPII:BCF III-1340

Primitive Classification (Durkheim *and* Mauss) MPII:NF III-1190

Primo Basílio, O. *See* Cousin Bazilio

Prince, The (Machiavelli) MP IX-5314

Prince and the Pauper, The (Twain) CLC II-915; MP IX-5317; MP:AF II-986

"Prince of Darkness" (Powers) MPII:SS IV-1848

Prince of Homburg, The (Kleist) CLC II-916; MP IX-5321

Princess, The (Tennyson) MP IX-5324

Princess Casamassima, The (James, H.) MP IX-5327; MP:AF II-990

Princess Iwona. *See* Ivona, Princess of Burgundia

Princess of Clèves, The (La Fayette) CLC II-917; MP IX-5330; MP:EF III-1034

Principle of Hope, The (Bloch) MPII:NF III-1196

Principles of Literary Criticism (Richards) MP IX-5334

Principles of Political Economy (Mill) MP IX-5337

Printer of Malgudi, The (Narayan) CLCII III-1236; MPII:BCF III-1346

Prinzip Hoffnung, Das. *See* Principle of Hope, The

Prison Notebooks (Gramsci) MPII:NF III-1200

Prisoner for God. *See* Letters and Papers from Prison

Prisoner of Grace. *See* Second Trilogy

Prisoner of Zenda, The (Hope) CLC II-917; MP IX-5340; MP:BF III-1266

Prisons (Settle) CLCII III-1237. *See also* Beulah Quintet, The

"Private Domain" (McPherson) MPII:SS IV-1852

Private Life of the Master Race, The (Brecht) CLC II-918; MP IX-5344

Private Lives (Coward) CLC II-919; CLCII III-1239; MP IX-5347; MPII:D III-1288

Private Papers of Henry Ryecroft, The (Gissing) CLC II-920; MP IX-5350; MP:BF III-1270

Privileged Ones. *See* Children of Crisis

Privy Seal. *See* Fifth Queen, The

"Problem of Cell 13, The" (Futrelle) MPII:SS IV-1856

Professor, The (Brontë, C.) CLC II-920; MP IX-5353; MP:BF III-1274

Professor's House, The (Cather) CLC II-922; MP IX-5357; MP:AF II-994

Prologue to an Autobiography (Naipaul) MPII:NF III-1204

Prometheus Bound (Aeschylus) CLC II-924; MP IX-5361

Prometheus Unbound (Shelley, P.) CLC II-925; MP IX-5365

Promise, The (Potok) CLCII I-281;
MPII:AF I-295

Promised Land, The (Pontoppidan) CLC
II-926; MP IX-5368; MP:EF III-1038

Proper Marriage, A. *See* Children of
Violence

Prophet, The (Gibran) MP IX-5372

Proserpine and Ceres (Unknown) CLC II-
926; MP IX-5374; MP:EF III-1042

Proshchanie iz niotkuda. *See* Farewell
from Nowhere

Prospero's Cell (Durrell) MPII:NF III-
1210

"Proszę państwa do gazu." *See* "This
Way for the Gas, Ladies and
Gentlemen"

Protestant Ethic and the Spirit of
Capitalism, The (Weber) MPII:NF III-
1214

Protestantische Ethik und der Geist des
Kapitalismus, Die. *See* Protestant Ethic
and the Spirit of Capitalism, The

Proust (Beckett) MPII:NF III-1219

"Prussian Officer, The" (Lawrence)
MPII:SS V-1859

"Psychiatrist, The" (Machado de Assis)
MPII:SS V-1862

Psycholog erlebt das Konzentrationslager,
Ein. *See* Man's Search for Meaning

Publikumsbeschimpfung. *See* Offending
the Audience

"Pupil, The" (James, H.) MPII:SS V-1865

"Purloined Letter, The" (Poe) MPII:SS V-
1868

Purple Dust (O'Casey) CLC II-927; MP
IX-5378

Purple Land, The (Hudson) CLC II-928;
MP IX-5382; MP:BF III-1278

"Pustoy sluchay." *See* "Trifling
Occurrence, A"

Puteshestviye v Armeniyu. *See* Journey to
Armenia

Pygmalion (Shaw) CLC II-928; MP IX-
5385

Pylon (Faulkner) CLCII III-1239;
MPII:AF III-1291

Q

Quaderni del carcere. *See* Prison Notebooks

Quality of Mercy, A (West, P.) CLCII III-1240; MPII:BCF III-1351

Quality Street (Barrie) CLC II-930; MP IX-5387

"Quando si comprende." *See* "War"

Quare Fellow, The (Behan) CLCII III-1241; MPII:D III-1294

Quartet in Autumn (Pym) CLCII III-1243; MPII:BCF III-1355

Que ma joie demeure. *See* Joy of Man's Desiring

Queen of Air and Darkness, The. *See* Once and Future King, The

"Queen of Spades, The" (Pushkin) CLCII III-1244; MPII:SS V-1872

Queen Victoria (Strachey) MP IX-5390

Queen's Necklace, The (Dumas, *père*) CLC II-930; MP IX-5394; MP:EF III-1046

Quel beau dimanche. *See* What a Beautiful Sunday!

Quentin Durward (Scott, Sir W.) CLC II-931; MP IX-5398; MP:BF III-1282

Quer pasticciaccio brutto de via Merulana. *See* That Awful Mess on Via Merulana

Quest for Christa T., The (Wolf) CLCII III-1245; MPII:WF III-1230

Quest of the Absolute, The (Balzac) CLCII III-1246; MPII:WF III-1236

Questa sera si recita a soggetto. *See* Tonight We Improvise

Question of Power, A (Head) CLCII III-1247; MPII:BCF III-1360

Question of Upbringing, A. *See* Dance to the Music of Time, A

Questionnaire, The (Gruša) CLCII III-1249; MPII:WF III-1240

Quicksand (Larsen) CLCII III-1250; MPII:AF III-1296

Quiet American, The (Greene) CLCII III-1252; MPII:BCF III-1364

Quincas Borba. *See* Philosopher or Dog?

Quo Vadis? (Sienkiewicz) CLC II-933; MP IX-5404; MP:EF III-1050

R

Rabbit Angstrom novels, The (Updike) MPII:AF III-1300

Rabbit Is Rich (Updike) CLCII III-1253. *See also* Rabbit Angstrom novels, The

Rabbit Redux (Updike) CLCII III-1254. *See also* Rabbit Angstrom novels, The

Rabbit, Run (Updike) CLCII III-1257; MP IX-5407; MP:AF II-998. *See also* Rabbit Angstrom novels, The

Radcliffe (Storey) CLCII III-1257; MPII:BCF III-1370

Radiance of the King, The (Laye) CLCII III-1258; MPII:WF III-1245

Radical Chic and Mau-Mauing the Flak Catchers (Wolfe) MPII:NF III-1225

"Ragman's Daughter, The" (Sillitoe) MPII:SS V-1876

Ragtime (Doctorow) CLCII III-1259; MPII:AF III-1310

"Raid, The" (Tolstoy) CLCII III-1261; MPII:SS V-1880

"Rain" (Maugham) MPII:SS V-1883

Rainbow, The (Lawrence, D. H.) CLC II-935; MP IX-5410; MP:BF III-1288

Raintree County (Lockridge) CLC II-936; MP IX-5415; MP:AF II-1001

"Rainy Moon, The" (Colette) MPII:SS V-1887

Raisin in the Sun, A (Hansberry) CLCII III-1262; MPII:D III-1300

Raj Quartet, The (Scott, P.) CLCII III-1263; MPII:BCF III-1376

Rakovy korpus. *See* Cancer Ward

Ralph Roister Doister (Udall) CLC II-937; MP IX-5418

"Ram in the Thicket, The" (Morris) MPII:SS V-1890

Ramayana, The (Valmiki) CLC II-938; MP IX-5421

Rambler, The (Johnson, S.) MP IX-5426

Rameau's Nephew (Diderot) CLC II-939; MP IX-5429; MP:EF III-1054

"Ransom of Red Chief, The" (O. Henry) MPII:SS V-1894

Rape of Lucrece, The (Shakespeare) CLC II-940; MP IX-5432

Rape of the Lock, The (Pope) CLC II-940; MP IX-5436

"Rappaccini's Daughter" (Hawthorne) MPII:SS V-1897

"Rashōmon" (Akutagawa) CLCII III-1265; MPII:SS V-1901

Rasselas (Johnson, S.) CLC II-941; MP IX-5441; MP:BF III-1293

Rat, The (Grass) CLCII III-1266; MPII:WF III-1252

Rat Man of Paris (West, P.) CLCII III-1267; MPII:BCF III-1386

Rat's Mass, A (Kennedy, A.) CLCII III-1269; MPII:D III-1305

Rates of Exchange (Bradbury, M.) CLCII III-1268; MPII:BCF III-1390

Rättin, Die. *See* Rat, The

Ravenshoe (Kingsley, H.) CLC II-942; MP IX-5446; MP:BF III-1298

Ravishing of Lol Stein, The (Duras) CLCII III-1270; MPII:WF III-1257

Ravissement de Lol V. Stein, Le. *See* Ravishing of Lol Stein, The

Raw Youth, A (Dostoevski) CLCII III-1271; MPII:WF III-1262

Rayuela. *See* Hopscotch

"Razgover o Dante." *See* Conversation About Dante

Razor's Edge, The (Maugham) CLCII III-1273; MPII:BCF III-1394

R. E. Lee (Freeman) MP IX-5497

Real Life of Sebastian Knight, The (Nabokov) MP IX-5450; MP:AF III-1005

"Real Thing, The" (James, H.) MPII:SS V-1905

Real Thing, The (Stoppard) CLCII III-1274; MPII:D III-1310

"Reasonable Facsimile, A" (Stafford) MPII:SS V-1908

Rebecca (du Maurier, D.) CLC II-943; MP IX-5452; MP:BF III-1302

Rebel, The (Camus) MPII:NF III-1231

Rebel Angels, The (Davies) CLCII III-1275; MPII:BCF III-1399

Rebel Generation, The (Ammers-Küller) MP IX-5456; MP:EF III-1058

Rebel Generation, The (Farquhar) CLC II-944

Rebellion in the Backlands (Cunha) CLCII III-1276; MPII:AF III-1317

Recherche de l'absolu, La. *See* Quest of the Absolute, The

"Recluse, A" (de la Mare) MPII:SS V-1913

Recognitions, The (Gaddis) CLCII III-1277; MPII:AF III-1324

Recruiting Officer, The (Farquhar) CLC II-945; MP IX-5459

Rector of Justin, The (Auchincloss) CLCII III-1279; MPII:AF III-1329

Red and the Black, The (Stendhal) CLC II-947; MP IX-5463; MP:EF III-1062

Red Badge of Courage, The (Crane, S.) CLC II-948; MP IX-5468; MP:AF III-1008

"Red-Headed League, The" (Doyle) MPII:SS V-1922

"Red Leaves" (Faulkner) MPII:SS V-1918

Red Pony, The (Steinbeck) CLCII III-1281; MPII:AF III-1334

Red Room, The (Strindberg) CLC II-949; MP IX-5473; MP:EF III-1067

Red Roses for Me (O'Casey) CLCII III-1282; MPII:D III-1315

Red Rover, The (Cooper) CLC II-950; MP IX-5477; MP:AF III-1013

Redburn (Melville) CLC II-951; MP IX-5481; MP:AF III-1017

Redskins, The (Cooper) CLC II-951; MP IX-5484; MP:AF III-1021

Reflections from a Diary Kept in 1909. *See* Autobiography of William Butler Yeats, The

Regard du roi, Le. *See* Radiance of the King, The

Regenta, La (Alas) CLCII III-1284; MPII:WF III-1267

Región más transparente, La. *See* Where the Air Is Clear

Reigen. *See* Ronde, La

Reino de este mundo, El. *See* Kingdom of This World, The

Reinvindicación del Conde Don Julián. *See* Count Julian

Reivers, The (Faulkner) MP IX-5489; MP:AF III-1027

Relapse, The (Vanbrugh) CLC II-952; MP IX-5493

Relations in Public (Goffman) MPII:NF III-1236

"Rembrandt's Hat" (Malamud) MPII:SS V-1926

Remembrance of Things Past (Proust) CLC II-953; MP IX-5500; MP:EF III-1072

Remembrance Rock (Sandburg) CLC II-955; MP IX-5505; MP:AF III-1032

Removalists, The (Williamson) CLCII III-1285; MPII:D III-1320

Renaissance, The (Pater) MP IX-5511

Renée Mauperin (Goncourt *and* Goncourt) CLC II-957; MP IX-5514; MP:EF III-1078

"Report to an Academy, A" (Kafka) MPII:SS V-1929

Representative Men (Emerson) MP IX-5518

Reprieve, The. *See* Roads to Freedom, The

Republic, The (Plato) MP IX-5522

Requiem for a Nun (Faulkner) MP X-5525; MP:AF III-1040

"Resemblance Between a Violin Case and a Coffin, The" (Williams, T.) MPII:SS V-1933

Responsibilities of the Novelist, The (Norris) MP X-5528

Restless Heart (Anouilh) CLCII III-1286; MPII:D III-1325

Restless Years, The. *See* Story of a Life, The

Resurrection (Tolstoy) CLC II-958; MP X-5531; MP:EF III-1082

Return, The (de la Mare) CLC II-958; MP X-5536; MP:BF III-1307

"Return of a Private, The" (Garland) MPII:SS V-1937

"Return of Chorb, The" (Nabokov) MPII:SS V-1941

Return of the King, The (Tolkien) MP X-5540; MP:BF III-1311

Return of the Native, The (Hardy) CLC II-959; MP X-5545; MP:BF III-1317

Return of the Soldier, The (West, R.) CLCII III-1288; MPII:BCF III-1404

Return to Región (Benet) CLCII III-1289; MPII:WF III-1272

"Revelation" (O'Connor, Flannery) MPII:SS V-1945

"Revenant, A" (de la Mare) MPII:SS V-1948

Revenge for Love, The (Lewis, W.) CLCII III-1290; MPII:BCF III-1410

Revenge of Bussy d'Ambois, The (Chapman) CLC II-961; MP X-5550

Revenger's Tragedy, The (Tourneur) CLC II-961; MP X-5554

Reveries over Childhood and Youth. See Autobiography of William Butler Yeats, The

Revolt of the Angels, The (France) CLC II-963; MP X-5558; MP:EF III-1088

Revolt of the Masses, The (Ortega y Gasset) MP X-5562

Revolving Lights. See Pilgrimage

Reynard the Fox (Unknown) CLC II-963; MP X-5565; MP:EF III-1092

Rhadamistus and Zenobia (Crébillon) CLC II-964; MP X-5570

Rhinoceros (Ionesco) MP X-5574

Riceyman Steps (Bennett) CLC II-965; MP X-5577; MP:BF III-1323

"Rich Boy, The" (Fitzgerald) MPII:SS V-1952

Richard the Second (Shakespeare) CLC II-965; MP X-5580

Richard the Third (Shakespeare) CLC II-967; MP X-5585

Rickshaw (Lao She) CLCII III-1291; MPII:WF III-1278

Ride Across Lake Constance, The (Handke) CLCII III-1292; MPII:D III-1330

Riders in the Chariot (White, P.) MP X-5590; MP:BF III-1327

Riders to the Sea (Synge) CLCII III-1294; MPII:D III-1337

Rigadoon (Céline) CLCII I-241; MPII:WF I-221

Right Stuff, The (Wolfe) MPII:NF III-1241

Right to an Answer, The (Burgess) CLCII III-1295; MPII:BCF III-1416

Right You Are--If You Think So (Pirandello) CLC II-970; MP X-5593

Rigodon. See Rigadoon

Rihlah ila al-ghad. See Voyage to Tomorrow

Riket grundlœgges. See Giants in the Earth

Rime of Petrarch, Le (Petrarch) MP X-5597

Rime of the Ancient Mariner, The (Coleridge) MP X-5600

Rimers of Eldritch, The (Wilson, L.) CLCII III-1296; MPII:D IV-1343

Ring and the Book, The (Browning, R.) CLC II-970; MP X-5603

Ring Round the Moon (Anouilh) CLC II-972; MP X-5608

"Rip Van Winkle" (Irving) CLC II-972; MP X-5611; MP:AF III-1044; MPII:SS V-1957

Ripening Corn, The. See Ripening Seed, The

Ripening Seed, The (Colette) CLCII III-1297; MPII:WF III-1282

Ripple from the Storm, A. See Children of Violence

Rise and Fall of César Birotteau. See César Birotteau

Rise and Fall of the City of Mahagonny (Brecht) CLCII III-1298; MPII:D IV-1350

Rise of American Civilization, The (Beard *and* Beard) MP X-5614

"Rise of Maud Martha, The" (Brooks) MPII:SS V-1961

Rise of Silas Lapham, The (Howells) CLC II-973; MP X-5618; MP:AF III-1047

Rites of Passage (Golding) CLCII III-1299; MPII:BCF III-1422

Ritt über den Bodensee, Der. *See* Ride Across Lake Constance, The

"Ritter Gluck" (Hoffmann) MPII:SS V-1964

Rivals, The (Sheridan) CLC II-974; MP X-5624

River Between, The (Ngugi) CLCII III-1300; MPII:BCF III-1428

River of Earth (Still) CLC II-975; MP X-5629; MP:AF III-1054

Rivet in Grandfather's Neck, The (Cabell) CLC II-976; MP X-5632; MP:AF III-1058

Road, The (Soyinka) CLCII III-1302; MPII:D IV-1356

Road to Mecca, The (Fugard) CLCII III-1303; MPII:D IV-1362

"Road to the Isles" (West, J.) MPII:SS V-1968

Road to Wigan Pier, The (Orwell) MPII:NF III-1247

Roads to Freedom, The (Sartre) CLCII III-1303; MPII:WF III-1288

Roadside Picnic (Strugatsky *and* Strugatsky) CLCII III-1306; MPII:WF III-1295

Roan Stallion (Jeffers) CLC II-977; MP X-5636

Rob Roy (Scott, Sir W.) CLC II-977; MP X-5638; MP:BF III-1331

Robber Bridegroom, The (Welty) CLCII III-1307; MPII:AF III-1339

Robin Hood's Adventures (Unknown) CLC II-978; MP X-5642; MP:BF III-1336

Robinson Crusoe (Defoe) CLC II-979; MP X-5647; MP:BF III-1341

Rock Cried Out, The (Douglas) CLCII III-1309; MPII:AF III-1344

"Rocking-Horse Winner, The" (Lawrence) MPII:SS V-1971

Roderick Hudson (James, H.) MP X-5652; MP:AF III-1062

Roderick Random (Smollett) CLC II-979; MP X-5656; MP:BF III-1347

Rodzinnia Europa. *See* Native Realm

Rogue Herries (Walpole, Hugh) CLC II-981; MP X-5661; MP:BF III-1353

Roi des aulnes, Le. *See* Ogre, The

Roi se meurt, Le. *See* Exit the King

Roman Actor, The (Massinger) CLC II-982; MP X-5665

"Roman Fever" (Wharton) MPII:SS V-1974

Romance of a Schoolmaster, The (Amicis) CLC II-983; MP X-5669; MP:EF III-1097

Romance of Leonardo da Vinci, The (Merezhkowsky) CLC II-984; MP X-5672; MP:EF III-1101

Romance of the Forest, The (Radcliffe) CLC II-984; MP X-5675; MP:BF III-1358

Romance of the Three Kingdoms (Lo Kuan-chung) CLC II-985; MP X-5681; MP:EF III-1105

Romantic Comedians, The (Glasgow) CLC II-986; MP X-5684; MP:AF III-1067

Romantic Ladies, The (Molière) CLC II-988; MP X-5689

Romany Rye, The (Borrow) CLC II-988; MP X-5693; MP:BF III-1365

Rome Haul (Edmonds) CLC II-989; MP X-5697; MP:AF III-1072

Romeo and Juliet (Shakespeare) CLC II-990; MP X-5700

Romola (Eliot, G.) CLC II-992; MP X-5705; MP:BF III-1369

Romulus der Grosse. *See* Romulus the Great

Romulus the Great (Dürrenmatt) CLCII III-1310; MPII:D IV-1367

Ronde, La (Schnitzler) CLCII III-1312; MPII:D IV-1372

Room at the Top (Braine) MP X-5709; MP:BF III-1373

Room on the Hill, A (St. Omer) CLCII III-1312; MPII:BCF III-1435

Room with a View, A (Forster) CLC II-994; MP X-5712; MP:BF III-1376

Roots (Haley) MPII:NF III-1251

"Rope" (Porter) MPII:SS V-1978

Rory O'More (Lover) CLC II-995; MP X-5715; MP:BF III-1380

"Rosa" (Ozick) MPII:SS V-1982

Rose and Crown. *See* Mirror in My House

"Rose for Emily, A" (Faulkner) MPII:SS V-1986

"Rose in the Heart of New York, A" (O'Brien, E.) MPII:SS V-1990

Rosencrantz and Guildenstern Are Dead (Stoppard) CLCII III-1314; MPII:D IV-1378

Rosmersholm (Ibsen) CLC II-995; MP X-5718

Rosshalde (Hesse) CLCII III-1314; MPII:WF III-1300

"Rothschild's Fiddle" (Chekhov) MPII:SS V-1994

Roughing It (Twain) MP X-5722

"Round by Round" (Aiken) MPII:SS V-1998

Route des Flandres, La. *See* Flanders Road, The

Roxana (Defoe) CLC II-996; MP X-5725; MP:BF III-1384

Royal Hunt of the Sun, The (Shaffer, P.) CLCII III-1316; MPII:D IV-1384

Royal Way, The (Malraux) CLCII III-1317; MPII:WF III-1305

Rubáiyát of Omar Khayyám, The (FitzGerald, E.) MP X-5730

Rubyfruit Jungle (Brown) CLCII III-1318; MPII:AF III-1349

Rudin (Turgenev) CLCII III-1319; MPII:WF III-1310

"Ruinas circulares, Las." *See* "Circular Ruins, The"

Ruined Map, The (Abe) CLCII III-1321; MPII:WF III-1315

Rule a Wife and Have a Wife (Fletcher) CLC II-996; MP X-5732

Ruling Class, The (Barnes, P.) CLCII III-1322; MPII:D IV-1390

Runaway Horse (Walser) CLCII III-1323; MPII:WF III-1321

Runaway Horses. *See* Sea of Fertility, The

Runner Mack (Beckham) CLCII III-1324; MPII:AF III-1353

R.U.R. (Čapek) CLC II-997; MP X-5736

Ruslan and Lyudmila (Pushkin) MP X-5740; MPII:NF III-1257

Russian Thinkers (Berlin) MPII:NF III-1257

S

S/Z (Barthes) MPII:NF III-1263
Sacred Families (Donoso) CLCII III-1325;
MPII:AF III-1357
Sacred Fount, The (James, H.) MP X-
5743; MP:AF III-1076
Sacred Journey, The (Buechner) MPII:NF
III-1269
Sacred Wood: Essays on Poetry and
Criticism, The (Eliot, T. S.) MP X-
5748
"Sad Fate of Mr. Fox, The" (Harris)
MPII:SS V-2002
Sad idzie. *See* Trial Begins, The
Safe-Conduct, A (Pasternak) MPII:NF III-
1274
Safety Net, The (Böll) CLCII III-1326;
MPII:WF III-1326
"Sailor Off the *Bremen*" (Shaw) MPII:SS
V-2005
Sailor Who Fell from Grace with the Sea,
The (Mishima) CLCII III-1328;
MPII:WF III-1332
Saint, The (Fogazzaro) CLC II-998; MP
X-5751; MP:EF III-1109
"Saint Augustine's Pigeon" (Connell, E.)
MPII:SS V-2008
Saint Jack (Theroux) CLCII III-1329;
MPII:AF III-1362
Saint Joan (Shaw) CLC II-998; MP X-
5755
Saint Manuel Bueno, Martyr (Unamuno)
CLCII III-1329; MPII:WF III-1338
"Saint Marie" (Erdrich) MPII:SS V-2012
St. Peter's Umbrella (Mikszáth) CLC II-
999; MP X-5757; MP:EF III-1113
St. Petersburg. *See* Petersburg
St. Ronan's Well (Scott, Sir W.) CLC II-
1000; MP X-5761; MP:BF III-1389
St. Urbain's Horseman (Richler) CLCII
III-1330; MPII:BCF III-1440
Sakuntala (Kalidasa) CLC II-1001; MP X-
5765
Salammbô (Flaubert) CLC II-1001; MP X-
5769; MP:EF III-1118

Salar the Salmon (Williamson) MP X-
5773; MP:BF III-1394
Salvador (Didion) MPII:NF III-1280
Samson Agonistes (Milton) CLC II-1002;
MP X-5776
Samurai, The (Endō) CLCII III-1332;
MPII:WF III-1345
San Manuel Bueno, mártir. *See* Saint
Manuel Bueno, Martyr
"Sanatorium Under the Sign of the
Hourglass" (Schulz) MPII:SS V-2016
Sanctuary (Faulkner) CLC II-1003; MP X-
5780; MP:AF III-1082
Sand Mountain (Linney) CLCII III-1333;
MPII:D IV-1396
Sandcastle, The (Murdoch) CLCII III-
1334; MPII:BCF III-1444
Sandford and Merton (Day, T.) CLC II-
1004; MP X-5784; MP:BF III-1398
"Sandman, The" (Hoffmann) MPII:SS V-
2020
Sanine (Artsybashev) CLC II-1004; MP X-
5787; MP:EF III-1123
Sapphira and the Slave Girl (Cather)
CLCII III-1335; MPII:AF III-1366
Sappho (Daudet) CLC II-1005; MP X-
5790; MP:EF III-1127
Sappho (Grillparzer) CLC II-1006; MP X-
5793
Saragossa (Pérez Galdós) CLC II-1006;
MP X-5796; MP:EF III-1131
Sarrasine (Balzac) CLCII III-1337;
MPII:WF III-1351
Sartor Resartus (Carlyle) MP X-5799
Sartoris (Faulkner) MP X-5801; MP:AF
III-1086
Sasame-yuki. *See* Makioka Sisters, The
Satanstoe (Cooper) CLC II-1007; MP X-
5804; MP:AF III-1090
Satin Slipper, The (Claudel) CLCII III-
1338; MPII:D IV-1401
Satires (Boileau-Despréaux) MP X-5809
Satires (Juvenal) MP X-5812
Satires (Lucian) MP X-5814

Satiromastix (Dekker) CLC II-1008; MP X-5817

"Saturday Night" (Farrell) MPII:SS V-2025

Saturday Night and Sunday Morning (Sillitoe) CLCII III-1339; MPII:BCF III-1449

Satyricon, The (Arbiter) CLC II-1008

Satyricon, The (Petronius) MP X-5820; MP:EF III-1135

Sauvage, La. *See* Restless Heart

Save Me the Waltz (Fitzgerald, Z.) CLCII III-1340; MPII:AF III-1370

Saved (Bond) CLCII III-1341; MPII:D IV-1406

Saving the Appearances (Barfield) MPII:NF III-1286

Sawbones Memorial (Ross) CLCII III-1342; MPII:BCF III-1455

"Scandal in Bohemia, A" (Doyle) MPII:SS V-2029

"Scandalous Woman, A" (O'Brien, E.) MPII:SS V-2033

"Scapegoat, The" (Dunbar) MPII:SS V-2037

Scapegoat, The (Girard) MPII:NF III-1293

Scapegoat, The (Settle) CLCII III-1343. *See also* Beulah Quintet, The

Scarlet Letter, The (Hawthorne) CLC II-1009; MP X-5826; MP:AF III-1096

Scenes from American Life (Gurney) CLCII III-1345; MPII:D IV-1411

Scepticism and Animal Faith (Santayana) MP X-5831

"Schakale und Araber." *See* "Jackals and Arabs"

Schlaflose Tage. *See* Sleepless Days

School for Fools, A (Sokolov) CLCII III-1347; MPII:WF III-1356

School for Husbands, The (Molière) CLC II-1010; MP X-5834

School for Scandal, The (Sheridan) CLC II-1011; MP X-5838

School for Wives, The (Molière) CLC II-1012; MP X-5843

"Schreuderspitze, The" (Helprin) MPII:SS V-2041

Schwanenhaus, Das. *See* Swan Villa, The

Scorched-Wood People, The (Wiebe) CLCII III-1348; MPII:BCF III-1460

Scornful Lady, The (Beaumont *and* Fletcher) CLC II-1012; MP X-5848

Scots Quair, A (Gibbon) CLCII III-1349; MPII:BCF III-1465

Scottish Chiefs, The (Porter, J.) CLC II-1013; MP X-5851; MP:BF III-1402

Scott's Last Expedition (Scott, Captain R.) MP X-5855

Screens, The (Genet) CLCII III-1352; MPII:D IV-1416

Sculpting in Time (Tarkovsky) MPII:NF III-1298

"Sculptor's Funeral, The" (Cather) MPII:SS V-2045

Se non ora, quando? *See* If Not Now, When?

Se questo è un uomo. *See* If This Is a Man

Se una notte d'inverno un viaggiatore. *See* If on a Winter's Night a Traveler

Sea and Sardinia (Lawrence) MPII:NF III-1303

Sea and the Jungle, The (Tomlinson) MP X-5858

Sea of Cortez (Steinbeck *and* Ricketts) MPII:NF III-1309

Sea of Fertility, The (Mishima) CLCII III-1354; MPII:WF III-1361

Sea of Grass, The (Richter) CLC II-1014; MP X-5861; MP:AF III-1102

Sea of Troubles, A. *See* Sea Wall, The

Sea Wall, The (Duras) CLCII III-1355; MPII:WF III-1367

Sea Wolf, The (London) CLC II-1015; MP X-5865; MP:AF III-1106

Seagull, The (Chekhov) CLC II-1015; MP X-5868

Seamarks (Perse) MP X-5874

Search for America, A (Grove) CLCII III-1356; MPII:BCF III-1472

Search for Signs of Intelligent Life in the Universe, The (Wagner) CLCII III-1357; MPII:D IV-1421

Seascape (Albee) CLCII III-1359; MPII:D IV-1427

Season in Hell, A (Rimbaud) MP X-5876

Season of Adventure (Lamming) CLCII III-1360; MPII:BCF III-1476

Season of Anomy (Soyinka) CLCII III-1362; MPII:BCF III-1482

Seasons, The (Thomson) MP X-5879

"Seaton's Aunt" (de la Mare) MPII:SS V-2049

Second Coming, The (Percy) CLCII III-1363; MPII:AF III-1376

Second Common Reader, The. *See* Literary Essays of Virginia Woolf, The

Second Foundation. *See* Foundation trilogy, The

Second Jungle Book, The. *See* Jungle Books, The

Second Man, The (Behrman) CLCII III-1364; MPII:D IV-1433

Second Mrs. Tanqueray, The (Pinero) CLC II-1017; MP X-5882

Second Sex, The (de Beauvoir) MPII:NF III-1314

Second Shepherd's Play, The (Unknown) CLC II-1017; MP X-5886

Second Trilogy (Cary) CLCII III-1365; MPII:BCF IV-1489

Second World War, The (Churchill, W. S.) MP X-5890

Secret Agent, The (Conrad) CLC II-1018; MP X-5893; MP:BF III-1407

Secret History of the Lord of Musashi, The (Tanizaki) CLCII III-1367; MPII:WF III-1372

Secret House, The (Bodanis) MPII:NF IV-1319

"Secret Integration, The" (Pynchon) MPII:SS V-2053

Secret Ladder, The. *See* Guyana Quartet, The

"Secret Life of Walter Mitty, The" (Thurber) MPII:SS V-2057

"Secret Sharer, The" (Conrad) CLCII III-1368; MPII:SS V-2061

Seduction and Betrayal (Hardwick) MPII:NF IV-1324

"See the Moon?" (Barthelme, D.) MPII:SS V-2064

Seize the Day (Bellow) CLCII III-1369; MPII:AF III-1382

Seizure of Power, The (Miłosz) CLCII III-1370; MPII:WF IV-1377

Sejanus, His Fall (Jonson) CLC II-1019; MP X-5896

Selected Poems (Ransom) MP X-5899

Self Condemned (Lewis, W.) CLCII III-1371; MPII:BCF IV-1496

Self-Tormentor, The (Terence) CLC II-1021; MP X-5902

Sem dnei tvoreniia. *See* Seven Days of Creation, The

Sembazuru. *See* Thousand Cranes

"Semejante a la noche." *See* "Like the Night"

Semeynoye schast'ye. *See* Family Happiness

Señas de identidad. *See* Marks of Identity

Senilità. *See* As a Man Grows Older

Sennik współczesny. *See* Dreambook for Our Time, A

Señor de Tacuru, El. *See* Lizard's Tail, The

Señor Presidente, El (Asturias) MP:AF III-1110

Sense and Sensibility (Austen) CLC II-1022; MP X-5905; MP:BF III-1411

Sent for You Yesterday. *See* Homewood trilogy, The

Sentiero dei nidi di ragno, Il. *See* Path to the Nest of Spiders, The

Sentimental Education, A (Flaubert) CLC II-1023; MP X-5909; MP:EF III-1141

Sentimental Journey, A (Shklovsky) CLCII III-1372; MPII:WF IV-1382

Sentimental Journey, A (Sterne) CLC II-1024; MP X-5914; MP:BF III-1415

Sentimental'noye puteshestviye. *See* Sentimental Journey, A

Separate Peace, A (Knowles) CLCII III-1373; MPII:AF III-1387

September Light. *See* Silesian Tetralogy, The

Septemberlicht. *See* Silesian Tetralogy, The

"Serapionsbrüder, Die." *See* "Story of Serapion, The"

Serebryagolub. *See* Silver Dove, The

Serebryanny golub. *See* Silver Dove, The

Serious Money (Churchill) CLCII III-1374; MPII:D IV-1438

Serjeant Musgrave's Dance (Arden) CLCII III-1375; MPII:D IV-1444

Serment de Kolvillàg, Le. *See* Oath, The

Serpent and the Rope, The (Rao) CLCII IV-1377; MPII:BCF IV-1501

Serpiente de oro, La. *See* Golden Serpent, The

Sertões, Os. *See* Rebellion in the Backlands

Set This House on Fire (Styron) MP X-5919; MP:AF III-1113

Setting Free the Bears (Irving) CLCII IV-1378; MPII:AF III-1392

Setting Sun, The (Dazai) CLCII IV-1379; MPII:WF IV-1388

Settlers of the Marsh (Grove) CLCII IV-1380; MPII:BCF IV-1506

Seven Against Thebes (Aeschylus) CLC II-1025; MP X-5922

Seven Ages, The (Figes) CLCII IV-1381; MPII:BCF IV-1510

Seven Days of Creation, The (Maximov) CLCII IV-1383; MPII:WF IV-1393

Seven Gothic Tales (Dinesen) MP X-5926; MP:EF III-1147

Seven Madmen, The (Arlt) CLCII IV-1384; MPII:AF IV-1397

Seven Pillars of Wisdom (Lawrence, T. E.) MP X-5929

Seven Short Plays (Gregory) MP X-5932

Seven Storey Mountain, The (Merton) MPII:NF IV-1330

Seven Types of Ambiguity (Empson) MPII:NF IV-1335

Seven Who Fled, The (Prokosch) CLC II-1026; MP X-5934; MP:AF III-1117

Seven Who Were Hanged, The (Andreyev) CLC II-1027; MP X-5939; MP:EF III-1151

Seventeen (Tarkington) CLC II-1027; MP X-5942; MP:AF III-1122

Severed Head, A (Murdoch) CLCII IV-1385; MPII:BCF IV-1516

Sexual Perversity in Chicago (Mamet) CLCII IV-1386; MPII:D IV-1449

Shadow of a Gunman, The (O'Casey) CLCII IV-1387; MPII:D IV-1454

Shadow of Night, The (Chapman) MP X-5945

Shadows on the Rock (Cather) CLC II-1028; MP X-5948; MP:AF III-1126

Shah of Shahs (Kapuściński) MPII:NF IV-1341

Shakespeare's Dog (Rooke) CLCII IV-1388; MPII:BCF IV-1523

Shame (Rushdie) CLCII IV-1389; MPII:BCF IV-1528

Shank's Mare. *See* Hizakurige

"Shape of Light, A" (Goyen) MPII:SS V-2068

Shayō. *See* Setting Sun, The

She (Haggard) CLC II-1029; MP X-5952; MP:BF III-1421

She Stoops to Conquer (Goldsmith) CLC II-1030; MP X-5957

"She-Wolf, The" (Verga) MPII:SS V-2076

Sheep Well, The (Vega) CLC II-1031; MP X-5962

Shelburne Essays (More, P.) MP X-5966

Sheltered Life, The (Glasgow) CLC II-1033; MP X-5969; MP:AF III-1130

Sheltering Sky, The (Bowles) CLCII IV-1390; MPII:AF IV-1402

Shepheardes Calendar, The (Spenser) MP X-5972

"Sheriff's Children, The" (Chesnutt) MPII:SS V-2072

Shih Ching, The (Confucius) MP X-5976

"Shiiku." *See* "Catch, The"

Shikasta (Lessing) CLCII IV-1391; MPII:BCF IV-1533

"Shinel." *See* "Overcoat, The"

Shining, The (King) CLCII IV-1393; MPII:AF IV-1407

Ship of Fools (Porter, K.) MP X-5979; MP:AF III-1134

Ship of the Line, A. *See* Captain Horatio Hornblower

Shipyard, The (Onetti) CLCII IV-1394; MPII:AF IV-1411

Shirley (Brontë, C.) CLC II-1034; MP X-5985; MP:BF III-1427

Shkola dlia durakov. *See* School for Fools, A

"Shoemaker Arnold" (Lovelace) MPII:SS V-2080

Shoemaker's Holiday, The (Dekker) CLC II-1035; MP X-5988

"Short Friday" (Singer) MPII:SS V-2084

"Short Happy Life of Francis Macomber, The" (Hemingway) MPII:SS V-2088

Short Letter, Long Farewell (Handke) CLCII IV-1395; MPII:WF IV-1398

Short Stories of A. E. Coppard, The (Coppard) MP X-5993; MP:BF III-1431

Short Stories of D. H. Lawrence (Lawrence, D. H.) MP X-5995; MP:BF III-1439

Short Stories of E. M. Forster, The (Forster) MP X-5998; MP:BF III-1434

Short Stories of Ernest Hemingway, The (Hemingway) MP X-6002; MP:AF III-1145

Short Stories of Eudora Welty, The (Welty) MP X-6005; MP:AF III-1164

Short Stories of Flannery O'Connor, The (O'Connor) MP X-6008; MP:AF III-1152

Short Stories of John Cheever, The (Cheever) MP X-6011; MP:AF III-1141

Short Stories of John Updike, The (Updike) MP X-6014; MP:AF III-1160

Short Stories of Katherine Mansfield, The (Mansfield) MP X-6018; MP:BF III-1442

Short Stories of O. Henry, The (O. Henry) MP X-6021; MP:AF III-1149

Short Stories of Peter Taylor (Taylor, P.) MP X-6024; MP:AF III-1156

Short Stories of Saki, The (Saki) MP X-6027; MP:BF III-1445

Shosha (Singer) CLCII IV-1396; MPII:AF IV-1417; MPII:WF IV-1404

"Shot, The" (Pushkin) MPII:SS V-2093

"Shower of Gold" (Welty) MPII:SS V-2097

Shropshire Lad, A (Housman) MP X-6030

Shrouded Woman, The (Bombal) CLCII IV-1397; MPII:AF IV-1422

Shum vremeni. *See* Noise of Time, The

Shuttlecock (Swift) CLCII IV-1398; MPII:BCF IV-1538

Sibyl, The (Lagerkvist) CLCII IV-1399; MPII:WF IV-1409

Sibyllan. *See* Sibyl, The

"Sick Call, A (Callaghan) MPII:SS V-2101

"Sick Child, The" (Colette) MPII:SS V-2104

Sickness unto Death, The (Kierkegaard) MP X-6032

Siddhartha (Hesse) CLCII IV-1400; MPII:WF IV-1414

Siege of Krishnapur, The (Farrell) CLCII IV-1401; MPII:BCF IV-1543

Siege of Rhodes, The (Davenant) CLC II-1036; MP X-6035

Siete locos, Los. *See* Seven Madmen, The

Sigismund (Gustafsson) CLCII IV-1403; MPII:WF IV-1419

Siglo de las luces, El. *See* Explosion in a Cathedral

Sign in Sidney Brustein's Window, The (Hansberry) CLCII IV-1404; MPII:D IV-1458

Sign of Four, The (Doyle) CLC II-1037; MP X-6037; MP:BF III-1449

Silas Marner (Eliot, G.) CLC II-1038; MP X-6043; MP:BF III-1455

Silence (Endō) CLCII IV-1405; MPII:WF IV-1425

Silences (Olsen) MPII:NF IV-1346

Silent Cry, The (Ōe) CLCII IV-1407; MPII:WF IV-1431

Silent Don, The. *See* And Quiet Flows the Don *and* Don Flows Home to the Sea, The

"Silent Snow, Secret Snow" (Aiken) MPII:SS V-2108

Silent Spring (Carson) MPII:NF IV-1351

Silent Woman, The (Jonson) CLC II-1039; MP X-6046

Silesian Tetralogy, The (Bienek) CLCII IV-1408; MPII:WF IV-1436

Silmarillion, The (Tolkien) CLCII IV-1410; MPII:BCF IV-1548

"Silver Dish, A" (Bellow) MPII:SS V-2112

Silver Dove, The (Bely) CLCII IV-1413; MPII:WF IV-1442

"Silver Mine, The" (Lagerlöf) MPII:SS V-2116

Silver Tassie, The (O'Casey) CLCII IV-1413; MPII:D IV-1465

"Simple Heart, A" (Flaubert) MPII:SS V-2120

Simple Honorable Man, A (Richter) MP X-6050; MP:AF III-1168

Simple Story, A (Agnon) CLCII IV-1415; MPII:WF IV-1448

Simplicissimus the Vagabond (Grimmelshausen) CLC II-1040; MP X-6053; MP:EF III-1155

Singapore Grip, The (Farrell) CLCII IV-1416; MPII:BCF IV-1558

Singer of Tales, The (Lord) MPII:NF IV-1356

Sipur pashut. *See* Simple Story, A

Sir Charles Grandison (Richardson, S.) CLC II-1041; MP X-6056; MP:BF III-1459

Sir Gawain and the Green Knight (Unknown) CLC II-1042; MP X-6060

Sir John van Olden Barnavelt (Fletcher *and* Massinger) CLC II-1042; MP X-6063

Sir Roger de Coverley Papers, The (Addison, Budgell, *and* Steele) CLC II-1044; MP X-6067

Sirens of Titan, The (Vonnegut) CLCII IV-1418; MPII:AF IV-1427

Sistema periodico, Il. *See* Periodic Table, The

Sister Carrie (Dreiser) CLC II-1045; MP X-6070; MP:AF III-1171

Sister Mary Ignatius Explains It All for You (Durang) CLCII IV-1419; MPII:D IV-1471

Sister Philomène (Goncourt *and* Goncourt) CLC II-1046; MP X-6075; MP:EF III-1159

"Sisters, The" (Joyce) MPII:SS V-2124

Six Characters in Search of an Author (Pirandello) CLC II-1047; MP X-6079

6,810,000 Litres d'eau par seconde. *See* Niagara

62: A Model Kit (Cortázar) CLCII IV-1420; MPII:AF IV-1433

Sketchbook, 1946-1949, *and* Sketchbook, 1966-1971 (Frisch) MPII:NF IV-1361

Skin of Our Teeth, The (Wilder) CLC II-1048; MP X-6084

"Skverny anekdot." *See* "Nasty Story, A"

"Sky Is Gray, The" (Gaines) MPII:SS V-2128

"Skylepy cynamanowe." *See* "Cinnamon Shops"

Slaughterhouse-Five (Vonnegut) CLCII IV-1421; MPII:AF IV-1438

Slave, The (Singer) CLCII IV-1422; MPII:AF IV-1443; MPII:WF IV-1453

Śledztwo. *See* Investigation, The

Sleep of Reason, The. *See* Strangers and Brothers

Sleepless Days (Becker) CLCII IV-1423; MPII:WF IV-1458

Sleepwalkers, The (Broch) CLC II-1049; MP X-6089; MP:EF III-1164

Sleepy Hollow. *See* Legend of Sleepy Hollow, The

Sleuth (Shaffer, A.) CLCII IV-1424; MPII:D IV-1477

"Slide Area, The" (Lambert) MPII:SS V-2132

Slipknot, The (Plautus) CLC II-1050; MP X-6094

Slouching Towards Bethlehem (Didion) MPII:NF IV-1366

Slow Approach of Thunder. *See* Story of a Life, The

Slow Homecoming (Handke) CLCII IV-1425; MPII:WF IV-1462

Ślub. *See* Marriage, The

Small Changes (Piercy) CLCII IV-1426; MPII:AF IV-1448

"Small, Good Thing, A" (Carver) MPII:SS V-2135

Small House at Allington, The (Trollope) CLC II-1050; MP X-6097; MP:BF III-1463

Small Is Beautiful (Schumacher) MPII:NF IV-1372

Small Room, The (Sarton) CLCII IV-1427; MPII:AF IV-1454

Small Souls (Couperus) CLC II-1052; MP X-6101; MP:EF III-1170

Small World (Lodge) CLCII IV-1429; MPII:BCF IV-1563

"Smallest Woman in the World, The" (Lispector) MPII:SS V-2138

"Smell of Death and Flowers, The" (Gordimer) MPII:SS V-2142

"Smert Ivana Ilicha." *See* "Death of Ivan Ilyich, The"

"Smiles of Konarak, The" (Dennison) MPII:SS V-2146

Smiley's People (le Carré) CLCII II-694; MPII:BCF IV-1710

Smoke (Turgenev) CLC II-1053; MP X-6105; MP:EF III-1174

Snail on the Slope, The (Strugatsky *and* Strugatsky) CLCII IV-1430; MPII:WF IV-1469

"Snake Charmer, The" (Shalamov) MPII:SS V-2150

Snake Pit, The (Undset) CLC II-1055; MP X-6109; MP:EF III-1178

"Sniper, The" (O'Flaherty) MPII:SS V-2154

"Sniper, The" (Sillitoe) MPII:SS V-2158

Snooty Baronet (Lewis, W.) CLCII IV-1432; MPII:BCF IV-1567

Snopes trilogy, The. *See* Hamlet, The; Mansion, The; *and* Town, The

Snow-Bound (Whittier) CLC II-1056; MP X-6113

Snow Country (Kawabata) CLCII IV-1433; MPII:WF IV-1475

Snow Leopard, The (Matthiessen) MPII:NF IV-1378

"Snow-Storm, The" (Tolstoy) MPII:SS V-2163

Snow Was Black, The (Simenon) CLCII IV-1434; MPII:WF IV-1481

So Big (Ferber) MP X-6115; MP:AF III-1176

So Red the Rose (Young, S.) CLC II-1056; MP X-6118; MP:AF III-1180

Sobache serdtse. *See* Heart of a Dog, The

Sobre héroes y tumbas. *See* On Heroes and Tombs

Society and Solitude (Emerson) MP X-6122

Society of Mind, The (Minsky) MPII:NF IV-1383

Sohrab and Rustum (Arnold) CLC II-1057; MP X-6125

Soil, The. *See* Earth

Solaris (Lem) CLCII IV-1435; MPII:WF IV-1486

Soldier's Art, The. *See* Dance to the Music of Time, A

"Soldier's Embrace, A" (Gordimer) MPII:SS V-2166

Soldier's Fortune, The (Otway) CLC II-1057; MP X-6128

"Soldier's Home" (Hemingway) MPII:SS V-2170

Soldiers' Pay (Faulkner) CLCII IV-1437; MPII:AF IV-1459

Solid Mandala, The (White) CLCII IV-1438; MPII:BCF IV-1572

Solo (Morris) MPII:NF IV-1696

Some Americans (Tomlinson) MPII:NF IV-1388

Some Do Not. *See* Parade's End

"Some Like Them Cold" (Lardner) MPII:SS V-2173

"Some of Us Had Been Threatening Our Friend Colby" (Barthelme, D.) MPII:SS V-2177

Some People (Nicolson) MP X-6132

Some Prefer Nettles (Tanizaki) CLCII IV-1439; MPII:WF IV-1491

Something Happened (Heller) CLCII IV-1440; MPII:AF IV-1465

"Something Out There" (Gordimer) MPII:SS V-2182

Something Wicked This Way Comes (Bradbury, R.) CLCII IV-1441; MPII:AF IV-1471

Sometimes a Great Notion (Kesey) CLCII IV-1442; MPII:AF IV-1476

Sommersi e i salvati, I. See Drowned and the Saved, The

Son Avenger, The (Undset) CLC II-1058; MP X-6134; MP:EF III-1182

Son of Man (Roa Bastos) CLCII IV-1444; MPII:AF IV-1481

Son of the Middle Border, A (Garland) MP X-6138

"Son smeshnogo cheloveka." See "Dream of a Ridiculous Man, The"

Sonezaki Shinjû (Chikamatsu Monzaemon) CLC II-1059; MP XI-6141

Song of a Goat (Clark) CLCII IV-1444; MPII:D IV-1483

Song of Bernadette, The (Werfel) CLC II-1060; MP XI-6144; MP:EF III-1186

Song of Hiawatha, The (Longfellow) CLC II-1060; MP XI-6147

Song of Roland, The (Unknown) CLC II-1061; MP XI-6150; MP:EF III-1190

Song of Solomon (Morrison) CLCII IV-1445; MPII:AF IV-1485

Song of Songs, The (Sudermann) CLC II-1063; MP XI-6156; MP:EF III-1197

Song of the Lark, The (Cather) CLC II-1064; MP XI-6159; MP:AF III-1184

Song of the World, The (Giono) CLC II-1067; MP XI-6163; MP:EF III-1201

Sonim de Geshichte fun a Liebe. See Enemies

Sonnets from the Portuguese (Browning, E.) MP XI-6168

Sonnets of Shakespeare, The (Shakespeare) MP XI-6170

Sonnets to Orpheus (Rilke) MP XI-6175

"Sonny's Blues" (Baldwin) MPII:SS V-2186

Sons and Lovers (Lawrence, D. H.) CLC II-1067; MP XI-6177; MP:BF III-1468

Sophie's Choice (Styron) CLCII IV-1446; MPII:AF IV-1492

"Sorrow-Acre" (Dinesen) MPII:SS V-2190

Sorrow Beyond Dreams, A (Handke) CLCII IV-1448; MPII:WF IV-1496

Sorrows of Werther, The. See Sorrows of Young Werther, The

Sorrows of Young Werther, The (Goethe) CLC II-1069; MP XI-6182; MP:EF III-1206

Sort of Life, A (Greene) MPII:NF IV-1393

Sotileza (Pereda) CLC II-1070; MP XI-6186; MP:EF III-1211

Sot-Weed Factor, The (Barth) MP XI-6190; MP:AF III-1188

Soulier de satin, Le. See Satin Slipper, The

Souls and Bodies (Lodge) CLCII IV-1448; MPII:BCF IV-1577

Sound and the Fury, The (Faulkner) CLC II-1070; MP XI-6194; MP:AF III-1193

"Sound of Silver, The." See "Black Prince, The"

Sound of the Mountain, The (Kawabata) CLCII IV-1450; MPII:WF IV-1501

Sound of Waves, The (Mishima) MP XI-6199; MP:EF III-1215

Sound-Shadows of the New World (Mehta) MPII:NF IV-1398

Sour Sweet (Mo) CLCII IV-1451; MPII:BCF IV-1581

Source, The (Michener) CLCII IV-1452; MPII:AF IV-1498

Sous le soleil de Satan. *See* Under the Sun of Satan

"South, The" (Borges) MPII:SS V-2194

South Goes North, The. *See* Children of Crisis

South Wind (Douglas, N.) CLC II-1072; MP XI-6202; MP:BF III-1473

Southern Adventure. *See* Story of a Life, The

"Southern Thruway, The" (Cortázar) MPII:SS V-2198

Southpaw, The (Harris, M.) CLCII IV-1455; MPII:AF IV-1505

Sovereignty of Good, The (Murdoch) MPII:NF IV-1402

Space, Time, and Architecture (Giedion) MPII:NF IV-1408

Space Trilogy, The (Lewis, C. S.) CLCII IV-1456; MPII:BCF IV-1588

Spanish Bawd, The. *See* Celestina

Spanish Friar, The (Dryden) CLC II-1073; MP XI-6205

Spanish Gipsy, The (Ford, Middleton, *and* Rowley) CLC II-1074; MP XI-6208

Spanish Rogue, The. *See* Guzmán de Alfarache

Spanish Tragedy, The (Kyd) CLC II-1076; MP XI-6211

"Spaziergang, Der." *See* "Walk, The"

Speak, Memory (Nabokov) MPII:NF IV-1414

Specimen Days (Whitman) MP XI-6216

Speculations About Jakob (Johnson, U.) MP XI-6219; MP:EF III-1218

Speed-the-Plow (Mamet) CLCII IV-1458; MPII:D IV-1486

Speedboat (Adler) CLCII IV-1459; MPII:AF IV-1511

Spell, The (Broch) CLCII IV-1460; MPII:WF IV-1506

Speranza (Delblanc) CLCII IV-1461; MPII:WF IV-1510

"Spinoza of Market Street, The" (Singer) MPII:SS V-2202

Spire, The (Golding) CLCII IV-1462; MPII:BCF IV-1593

Spirit of the Laws, The (Montesquieu) MP XI-6222

Splendeurs et misères des courtisanes. *See* Splendors and Miseries of Courtesans, The

Splendors and Miseries of Courtesans, The (Balzac) CLCII IV-1463; MPII:WF IV-1516

"Split Cherry Tree" (Stuart) MPII:SS V-2206

Spoilers, The (Beach) CLC II-1077; MP XI-6225; MP:AF III-1198

Spoils of Poynton, The (James, H.) CLC II-1078; MP XI-6228; MP:AF III-1202

Spoilt City, The. *See* Balkan trilogy, The

Spokoinoi nochi (Sinyavsky) MPII:WF IV-1524. *See also* Goodnight!

Spöksonaten. *See* Ghost Sonata, The

Spoon River Anthology (Masters) MP XI-6233

Sport of the Gods, The (Dunbar) CLCII IV-1465; MPII:AF IV-1516

Sporting Club, The (McGuane) CLCII IV-1466; MPII:AF IV-1521

"Spotted Horses" (Faulkner) MPII:SS V-2210

Sprightly Running (Wain) MPII:NF IV-1421

Spring Floods. *See* Torrents of Spring, The (Turgenev)

Spring Snow. *See* Sea of Fertility, The

"Spring Victory" (Stuart) MPII:SS V-2214

Spy, The (Cooper) CLC II-1079; MP XI-6236; MP:AF III-1208

Spy in the House of Love, A (Nin) CLCII IV-1468; MPII:AF IV-1527

Spy Who Came in from the Cold, The (le Carré) CLCII IV-1469; MPII:BCF IV-1599

"Sredni Vashtar" (Saki) MPII:SS V-2217

Stand, The (King, S.) CLCII IV-1470; MPII:AF IV-1532

Stanley and the Women (Amis) CLCII IV-1472; MPII:BCF IV-1604

"Stantsionnyi smotritel." *See* "Stationmaster, The"

Star of Satan, The. *See* Under the Sun of Satan

Star of Seville, The (Unknown) CLC II-1079; MP XI-6242

Starik. *See* Old Man, The

Staring at the Sun (Barnes, J.) CLCII IV-1472; MPII:BCF IV-1609

"Starosvetskiye pomeshchiki." *See* "Old-World Landowners"

Starry Ticket, A. *See* Ticket to the Stars, A

Start in Life, A. *See* Debut, The

Starting Out in the Thirties (Kazin) MPII:NF IV-1427

State Fair (Stong) CLC II-1080; MP XI-6246; MP:AF III-1215

"Station-master, The" (Pushkin) MPII:SS V-2220

"Steel Flea, The." *See* "Lefty"

Stellvertreter, Der. *See* Deputy, The

Step. *See* Steppe, The

"Steppe, The" (Chekhov) CLCII IV-1474; MPII:SS V-2224

Steppenwolf (Hesse) CLC II-1081; MP XI-6250; MP:EF III-1221

"Stick of Green Candy, A" (Bowles, J.) MPII:SS V-2228

Stiller. *See* I'm Not Stiller

Stoic, The (Dreiser) CLC II-1081; MP XI-6255; MP:AF III-1219

Stone Angel, The (Laurence) CLCII IV-1475; MPII:BCF IV-1614

"Stone Boy, The" (Berriault) MPII:SS V-2232

Stone Desert (Wast) CLC II-1082; MP XI-6259; MP:AF III-1223

Stones of Venice, The (Ruskin) MP XI-6262

Stop-Time (Conroy) MPII:NF IV-1432

Stopfkuchen. *See* Tubby Schaumann

Storia, La. *See* History

"Storm, The" (Chopin) MPII:SS V-2235

Stormy Weather (Strindberg) CLCII IV-1476; MPII:D IV-1491

"Story by Maupassant, A" (O'Connor, Frank) MPII:SS V-2238

Story of a Bad Boy, The (Aldrich) CLC II-1082; MP XI-6265; MP:AF III-1227

Story of a Country Town, The (Howe) CLC II-1083; MP XI-6268; MP:AF III-1231

Story of a Life, The (Paustovsky) MPII:NF IV-1437

Story of an African Farm, The (Schreiner) CLC II-1084; MP XI-6272; MP:EF III-1227

"Story of an Hour, The" (Chopin) MPII:SS V-2241

Story of Burnt Njal, The (Unknown) CLC II-1085; MP XI-6276; MP:EF III-1231

Story of Gösta Berling, The (Lagerlöf) CLC II-1087; MP XI-6281; MP:EF III-1236

Story of Manon Lescaut and the Chevalier des Grieux. *See* Manon Lescaut

Story of My Boyhood and Youth, The (Muir) MP XI-6286

"Story of My Dovecot, The" (Babel) MPII:SS V-2244

"Story of Serapion, The" (Hoffmann) MPII:SS V-2248

Story of the Guitar (Kao Tse-ch'eng) CLC II-1088; MP XI-6288

Story Teller's Story, A (Anderson, S.) MP XI-6291

Storyteller, The (Benjamin) MPII:NF IV-1447

Storyteller (Silko) MPII:NF IV-1442

Strait Is the Gate (Gide) CLCII IV-1477; MPII:WF IV-1529

Strange Case of Dr. Jekyll and Mr. Hyde. *See* Dr. Jekyll and Mr. Hyde

Strange Interlude (O'Neill) CLC II-1089; MP XI-6294

"Strange Ride of Morrowbie Jukes, The" (Kipling) MPII:SS V-2252

Strange Stories from a Chinese Studio (P'u Sung-ling) MP XI-6299; MP:EF III-1241

Stranger, The (Camus) MP XI-6301; MP:EF III-1244

Stranger in a Strange Land (Heinlein) CLCII IV-1478; MPII:AF IV-1536

Strangers All Are Gone, The. *See* To Keep the Ball Rolling

Strangers and Brothers (Snow) CLCII IV-1480; MPII:BCF IV-1619. *See also* Affair, The; Conscience of the Rich, The; Corridors of Power; George Passant; Homecomings; Last Things; Light and the Dark, The; Masters, The; New Men, The; Sleep of Reason, The; *and* Time of Hope

Streamers (Rabe) CLCII IV-1483; MPII:D IV-1496

"Street of Crocodiles, The" (Schulz) MPII:SS V-2256

Street Scene (Rice) CLC II-1090; MP XI-6304

Streetcar Named Desire, A (Williams, T.) MP XI-6308

Strife (Galsworthy) CLC II-1091; MP XI-6311

Strike the Father Dead (Wain) CLCII IV-1484; MPII:BCF IV-1633

"Strong Horse Tea" (Walker) MPII:SS V-2259

Strong Wind (Asturias) CLCII IV-1485; MPII:AF IV-1541

Structure of Scientific Revolution, The (Kuhn) MPII:NF IV-1452

Studies in Classic American Literature (Lawrence, D. H.) MP XI-6314

Studies on Hysteria (Breuer *and* Freud) MP XI-6317

Studs Lonigan: A Trilogy (Farrell) CLC II-1091; MP XI-6320; MP:AF III-1235

Study in Scarlet, A (Doyle) CLC II-1092; MP XI-6322; MP:BF III-1477

Study of History, A (Toynbee) MP XI-6326

Stunde der wahren Empfindung, Die. *See* Moment of True Feeling, A

Subject Was Roses, The (Gilroy) CLCII IV-1486; MPII:D IV-1503

Such Is My Beloved (Callaghan) CLCII IV-1487; MPII:BCF IV-1638

Suddenly Last Summer (Williams, T.) CLCII IV-1488; MPII:D IV-1508

Sugar Cane Cycle, The. *See* Plantation Boy

"Suicide Club, The" (Stevenson) MPII:SS V-2262

Suicide's Wife, The (Madden) CLCII IV-1489; MPII:AF IV-1545

Sula (Morrison) CLCII IV-1490; MPII:AF IV-1550

Summa Theologica (Aquinas) MP XI-6329

Summer and Smoke (Williams, T.) CLCII IV-1492; MPII:D IV-1514

"Summer Evening" (Boyle, K.) MPII:SS V-2267

"Summer Night" (Bowen) MPII:SS V-2271

"Summer of the Beautiful White Horse, The" (Saroyan) MPII:SS V-2275

Summer of the Seventeenth Doll (Lawler) CLCII IV-1493; MPII:D IV-1520

Summing Up, The (Maugham) MP XI-6332

"Sun" (Lawrence) MPII:SS V-2278

Sun Also Rises, The (Hemingway) CLC II-1093; MP XI-6335; MP:AF III-1238

Sun and Steel (Mishima) MPII:NF IV-1457

Suna no onna. *See* Woman in the Dunes, The

Sunday of Life, The (Queneau) CLCII IV-1494; MPII:WF IV-1533

Sunken Bell, The (Hauptmann) CLC II-1094; MP XI-6341

Sunlight Dialogues, The (Gardner) CLCII IV-1495; MPII:AF IV-1555

Sunset and Evening Star. *See* Mirror in My House

Sunset Song. *See* Scots Quair, A

"Supper at Elsinore, The" (Dinesen) MPII:SS V-2281

Suppliants, The (Aeschylus) CLC II-1094; MP XI-6345

Suppliants, The (Euripides) CLC II-1096; MP XI-6349

Suppositi, I (Ariosto) CLC II-1097; MP XI-6352

"Supremacy of the Hunza, The" (Greenberg) MPII:SS V-2285

"Sur, El." *See* "South, The"

"Sur" (Le Guin) MPII:SS V-2288

Surfacing (Atwood) CLCII IV-1498; MPII:BCF IV-1643

Surprised by Joy (Lewis, C. S.) MPII:NF IV-1462

Surry of Eagle's-Nest (Cooke) CLC II-1097; MP XI-6355; MP:AF III-1244

Sursis, Le. *See* Roads to Freedom, The

Survival in Auschwitz. *See* If This Is a Man

Survivor, The (Keneally) CLCII IV-1499; MPII:BCF IV-1649

Sutter's Gold (Cendrars) CLCII IV-1500; MPII:WF IV-1538

Suttree (McCarthy, C.) CLCII IV-1501; MPII:AF IV-1559

Swallow Barn (Kennedy) CLC II-1098; MP XI-6359; MP:AF III-1248

Swamp Angel (Wilson, E.) CLCII IV-1503; MPII:BCF IV-1654

Swan Villa, The (Walser) CLCII IV-1504; MPII:WF IV-1542

"Sweat" (Hurston) MPII:SS V-2293

Sweet Bird of Youth (Williams, T.) CLCII IV-1505; MPII:D IV-1524

Sweet Dove Died, The (Pym) CLCII IV-1507; MPII:BCF IV-1659

Sweet-Vendor, The. *See* Vendor of Sweets, The

"Swimmer, The" (Cheever) MPII:SS V-2297

Swiss Family Robinson, The (Wyss *and* Wyss) CLC II-1099; MP XI-6363; MP:EF III-1248

Sword in the Stone, The. *See* Once and Future King, The

Sword of Honour (Waugh) CLCII IV-1508; MPII:BCF IV-1664

System of Dante's Hell, The (Baraka) CLCII IV-1510; MPII:AF IV-1564

Szachinszach. *See* Shah of Shahs

T

"Tables of the Law, The" (Yeats) MPII:SS V-2300

Tade kuu mushi. *See* Some Prefer Nettles

Tagebuch, 1946-1949, *and* Tagebuch, 1966-1971. *See* Sketchbook, 1946-1949, *and* Sketchbook, 1966-1971

Tagebücher von Paul Klee. *See* Diaries of Paul Klee, The

Taiyö to tetsu. *See* Sun and Steel

Take a Girl Like You (Amis) CLCII IV-1511; MPII:BCF IV-1671

Takeover, The (Spark) CLCII IV-1513; MPII:BCF IV-1677

Tale of a Tub, A (Swift) MP XI-6366; MP:BF III-1481

Tale of Genji, The (Murasaki Shikibu) CLC II-1100; MP XI-6369; MP:EF III-1252

"Tale of the Squint-eyed Left-handed Gunsmith from Tula and the Steel Flea, The." *See* "Lefty"

Tale of Two Cities, A (Dickens) CLC II-1100; MP XI-6373; MP:BF III-1485

Tales of Arabian Nights, The. *See* Arabian Nights' Entertainments, The

Tales of Ise (Arihara no Narihira) MP XI-6378; MP:EF III-1257

Tales of Jacob, The. *See* Joseph and His Brothers

Tales of Soldiers and Civilians (Bierce) MP XI-6381; MP:AF III-1252

Tales of Uncle Remus (Harris) MP XI-6384; MP:AF III-1256

Tali` al-shajarah, Ya. *See* Tree Climber, The

Talisman, The (Scott, Sir W.) CLC II-1102; MP XI-6387; MP:BF III-1490

Talley's Folly (Wilson, L.) CLCII IV-1514; MPII:D IV-1529

Tamar (Jeffers) CLC II-1103; MP XI-6393

Tamburlaine the Great (Marlowe) CLC II-1104; MP XI-6396

Taming of the Shrew, The (Shakespeare) CLC II-1106; MP XI-6401

Tango (Mrożek) CLCII IV-1515; MPII:D IV-1534

Taps for Private Tussie (Stuart) CLC II-1107; MP XI-6405; MP:AF III-1259

"Taqāsīm al-layl wa-al-nahār." *See* Mudun al-milh

Taras Bulba (Gogol) CLC II-1108; MP XI-6408; MP:EF III-1260

Tarka the Otter (Williamson) MP XI-6411; MP:BF III-1497

Tarr (Lewis, W.) CLC II-1109; MP XI-6413; MP:BF III-1500

Tartar Steppe, The (Buzzati) CLCII IV-1516; MPII:WF IV-1548

Tartarin of Tarascon (Daudet) CLC II-1110; MP XI-6417; MP:EF III-1264

Tartuffe (Molière) CLC II-1111; MP XI-6421

Task, The (Cowper) MP XI-6425

Taste of Honey, A (Delaney) CLCII IV-1517; MPII:D IV-1538

"Tatuana's Tale" (Asturias) MPII:SS V-2305

Tea and Sympathy (Anderson, R.) CLCII IV-1518; MPII:D IV-1543

Teachings of Don Juan, The (Castaneda) MPII:NF IV-1468

Teahouse of the August Moon, The (Patrick) CLCII IV-1519; MPII:D IV-1548

Technique, La. *See* Technological Society, The

Technological Society, The (Ellul) MPII:NF IV-1473

Telegraph, The. *See* Lucien Leuwen

"Tell Me a Riddle" (Olsen) MPII:SS V-2308

Tell Me That You Love Me, Junie Moon (Kellogg) CLCII IV-1520; MPII:AF IV-1568

"Tell-Tale Heart, The" (Poe) MPII:SS V-2312

"Tema del traidor y del héroe." *See* "Theme of the Traitor and the Hero"

Tempest, The (Shakespeare) CLC II-1112; MP XI-6427

Temple, The (Herbert) MP XI-6432

Temple Beau, The (Fielding) CLC II-1113; MP XI-6435

Temple of Dawn, The. *See* Sea of Fertility, The

Temple of the Golden Pavilion, The (Mishima) CLCII IV-1522; MPII:WF IV-1554

Temporary Kings. *See* Dance to the Music of Time, A

Temptation (Havel) CLCII IV-1523; MPII:D IV-1554

Temptation of Saint Anthony, The (Flaubert) CLC II-1114; MP XI-6438; MP:EF III-1268

Ten North Frederick (O'Hara) CLCII IV-1524; MPII:AF IV-1573

Tenant of Wildfell Hall, The (Brontë, A.) CLC II-1115; MP XI-6442; MP:BF III-1505

Tenants of Moonbloom, The (Wallant) MP XI-6445; MP:AF III-1263

Tenda dos milagres. *See* Tent of Miracles

Tender Is the Night (Fitzgerald, F.) CLC II-1117; MP XI-6448; MP:AF III-1266

"Tender Shoot, The" (Colette) MPII:SS V-2316

"Tendron, Le." *See* "Tender Shoot, The"

Tennin gosui. *See* Sea of Fertility, The

Tennis Players, The (Gustafsson) CLCII IV-1525; MPII:WF IV-1560

Tennisspelarna. *See* Tennis Players, The

Tent of Miracles (Amado) CLCII IV-1526; MPII:AF IV-1578

Tents of Wickedness, The (De Vries) CLCII IV-1528; MPII:AF IV-1583

Terms of Endearment (McMurtry) CLCII IV-1529; MPII:AF IV-1587

Terra Nostra (Fuentes) CLCII IV-1530; MPII:AF IV-1593

Terras do sem fin. *See* Violent Land, The

"Territory" (Leavitt) MPII:SS V-2320

Teseide, La (Boccaccio) MP XI-6453

Tess of the D'Urbervilles (Hardy) CLC II-1118; MP XI-6457; MP:BF III-1509

Testament of Experience (Brittain) MPII:NF IV-1479

Testament of Friendship (Brittain) MPII:NF IV-1479

Testimony (Shostakovich) MPII:NF IV-1485

Thaddeus of Warsaw (Porter, J.) CLC II-1120; MP XI-6462; MP:BF III-1514

"Thank You, M'am" (Hughes) MPII:SS VI-2323

That Awful Mess on Via Merulana (Gadda) CLCII IV-1532; MPII:WF IV-1565

"That Evening Sun" (Faulkner) MPII:SS VI-2325

That Hideous Strength. *See* Space trilogy, The

That Uncertain Feeling (Amis) MP XI-6466; MP:BF III-1519

That Voice (Pinget) CLCII IV-1532; MPII:WF IV-1570

Thaw, The (Ehrenburg) CLCII IV-1533; MPII:WF IV-1575

Theatre and Its Double, The (Artaud) MPII:NF IV-1490

Théâtre et son double, Le. *See* Theater and Its Double, The

Thebais, The (Statius) MP XI-6469

Their Eyes Were Watching God (Hurston) CLCII IV-1534; MPII:AF IV-1598

them (Oates) CLCII IV-1535; MPII:AF IV-1604

"Theme of the Traitor and the Hero" (Borges) MPII:SS VI-2329

Theophilus North (Wilder) CLCII IV-1536; MPII:AF IV-1609

Theory of the Leisure Class, The (Veblen) MP XI-6471

There Are Crimes and Crimes (Strindberg) CLC II-1121; MP XI-6473

There Is a Tree More Ancient than Eden (Forrest) CLCII IV-1538; MPII:AF IV-1615

"There Will Come Soft Rains" (Bradbury)
MPII:SS VI-2333

Thérèse (Mauriac, F.) CLC II-1121; MP
XI-6477; MP:EF III-1273

Thérèse Raquin (Zola) CLCII IV-1539;
MPII:WF IV-1579

These the Companions (Davie) MPII:NF
IV-1495

These Thousand Hills (Guthrie) CLCII IV-
1541; MPII:AF IV-1620

Thesmophoriazusae, The (Aristophanes)
CLC II-1122; MP XI-6483

"They" (Kipling) MPII:SS VI-2337

They Shoot Horses, Don't They? (McCoy)
MP XI-6486; MP:AF III-1271

Thin Man, The (Hammett) CLC II-1123;
MP XI-6489; MP:AF III-1275

Thin Red Line, The (Jones, J.) CLCII IV-
1542; MPII:AF IV-1624

Things as They Are. See Caleb Williams

Things Fall Apart (Achebe) CLCII IV-
1544; MPII:BCF IV-1681

Third and Oak: The Laundromat (Norman)
CLCII IV-1546; MPII:D IV-1562

"Third Bank of the River, The"
(Guimarães Rosa) MPII:SS VI-2341

Third Factory (Shklovsky) CLCII IV-1546;
MPII:WF IV-1584

Third Life of Grange Copeland, The
(Walker, A.) CLCII IV-1547; MPII:AF
IV-1629

Third Policeman, The (O'Brien, F.) CLCII
IV-1548; MPII:BCF IV-1686

"Third Prize, The" (Coppard) MPII:SS VI-
2344

Thirties, The (Wilson) MPII:NF IV-1500

Thirty-nine Steps, The (Buchan) CLC II-
1124; MP XI-6493; MP:BF III-1523

This Above All (Knight) CLC II-1124; MP
XI-6497; MP:BF III-1528

This Business of Living. See Burning
Brand, The

This Side of Paradise (Fitzgerald, F. S.)
CLCII IV-1550; MPII:AF IV-1635

This Sporting Life (Storey) CLCII IV-
1551; MPII:BCF IV-1690

This Sunday (Donoso) CLCII IV-1552;
MPII:AF IV-1630

"This Way for the Gas, Ladies and
Gentlemen" (Borowski) MPII:SS VI-
2348

Thought and Language (Vygotsky)
MPII:NF IV-1507

Thousand and One Nights, The. See
Arabian Nights' Entertainments, The

Thousand Cranes (Kawabata) CLCII IV-
1554; MPII:WF IV-1589

Thread That Runs So True, The (Stuart)
MPII:NF IV-1513

Three Black Pennys, The (Hergesheimer)
CLC II-1126; MP XI-6500; MP:AF III-
1279

Three-Cornered Hat, The (Alarcón) CLC
II-1126; MP XI-6505; MP:EF III-1286

Three-Cornered World, The (Natsume)
CLCII IV-1555; MPII:WF IV-1595

"Three-Day Blow, The" (Hemingway)
MPII:SS VI-2358

"Three Deaths" (Tolstoy) MPII:SS VI-
2351

"Three Hermits, The" (Tolstoy) MPII:SS
VI-2355

365 Days (Glasser) MPII:NF IV-1518

Three Lives (Stein) CLCII IV-1555;
MPII:AF IV-1643

Three Marias, The (Queiroz) CLCII IV-
1557; MPII:AF IV-1648

Three Men in a Boat (Jerome) CLC II-
1127; MP XI-6508; MP:BF III-1532

"Three Mendicants." See "Three Hermits,
The"

Three Musketeers, The (Dumas, père)
CLC II-1127; MP XI-6511; MP:EF III-
1279

"Three Old Men, The." See "Three
Hermits, The"

Three Sisters, The (Chekhov) CLC II-
1129; MP XI-6518

Three Sisters, The (Sinclair) CLCII IV-
1558; MPII:BCF IV-1695

Three Soldiers (Dos Passos) CLC II-1130;
MP XI-6522; MP:AF III-1285

Three Trapped Tigers (Cabrera Infante) CLCII IV-1559; MPII:AF IV-1652

Threepenny Opera, The (Brecht) CLCII IV-1560; MPII:D IV-1568

Through the Looking-Glass (Carroll) CLC II-1130; MP XI-6526; MP:BF III-1536

"Thrown Away" (Kipling) MPII:SS VI-2362

Thus Spake Zarathustra (Nietzsche) MP XI-6532

Thyestes (Seneca) CLC II-1131; MP XI-6535

Tía Julia y el escribidor, La. *See* Aunt Julia and the Scriptwriter

Ticket to the Stars, A (Aksyonov) CLCII IV-1561; MPII:WF IV-1600

"Tickets, Please" (Lawrence) MPII:SS VI-2365

Tidings Brought to Mary, The (Claudel) CLCII IV-1563; MPII:D IV-1574

Tierras flacas, Las. *See* Lean Lands, The

Tieta, the Goat Girl (Amado) CLCII IV-1564; MPII:AF IV-1657

Tiêta do Agreste. *See* Tieta, the Goat Girl

Tiger at the Gates (Giraudoux) MP XI-6539

Tīh, al-. *See* Mudun al-milh

Till We Have Faces (Lewis, C. S.) CLCII IV-1565; MPII:BCF IV-1700

Tilted Cross, The (Porter) CLCII IV-1566; MPII:BCF IV-1705

Time and the Conways (Priestley) CLCII IV-1567; MPII:D IV-1579

Time and Western Man (Lewis, W.) MPII:NF IV-1523

Time Machine, The (Wells) CLC II-1131; MP XI-6542; MP:BF III-1543

Time of Hope. *See* Strangers and Brothers

Time of Indifference, The (Moravia) CLCII IV-1568; MPII:WF IV-1605

Time of Man, The (Roberts, E.) CLC II-1132; MP XI-6545; MP:AF III-1289

Time of the Hero, The (Vargas Llosa) CLCII IV-1569; MPII:AF IV-1663

Time of Your Life, The (Saroyan) CLCII IV-1571; MPII:D IV-1585

"Time the Tiger" (Lewis, W.) MPII:SS VI-2369

Time to Dance, No Time to Weep, A (Godden) MPII:NF IV-1527

Time Without Bells. *See* Silesian Tetralogy, The

Timebends (Miller) MPII:NF IV-1533

Timon of Athens (Shakespeare) CLC II-1133; MP XI-6549

Tin Drum, The (Grass) MP XI-6553; MP:EF III-1290

Tinker, Tailor, Soldier, Spy (le Carré) CLCII II-694; MPII:BCF IV-1710

Tiny Alice (Albee) CLCII IV-1572; MPII:D IV-1590

Tirra Lirra by the River (Anderson, J.) CLCII IV-1573; MPII:BCF IV-1716

'Tis Pity She's a Whore (Ford, J.) CLC II-1134; MP XI-6556

Titan, The (Dreiser) CLC II-1135; MP XI-6560; MP:AF III-1293

Titan (Jean Paul) CLCII IV-1574; MPII:WF IV-1610

Titus Alone. *See* Gormenghast trilogy, The

Titus Andronicus (Shakespeare) CLC II-1135; MP XI-6565

Titus Groan. *See* Gormenghast trilogy, The

"Tlön, Uqbar, Orbis Tertius" (Borges) MPII:SS VI-2373

To Be a Pilgrim (Cary) CLC II-1137; MP XI-6570; MP:BF III-1547

"To Build a Fire" (London) MPII:SS VI-2377

To Have and Have Not (Hemingway) CLCII IV-1577; MPII:AF IV-1668

To Have and to Hold (Johnston) CLCII IV-1578; MPII:AF IV-1673

To Keep the Ball Rolling (Powell) MPII:NF IV-1538

To Kill a Mockingbird (Lee) CLCII IV-1580; MPII:AF IV-1677

To Let. *See* Forsyte Saga, The

To the Land of the Cattails (Appelfeld) CLCII IV-1581; MPII:WF IV-1616

To the Lighthouse (Woolf) CLC II-1138; MP XI-6573; MP:BF III-1551

Tobacco Road (Caldwell) CLC II-1140; MP XI-6578; MP:AF III-1299

Tobacco Road (Kirkland) CLCII IV-1582; MPII:D IV-1596

Tobias Trilogy, The (Lagerkvist) CLCII IV-1583; MPII:WF IV-1623

"Tod in Venedig, Der." See "Death in Venice"

Todo verdor perecerá. See All Green Shall Perish

"Together and Apart" (Woolf) MPII:SS VI-2381

Toilers of the Sea, The (Hugo) CLC II-1140; MP XI-6581; MP:EF III-1293

Tokaido Circuit. See Hizakurige

"Tokyo hakkei." See "Eight Views of Tokyo"

Told by an Idiot (Macaulay) CLCII IV-1585; MPII:BCF IV-1721

Tom and Jerry. See Life in London

Tom Brown's School Days (Hughes, T.) CLC II-1141; MP XI-6585; MP:BF III-1556

Tom Burke of Ours (Lever) CLC II-1141; MP XI-6588; MP:BF III-1560

Tom Cringle's Log (Scott, M.) CLC II-1142; MP XI-6594; MP:BF III-1567

Tom Jones (Fielding) CLC II-1143; MP XI-6598; MP:BF III-1571

Tom Sawyer. See Adventures of Tom Sawyer, The

Tom Thumb the Great (Fielding) CLC II-1146; MP XI-6609

Tomb for Boris Davidovich, A (Kiš) CLCII IV-1586; MPII:WF IV-1629

"Tommy" (Wideman) MPII:SS VI-2385

"Tomorrow and Tomorrow and So Forth" (Updike) MPII:SS VI-2389

Tongue Set Free, The (Canetti) MPII:NF IV-1546

Tonight We Improvise (Pirandello) CLCII IV-1588; MPII:D IV-1601

"Tonio Kröger" (Mann) MPII:SS VI-2393

Tono-Bungay (Wells) CLC II-1146; MP XI-6613; MP:BF III-1578

Tooth of Crime, The (Shepard) CLCII IV-1589; MPII:D IV-1607

Top Girls (Churchill) CLCII IV-1591; MPII:D IV-1613

Torch in My Ear, The (Canetti) MPII:NF IV-1546

Torch Song Trilogy (Fierstein) CLCII IV-1592; MPII:D IV-1618

Tor-ha-pela'ot. See Age of Wonders, The

Torrents of Spring, The (Hemingway) CLCII IV-1593; MPII:AF IV-1682

Torrents of Spring, The (Turgenev) CLCII IV-1594; MPII:WF IV-1634

Tortilla Flat (Steinbeck) CLCII IV-1595; MPII:AF IV-1688

Totem and Taboo (Freud) MPII:NF IV-1553

Totem und Tabu. See Totem and Taboo

Totenschiff, Das. See Death Ship, The

Tour du monde en quatre-vingts jours, Le. See Around the World in Eighty Days

Tower of Babel, The. See Auto-da-Fé

Tower of London, The (Ainsworth) CLC II-1148; MP XI-6618; MP:BF III-1583

Towers of Silence, The. See Raj Quartet, The

Towers of Trebizond, The (Macaulay) CLCII IV-1596; MPII:BCF IV-1726

Town, The (Faulkner) CLC II-1149; MP XI-6623; MP:AF III-1302

Town, The (Richter) CLC II-1150; MP XI-6628; MP:AF III-1308

"Town and Country Lovers" (Gordimer) MPII:SS VI-2397

"Town Poor, The" (Jewett) MPII:SS VI-2401

Tra donne sole. See Among Women Only

Trachinai. See Women of Trachis

Track of the Cat, The (Clark, Walter) CLC II-1151; MP XI-6633; MP:AF III-1313

Tragédie du Roi Christophe, La. See Tragedy of King Christophe, The

Tragedy of King Christophe, The (Césaire) CLCII IV-1598; MPII:D IV-1623

Tragic Muse, The (James, H.) MP XI-6636; MP:AF III-1317

Tragic Sense of Life in Men and in Peoples, The (Unamuno y Jugo) MP XI-6640

Traición de Rita Hayworth, La. *See* Betrayed by Rita Hayworth

Traitor, The (Shirley) CLC II-1151; MP XI-6643

Transfiguration of Benno Blimpie, The (Innaurato) CLCII IV-1599; MPII:D IV-1629

Transformation of Lucius Apuleius of Madaura. *See* Golden Ass of Lucius Apuleius, The

Translations (Friel) CLCII IV-1600; MPII:D IV-1634

Transposed Heads, The (Mann) CLCII IV-1602; MPII:WF IV-1639

Trap, The. *See* Pilgrimage

Travelling North (Williamson) CLCII IV-1603; MPII:D IV-1639

Travels in Arabia Deserta (Doughty) MP XI-6647

Travels into Several Remote Nations of the World, in Four Parts, by Lemuel Gulliver, First Surgeon, and then a Captain of Several Ships. *See* Gulliver's Travels

Travels of Lao Ts'an, The (Liu E) CLCII IV-1604; MPII:WF IV-1646

Travels of Marco Polo, The (Polo) MP XI-6650

Travels to the Interior Districts of Africa (Park) MP XI-6656

Travels with a Donkey (Stevenson) MP XI-6659

Travesties (Stoppard) CLCII IV-1606; MPII:D IV-1643

Travnička hronika. *See* Bosnian Chronicle

Treasure Hunt. *See* Book of Bebb, The

Treasure Island (Stevenson) CLC II-1152; MP XI-6662; MP:BF III-1589

Treatise on Painting. *See* Notebooks of Leonardo da Vinci, The

Treatises of Cicero, The (Cicero) MP XI-6669

"Tree. A Rock. A Cloud., A" (McCullers) MPII:SS VI-2404

Tree Climber, The (Hakim) CLCII IV-1607; MPII:D IV-1648

Tree Grows in Brooklyn, A (Smith, B.) CLC II-1152; MP XI-6672; MP:AF III-1322

Tree of Knowledge, The (Baroja) CLCII IV-1608; MPII:WF IV-1650

"Tree of Knowledge, The" (James, H.) MPII:SS VI-2407

Tree of Man, The (White, P.) MP XI-6676; MP:BF III-1597

Tree of the Folkungs, The (Heidenstam) CLC II-1153; MP XI-6679; MP:EF III-1297

Trees, The (Richter) CLC II-1154; MP XI-6683; MP:AF III-1326

Treffen in Telgte, Das. *See* Meeting at Telgte, The

Trembling of the Veil, The. *See* Autobiography of William Butler Yeats, The

Tremor of Intent (Burgess) CLCII IV-1609; MPII:BCF IV-1732

Três Marias, As. *See* Three Marias, The

Tres novelitas burguesas. *See* Sacred Families

Tres tristes tigres. *See* Three Trapped Tigers

Tretya fabrika. *See* Third Factory

"Tri smerti." *See* "Three Deaths"

"Tri startsa." *See* "Three Hermits, The"

Trial, The (Kafka) CLC II-1155; MP XI-6687; MP:EF III-1302

Trial Begins, The (Sinyavsky) CLCII IV-1610; MPII:WF IV-1656

Trial by Jury (Gilbert) CLC II-1156; MP XI-6692

Tribute to Freud (H. D.) MPII:NF IV-1558

Trick of the Ga Bolga, The (McGinley) CLCII IV-1612; MPII:BCF IV-1737

Trick to Catch the Old One, A (Middleton) CLC II-1156; MP XI-6695

Trickster, The (Plautus) CLC II-1157; MP XI-6698

"Trifling Occurrence, A" (Chekhov) MPII:SS VI-2411

Trilby (du Maurier, G.) CLC II-1158; MP XI-6701; MP:BF III-1600

Trilogy, The (Beckett) MPII:BCF IV-1742; MPII:WF IV-1661. *See also* Unnamable, The

Triptych (Simon, C.) CLCII IV-1613; MPII:WF IV-1666

"Tristan" (Mann) MPII:SS VI-2417

Tristan and Isolde (Strassburg) CLC II-1159; MP XI-6705

Tristes Tropiques (Lévi-Strauss) MPII:NF IV-1563

Tristram (Robinson, E.) MP XI-6709

Tristram Shandy (Sterne) CLC II-1159; MP XI-6712; MP:BF III-1605

Triton (Delany) CLCII IV-1614; MPII:AF IV-1692

Triumph of Death, The (D'Annunzio) CLC II-1161; MP XI-6717; MP:EF III-1307

Troilus and Cressida (Shakespeare) CLC II-1162; MP XI-6720

Troilus and Criseyde (Chaucer) CLC II-1164; MP XI-6725

Trojan Women, The (Euripides) CLC II-1164; MP XI-6729

Troops Return, The. *See* November 1918

Tropic of Cancer (Miller, H.) CLCII IV-1615; MPII:AF IV-1697

Tropic of Capricorn (Miller, H.) MP XI-6733; MP:AF III-1330

Trouble in Mind (Childress) CLCII IV-1616; MPII:D IV-1654

Troubled Sleep. *See* Roads to Freedom, The

Troubles (Farrell) CLCII IV-1617; MPII:BCF IV-1747

Trout Fishing in America (Brautigan) CLCII IV-1619; MPII:AF IV-1702

True Confessions of an Albino Terrorist, The (Breytenbach) MPII:NF IV-1569

True History, The (Lucian) MP XI-6737; MP:EF III-1311

True Story of Ah Q, The (Lu Hsün) CLCII IV-1620; MPII:WF IV-1671

True West (Shepard) CLCII IV-1621; MPII:D IV-1660

"Trumpet, The" (de la Mare) MPII:SS VI-2421

"Truth and Lies" (Price) MPII:SS VI-2425

Truth and Life of Myth, The (Duncan) MPII:NF IV-1574

Truth and Method (Gadamer) MPII:NF IV-1580

Truth Suspected (Ruiz de Alarcón) CLC II-1166; MP XI-6740

Tubby Schaumann (Raabe) CLCII IV-1622; MPII:WF IV-1676

Tueur sans gages. *See* Killer, The

Túnel, El. *See* Outsider, The (Sábato)

Tung-chou lieh-kuo chih. *See* Lieh-kuo chih

Tunnel, The. *See* Pilgrimage

Turcaret (Le Sage) CLC II-1166; MP XI-6744

Turn of the Screw, The (James, H.) CLC II-1167; MP XI-6748; MP:AF III-1335

Turvey (Birney) CLCII IV-1623; MPII:BCF IV-1751

Tutti i nostri ieri. *See* All Our Yesterdays

Twelfth Night (Shakespeare) CLC II-1168; MP XII-6753

Twelve Years (Agee) MPII:NF IV-1586

Twenty-seven Wagons Full of Cotton (Williams, T.) CLCII IV-1624; MPII:D IV-1665

"Twenty-six Men and a Girl" (Gorky) MPII:SS VI-2429

Twenty Thousand Leagues Under the Sea (Verne) CLC II-1169; MP XII-6758; MP:EF III-1315

Twenty Years After (Dumas, *père*) CLC II-1169; MP XII-6762; MP:EF III-1319

Twice Round the Black Church (Clarke) MPII:NF IV-1592

Twilight in Italy (Lawrence, D. H.) MP XII-6766

"Two Drovers, The" (Scott) MPII:SS VI-2432

"Two Elenas, The" (Fuentes) MPII:SS VI-2436

Two Essays on Analytical Psychology (Jung) MP XII-6769

Two for the Seesaw (Gibson) CLCII IV-1625; MPII:D IV-1670

"Two Gallants" (Joyce) MPII:SS VI-2439

Two Gentlemen of Verona (Shakespeare) CLC II-1170; MP XII-6772

"Two Little Soldiers" (Maupassant) MPII:SS VI-2442

"Two Lovely Beasts (O'Flaherty) MPII:SS VI-2445

Two Noble Kinsmen, The (Shakespeare and Fletcher) CLC II-1172; MP XII-6775

Two Solitudes (MacLennan) CLCII IV-1625; MPII:BCF IV-1756

2001: A Space Odyssey (Clarke, Arthur C.) CLCII IV-1627; MPII:AF IV-1707

Two Thousand Seasons (Armah) CLCII IV-1628; MPII:BCF IV-1761

Two Towers, The (Tolkien) MP XII-6778; MP:BF III-1611

Two Women (Moravia) MP XII-6782; MP:EF III-1323

Two Worlds (Daiches) MPII:NF IV-1597

Two Years Before the Mast (Dana) MP XII-6785

Typee (Melville) CLC II-1173; MP XII-6791; MP:AF III-1340

"Typhoon" (Conrad) CLCII IV-1629; MPII:SS VI-2448

Tzili (Appelfeld) CLCII IV-1630; MPII:WF IV-1682

U

Ubu Roi (Jarry) CLCII IV-1631; MPII:D IV-1676

"Uezdnyi lekar." *See* "District Doctor, The"

Ugly Duchess, The (Feuchtwanger) CLC II-1174; MP XII-6796; MP:EF III-1326

Ukhdūd, al-. *See* Mudun al-milh

"Ulica krokodyli." *See* "Street of Crocodiles, The"

Ulitka na sklone. *See* Snail on the Slope, The

Última niebla, La. *See* Final Mist, The

Ultima Thule. *See* Fortunes of Richard Mahony, The

Ultramarine (Lowry) CLCII IV-1632; MPII:BCF IV-1766

Ulysses (Joyce) CLC II-1175; MP XII-6799; MP:BF III-1616

Umarła Klasa. *See* Dead Class, The

Un di Velt hot geshvign. *See* Night

Un día en la vida. *See* One Day of Life

Unbearable Bassington, The (Saki) CLC II-1177; MP XII-6804; MP:BF III-1622

Unbearable Lightness of Being, The (Kundera) CLCII IV-1633; MPII:WF IV-1689

"Uncle" (Narayan) MPII:SS VI-2452

Uncle Remus. *See* Tales of Uncle Remus

Uncle Silas (Le Fanu) CLC II-1177; MP XII-6808; MP:BF III-1627

Uncle Tom's Cabin (Stowe) CLC II-1178; MP XII-6814; MP:AF III-1345

Uncle Vanya (Chekhov) CLC II-1179; MP XII-6818

"Uncle Wiggily in Connecticut" (Salinger) MPII:SS VI-2457

Unconditional Surrender. *See* Sword of Honour

"Under a Glass Bell" (Nin) MPII:SS VI-2461

Under Fire (Barbusse) CLC II-1180; MP XII-6822; MP:EF III-1330

Under Milk Wood (Thomas) MP XII-6825

Under the Greenwood Tree (Hardy) CLC II-1181; MP XII-6829; MP:BF III-1634

"Under the Rose" (Pynchon) MPII:SS VI-2464

Under the Sun of Satan (Bernanos) CLCII IV-1634; MPII:WF IV-1694

Under the Volcano (Lowry) MP XII-6833; MP:BF III-1639

Under the Yoke (Vazov) CLC II-1182; MP XII-6836; MP:EF III-1334

Under Two Flags (Ouida) CLC II-1183; MP XII-6840; MP:BF III-1643

Under Western Eyes (Conrad) CLC II-1184; MP XII-6844; MP:BF III-1647

Underdogs, The (Azuela) CLC II-1185; MP XII-6847; MP:AF III-1349

Underground Man, The (Macdonald) CLCII IV-1636; MPII:AF IV-1711

Understanding Media (McLuhan) MPII:NF IV-1601

Undine (La Motte-Fouqué) CLC II-1186; MP XII-6852; MP:EF III-1338

Undying Grass, The (Kemal) CLCII IV-1718; MPII:WF IV-1754

Unfinished Woman, An (Hellman) MPII:NF IV-1607

Unfortunate Traveller, The (Nash) CLC II-1186; MP XII-6855; MP:BF III-1650

Unframed Originals (Merwin) MPII:NF IV-1612

Unholy Loves (Oates) CLCII IV-1637; MPII:AF IV-1717

Unhuman Tour. *See* Three-Cornered World, The

Unicorn, The (Murdoch) CLCII IV-1639; MPII:BCF IV-1771

Union Street (Barker) CLCII IV-1640; MPII:BCF IV-1775

Universal Baseball Association, Inc., J. Henry Waugh, Prop., The (Coover) CLCII IV-1642; MPII:AF IV-1723

Unizhennye i oskorblyonnye. *See* Insulted and the Injured, The

"Unknown Masterpiece, The" (Balzac) MPII:SS VI-2468

"Unmailed, Unwritten Letters" (Oates) MPII:SS VI-2471

Unnamable, The (Beckett) CLCII IV-1643. *See also* Trilogy, The

"Unordnung und frühes Leid." *See* "Disorder and Early Sorrow"

Unquiet Grave, The (Connolly) MPII:NF IV-1617

Untergeher, Der (Bernhard) CLCII IV-1644; MPII:WF IV-1700

Unvanquished, The (Faulkner) MP XII-6860; MP:AF III-1354

"Up the Bare Stairs" (O'Faoláin) MPII:SS VI-2474

"Upon the Sweeping Flood" (Oates) MPII:SS VI-2478

Ursache, Die. *See* Gathering Evidence

U.S.A. (Dos Passos) CLC II-1187; MP XII-6863; MP:AF III-1358

"Use of Force, The" (Williams, W.) MPII:SS VI-2482

Ushant (Aiken) MPII:NF IV-1622

Utage no ato. *See* After the Banquet

Utopia (More, T.) CLC II-1189; MP XII-6868

Utsukushisa to kanashimi to. *See* Beauty and Sadness

V

V. (Pynchon) CLCII IV-1646; MPII:AF IV-1727

V kruge pervom. *See* First Circle, The

Vagabond, The (Colette) CLCII IV-1649; MPII:WF IV-1705

Valle negro. *See* Black Valley

Valley of Bones, The. *See* Dance to the Music of Time, A

Valley of Decision, The (Wharton) CLCII IV-1650; MPII:AF IV-1733

Valse aux adieux, La. *See* Farewell Party, The

Vanessa (Walpole, Hugh) CLC II-1189; MP XII-6871; MP:BF III-1656

Vanished World, The (Bates) MPII:NF IV-1628

Vanity Fair (Thackeray) CLC II-1190; MP XII-6875; MP:BF III-1660

Városalapító, A. *See* City Builder, The

Vathek (Beckford) CLC II-1194; MP XII-6881; MP:BF III-1667

Vatican Swindle, The. *See* Lafcadio's Adventures

Vedi (Mehta) MPII:NF IV-1635

Vein of Iron (Glasgow) CLCII IV-1651; MPII:AF IV-1738

"Veldt, The" (Bradbury) MPII:SS VI-2485

Velvet Horn, The (Lytle) MP XII-6884; MP:AF III-1363

Vendor of Sweets, The (Narayan) CLCII IV-1653; MPII:BCF IV-1780

Vendredi. *See* Friday

Venetian Glass Nephew, The (Wylie) CLC II-1194; MP XII-6887; MP:AF III-1367

Venice Preserved (Otway) CLC II-1195; MP XII-6890

Vent, Le. *See* Wind, The

Venus and Adonis (Shakespeare) CLC II-1196; MP XII-6893

"Venus, Cupid, Folly, and Time" (Taylor) MPII:SS VI-2489

Venusberg (Powell) CLCII IV-1654; MPII:BCF IV-1785

Verfolgung und Ermordung Jean-Paul Marats, dargestellt durch die Schauspielgruppe des Hospizes zu Charenton unter der Anleitung des Herrn de Sade, Die. *See* Marat/Sade

"Verlobung in St. Domingo, Der." *See* "Engagement in Santo Domingo, The"

Verlorene Ehre der Katharina Blum, Die. *See* Lost Honor of Katharina Blum, The

Vermischte Bemerkungen. *See* Culture and Value

Verratenes Volk. *See* November 1918

Versiegelte Zeit, Die. *See* Sculpting in Time

Verstoorde leven, Het. *See* Interrupted Life, An

Verstörung. *See* Gargoyles

Vertauschten Köpfe, Die. *See* Transposed Heads, The

"Vertical Ladder, The" (Sansom) MPII:SS VI-2493

"Verwandlung, Die." *See* "Metamorphosis, The"

Verwirrungen des Zöglings Törless, Die. *See* Young Törless

Very Private Eye, A (Pym) MPII:NF IV-1641

Verzauberung, Die. *See* Spell, The

Veshniye vody. *See* Torrents of Spring, The (Turgenev)

Vicar of Bullhampton, The (Trollope) CLC II-1197; MP XII-6897; MP:BF III-1670

Vicar of Wakefield, The (Goldsmith) CLC II-1198; MP XII-6901; MP:BF III-1674

Vicomte de Bragelonne, The (Dumas, père) CLC II-1199; MP XII-6904; MP:EF III-1341

Victim, The (Bellow) MP XII-6911; MP:AF III-1371

Victoria (Hamsun) CLCII IV-1655; MPII:WF IV-1709

Victory (Conrad) CLC II-1200; MP XII-6914; MP:BF III-1678

"Victrola" (Morris) MPII:SS VI-2497

Vida a plazos de Don Jacobo Lerner, La. *See* Fragmented Life of Don Jacobo Lerner, The

Vida breve, La. *See* Brief Life, A

Vida de Lazarillo de Tormes y de sus fortunatas y adversidades, La. *See* Lazarillo de Tormes

Vida inútil de Pito Pérez, La. *See* Futile Life of Pito Pérez, The

Vie est ailleurs, La. *See* Life Is Elsewhere

Vienna: Lusthaus (Clarke, M.) CLCII IV-1655; MPII:D IV-1682

Viento fuerte. *See* Strong Wind

"Views of My Father Weeping" (Barthelme, D.) MPII:SS VI-2500

Vile Bodies (Waugh) CLC II-1202; MP XII-6918; MP:BF III-1682

Village, The (Bunin) CLC II-1203; MP XII-6922; MP:EF III-1349

Village, The (Crabbe) MP XII-6927

Villagers, The (Icaza) MP:AF III-1375. *See also* Huasipungo

Villette (Brontë, C.) CLC II-1204; MP XII-6929; MP:BF III-1686

"Villon's Wife" (Dazai) MPII:SS VI-2504

Vindication of Natural Society, A (Burke) MP XII-6934

Violent Bear It Away, The (O'Connor) MP XII-6937; MP:AF III-1380

Violent Land, The (Amado) CLC II-1206; MP XII-6939; MP:AF III-1383

Violins of Saint-Jacques, The (Fermor) CLCII IV-1656; MPII:BCF IV-1790

Vipers' Tangle (Mauriac) CLCII IV-1657; MPII:WF IV-1715

Virgin and the Gipsy, The (Lawrence) CLCII IV-1658; MPII:BCF IV-1797

Virgin Soil (Turgenev) CLC II-1206; MP XII-6944; MP:EF III-1354

Virginia Comedians, The (Cooke) CLC II-1208; MP XII-6949; MP:AF III-1388

Virginian, The (Wister) CLC II-1208; MP XII-6952; MP:AF III-1392

Virginians, The (Thackeray) CLC II-1209; MP XII-6956; MP:BF III-1692

Visconte dimezzato, Il. *See* Cloven Viscount, The

Visión de Anáhuac (Reyes) MP XII-6961

Vision of William, Concerning Piers the Plowman (Langland) CLC II-1212; MP XII-6965

Visit, The (Dürrenmatt) CLCII IV-1659; MPII:D IV-1688

"Visit of Charity, A" (Welty) MPII:SS VI-2507

"Visit to Grandmother, A" (Kelley) MPII:SS VI-2510

Visitants (Stow) CLCII IV-1661; MPII:BCF IV-1802

Vita Nuova, The (Dante Alighieri) MP XII-6968

Vivian Grey (Disraeli) CLC II-1212; MP XII-6971; MP:BF III-1698

Vivisector, The (White) CLCII IV-1662; MPII:BCF IV-1806

"Viy" (Gogol) MPII:SS VI-2513

"Viyon no tsuma." *See* "Villon's Wife"

Voice from the Chorus, A (Sinyavsky) MPII:NF IV-1646

Voices in Time (MacLennan) CLCII IV-1663; MPII:BCF IV-1812

Voices of Silence, The (Malraux) MP XII-6975

Voie royale, La. *See* Royal Way, The

Volpone (Jonson) CLC II-1213; MP XII-6978

Volunteers (Friel) CLCII IV-1665; MPII:D IV-1695

Volupté (Sainte-Beuve) CLC II-1215; MP XII-6983; MP:EF III-1360

Volverás a Región. *See* Return to Región

Von Berlin nach Jerusalem. *See* From Berlin to Jerusalem

Voraussetzungen einer Erzählung. *See* Cassandra

Vospominaniya. *See* Hope Against Hope

Voss (White) CLCII IV-1666; MPII:BCF IV-1817

Voyage au centre de la terre. *See* Journey to the Center of the Earth

Voyage of the Beagle, The (Darwin) MP XII-6987

Voyage Out, The (Woolf) CLCII IV-1667; MPII:BCF IV-1823

Voyage Round My Father, A (Mortimer) CLCII IV-1668; MPII:D IV-1701

Voyage to Tomorrow (Hakim) CLCII IV-1669; MPII:D IV-1706

"Vozvrashchenie Chorba. *See* Return of Chorb, The

Vremya bolshikh ozhidany. *See* Story of a Life, The

Vtoraia kniga. *See* Hope Abandoned

Vyrozumění. *See* Memorandum, The

"Vystrel." *See* "Shot, The"

W

Wagahai wa neko de aru. *See* I Am a Cat

Wahrheit und Methode. *See* Truth and Method

"Waiting" (Oates) MPII:SS VI-2517

Waiting for Godot (Beckett) CLC II-1215; MP XII-6991

Waiting for the Barbarians (Coetzee) CLCII IV-1671; MPII:BCF IV-1830

"Wakefield" (Hawthorne) MPII:SS VI-2521

Walden (Thoreau) MP XII-6996

"Walk, The" (Walser) MPII:SS VI-2525

Walk in the Night, A (La Guma) CLCII IV-1672; MPII:BCF IV-1837

Walk on the Wild Side, A (Algren) CLCII IV-1673; MPII:AF IV-1743

Walker in the City, A (Kazin) MPII:NF IV-1651

Wall, The (Hersey) CLCII IV-1674; MPII:AF IV-1748

"Wall, The" (Sansom) MPII:SS VI-2530

"Wall, The" (Sartre) MPII:SS VI-2534

Wall Jumper, The (Schneider) CLCII IV-1676; MPII:WF IV-1720

Wallenstein (Schiller) CLC II-1216; MP XII-7001

"Walter Briggs" (Updike) MPII:SS VI-2537

Wanderer, The (Alain-Fournier) CLC II-1217; MP XII-7006; MP:EF III-1365

"Wanderers, The" (Lewis, A.) MPII:SS VI-2541

Wanderers, The (Mphahlele) CLCII IV-1677; MPII:BCF IV-1843

Wandering Jew, The (Sue) CLC II-1218; MP XII-7010; MP:EF III-1370

Wandering Scholar from Paradise, The (Sachs) CLC II-1219; MP XII-7014

Waning of the Middle Ages, The (Huizinga) MP XII-7017

Wapshot Chronicle, The (Cheever) MP XII-7020; MP:AF III-1396

Wapshot Scandal, The (Cheever) MP XII-7024; MP:AF III-1400

"War" (Pirandello) MPII:SS VI-2544

War and Peace (Tolstoy) CLC II-1220; MP XII-7028; MP:EF III-1374

War and Remembrance (Wouk) CLCII IV-1678; MPII:AF IV-1754

War Between the Tates, The (Lurie) CLCII IV-1681; MPII:AF IV-1759

War of the End of the World, The (Vargas Llosa) CLCII IV-1682; MPII:AF IV-1764

War of the Worlds, The (Wells) CLC II-1222; MP XII-7035; MP:BF III-1702

War Years, The. *See* Abraham Lincoln

"Ward No. 6" (Chekhov) MPII:SS VI-2548

Warden, The (Trollope) CLC II-1222; MP XII-7038; MP:BF III-1706

Wariat i zakonnica. *See* Madman and the Nun, The

Wars, The (Findley) CLCII IV-1683; MPII:BCF IV-1848

Was soll aus dem Jungen bloss werden? *See* What's to Become of the Boy?

"Wash" (Faulkner) MPII:SS VI-2552

Washington Square (James, H.) CLC II-1224; MP XII-7041; MP:AF III-1405

Wasps, The (Aristophanes) CLC II-1225; MP XII-7044

Wasserfälle von Slunj, Die. *See* Waterfalls of Slunj, The

Waste Land, The (Eliot, T. S.) MP XII-7047

Watch on the Rhine (Hellman) CLCII IV-1684; MPII:D IV-1712

Watch That Ends the Night, The (MacLennan) CLCII IV-1685; MPII:BCF IV-1854

"Watcher, The" (Calvino) MPII:SS VI-2556

Watchmaker of Everton, The (Simenon) CLCII IV-1686; MPII:WF IV-1725

Water Hen, The (Witkiewicz) CLCII IV-1687; MPII:D IV-1718

Waterfall, The (Drabble) CLCII IV-1688; MPII:BCF IV-1859

123

Waterfalls of Slunj, The (Doderer) CLCII IV-1689; MPII:WF IV-1729

Waterland (Swift) CLCII IV-1691; MPII:BCF IV-1865

Waters of Kronos, The (Richter) MP XII-7049; MP:AF III-1409

Watership Down (Adams) CLCII IV-1692; MPII:BCF IV-1870

Watt (Beckett) CLCII IV-1694; MPII:BCF IV-1875

Wave, The (Scott, E.) CLCII IV-1695; MPII:AF IV-1769

Waverley (Scott, Sir W.) CLC II-1226; MP XII-7052; MP:BF III-1710

Waves, The (Woolf) CLC II-1227; MP XII-7057; MP:BF III-1716

Way Home, The. *See* Fortunes of Richard Mahony, The

Way of All Flesh, The (Butler) CLC II-1228; MP XII-7061; MP:BF III-1721

Way of the World, The (Congreve) CLC II-1230; MP XII-7066

Way That Girls Love, The. *See* Splendors and Miseries of Courtesans, The

Way the Future Was, The (Pohl) MPII:NF IV-1656

Way to Rainy Mountain, The (Momaday) MPII:NF IV-1660

Way West, The (Guthrie) CLCII IV-1698; MPII:AF IV-1773

Ways of Escape (Green) MPII:NF IV-1665

Ways of Seeing (Berger) MPII:NF IV-1670

We (Zamyatin) CLCII IV-1700; MPII:WF IV-1734

Wealth of Nations, The (Smith, A.) MP XII-7070

Weather in the Streets, The (Lehmann) CLCII IV-1701; MPII:BCF IV-1880

Weavers, The (Hauptmann) CLC II-1231; MP XII-7073

Web and the Rock, The (Wolfe) CLC II-1232; MP XII-7077; MP:AF III-1412

Weeds (Kelley, E.) CLCII IV-1702; MPII:AF IV-1777

Week on the Concord and Merrimack Rivers, A (Thoreau) MP XII-7081

Weight of the World, The (Handke) MPII:NF IV-1675

Well, The (Jolley) CLCII IV-1703; MPII:BCF IV-1885

West with the Night (Markham) MPII:NF IV-1681

Westward Ho! (Kingsley, C.) CLC II-1233; MP XII-7084; MP:BF III-1726

"Wet Saturday" (Collier) MPII:SS VI-2562

What a Beautiful Sunday! (Semprun) CLCII IV-1704; MPII:WF IV-1739

What Every Woman Knows (Barrie) CLC II-1234; MP XII-7089

What I'm Going to Do, I Think (Woiwode) CLCII IV-1705; MPII:AF IV-1784

"What Is the Connection Between Men and Women?" (Oates) MPII:SS VI-2565

What Maisie Knew (James, H.) CLC II-1235; MP XII-7094; MP:AF III-1416

What Price Glory? (Anderson, M., *and* Laurence Stallings) CLCII IV-1706; MPII:D IV-1723

What the Butler Saw (Orton) CLCII IV-1707; MPII:D IV-1728

What's Bred in the Bone (Davies) CLCII IV-1708; MPII:BCF IV-1890

What's to Become of the Boy? (Böll) MPII:NF IV-1687

"When I Was Thirteen" (Welch) MPII:SS VI-2569

When I Whistle (Endō) CLCII IV-1709; MPII:WF IV-1745

"When the Light Gets Green" (Warren) MPII:SS VI-2573

When the Mountain Fell (Ramuz) CLC II-1235; MP XII-7097; MP:EF III-1383

When We Dead Awaken (Ibsen) CLC II-1236; MP XII-7100

When You Comin' Back, Red Ryder? (Medoff) CLCII IV-1710; MPII:D IV-1733

Where Angels Fear to Tread (Forster) CLC II-1236; MP XII-7104; MP:BF III-1731

"Where Are You Going, Where Have You Been?" (Oates) MPII:SS VI-2577

Where Has Tommy Flowers Gone? (McNally) CLCII IV-1711; MPII:D IV-1739

Where the Air Is Clear (Fuentes) MP XII-7107; MP:AF III-1420

White Company, The (Doyle) CLC II-1237; MP XII-7111; MP:BF III-1735

White Devil, The (Webster) CLC II-1238; MP XII-7115

White Goddess, The (Graves) MPII:NF IV-1692

"White Heron, A" (Jewett) MPII:SS VI-2581

"White Horses of Vienna, The" (Boyle, K.) MPII:SS VI-2585

White-Jacket (Melville) CLC II-1239; MP XII-7118; MP:AF III-1425

"White Nights" (Dostoevski) MPII:SS VI-2589

"White Stocking, The" (Lawrence) MPII:SS VI-2593

Who Has Seen the Wind (Mitchell) CLCII IV-1712; MPII:BCF IV-1895

Whole Armour, The. See Guyana Quartet, The

"Whole Loaf, A" (Agnon) MPII:SS VI-2597

"Whore of Mensa, The" (Allen) MPII:SS VI-2602

Who's Afraid of Virginia Woolf? (Albee) MP XII-7121

"Why Don't You Dance?" (Carver) MPII:SS VI-2605

"Why I Live at the P.O." (Welty) MPII:SS VI-2608

Wickford Point (Marquand) CLC II-1240; MP XII-7126; MP:AF III-1429

"Wide Net, The" (Welty) MPII:SS VI-2612

Wide Sargasso Sea (Rhys) CLCII IV-1714; MPII:BCF IV-1899

Widerstand und Ergebung. See Letters and Papers from Prison

Widmung, Die. See Devotion

Widower's Son, The (Sillitoe) CLCII IV-1715; MPII:BCF IV-1904

"Widow's Son, The" (Lavin) MPII:SS VI-2616

Wieland (Brown) CLC II-1241; MP XII-7129; MP:AF III-1433

Wielopole, Wielopole (Kantor) CLCII IV-1717; MPII:D IV-1745

Wild Ass's Skin, The (Balzac) CLC II-1241; MP XII-7133; MP:EF III-1386

Wild Duck, The (Ibsen) CLC II-1242; MP XII-7137

Wild Palms, The (Faulkner) MP XII-7142; MP:AF III-1437

"Wild Swans" (Munro, A.) MPII:SS VI-2619

Wild Wales (Borrow) MP XII-7145

Wilhelm Meister's Apprenticeship (Goethe) CLC II-1243; MP XII-7148; MP:EF III-1390

Wilhelm Meister's Travels (Goethe) CLC II-1245; MP XII-7152; MP:EF III-1395

"Will, The" (Lavin) MPII:SS VI-2623

"Will You Please Be Quiet, Please?" (Carver) MPII:SS VI-2627

Will's Boy (Morris) MPII:NF IV-1696

William Tell (Schiller) CLC II-1246; MP XII-7156

"William Wilson" (Poe) MPII:SS VI-2630

"Willis Carr at Bleak House" (Madden) MPII:SS VI-2634

"Willows, The" (Blackwood) MPII:SS VI-2638

Wind, The (Simon, C.) CLCII IV-1717; MPII:WF IV-1750

"Wind and the Snow of Winter, The" (Clark) MPII:SS VI-2642

Wind from the Plain, The (Kemal) CLCII IV-1718; MPII:WF IV-1754

Wind in the Willows, The (Grahame) CLC II-1247; MP XII-7159; MP:BF III-1739

Wind, Sand, and Stars (Saint-Exupéry) MP XII-7163; MP:EF III-1400

Winds of War, The (Wouk) CLCII IV-1720; MPII:AF IV-1790

Windsor Castle (Ainsworth) CLC II-1248; MP XII-7166; MP:BF III-1743

Wine of Astonishment, The (Lovelace) CLCII IV-1723; MPII:BCF IV-1909

Winesburg, Ohio (Anderson, S.) CLC II-1249; MP XII-7171; MP:AF III-1440

Wings (Kopit) CLCII IV-1725; MPII:D IV-1751

Wings of the Dove, The (James, H.) CLC II-1250; MP XII-7176; MP:AF III-1445

Winners, The (Cortázar) CLCII IV-1726; MPII:AF IV-1795

"Winter Dreams" (Fitzgerald) MPII:SS VI-2645

"Winter Night" (Boyle, K.) MPII:SS VI-2649

"Winter: 1978" (Beattie) MPII:SS VI-2652

Winter's Tale, The (Shakespeare) CLC II-1251; MP XII-7181

Winterset (Anderson, M.) CLC II-1252; MP XII-7186

"Wireless" (Kipling) MPII:SS VI-2656

Wisdom of the Sands, The (Saint-Exupéry) MP XII-7189

Wise Blood (O'Connor) MP XII-7192; MP:AF III-1450

Wise Virgin (Wilson, A. N.) CLCII IV-1727; MPII:BCF IV-1915

"Wish House, The" (Kipling) MPII:SS VI-2660

"Wissler Remembers" (Stern) MPII:SS VI-2664

Wit and Its Relation to the Unconscious (Freud) MPII:NF IV-1704

Witch in the Wood (The Queen of Air and Darkness), The. See Once and Future King, The

"Witch's Money" (Collier) MPII:SS VI-2668

With Fire and Sword (Sienkiewicz) CLC II-1253; MP XII-7195; MP:EF III-1404

"Within and Without" (Hesse) MPII:SS VI-2672

Within the Gates (O'Casey) CLC II-1254; MP XII-7199

Witz und sein Beziehung zum Unbewussten, Der. See Wit and Its Relation to the Unconscious

Wolf Solent (Powys, J.) CLC II-1255; MP XII-7203; MP:BF III-1749

"Woman at the Store, The" (Mansfield) MPII:SS VI-2676

Woman from Sarajevo, The (Andrić) CLCII IV-1728; MPII:WF IV-1764

Woman Hater, The (Beaumont and Fletcher) CLC II-1255; MP XII-7207

Woman in the Dunes, The (Abe) CLCII IV-1729; MPII:WF IV-1769

Woman in White, The (Collins, Wilkie) CLC II-1256; MP XII-7211; MP:BF III-1753

Woman Killed with Kindness, A (Heywood) CLC II-1257; MP XII-7217

Woman of Rome, The (Moravia) CLC II-1259; MP XII-7221; MP:EF III-1409

Woman of the Pharisees, A (Mauriac) CLCII IV-1730; MPII:WF IV-1774

Woman on the Edge of Time (Piercy) CLCII IV-1732; MPII:AF IV-1800

Woman Warrior, The (Kingston) MPII:NF IV-1709

"Woman Who Rode Away, The" (Lawrence) MPII:SS VI-2680

Woman's Life, A (Maupassant) CLC II-1259; MP XII-7224; MP:EF III-1413

Woman's Prize, The (Fletcher) CLC II-1260; MP XII-7229

Women at the Pump, The (Hamsun) CLCII IV-1733; MPII:WF IV-1779

Women Beware Women (Middleton) CLC II-1261; MP XII-7235

Women in Love (Lawrence, D. H.) MP XII-7239; MP:BF III-1760

Women of Brewster Place, The (Naylor) CLCII IV-1734; MPII:AF IV-1805

Women of Messina (Vittorini) CLCII IV-1736; MPII:WF IV-1784

Women of Trachis (Sophocles, trans. by Pound) CLCII IV-1736; MPII:D IV-1757

Women of Trachis, The (Sophocles) CLC II-1262; MP XII-7242

Women's Room, The (French) CLCII IV-1737; MPII:AF IV-1810

Wonder-Worker, The (Jacobson) CLCII IV-1738; MPII:BCF IV-1921

Wonderful Fool (Endō) CLCII IV-1740; MPII:WF IV-1789

"Wonderful Tar-Baby Story, The" (Harris) MPII:SS VI-2684

Wonderland (Oates) CLCII IV-1741; MPII:AF IV-1815

"Wondersmith, The" (O'Brien, F.) MPII:SS VI-2687

Woodcutters (Bernhard) CLCII IV-1742. *See also* Holzfällen

Woodlanders, The (Hardy) CLC II-1263; MP XII-7247; MP:BF II-1764

Woods, The (Mamet) CLCII IV-1743; MPII:D IV-1762

Woodstock (Scott, W.) CLC II-1265; MP XII-7251; MP:BF III-1768

Word Child, A (Murdoch) CLCII IV-1744; MPII:BCF IV-1926

Words, The (Sartre) MPII:NF IV-714

Words and Music (Beckett) CLCII IV-1745; MPII:D IV-1766

Words upon the Window-Pane, The (Yeats) CLCII IV-1746; MPII:D IV-1772

"Work" (Plante) MPII:SS VI-2692

Work of Art in the Age of Mechanical Reproduction, The (Benjamin) MPII:NF IV-1719

Workhouse Ward, The (Gregory) CLCII IV-1748; MPII:D IV-1778

Works and Days (Hesiod) MP XII-7254

Works of Jonathan Edwards (Edwards) MP XII-7256

Works of Love, The (Morris) CLCII IV-1749; MPII:AF IV-1820

World According to Garp, The (Irving) CLCII IV-1749; MPII:AF IV-1825

"World According to Hsü, The" (Mukherjee) MPII:SS VI-2696

World as Will and Idea, The (Schopenhauer) MP XII-7259

"World Ends, A" (Hildesheimer) MPII:SS VI-2701

World Enough and Time (Warren) CLC II-1266; MP XII-7262; MP:AF III-1454

World in Ripeness, The (Bates) MPII:NF IV-1628

World My Wilderness, The (Macaulay) CLCII IV-1752; MPII:BCF IV-1930

"World of Apples, The" (Cheever) MPII:SS VI-2705

World of Love, A (Bowen) CLCII IV-1753; MPII:BCF IV-1935

"World of Stone, The" (Borowski) MPII:SS VI-2709

World of Strangers, A (Gordimer) CLCII IV-1754; MPII:BCF IV-1940

World of the Thibaults, The (Martin du Gard) CLC II-1267; MP XII-7266; MP:EF III-1419

World of Wonders. *See* Deptford Trilogy, The

World on the Wane, A. *See* Tristes Tropiques

World's Illusion, The (Wassermann) CLC II-1268; MP XII-7271; MP:EF III-1425

"Worn Path, A" (Welty) MPII:SS VI-2713

Woyzeck (Büchner) CLC II-1269; MP XII-7275

"Wrack" (Barthelme, D.) MPII:SS VI-2716

Wreath for Udomo, A (Abrahams) CLCII IV-1755; MPII:BCF IV-1945

Wreath of Roses, A (Taylor) CLCII IV-1756; MPII:BCF IV-1950

Wreck of the Grosvenor, The (Russell, W.) CLC II-1269; MP XII-7278; MP:BF III-1772

Wreckage of Agathon, The (Gardner) CLCII IV-1758; MPII:AF IV-1830

Wretched of the Earth, The (Fanon) MPII:NF IV-1725

XYZ

Xala (Sembène) CLCII IV-1759; MPII:WF IV-1793

". . . y no se lo tragó la tierra." *See* ". . . and the earth did not part"

Yama no oto. *See* Sound of the Mountain, The

Year of Living Dangerously, The (Koch) CLCII IV-1760; MPII:BCF IV-1955

Year of the Dragon, The (Chin) CLCII IV-1761; MPII:D IV-1783

Yearling, The (Rawlings) CLC II-1272; MP XII-7286; MP:AF III-1459

Years, The (Woolf) CLC II-1273; MP XII-7290; MP:BF III-1781

Years of Hope. *See* Story of a Life, The

Years with Ross, The (Thurber) MPII:NF IV-1736

Yellow Back Radio Broke-Down (Reed) CLCII IV-1762; MPII:AF IV-1835

"Yellow Woman" (Silko) MPII:SS VI-2724

Yemassee, The (Simms) CLC II-1274; MP XII-7295; MP:AF III-1463

"Yentl the Yeshiva Boy" (Singer) MPII:SS VI-2729

Yer demir, gök bakir. *See* Iron Earth, Copper Sky

"Yermolai and the Miller's Wife" (Turgenev) MPII:SS VI-2733

Yonnondio (Olsen) CLCII IV-1763; MPII:AF IV-1841

You Can't Go Home Again (Wolfe) CLC II-1275; MP XII-7299; MP:AF III-1467

You Can't Take It with You (Kaufman *and* Hart) CLCII IV-1764; MPII:D IV-1788

You Know Me Al (Lardner) CLC II-1276; MP XII-7303; MP:AF III-1472

Youma (Hearn) CLC II-1277; MP XII-7306; MP:AF III-1476

"Young Goodman Brown" (Hawthorne) MPII:SS VI-2737

Young Joseph, The. *See* Joseph and His Brothers

Young Lions, The (Shaw, I.) CLCII IV-1765; MPII:AF IV-1846

Young Lonigan. *See* Studs Lonigan

Young Man in Search of Love, A (Singer) MPII:NF II-835

Young Manhood of Studs Lonigan, The. *See* Studs Lonigan: A Trilogy

Young Törless (Musil) CLCII IV-1766; MPII:WF IV-1797

"Youth" (Conrad) MPII:SS VI-2741

Yukiguni. *See* Snow Country

"Yūkoku." *See* "Patriotism"

"Yume no ukihashi." *See* "Bridge of Dreams, The"

Yvain (Chrétien de Troyes) CLC II-1277; MP XII-7309

Zababělci. *See* Cowards, The

Zadig (Voltaire) CLC II-1278; MP XII-7314; MP:EF III-1430

Zahradní slavnost. *See* Garden Party, The

Zaïre (Voltaire) CLC II-1279; MP XII-7318

"Zaklinatel zmei." *See* "Snake Charmer, The"

Zapiski iz myortvogo doma. *See* House of the Dead, The

"Zapiski sumasshedshego." *See* "Diary of a Madman, The"

Zarco, El (Altamirano) CLC II-1279; MP XII-7323; MP:AF III-1480

Zashchita Luzhina. *See* Defense, The

Zavist. *See* Envy

Zazie dans le métro. *See* Zazie in the Metro

Zazie in the Metro (Queneau) CLCII IV-1767; MPII:WF IV-1803

Zbabělci. *See* Cowards, The

Zdobycie władzy. *See* Seizure of Power, The

Zeit ohne Glocken. *See* Silesian Tetralogy, The

Zen and the Art of Motorcycle Maintenance (Pirsig) MPII:NF IV-1741

Zero (Loyola Brandão) CLCII IV-1769; MPII:AF IV-1852

Žert. *See* Joke, The

"Zhivye Moshchi." *See* "Living Relic, A"

Zhizn'i neobychainye priklyucheniya soldata Ivana Chonkina. *See* Life and Extraordinary Adventures of Private Ivan Chonkin, The

Zhizn' cheloveka. *See* Life of Man, The

Ziemia Ulro. *See* Land of Ulro, The

Zincali, The (Borrow) MP XII-7328

Zniewolony umysł. *See* Captive Mind, The

Zona sagrada. *See* Holy Place

Zona. *See* Zone, The

Zone, The (Dovlatov) CLCII IV-1770; MPII:WF IV-1808

Zoo (Shklovsky) CLCII IV-1771; MPII:WF IV-1814

Zoo Story, The (Albee) CLCII IV-1772; MPII:D IV-1794

Zoot Suit (Valdez) CLCII IV-1773; MPII:D IV-1799

Zorba the Greek (Kazantzakis) MP XII-7331; MP:EF III-1435

Ztížená možnost soustředění. *See* Increased Difficulty of Concentration, The

Zuckerman Bound (Roth) MPII:AF IV-1856

Zuckerman Unbound (Roth, P.) CLCII IV-1774. *See also* Zuckerman Bound

Zuleika Dobson (Beerbohm) CLC II-1280; MP XII-7334; MP:BF III-1787

"Zulu and the Zeide, The" (Jacobson) MPII:SS VI-2745

Zvezdnyi bilet. *See* Ticket to the Stars, A

Zvyozdnyi bilet. *See* Ticket to the Stars, A

AUTHOR INDEX

A

ABBEY, EDWARD, CWAII I-1
Desert Solitaire, MPII:NF I-342
ABE, KŌBŌ, CWAII I-3
Inter Ice Age 4, CLCII II-770;
MPII:WF II-711
Ruined Map, The, CLCII III-1321;
MPII:WF III-1315
Woman in the Dunes, The, CLCII IV-1729; MPII:WF IV-1769
ABEL, LIONEL
Intellectual Follies, The, MPII:NF II-742
ABÉLARD, PIERRE, CWA I-1
Historia calamitatum, MP V-2624
ABOUT, EDMOND FRANÇOIS, CWA I-2
King of the Mountains, The, CLC I-575; MP VI-3156; MP:EF II-724
ABRAHAM, NELSON AHLGREN. *See* ALGREN, NELSON
ABRAHAMS, PETER, CWAII I-6
Wreath for Udomo, A, CLCII IV-1755; MPII:BCF IV-1945
ACHEBE, CHINUA, CWAII I-8
Arrow of God, CLCII I-69; MPII:BCF I-67
No Longer at Ease, CLCII III-1105; MPII:BCF III-1219
Things Fall Apart, CLCII IV-1544; MPII:BCF IV-1681
ADAMOV, ARTHUR, CWA I-3; CWAII I-11
Ping-Pong, MP VIII-4719
ADAMS, ALICE, CWAII I-13
"Greyhound People," MPII:SS III-948
ADAMS, HENRY, CWA I-5
Education of Henry Adams, The, MP III-1708
Mont-Saint-Michel and Chartres, MP VII-4049
ADAMS, JOHN, CWA I-7
Defense of the Constitutions of Government of the United States of America, A, MP III-1426

ADAMS, RICHARD, CWAII I-15
Watership Down, CLCII IV-1692; MPII:BCF IV-1870
ADDISON, JOSEPH, CWA I-11
ADDISON, JOSEPH, SIR RICHARD STEELE, *and* EUSTACE BUDGELL
Sir Roger de Coverley Papers, The, CLC II-1044; MP X-6067
ADLER, RENATA, CWAII I-17
Pitch Dark, CLCII III-1209; MPII:AF III-1258
Speedboat, CLCII IV-1459; MPII:AF IV-1511
Æ, CWA I-14
Poetry of "A. E.," The, MP VIII-4795
AESCHYLUS, CWA I-16
House of Atreus, The, CLC I-486; MP V-2719
Persians, The, CLC II-862; MP VIII-4609
Prometheus Bound, CLC II-924; MP IX-5361
Seven Against Thebes, CLC II-1025; MP X-5922
Suppliants, The, CLC II-1094; MP XI-6345
AESOP, CWA I-19
Aesop's Fables, MP I-51; MP:EF I-10
AGEE, JAMES, CWA I-20; CWAII I-19
Death in the Family, A, MP III-1354; MP:AF I-269
Let Us Now Praise Famous Men, MP VI-3330
Morning Watch, The, CLCII III-1039; MPII:AF III-1050
AGEE, JOEL
Twelve Years, MPII:NF IV-1586
AGNON, SHMUEL YOSEF, CWAII I-21
Bridal Canopy, The, CLCII I-200; MPII:WF I-194
Guest for the Night, A, CLCII II-645; MPII:WF I-194
In the Heart of the Seas, CLCII II-749; MPII:WF I-194

"Kerchief, The," MPII:SS III-1255
Simple Story, A, CLCII IV-1415;
MPII:WF IV-1448
"Whole Loaf, A," MPII:SS VI-2597
AGUILERA MALTA, DEMETRIO
Don Goyo, CLCII II-416; MPII:AF I-434
AIKEN, CONRAD POTTER, CWA I-22;
CWAII I-23
"Dark City, The," MPII:SS II-488
"Impulse," MPII:SS III-1126
Poetry of Aiken, The, MP VIII-4798
"Round by Round," MPII:SS V-1998
"Silent Snow, Secret Snow," MPII:SS
V-2108
Ushant, MPII:NF IV-1622
AINSWORTH, WILLIAM HARRISON,
CWA I-24
Jack Sheppard, CLC I-538; MP V-2969; MP:BF II-676
Old St. Paul's, CLC II-807; MP VIII-4341; MP:BF II-1096
Tower of London, The, CLC II-1148;
MP XI-6618; MP:BF III-1583
Windsor Castle, CLC II-1248; MP XII-7166; MP:BF III-1743
AKALAITIS, JOANNE, CWAII I-26
Green Card, CLCII II-631; MPII:D II-711
AKSYONOV, VASSILY, CWAII I-28
Burn, The, CLCII I-215; MPII:WF I-200
Island of Crimea, The, CLCII II-778;
MPII:WF II-737
Ticket to the Stars, A, CLCII IV-1561;
MPII:WF IV-1600
AKUTAGAWA, RYŪNOSUKE, CWAII
I-31
"Rashōmon," CLCII III-1265; MPII:SS
V-1901
ALAIN-FOURNIER, CWA I-26
Wanderer, The, CLC II-1217; MP XII-7006; MP:EF III-1365
ALARCÓN Y MENDOZA, JUAN RUIZ
DE. See RUIZ DE ALARCÓN,
JUAN

ALARCÓN, PEDRO ANTONIO DE,
CWA I-27
"Nun, The," MPII:SS IV-1637
Three-Cornered Hat, The, CLC II-1126;
MP XI-6505; MP:EF III-1286
ALAS, LEOPOLDO
Regenta, La, MPII:WF III-1267; CLCII
III-1284
ALBEE, EDWARD, CWA I-29; CWAII
I-34
American Dream, The, CLCII I-39;
MPII:D I-55
Delicate Balance, A, CLCII I-385;
MPII:D II-475
Seascape, CLCII III-1359; MPII:D IV-1427
Tiny Alice, CLCII IV-1572; MPII:D
IV-1590
Who's Afraid of Virginia Woolf? MP
XII-7121
Zoo Story, The, CLCII IV-1772;
MPII:D IV-1794
ALCAYAGA, LUCILA GODOY. See
MISTRAL, GABRIELA
ALCOTT, LOUISA MAY, CWA I-32
Little Women, CLC I-622; MP VI-3458; MP:AF II-687
ALDINGTON, RICHARD, CWA I-34;
CWAII I-36
All Men Are Enemies, CLCII I-28;
MPII:BCF I-37
Death of a Hero, CLC I-254; MP III-1362; MP:BF I-291
ALDISS, BRIAN W., CWAII I-38
Barefoot in the Head, CLCII I-114;
MPII:BCF I-98
Frankenstein Unbound, CLCII II-544;
MPII:BCF II-542
ALDRICH, THOMAS BAILEY, CWA I-36
Story of a Bad Boy, The, CLC II-1082;
MP XI-6265; MP:AF III-1227
ALEGRÍA, CIRO, CWA I-38; CWAII I-41
Broad and Alien Is the World, CLC I-126; MP II-666; MP:AF I-144

Golden Serpent, The, CLCII II-607; MPII:AF II-645

ALEICHEM, SHOLOM, CWAII I-44
"Hodel," MPII:SS III-1029
"On Account of a Hat," MPII:SS IV-1692

ALEMÁN, MATEO, CWA I-39
Guzmán de Alfarache, CLC I-435; MP IV-2437; MP:EF II-613

ALESHKOVSKY, YUZ, CWAII I-47
Kangaroo, CLCII II-811; MPII:WF II-790

ALGREN, NELSON, CWAII I-49
"Bottle of Milk for Mother, A," MPII:SS I-285
"How the Devil Came Down Division Street," MPII:SS III-1073
Man with the Golden Arm, The, CLCII III-961; MPII:AF III-971
Never Come Morning, CLCII III-1085; MPII:AF III-1124
Walk on the Wild Side, A, CLCII IV-1673; MPII:AF IV-1743

AL-HAKIM, TAWFIQ. See HAKIM, TAWFIQ AL-

ALIGHIERI, DANTE. See DANTE ALIGHIERI

ALLEN, HERVEY, CWA I-41
Anthony Adverse, CLC I-47; MP I-246; MP:AF I-58

ALLEN, WOODY, CWAII I-51
"Kugelmass Episode, The," MPII:SS III-1276
"Whore of Mensa, The," MPII:SS VI-2602

ALTAMIRANO, IGNACIO MANUEL, CWA I-43
Zarco, El, CLC II-1279; MP XII-7323; MP:AF III-1480

AMADI, ELECHI, CWAII I-53
Great Ponds, The, CLCII II-629; MPII:BCF II-665

AMADO, JORGE, CWA I-45; CWAII I-55
Dona Flor and Her Two Husbands, CLCII II-416; MPII:AF I-439

Gabriela, Clove and Cinnamon, MP IV-2192; MP:AF I-425
Jubiabá, CLCII II-804; MPII:AF II-819
Tent of Miracles, CLCII IV-1526; MPII:AF IV-1578
Tieta, the Goat Girl, CLCII IV-1564; MPII:AF IV-1657
Violent Land, The, CLC II-1206; MP XII-6939; MP:AF III-1383

AMBLER, ERIC, CWAII I-58
Coffin for Dimitrios, A, CLCII I-303; MPII:BCF I-276
Journey into Fear, CLCII II-799; MPII:BCF II-862

AMBROGINI, ANGELO. See POLITIAN

AMICIS, EDMONDO DE, CWA I-46
Romance of a Schoolmaster, The, CLC II-983; MP X-5669

AMIS, KINGSLEY, CWA I-48; CWAII I-60
Girl, 20, CLCII II-590; MPII:BCF II-602
Green Man, The, CLCII II-633; MPII:BCF II-670
I Like It Here, CLCII II-728; MPII:BCF II-777
Jake's Thing, CLCII II-787; MPII:BCF II-852
Lucky Jim, MP VI-3554; MP:BF II-843
Old Devils, The, CLCII III-1136; MPII:BCF III-1253
Stanley and the Women, CLCII IV-1472; MPII:BCF IV-1604
Take a Girl Like You, CLCII IV-1511; MPII:BCF IV-1671
That Uncertain Feeling, MP XI-6466; MP:BF III-1519

AMMERS-KÜLLER, JOHANNA VAN, CWA I-50
Rebel Generation, The, CLC II-944; MP IX-5456; MP:EF III-1058

ANACREON
Poetry of Anacreon, The, MP VIII-4801

ANDERSEN, HANS CHRISTIAN, CWA I-52

Andersen's Fairy Tales, MP I-205;
MP:EF I-34
ANDERSEN NEXÖ, MARTIN. See
NEXÖ, MARTIN ANDERSEN
ANDERSON, JESSICA
Tirra Lirra by the River, CLCII IV-
1573; MPII:BCF IV-1716
ANDERSON, MAXWELL, CWA I-55;
CWAII I-62
Anne of the Thousand Days, CLCII I-
52; MPII:D I-71
Winterset, CLC II-1252; MP XII-7186
ANDERSON, MAXWELL, and
LAURENCE STALLINGS
What Price Glory? CLCII IV-1706;
MPII:D IV-1723
ANDERSON, ROBERT, CWAII I-64
Tea and Sympathy, CLCII IV-1518;
MPII:D IV-1543
ANDERSON, SHERWOOD, CWA I-57
Dark Laughter, CLC I-241; MP III-
1317; MP:AF I-255
"Death in the Woods," MPII:SS II-528
"Egg, The," MPII:SS II-668
"I Want to Know Why," MPII:SS III-
1095
"I'm a Fool," MPII:SS III-1116
Poor White, CLC II-901; MP IX-5241;
MP:AF II-961
Story Teller's Story, A, MP XI-6291
Winesburg, Ohio, CLC II-1249; MP
XII-7171; MP:AF III-1440
ANDRADE, MÁRIO DE, CWAII I-66
Macunaíma, CLCII III-940; MPII:AF
III-948
ANDREYEV, LEONID, CWA I-60
Life of Man, The, CLCII II-889;
MPII:D III-975
Seven Who Were Hanged, The, CLC II-
1027; MP X-5939; MP:EF III-1151
ANDRIĆ, IVO, CWA I-62; CWAII I-68
Bosnian Chronicle, CLCII I-195;
MPII:WF I-182
Bridge on the Drina, The, MP II-656;
MP:EF I-136

Woman from Sarajevo, The, CLCII IV-
1728; MPII:WF IV-1764
ANDRZEJEWSKI, JERZY, CWAII I-70
Ashes and Diamonds, CLCII I-75;
MPII:WF I-80
ANGELOU, MAYA, CWAII I-72
All God's Children Need Traveling
Shoes, MPII:NF I-34
I Know Why the Caged Bird Sings,
MPII:NF II-673
ANNUNZIO, GABRIELE D'. See
D'ANNUNZIO, GABRIELE
ANOUILH, JEAN, CWA I-65; CWAII I-
74
Antigone, CLCII I-58; MPII:D I-77
Becket, CLCII I-130; MPII:D I-139
Restless Heart, CLCII III-1286; MPII:D
III-1325
Ring Round the Moon, CLC II-972; MP
X-5608
ANTHONY, MICHAEL, CWAII I-77
Games Were Coming, The, CLCII II-
563; MPII:BCF II-572
APOLLINAIRE, GUILLAUME, CWA I-
67
Poetry of Apollinaire, The, MP VIII-
4805
APPELFELD, AHARON, CWAII I-79
Age of Wonders, The, CLCII I-22;
MPII:WF I-29
Badenheim 1939, CLCII I-101;
MPII:WF I-101
To the Land of the Cattails, CLCII IV-
1581; MPII:WF IV-1616
Tzili, CLCII IV-1630; MPII:WF IV-
1682
APULEIUS, LUCIUS, CWA I-69
Golden Ass of Lucius Apuleius, The,
CLC I-406; MP IV-2292; MP:EF II-
575
AQUINAS, THOMAS, CWA I-71
Summa Theologica, MP XI-6329
ARBLEY, MADAM. See BURNEY,
FANNY

ARDEN, JOHN, CWAII I-81
Serjeant Musgrave's Dance, CLCII III-1375; MPII:D IV-1444
ARENDT, HANNAH, CWAII I-83
Eichmann in Jerusalem, MPII:NF I-431
Origins of Totalitarianism, The, MPII:NF III-1107
ARETINO, PIETRO, CWA I-73
Courtesan, The, CLC I-212; MP II-1168
Discourses, MP III-1524
ARGUETA, MANLIO
One Day of Life, CLCII III-1148; MPII:AF III-1198
ARIHARA NO NARIHIRA, CWA I-75
Tales of Ise, MP XI-6378; MP:EF III-1257
ARIOSTO, LUDOVICO, CWA I-76
Orlando Furioso, CLC II-816; MP VIII-4404
Suppositi, I, CLC II-1097; MP XI-6352
ARISTOPHANES, CWA I-78
Acharnians, The, CLC I-6; MP I-26
Birds, The, CLC I-105; MP I-547
Clouds, The, CLC I-189; MP II-1006
Ecclesiazusae, The, CLC I-314; MP III-1699
Frogs, The, CLC I-388; MP IV-2178
Knights, The, CLC I-582; MP VI-3189
Lysistrata, CLC I-640; MP VI-3578
Peace, The, CLC II-844; MP VIII-4541
Plutus, CLC II-896; MP VIII-4770
Thesmophoriazusae, The, CLC II-1122; MP XI-6483
Wasps, The, CLC II-1225; MP XII-7044
ARISTOTLE, CWA I-81
Poetics, The, MP VIII-4789
ARIZA, PEDRO ANTONIO DE ALARCÓN Y. See ALARCÓN, PEDRO ANTONIO DE
ARLEN, MICHAEL J.
Exiles, MPII:NF II-476
ARLT, ROBERTO
Seven Madmen, The, CLCII IV-1384; MPII:AF IV-1397

ARMAH, AYI KWEI, CWAII I-85
Beautyful Ones Are Not Yet Born, The, CLCII I-129; MPII:BCF I-118
Healers, The, CLCII II-666; MPII:BCF II-705
Two Thousand Seasons, CLCII IV-1628; MPII:BCF IV-1761
ARNOLD, MATTHEW, CWA I-83
Culture and Anarchy, MP III-1242
Poetry of Arnold, The, MP VIII-4808
Sohrab and Rustum, CLC II-1057; MP X-6125
ARNOW, HARRIETTE, CWAII I-87
Dollmaker, The, CLCII II-414; MPII:AF I-428
ARRABAL, FERNANDO, CWAII I-89
Architect and the Emperor of Assyria, The, CLCII I-65; MPII:D I-82
ARREOLA, JUAN JOSÉ
Fair, The, CLCII II-483; MPII:AF II-505
ARTAUD, ANTONIN, CWAII I-92
Cenci, The, CLCII I-249; MPII:D I-293
Theatre and Its Double, The, MPII:NF IV-1490
ARTSYBASHEV, MIKHAIL, CWA I-86
Sanine, CLC II-1004; MP X-5787; MP:EF III-1123
ASCH, SHOLEM, CWA I-87; CWAII I-94
Apostle, The, CLC I-53; MP I-269; MP:AF I-62
Nazarene, The, CLC II-761; CLCII III-1081; MP VII-4161; MP:AF II-837; MPII:WF III-1085
ASIMOV, ISAAC, CWAII I-96
Foundation trilogy, The, CLCII II-536; MPII:AF II-565
In Joy Still Felt, MPII:NF II-709
In Memory Yet Green, MPII:NF II-714
"Nightfall," MPII:SS IV-1620
ASSÍS, JOAQUIM MARIA MACHADO DE. See MACHADO DE ASSÍS, JOAQUIM MARIA

ASTLEY, THEA
  Acolyte, The, CLCII I-9; MPII:BCF I-12
  Beachmasters, CLCII I-126; MPII:BCF I-114
ASTURIAS, MIGUEL ÁNGEL, CWA I-89; CWAII I-100
  Men of Maize, CLCII III-996; MPII:AF III-991
  Mulata, CLCII III-1054; MPII:AF III-1087
  Señor Presidente, El, MP III-1726; MP:AF III-1110
  Strong Wind, CLCII IV-1485; MPII:AF IV-1541
  "Tatuana's Tale," MPII:SS V-2305
ATWOOD, MARGARET, CWAII I-103
  Edible Woman, The, CLCII II-445; MPII:BCF I-432
  Handmaid's Tale, The, CLCII II-654; MPII:BCF II-690
  Life Before Man, CLCII II-885; MPII:BCF II-959
  Surfacing, CLCII IV-1498; MPII:BCF IV-1643
AUBREY, JOHN, CWA I-91
  Brief Lives, MP II-659
AUCHINCLOSS, LOUIS, CWAII I-105
  Embezzler, The, CLCII II-452; MPII:AF II-467
  Rector of Justin, The, CLCII III-1279; MPII:AF III-1329
AUDEN, W. H., CWA I-93; CWAII I-107
  Poetry of Auden, The, MP VIII-4811
AUDEN, W. H., and CHRISTOPHER ISHERWOOD

Dog Beneath the Skin, The, CLCII II-410; MPII:D II-507
AUE, HARTMANN VON. See HARTMANN, VON AUE
AUERBACH, ERICH, CWAII I-109
  Mimesis, MPII:NF III-960
AUGUSTINE, SAINT, CWA I-95
  Confessions, MP II-1057
AUGUSTINUS, AURELIUS. See AUGUSTINE, SAINT
AURELIUS, MARCUS. See MARCUS AURELIUS
AUSTEN, JANE, CWA I-97
  Emma, CLC I-324; MP III-1763; MP:BF I-363
  Mansfield Park, CLC I-666; MP VII-3704; MP:BF II-864
  Northanger Abbey, CLC II-782; MP VII-4238; MP:BF II-1068
  Persuasion, CLC II-863; MP VIII-4615; MP:BF II-1190
  Pride and Prejudice, CLC II-914; MP IX-5307; MP:BF III-1258
  Sense and Sensibility, CLC II-1022; MP X-5905; MP:BF III-1411
AYCKBOURN, ALAN
  Absurd Person Singular, CLCII I-4; MPII:D I-1
  Norman Conquests, The, CLCII III-1111; MPII:D III-1153
AZUELA, MARIANO, CWA I-100
  Flies, The, MP IV-2085; MP:AF I-395
  Underdogs, The, CLC II-1185; MP XII-6847; MP:AF III-1349

B

BABEL, ISAAC, CWAII I-112
"Crossing into Poland," MPII:SS II-463
"Di Grasso," MPII:SS II-600
"Guy de Maupassant," MPII:SS III-966
"How It Was Done in Odessa,"
MPII:SS III-1067
"Lyubka the Cossack," MPII:SS IV-1420
"My First Goose," MPII:SS IV-1552
"Story of My Dovecot, The," MPII:SS V-2244
BACCHELLI, RICCARDO, CWA I-101
Mill on the Po, The, CLC II-707; MP VII-3901; MP:EF II-861
BACHMAN, RICHARD. See KING, STEPHEN
BACON, SIR FRANCIS, CWA I-103
Essays, MP IV-1842
History of the Reign of King Henry VII, MP V-2660
New Atlantis, MP VII-4168
BAINBRIDGE, BERYL, CWAII I-114
Harriet Said, CLCII II-658; MPII:BCF II-700
BAKER, RUSSELL
Growing Up, MPII:NF II-606
BAKHTIN, MIKHAIL, CWAII I-116
Dialogic Imagination, The, MPII:NF I-355
BALDWIN, JAMES, CWA I-106; CWAII I-119
Another Country, CLCII I-55; MPII:AF I-43
Blues for Mister Charlie, CLCII I-179; MPII:D I-219
Fire Next Time, The, MPII:NF II-512
Giovanni's Room, CLCII II-586; MPII:AF II-623
Go Tell It on the Mountain, MP IV-2276; MP:AF I-458
"Going to Meet the Man," MPII:SS II-880
If Beale Street Could Talk, CLCII II-733; MPII:AF II-774

Just Above My Head, CLCII II-809; MPII:AF II-830
Notes of a Native Son, MPII:NF III-1029
"Sonny's Blues," MPII:SS V-2186
BALE, JOHN, CWA I-108
King John, CLC I-569; MP VI-3140
BALLARD, J. G., CWAII I-121
Crystal World, The, CLCII I-355; MPII:BCF I-339
Empire of the Sun, CLCII II-453; MPII:BCF I-437
BALZAC, HONORÉ DE, CWA I-109
César Birotteau, CLC I-165; MP II-876; MP:EF I-206
Chouans, The, CLC I-178; MP II-943; MP:EF I-232
Country Doctor, The, CLC I-209; MP II-1152; MP:EF I-285
Cousin Bette, CLC I-213; MP II-1175; MP:EF I-289
Cousin Pons, CLC I-215; MP II-1180; MP:EF I-294
Eugénie Grandet, CLC I-335; MP IV-1886; MP:EF I-480
Father Goriot, CLC I-359; MP IV-2007; MP:EF II-505
"Gobseck," MPII:SS II-867
Lost Illusions, CLC I-630; MP VI-3518; MP:EF II-798
Louis Lambert, CLCII III-922; MPII:WF II-896
Quest of the Absolute, The, CLCII III-1246; MPII:WF III-1236
Sarrasine, CLCII III-1337; MPII:WF III-1351
Splendors and Miseries of Courtesans, The, CLCII IV-1463; MPII:WF IV-1516
"Unknown Masterpiece, The," MPII:SS VI-2468
Wild Ass's Skin, The, CLC II-1241; MP XII-7133; MP:EF III-1386
BAMBARA, TONI CADE
"My Man Bovanne," MPII:SS IV-1560

BANVILLE, JOHN, CWAII I-123
Doctor Copernicus, CLCII II-409;
MPII:BCF I-388
Kepler, CLCII II-823; MPII:BCF II-899
BARAKA, AMIRI, CWAII I-125
Dutchman, CLCII II-434; MPII:D II-529
System of Dante's Hell, The, CLCII IV-1510; MPII:AF IV-1564
BARBUSSE, HENRI, CWA I-113
Under Fire, CLC II-1180; MP XII-6822; MP:EF III-1330
BARCA, PEDRO CALDERÓN DE LA.
See CALDERÓN DE LA BARCA, PEDRO
BARCLAY, JOHN, CWA I-115
Argenis, CLC I-59; MP I-302; MP:BF I-69
BARFIELD, OWEN, CWAII I-127
Saving the Appearances, MPII:NF III-1286
BARHAM, RICHARD HARRIS. See
INGOLDSBY, THOMAS
BARKER, GEORGE, CWA I-116
Poetry of Barker, The, MP VIII-4814
BARKER, PAT
Union Street, CLCII IV-1640;
MPII:BCF IV-1775
BARNARD, MARY
Assault on Mount Helicon, MPII:NF I-97
BARNES, DJUNA, CWAII I-129
Nightwood, CLCII III-1099; MPII:AF III-1139
BARNES, JULIAN, CWAII I-132
Flaubert's Parrot, CLCII II-521;
MPII:BCF II-526
Staring at the Sun, CLCII IV-1472;
MPII:BCF IV-1609
BARNES, PETER, CWAII I-134
Ruling Class, The, CLCII III-1322;
MPII:D IV-1390
BARNSLEY, ALAN GABRIEL. See
FIELDING, GABRIEL

BAROJA, PÍO, CWA I-118
Caesar or Nothing, CLC I-139; MP II-731; MP:EF I-163
King Paradox, CLC I-575; MP VI-3159; MP:EF II-728
Tree of Knowledge, The, CLCII IV-1608; MPII:WF IV-1650
BARRETT, ELIZABETH. See
BROWNING, ELIZABETH
BARRETT
BARRIE, JAMES M., CWA I-120
Admirable Crichton, The, CLC I-9; MP I-35
Dear Brutus, CLC I-249; MP III-1345
Little Minister, The, CLC I-621; MP VI-3454; MP:BF II-807
Peter Pan, CLC II-865; MP VIII-4622
Quality Street, CLC II-930; MP IX-5387
What Every Woman Knows, CLC II-1234; MP XII-7089
BARRIOS, EDUARDO, CWA I-123
Brother Ass, MP II-677; MP:AF I-149
BARRY, PHILIP, CWAII I-136
Philadelphia Story, The, CLCII III-1203; MPII:D III-1235
BARTH, JOHN, CWA I-125; CWAII I-138
End of the Road, The, MP III-1772;
MP:AF I-339
Floating Opera, The, CLCII II-524;
MPII:AF II-557
Giles Goat-Boy, CLCII II-584;
MPII:AF II-613
"Life-Story," MPII:SS II-1348
"Lost in the Funhouse," MPII:SS IV-1403
"Night-Sea Journey," MPII:SS IV-1624
Sot-Weed Factor, The, MP XI-6190;
MP:AF III-1188
BARTHELME, DONALD, CWAII I-140
"Critique de la Vie Quotidienne,"
MPII:SS I-459
"Indian Uprising, The," MPII:SS III-1165
"Lightning," MPII:SS III-1355

"Paraguay," MPII:SS IV-1764
"See the Moon?" MPII:SS V-2064
"Some of Us Had Been Threatening Our
Friend Colby," MPII:SS V-2177
"Views of My Father Weeping,"
MPII:SS VI-2500
"Wrack," MPII:SS VI-2716
BARTHELME, FREDERICK, CWAII I-
142
"Moon Deluxe," MPII:SS IV-1532
BARTHES, ROLAND, CWAII I-144
Camera Lucida, MPII:NF I-227
S/Z, MPII:NF III-1263
BASHÔ, MATSUO, CWA I-127
Poetry of Bashô, The, MP VIII-4816
BASOALTO, NEFTALÍ RICARDO
REYES. See NERUDA, PABLO
BASS, ROCHELLE. See OWENS,
ROCHELLE
BASSANI, GIORGIO, CWAII I-146
Garden of the Finzi-Continis, The,
CLCII II-566; MPII:WF II-511
Gold-Rimmed Eyeglasses, The, CLCII
II-604; MPII:WF II-557
BATES, H. E., CWAII I-148
Blossoming World, The, MPII:NF IV-
1628
"Cruise of The Breadwinner, The,"
MPII:SS II-471
"Death of a Huntsman," MPII:SS II-535
"Gleaner, The," MPII:SS II-860
"House with the Grape-vine, The,"
MPII:SS III-1049
Love for Lydia, CLCII III-924;
MPII:BCF III-1017
Vanished World, The, MPII:NF IV-
1628
World in Ripeness, The, MPII:NF IV-
1628
BAUDELAIRE, CHARLES, CWA I-129
Flowers of Evil, MP IV-2092
BAUM, VICKI, CWA I-131
Grand Hotel, CLC I-414; MP IV-2335;
MP:EF II-585

BEACH, REX, CWA I-132
Spoilers, The, CLC II-1077; MP XI-
6225; MP:AF III-1198
BEARD, CHARLES A., and MARY R.
BEARD, CWA I-133
Rise of American Civilization, The, MP
X-5614
BEATTIE, ANN, CWAII I-150
"Imagined Scenes," MPII:SS III-1122
"In the White Night," MPII:SS III-1158
"Jacklighting," MPII:SS III-1208
"Winter: 1978," MPII:SS VI-2652
BEAUCHAMP, KATHLEEN
MANSFIELD. See MANSFIELD,
KATHERINE
BEAUMARCHAIS, PIERRE AUGUSTIN
CARON DE, CWA I-135
Barber of Seville, The, CLC I-79; MP
I-423
Marriage of Figaro, The, CLC I-674;
MP VII-3745
BEAUMONT, FRANCIS
Knight of the Burning Pestle, The, CLC
I-581; MP VI-3185
BEAUMONT, FRANCIS, and JOHN
FLETCHER, CWA I-137
Coxcomb, The, CLC I-218; MP II-1185
King and No King, A, CLC I-569; MP
VI-3133
Maid's Tragedy, The, CLC I-654; MP
VI-3638
Philaster, CLC II-868; MP VIII-4639
Scornful Lady, The, CLC II-1012; MP
X-5848
Woman Hater, The, CLC II-1255; MP
XII-7207
BEAUVOIR, SIMONE DE, CWAII I-153
Memoirs of a Dutiful Daughter,
MPII:NF III-917
Prime of Life, The, MPII:NF III-1184
Second Sex, The, MPII:NF IV-1314
BECKER, JUREK, CWAII I-155
Sleepless Days, CLCII IV-1423;
MPII:WF IV-1458
BECKETT, SAMUEL, CWA I-141;
CWAII I-157

All That Fall, CLCII I-32; MPII:D I-33
Company, CLCII I-314; MPII:BCF I-303; MPII:WF I-291
"Dante and the Lobster," MPII:SS II-480
Embers, CLCII II-451; MPII:D II-557
"End, The," MPII:SS II-686
Endgame, CLCII II-458; MPII:D II-563
Happy Days, CLCII II-657; MPII:D II-742
How It Is, CLCII II-717; MPII:WF II-644
Ill Seen Ill Said, CLCII II-738; MPII:WF II-664
"Imagination Dead Imagine," MPII:SS III-1119
Krapp's Last Tape, CLCII II-841; MPII:D III-920
Malone Dies, CLCII III-951
Molloy, CLCII III-1028
Murphy, CLCII III-1059; MPII:BCF III-1157
Proust, MPII:NF III-1219
Trilogy, The, MPII:BCF IV-1742; MPII:WF IV-1661
Unnamable, The, CLCII IV-1643
Waiting for Godot, CLC II-1215; MP XII-6991
Watt, CLCII IV-1694; MPII:BCF IV-1875
Words and Music, CLCII IV-1745; MPII:D IV-1766
BECKFORD, WILLIAM, CWA I-143
Vathek, CLC II-1194; MP XII-6881; MP:BF III-1667
BECKHAM, BARRY, CWAII I-160
Runner Mack, CLCII III-1324; MPII:AF III-1353
BEDDOES, THOMAS LOVELL, CWA I-145
Poetry of Beddoes, The, MP VIII-4819
BEERBOHM, MAX, CWA I-147
"Enoch Soames," MPII:SS II-702
Essays of Max Beerbohm, The, MP IV-1866

"Mote in the Middle Distance, H*nry J*m*s, The," MPII:SS IV-1538
Zuleika Dobson, CLC II-1280; MP XII-7334; MP:BF III-1787
BEHAN, BRENDAN, CWAII I-162
Borstal Boy, MPII:NF I-190
Hostage, The, CLCII II-700; MPII:D II-778
Quare Fellow, The, CLCII III-1241; MPII:D III-1294
BEHN, APHRA, CWA I-149
Oroonoko, CLC II-823; MP VIII-4421; MP:BF II-1137
BEHRMAN, S. N., CWAII I-164
Second Man, The, CLCII III-1364; MPII:D IV-1433
BELLAMANN, HENRY, CWA I-151
King's Row, CLC I-579; MP VI-3179; MP:AF II-636
BELLAMY, EDWARD, CWA I-152
Looking Backward, CLC I-626; MP VI-3497; MP:AF II-702
BELLAY, JOACHIM DU, CWA I-154
Poetry of Du Bellay, The, MP IX-4914
BELLOC, HILAIRE, CWA I-156
Path to Rome, The, MP VIII-4521
BELLOW, SAUL, CWA I-158; CWAII I-166
Adventures of Augie March, The, MP I-43; MP:AF I-7
Dangling Man, CLCII I-363; MPII:AF I-366
Dean's December, The, CLCII I-375; MPII:AF I-378
"Gonzaga Manuscripts, The," MPII:SS II-896
Henderson the Rain King, MP V-2547; MP:AF II-547
Herzog, CLCII II-677; MPII:AF II-712
Humboldt's Gift, CLCII II-721; MPII:AF II-759
"Leaving the Yellow House," MPII:SS III-1317
"Looking for Mr. Green," MPII:SS IV-1395

Mr. Sammler's Planet, CLCII III-1020; MPII:AF III-1017
Seize the Day, CLCII III-1369; MPII:AF III-1382
"Silver Dish, A," MPII:SS V-2112
Victim, The, MP XII-6911; MP:AF III-1371
BELY, ANDREY, CWAII I-168
Petersburg, CLCII III-1199; MPII:WF IV-1442
Silver Dove, The, CLCII IV-1413; MPII:WF IV-1442
BENAVENTE, JACINTO, CWA I-160
Bonds of Interest, The, CLC I-115; MP I-589
Passion Flower, The, CLC II-840; MP VIII-4505
BENET, JUAN, CWAII I-170
Meditation, A, CLCII III-990; A, MPII:WF III-988
Return to Región, CLCII III-1289; MPII:WF III-1272
BENÉT, STEPHEN VINCENT, CWA I-162
"Devil and Daniel Webster, The," MPII:SS II-575
John Brown's Body, CLC I-549; MP V-3016
Poetry of Stephen Vincent Benét, The, MP IX-5159
BENJAMIN, WALTER, CWAII I-172
Storyteller, The, MPII:NF IV-1447
Work of Art in the Age of Mechanical Reproduction, The, MPII:NF IV-1719
BENNETT, ARNOLD, CWA I-164
Anna of the Five Towns, CLC I-46; MP I-233; MP:BF I-50
Clayhanger Trilogy, The, CLC I-185; MP II-984; MP:BF I-220
Old Wives' Tale, The, CLC II-808; MP VIII-4344; MP:BF II-1100
Riceyman Steps, CLC II-965; MP X-5577; MP:BF III-1323
BERDYAEV, NICHOLAS, CWA I-167
Dostoevsky, MP III-1621

BERGER, JOHN, CWAII I-175
Fortunate Man, A, MPII:NF II-521
G., CLCII II-560; MPII:BCF II-567
Painter of Our Time, A, CLCII III-1171; MPII:BCF III-1272
Ways of Seeing, MPII:NF IV-1670
BERGER, THOMAS, CWAII I-177
Little Big Man, CLCII III-893; MPII:AF III-891
BERGSON, HENRI, CWA I-169
Laughter, MP VI-3289
Matter and Memory, MP VII-3776
BERKELEY, GEORGE, CWA I-171
Essay Towards a New Theory of Vision, An, MP IV-1840
BERLIN, ISAIAH, CWAII I-179
Russian Thinkers, MPII:NF III-1257
BERNANOS, GEORGES, CWA I-173
Diary of a Country Priest, The, CLC I-270; MP III-1503; MP:EF I-394
Mouchette, CLCII III-1048; MPII:WF III-1045
Under the Sun of Satan, CLCII IV-1634; MPII:WF IV-1694
BERNHARD, THOMAS, CWAII I-182
Concrete, CLCII I-319; MPII:WF I-300
Correction, CLCII I-338; MPII:WF I-323
Gargoyles, CLCII II-568; MPII:WF II-516
Gathering Evidence, MPII:NF II-539
Lime Works, The, CLCII II-891; MPII:WF II-866
Untergeher, Der, CLCII IV-1644; MPII:WF IV-1700
Woodcutters, CLCII IV-1742; MPII:WF II-603
BERRIAULT, GINA
"Stone Boy, The," MPII:SS V-2232
BERRY, WENDELL, CWAII I-185
Gift of Good Land, The, MPII:NF II-555
BERRYMAN, JOHN, CWA I-175
Homage to Mistress Bradstreet, MP V-2678

BETI, MONGO, CWAII I-187
    Poor Christ of Bomba, The, CLCII III-
    1219; MPII:WF IV-1214
BETJEMAN, JOHN
    Poetry of Betjeman, The, MP VIII-4822
BEYLE, MARIE-HENRI. *See*
    STENDHAL
BIENEK, HORST
    Silesian Tetralogy, The, CLCII IV-
    1408; MPII:WF III-1436
BIERCE, AMBROSE, CWA I-177
    "Chickamauga," MPII:SS I-368
    "Occurrence at Owl Creek Bridge, An,"
    MPII:SS IV-1643
    "One of the Missing," MPII:SS IV-1701
    Tales of Soldiers and Civilians, MP XI-
    6381; MP:AF III-1252
BION
    Poetry of Bion, The, MP VIII-4825
BIOY CASARES, ADOLFO, CWAII I-
    189
    Diary of the War of the Pig, CLCII I-
    399; MPII:AF I-400
    Invention of Morel, The, CLCII II-772;
    MPII:AF II-798
BIRD, ROBERT MONTGOMERY, CWA
    I-179
    Nick of the Woods, CLC II-775; MP
    VII-4199; MP:AF II-841
BIRNEY, EARLE, CWAII I-191
    Turvey, CLCII IV-1623; MPII:BCF IV-
    1751
BIYIDI, ALEXANDRE. *See* BETI,
    MONGO
BJÖRNSON, BJÖRNSTJERNE, CWA I-
    180
    Arne, CLC I-61; MP I-310; MP:EF I-
    61
    Beyond Human Power, Two, CLC I-
    102; MP I-523
    Fisher Maiden, The, CLC I-371; MP
    IV-2079; MP:EF II-519
BLACKMORE, R. D., CWA I-183
    Lorna Doone, CLC I-628; MP VI-3508;
    MP:BF II-829

BLACKWOOD, ALGERNON, CWAII I-
    194
    "Willows, The," MPII:SS VI-2638
BLAIR, ERIC ARTHUR. *See* ORWELL,
    GEORGE
BLAIR, ERIC HUGH. *See* ORWELL,
    GEORGE
BLAKE, WILLIAM, CWA I-185
    Poetry of Blake, The, MP VIII-4827
BLASCO IBÁÑEZ, VICENTE, CWA I-
    188
    Cabin, The, CLC I-137; MP II-722;
    MP:EF I-156
BLIXEN-FINECKE, BARONESS
    KAREN. *See* DINESEN, ISAK
BLOCH, ERNST, CWAII I-196
    Principle of Hope, The, MPII:NF III-
    1196
BLOK, ALEKSANDR, CWA I-190
    Poetry of Blok, The, MP VIII-4830
BLOOM, ALLAN, CWAII I-198
    Closing of the American Mind, The,
    MPII:NF I-255
BLOOM, HAROLD, CWAII I-200
    Anxiety of Influence, The, MPII:NF I-
    75
BLUNDEN, EDMUND CHARLES, CWA
    I-192
    Poetry of Blunden, The, MP VIII-4833
BOAS, FRANZ, CWA I-193
    Mind of Primitive Man, The, MP VII-
    3906
BOCCACCIO, GIOVANNI, CWA I-195
    Decameron, The, MP III-1397; MP:EF
    I-371
    Filostrato, Il, MP IV-2062
    L'Amorosa Fiammetta, CLC I-591; MP
    VI-3240; MP:EF II-746
    Teseide, La, MP XI-6453
BODANIS, DAVID
    Secret House, The, MPII:NF IV-1319
BOETHIUS, ANICIUS MANLIUS
    SEVERINUS, CWA I-197
    Consolation of Philosophy, The, MP II-
    1104

BOIARDO, MATTEO MARIA, CWA I-198
Orlando Innamorato, CLC II-819; MP VIII-4410
BOILEAU-DESPRÉAUX, NICOLAS, CWA I-199
Dialogue des héros de roman, MP III-1479
Satires, MP X-5809
BOJER, JOHAN, CWA I-201
Emigrants, The, CLC I-321; MP III-1749; MP:EF I-473
Last of the Vikings, The, CLC I-597; MP VI-3266; MP:EF II-754
BÖLL, HEINRICH, CWAII I-203
Billiards at Half-Past Nine, CLCII I-153; MPII:WF I-152
Clown, The, CLCII I-300; MPII:WF I-281
Group Portrait with Lady, CLCII II-641; MPII:WF II-562
Lost Honor of Katharina Blum, The, CLCII III-919; MPII:WF II-870
"Murke's Collected Silences," MPII:SS IV-1548
Safety Net, The, CLCII III-1326; MPII:WF III-1326
What's to Become of the Boy? MPII:NF IV-1687
BOLT, ROBERT, CWAII I-205
Man for All Seasons, A, CLCII III-952; MPII:D III-1037
BOMBAL, MARÍA LUISA, CWAII I-207
Final Mist, The, CLCII II-503; MPII:AF II-537
"New Islands," MPII:SS IV-1612
Shrouded Woman, The, CLCII IV-1397; MPII:AF IV-1422
BOND, EDWARD, CWAII I-210
Lear, CLCII II-866; MPII:D III-949
Saved, CLCII III-1341; MPII:D IV-1406
BONHOEFFER, DIETRICH, CWAII I-212
Ethics, MPII:NF II-466

Letters and Papers from Prison, MPII:NF II-807
BONTEMPS, ARNA, CWAII I-215
Black Thunder, CLCII I-164; MPII:AF I-171
BOOTH, PHILIP, CWA I-203
Poetry of Booth, The, MP VIII-4835
BORGES, JORGE LUIS, CWA I-204; CWAII I-217
"Aleph, The," MPII:SS I-52
"Circular Ruins, The," MPII:SS I-399
Ficciones, MP IV-1040; MP:AF I-375
"Funes, the Memorious," MPII:SS II-820
"Garden of Forking Paths, The," MPII:SS II-824
"Gospel According to Mark, The," MPII:SS II-915
"Library of Babel, The," MPII:SS III-1342
"Pierre Menard, Author of the Quixote," MPII:SS IV-1814
"South, The," MPII:SS V-2194
"Theme of the Traitor and the Hero," MPII:SS VI-2329
"Tlön, Uqbar, Orbis Tertius," MPII:SS VI-2373
BOROWSKI, TADEUSZ, CWAII I-220
"This Way for the Gas, Ladies and Gentlemen," MPII:SS VI-2348
"World of Stone, The," MPII:SS VI-2709
BORROW, GEORGE HENRY, CWA I-209
Bible in Spain, The, MP I-528
Lavengro, CLC I-601; MP VI-3292; MP:BF II-787
Romany Rye, The, CLC II-988; MP X-5693; MP:BF II-1365
Wild Wales, MP XII-7145
Zinicali, The, MP XII-7328
BOSWELL, JAMES, CWA I-211
Boswell's London Journal: 1762-1763, MP I-608
Journal of a Tour to the Hebrides, MP V-3044

Life of Samuel Johnson, LL.D., The,
MP VI-3409
BOURGET, PAUL, CWA I-214
Disciple, The, CLC I-271; MP III-1519;
MP:EF I-402
BOWEN, ELIZABETH, CWA I-216;
CWAII I-222
Bowen's Court, MPII:NF I-201
Death of the Heart, The, CLC I-257;
MP III-1381; MP:BF I-295
"Demon Lover, The," MPII:SS II-565
Eva Trout, CLCII II-470; MPII:BCF I-461
"Happy Autumn Fields, The," MPII:SS
III-985
Heat of the Day, The, CLC I-453; MP
V-2523; MP:BF I-555
"Her Table Spread," MPII:SS III-1000
House in Paris, The, CLC I-486; MP
V-2714; MP:BF II-602
"Ivy Gripped the Steps," MPII:SS III-1201
Little Girls, The, CLCII III-895;
MPII:BCF II-971
"Mysterious Kôr," MPII:SS IV-1575
"Summer Night," MPII:SS V-2271
World of Love, A, CLCII IV-1753;
MPII:BCF IV-1935
BOWERING, GEORGE
Burning Water, CLCII I-217;
MPII:BCF I-211
BOWERS, CLAUDE G. CWA 1-218
Jefferson and Hamilton: The Struggle
for Democracy in America, MP V-2993
BOWLES, JANE, CWAII I-224
"Stick of Green Candy, A," MPII:SS V-2228
BOWLES, PAUL, CWAII I-226
"Delicate Prey, The," MPII:SS II-553
"Distant Episode, A," MPII:SS II-610
Sheltering Sky, The, CLCII IV-1390;
MPII:AF IV-1402
BOX, EDGAR. See VIDAL, GORE

BOYD, JAMES, CWA I-219
Drums, CLC I-307; MP III-1656;
MP:AF I-313
Marching On, CLC I-668; MP VII-3714; MP:AF II-761
BOYD, MARTIN
Lucinda Brayford, CLCII III-933;
MPII:BCF III-1033
BOYLE, KAY, CWAII I-228
"Summer Evening," MPII:SS V-2267
"White Horses of Vienna, The,"
MPII:SS VI-2585
"Winter Night," MPII:SS VI-2649
BOYLE, T. CORAGHESSAN, CWAII I-231
"Greasy Lake," MPII:SS III-925
"Overcoat II, The," MPII:SS IV-1749
BRACKENRIDGE, HUGH HENRY,
CWA I-220
Modern Chivalry, CLC II-728; MP VII-4001; MP:AF II-806
BRADBURY, MALCOLM, CWAII I-233
Eating People Is Wrong, CLCII II-439;
MPII:BCF I-418
History Man, The, CLCII II-680;
MPII:BCF II-721
Rates of Exchange, CLCII III-1268;
MPII:BCF III-1390
BRADBURY, RAY, CWAII I-235
"April Witch, The," MPII:SS I-103
Fahrenheit 451, CLCII II-482; MPII:AF
II-501
Martian Chronicles, The, CLCII III-979; MPII:AF III-986
Something Wicked This Way Comes,
CLCII IV-1441; MPII:AF IV-1471
"There Will Come Soft Rains,"
MPII:SS VI-2333
"Veldt, The," MPII:SS VI-2485
BRADFORD, GAMALIEL, CWA I-221
Damaged Souls, MP III-1273
BRADFORD, WILLIAM, CWA I-223
Of Plimouth Plantation, MP VIII-4297
BRADLEY, DAVID
Chaneysville Incident, The, CLCII I-256; MPII:AF I-274

BRAINE, JOHN, CWA I-225
Room at the Top, MP X-5709; MP:BF
III-1373
BRANDÃO, IGNÁCIO DE LOYOLA.
See LOYOLA BRANDÃO,
IGNÁCIO DE
BRAUTIGAN, RICHARD, CWAII I-240
Confederate General from Big Sur, A,
CLCII I-321; MPII:AF I-325
In Watermelon Sugar, CLCII II-754;
MPII:AF II-787
Trout Fishing in America, CLCII IV-
1619; MPII:AF IV-1702
BRECHT, BERTOLT, CWA I-227;
CWAII I-242
Baal, MP I-397
Caucasian Chalk Circle, The, CLCII I-
247; MPII:D I-288
Galileo, CLCII II-562; MPII:D II-650
Good Woman of Setzuan, The, CLCII
II-615; MPII:D II-689
Mother Courage and Her Children,
CLCII III-1046; MPII:D III-1105
Private Life of the Master Race, The,
CLC II-918; MP IX-5344
Rise and Fall of the City of Mahagonny,
CLCII III-1298; MPII:D IV-1350
Threepenny Opera, The, CLCII IV-
1560; MPII:D IV-1568
BRENTON, HOWARD, CWAII I-245
Bloody Poetry, CLCII I-172; MPII:D I-
207
BRENTON, HOWARD, and DAVID
HARE
Pravda, CLCII III-1232; MPII:D III-
1278
BRETON, ANDRÉ, CWA I-229
Poetry of André Breton, The, MP VIII-
4802
BRETON, NICHOLAS, CWA I-231
Poetry of Nicholas Breton, The, MP IX-
5103
BREUER, JOSEF, and SIGMUND
FREUD
Studies on Hysteria, MP XI-6317

BREYTENBACH, BREYTEN, CWAII I-
247
True Confessions of an Albino
Terrorist, The, MPII:NF IV-1569
BRINK, ANDRÉ, CWAII I-250
Chain of Voices, A, CLCII I-254;
MPII:BCF I-235
BRITTAIN, VERA, CWAII I-253
Testament of Youth, Testament of
Friendship, and Testament of
Experience, MPII:NF IV-1479
BROCH, HERMANN, CWA I-232;
CWAII I-255
Death of Virgil, The, CLC I-257; MP
III-1385; MP:EF I-363
Sleepwalkers, The, CLC II-1049; MP
X-6089; MP:EF III-1164
Spell, The, CLCII IV-1460; MPII:WF
IV-1506
BRODKEY, HAROLD, CWAII I-257
"His Son, in His Arms, in Light,
Aloft," MPII:SS III-1022
BRODSKY, JOSEPH, CWAII I-259
Less Than One, MPII:NF II-802
BROME, RICHARD, CWA I-234
Jovial Crew, A, CLC I-556; MP VI-
3075
Northern Lass, The, CLC II-783; MP
VII-4243
BROMFIELD, LOUIS, CWA I-235
Green Bay Tree, The, CLC I-424; MP
IV-2378; MP:AF II-509
BRONTË, ANNE, CWA I-237
Agnes Grey, CLC I-15; MP I-73;
MP:BF I-16
Tenant of Wildfell Hall, The, CLC II-
1115; MP XI-6442; MP:BF III-1505
BRONTË, CHARLOTTE, CWA I-237
Jane Eyre, CLC I-540; MP V-2976;
MP:BF II-681
Professor, The, CLC II-920; MP IX-
5353; MP:BF III-1274
Shirley, CLC II-1034; MP X-5985;
MP:BF III-1427
Villette, CLC II-1204; MP XII-6929;
MP:BF III-1686

BRONTË, EMILY, CWA I-237
Poetry of Emily Brontë, The, MP IX-4932
Wuthering Heights, CLC II-1270; MP XII-7281; MP:BF III-1775
BROOKE, HENRY, CWA I-241
Fool of Quality, The, CLC I-374; MP IV-2107; MP:BF I-434
BROOKE, RUPERT, CWA I-242
Poetry of Brooke, The, MP VIII-4838
BROOKNER, ANITA, CWAII I-261
Debut, The, CLCII I-383; MPII:BCF I-370
Hotel du Lac, CLCII II-702; MPII:BCF II-743
Look at Me, CLCII III-912; MPII:BCF III-1003
BROOKS, GWENDOLYN, CWA I-244; CWAII I-263
"Rise of Maud Martha, The," MPII:SS V-1961
BROOKS, VAN WYCK, CWA I-246
America's Coming-of-Age, MP I-179
BROWN, CHARLES BROCKDEN, CWA I-248
Wieland, CLC II-1241; MP XII-7129; MP:AF III-1433
BROWN, GEORGE DOUGLAS. See DOUGLAS, GEORGE
BROWN, RITA MAE, CWAII I-265
Rubyfruit Jungle, CLCII III-1318; MPII:AF III-1349
BROWNE, SIR THOMAS, CWA I-250
Hydriotaphia: Urn-Burial, MP V-2791
BROWNING, ELIZABETH BARRETT, CWA I-252
Sonnets from the Portuguese, MP XI-6168
BROWNING, ROBERT, CWA I-254
Blot in the 'Scutcheon, A, CLC I-112; MP I-578
Dramatic Monologues and Lyrics of Browning, MP III-1641
Dramatis Personae, MP III-1644
Men and Women, MP VII-3846

Ring and the Book, The, CLC II-970; MP X-5603
BRYANT, WILLIAM CULLEN, CWA I-257
Poetry of Bryant, The, MP VIII-4841
BRYCE, JAMES VISCOUNT, CWA I-260
American Commonwealth, The, MP I-169
BUCHAN, JOHN, CWA I-261
Thirty-Nine Steps, The, CLC II-1124; MP XI-6493; MP:BF III-1523
BÜCHNER, GEORG, CWA I-263
"Lenz," CLCII II-872; MPII:SS III-1335
Woyzeck, CLC II-1269; MP XII-7275
BUCK, PEARL S., CWA I-265
Dragon Seed, CLC I-302; MP III-1638; MP:AF I-309
Good Earth, The, CLC I-411; MP IV-2319; MP:AF I-478
BUCKLER, ERNEST, CWAII I-267
Mountain and the Valley, The, CLCII III-1051; MPII:BCF III-1143
BUCKLEY, WILLIAM F., JR., CWAII I-269
Cruising Speed, MPII:NF I-310
Overdrive, MPII:NF III-1113
BUDGELL, EUSTACE, JOSEPH ADDISON, and SIR RICHARD STEELE
Sir Roger de Coverley Papers, The, CLC II-1044; MP X-6067
BUECHNER, FREDERICK, CWAII I-272
Book of Bebb, The, CLCII I-187; MPII:AF I-196
Now and Then, MPII:NF III-1041
Sacred Journey, The, MPII:NF III-1269
BUGAEV, BORIS NIKOLAYEVICH. See BELY, ANDREY
BULGAKOV, MIKHAIL, CWAII I-275
Days of the Turbins, CLCII I-371; MPII:D II-449
Heart of a Dog, The, CLCII II-667; MPII:WF II-583

Master and Margarita, The, CLCII III-984; MPII:WF III-976
BULLEN, FRANK THOMAS, CWA I-268
Cruise of the Cachalot, The, CLC I-227; MP III-1232; MP:BF I-265
BULLINS, ED, CWAII I-278
In the Wine Time, CLCII II-753; MPII:D II-820
BULWER-LYTTON, EDWARD GEORGE EARLE, CWA I-269
Eugene Aram, CLC I-334; MP IV-1879; MP:BF I-378
Last Days of Pompeii, The, CLC I-594; MP VI-3249; MP:BF II-772
Last of the Barons, The, CLC I-595; MP VI-3257; MP:BF II-780
BUNIN, IVAN ALEXEYEVICH, CWA I-272
"Gentleman from San Francisco, The," MPII:SS II-835
Village, The, CLC II-1203; MP XII-6922; MP:EF III-1349
BUNYAN, JOHN, CWA I-274
Life and Death of Mr. Badman, The, CLC I-610; MP VI-3392; MP:BF II-796
Pilgrim's Progress, The, CLC II-882; MP VIII-4705; MP:BF III-1227
BUONARROTI, MICHELANGELO. See MICHELANGELO BUONARROTI
BURGESS, ANTHONY, CWAII I-280
Clockwork Orange, A, CLCII I-295; MPII:BCF I-271
Earthly Powers, CLCII II-437; MPII:BCF I-413
End of the World News, The, CLCII II-455; MPII:BCF I-447
Little Wilson and Big God, MPII:NF II-841
Napoleon Symphony, CLCII III-1075; MPII:BCF III-1171
Nothing Like the Sun, CLCII III-1116; MPII:BCF III-1233
Right to an Answer, The, CLCII III-1295; MPII:BCF III-1416

Tremor of Intent, CLCII IV-1609; MPII:BCF IV-1732
BURKE, EDMUND, CWA I-279
Vindication of Natural Society, A, MP XII-6934
BURKE, KENNETH, CWAII I-283
Grammar of Motives, A, MPII:NF II-573
BURNEY, FANNY, CWA I-281
Cecilia, CLC I-162; MP II-861; MP:BF I-193
Diary and Letters of Mme. d'Arblay, The, MP III-1499
Evelina, CLC I-341; MP IV-1913; MP:BF I-395
BURNS, ROBERT, CWA I-283
Poems, Chiefly in the Scottish Dialect, MP VIII-4783
BURROUGHS, WILLIAM S., CWAII I-286
Naked Lunch, CLCII III-1071; MPII:AF III-1114
BURTON, ROBERT, CWA I-286
Anatomy of Melancholy, The, MP I-200
BUTLER, SAMUEL (1612-1680) CWA I-288
Hudibras, CLC I-497; MP V-2760
BUTLER, SAMUEL (1835-1902) CWA I-289
Erewhon, CLC I-331; MP III-1822; MP:BF I-370
Way of All Flesh, The, CLC II-1228; MP XII-7061; MP:BF III-1721
BUTOR, MICHEL, CWAII I-288
Change of Heart, A, CLCII I-257; MPII:WF I-239
Mobile, CLCII III-1027; MPII:WF II-1021
Niagara, CLCII III-1089; MPII:WF III-1093
Passing Time, CLCII III-1183; MPII:WF III-1173
BUZZATI, DINO
Bàrnabo of the Mountains, CLCII I-117; MPII:WF I-116
"Count's Wife, The," MPII:SS I-448

Tartar Steppe, The, CLCII IV-1516; MPII:WF IV-1548

BYRNE, DONN, CWA I-291
Destiny Bay, CLC I-266; MP III-1463; MP:BF I-314
Hangman's House, CLC I-442; MP V-2473; MP:BF I-528
Messer Marco Polo, CLC I-698; MP VII-3863; MP:BF II-928

BYRNE, JOHN KEYES. *See* LEONARD, HUGH

BYRON, GEORGE GORDON, LORD, CWA I-293
Cain, CLC I-140; MP II-734
Childe Harold's Pilgrimage, MP II-921
Don Juan, CLC I-291; MP III-1590
Lyric Poetry of Byron, The, MP VI-3562
Manfred, CLC I-663; MP VII-3690

C

CABELL, JAMES BRANCH, CWA I-296
  Cream of the Jest, The, CLC I-220; MP
    II-1194; MP:AF I-231
  Jurgen, CLC I-563; MP VI-3105;
    MP:AF II-626
  Rivet in Grandfather's Neck, The, CLC
    II-976; MP X-5632; MP:AF III-1058
CABLE, GEORGE WASHINGTON,
    CWA I-299
  Grandissimes, The, CLC I-414; MP IV-
    2338; MP:AF I-483
  "Jean-ah Poquelin," MPII:SS III-1214
CABRERA INFANTE, GUILLERMO,
    CWAII I-290
  Infante's Inferno, CLCII II-760;
    MPII:AF II-792
  Three Trapped Tigers, CLCII IV-1559;
    MPII:AF IV-1652
CAESAR, CWA I-301
  Commentaries, MP II-1040
CAIN, GUILLERMO. See CABRERA
    INFANTE, GUILLERMO
CAIN, JAMES M., CWA I-303
  Postman Always Rings Twice, The, MP
    IX-5270; MP:AF II-978
CALDERÓN DE LA BARCA, PEDRO,
    CWA I-305
  Devotion of the Cross, The, CLC I-267;
    MP III-1471
  It Is Better than It Was, CLC I-534; MP
    V-2942
  It Is Worse than It Was, CLC I-534;
    MP V-2945
  Life Is a Dream, CLC I-611; MP VI-
    3398
  Mayor of Zalamea, The, CLC I-684;
    The, MP VII-3788
  Mock Astrologer, The, CLC II-728; MP
    VII-3998
CALDWELL, ERSKINE, CWA I-308;
    CWAII I-292
  God's Little Acre, CLCII II-603;
    MPII:AF II-639
  Tobacco Road, CLC II-1140; MP XI-
    6578; MP:AF III-1299

CALISHER, HORTENSE, CWAII I-295
  "In Greenwich There Are Many
    Gravelled Walks," MPII:SS III-1137
CALLAGHAN, MORLEY, CWAII I-297
  "All the Years of Her Life," MPII:SS I-
    60
  "Cap for Steve, A," MPII:SS I-326
  Loved and the Lost, The, CLCII III-
    928; MPII:BCF III-1022
  Passion in Rome, A, CLCII III-1184;
    MPII:BCF III-1298
  "Sick Call, A," MPII:SS V-2101
  Such Is My Beloved, CLCII IV-1487;
    MPII:BCF IV-1638
CALVINO, ITALO, CWAII I-300
  Baron in the Trees, The, CLCII I-119;
    MPII:WF I-121
  Castle of Crossed Destinies, The, CLCII
    I-240; MPII:WF I-216
  Cloven Viscount, The, CLCII I-299;
    MPII:WF I-277
  If on a Winter's Night a Traveler,
    CLCII II-736; MPII:WF II-659
  Invisible Cities, CLCII II-774;
    MPII:WF II-727
  Mr. Palomar, CLCII III-1020;
    MPII:WF III-1015
  Non-existent Knight, The, CLCII III-
    1110; MPII:WF III-1113
  Path to the Nest of Spiders, The, CLCII
    III-1186; MPII:WF III-1178
  "Watcher, The," MPII:SS VI-2556
CAMOËNS, LUIS DE, CWA I-310
  Lusiad, The, CLC I-639; MP VI-3557
CAMPBELL, JOSEPH, CWAII I-302
  Hero with a Thousand Faces, The,
    MPII:NF II-636
CAMPION, THOMAS, CWA I-312
  Poetry of Campion, The, MP VIII-4844
CAMUS, ALBERT, CWA I-314; CWAII
    I-304
  "Adulterous Woman, The," MPII:SS I-
    19
  Caligula, CLCII I-226; MPII:D I-278

Exile and the Kingdom, MP IV-1936; MP:EF II-489

Fall, The, MP IV-1965; MP:EF II-493

"Guest, The," MPII:SS III-952

Myth of Sisyphus, The, MP VII-4128

Plague, The, CLC II-889; MP VIII-4734; MP:EF III-1010

Possessed, The, CLCII III-1227; MPII:D III-1269

Rebel, The, MPII:NF III-1231

Stranger, The, MP XI-6301; MP:EF III-1244

CANETTI, ELIAS, CWAII I-306

Auto-da-Fé, CLCII I-91; MPII:WF I-95

Crowds and Power, MPII:NF I-304

Play of the Eyes, The, MPII:NF IV-1546

Tongue Set Free, The, MPII:NF IV-1546

Torch in My Ear, The, MPII:NF IV-1546

ČAPEK, KAREL, CWA I-316

R. U. R., CLC II-997; MP X-5736

CAPOTE, TRUMAN, CWAII I-308

"Children on Their Birthdays," MPII:SS I-376

"Headless Hawk, The," MPII:SS III-993

In Cold Blood, MPII:NF II-704

"My Side of the Matter," MPII:SS IV-1567

CARDUCCI, GIOSUÈ, CWA I-317

Poetry of Carducci, The, MP VIII-4847

CAREW, THOMAS, CWA I-319

Poetry of Carew, The, MP VIII-4850

CAREY, PETER

Illywhacker, CLCII II-739; MPII:BCF II-794

CARLETON, WILLIAM, CWA I-321

"Donagh, The," MPII:SS II-624

Emigrants of Ahadarra, The, CLC I-322; MP III-1752; MP:BF I-359

CARLYLE, THOMAS, CWA I-322

French Revolution, The, MP IV-2169

History of Frederick II of Prussia, MP V-2634

On Heroes, Hero-Worship and the Heroic in History, MP VIII-4368

Sartor Resartus, MP X-5799

CARPENTIER, ALEJO, CWAII I-310

Explosion in a Cathedral, CLCII II-477; MPII:AF II-496

Kingdom of This World, The, CLCII II-834; MPII:AF II-840

"Like the Night," MPII:SS III-1359

Lost Steps, The, CLCII III-921; MPII:AF II-927

Manhunt, CLCII III-965; MPII:AF III-977

CARROLL, LEWIS, CWA I-325

Alice's Adventures in Wonderland, CLC I-22; MP I-107; MP:BF I-30

Through the Looking Glass, CLC II-1130; MP:BF III-1536; MP XI-6526

CARSON, RACHEL

Silent Spring, MPII:NF IV-1351

CARVER, RAYMOND, CWAII I-313

"Careful," MPII:SS I-330

"Small, Good Thing, A," MPII:SS V-2135

"Why Don't You Dance?" MPII:SS VI-2605

"Will You Please Be Quiet, Please?" MPII:SS VI-2627

CARY, JOYCE, CWA I-328; CWAII I-315

Herself Surprised, CLC I-472; MP V-2603; MP:BF I-574

Horse's Mouth, The, CLC I-482; MP V-2699; MP:BF I-593

Second Trilogy, CLCII III-1365; MPII:BCF IV-1489

To Be a Pilgrim, CLC II-1137; MP XI-6570; MP:BF III-1547

CASANOVA, CWA I-330

Memoirs, MP VII-3823

CASEY, JOHN. See O'CASEY, SEAN

CASTANEDA, CARLOS, CWAII I-318

Teachings of Don Juan, The, MPII:NF IV-1468

CASTIGLIONE, BALDASSARE, CWA I-332

Book of the Courtier, The, MP I-596

CATHER, WILLA, CWA I-334; CWAII I-320

"Coming, Aphrodite," MPII:SS I-422

Death Comes for the Archbishop, CLC I-251; MP III-1349; MP:AF I-264

Lost Lady, A, CLC I-631; MP VI-3521; MP:AF II-706

Lucy Gayheart, CLCII III-936; MPII:AF III-943

My Ántonia, CLC II-749; MP VII-4103; MP:AF II-823

"Neighbor Rosicky," MPII:SS IV-1602

O Pioneers! CLC II-785; MP VII-4265; MP:AF II-856

One of Ours, CLCII III-1154; MPII:AF III-1213

"Paul's Case," MPII:SS IV-1779

Professor's House, The, CLC II-922; MP IX-5357; MP:AF II-994

Sapphira and the Slave Girl, CLCII III-1335; MPII:AF III-1366

"Sculptor's Funeral, The," MPII:SS V-2045

Shadows on the Rock, CLC II-1028; MP X-5948; MP:AF III-1126

Song of the Lark, The, CLC II-1064; MP XI-6159; MP:AF III-1184

CATULLUS, CWA I-338

Carmina, MP II-806

CAVAFY, CONSTANTINE P., CWA I-339

Poetry of Cavafy, The, MP VIII-4854

CAVENDISH, GEORGE, CWA I-340

Life and Death of Cardinal Wolsy, The, MP VI-3389

CELA, CAMILIO JOSÉ, CWA I-341

Family of Pascual Duarte, The, MP IV-1980; MP:EF II-501

Hive, The, MP V-2663; MP:EF II-641

CÉLINE, LOUIS-FERDINAND, CWA I-343; CWAII I-322

Castle to Castle, North, CLCII I-241; MPII:WF I-221

Death on the Installment Plan, CLCII I-380; MPII:WF I-353

Journey to the End of the Night, CLC I-555; MP VI-3068; MP:EF II-720

Rigadoon, CLCII I-241; MPII:WF I-221

CELLINI, BENVENUTO, CWA I-345

Autobiography of Benvenuto Cellini, The, MP I-368

CENDRARS, BLAISE, CWAII I-324

Sutter's Gold, CLCII IV-1500; MPII:WF IV-1538

CERVANTES, CWA I-347

Don Quixote de la Mancha, CLC I-294; MP III-1603; MP:EF I-431

Exemplary Novels, MP IV-1933; MP:EF II-485

CÉSAIRE, AIMÉ, CWAII I-326

Tragedy of King Christophe, The, CLCII IV-1598; MPII:D IV-1623

CHALLANS, MARY. See RENAULT, MARY

CHANDLER, RAYMOND, CWAII I-328

Big Sleep, The, CLCII I-151; MPII:AF I-166

Farewell, My Lovely, CLCII II-493; MPII:AF II-527

Long Goodbye, The, CLCII III-910; MPII:AF III-911

"Nevada Gas," MPII:SS IV-1608

CHAPMAN, GEORGE, CWA I-351

All Fools, CLC I-24; MP I-114

Bussy d'Ambois, CLC I-136; MP II-714

Gentleman Usher, The, CLC I-396; MP IV-2230

Monsieur d'Olive, CLC II-736; MP VII-4037

Revenge of Bussy d'Ambois, The, CLC II-961; MP X-5550

Shadow of Night, The, MP X-5945

CHAPMAN, GEORGE, BEN JONSON, and JOHN MARSTON

Eastward Ho! CLC I-313; MP III-1693

CHATEAUBRIAND, FRANÇOIS-AUGUSTE-RENÉ DE, CWA I-353

Atala, CLC I-69; MP I-349; MP:EF I-81

CHATTERTON, THOMAS, CWA I-355
Poetry of Chatterton, The, MP VIII-4857
CHATWIN, BRUCE, CWAII I-330
In Patagonia, MPII:NF II-725
CHAUCER, GEOFFREY, CWA I-357
Canterbury Tales, The, CLC I-146; MP II-769
Legend of Good Women, The, CLC I-605; MP VI-3311
Parliament of Fowls, The, MP VIII-4493
Troilus and Criseyde, CLC II-1164; MP XI-6725
CHEEVER, JOHN, CWA I-360; CWAII I-332
"Angel of the Bridge, The," MPII:SS I-95
"Brigadier and the Golf Widow, The," MPII:SS I-308
Bullet Park, CLCII I-210; MPII:AF I-216
"Country Husband, The," MPII:SS I-440
"Enormous Radio, The," MPII:SS II-706
Falconer, CLCII II-488; MPII:AF II-515
"Five-Forty-Eight, The," MPII:SS II-785
"Goodbye, My Brother," MPII:SS II-907
"Housebreaker of Shady Hill, The," MPII:SS II-1052
"Metamorphoses," MPII:SS IV-1489
Oh What a Paradise It Seems, CLCII III-1134; MPII:AF III-1180
Short Stories of John Cheever, The, MP X-6011; MP:AF III-1141
"Swimmer, The," MPII:SS V-2297
Wapshot Chronicle, The, MP XII-7020; MP:AF III-1396
Wapshot Scandal, The, MP XII-7024; MP:AF III-1400
"World of Apples, The," MPII:SS VI-2705

CHEKHOV, ANTON, CWA I-361
"Bet, The," MPII:SS I-192
"Bishop, The," MPII:SS I-214
"Chemist's Wife, The," MPII:SS I-364
Cherry Orchard, The, CLC I-173; MP II-908
"Darling, The," MPII:SS II-492
"Duel, The," CLCII II-428; MPII:SS II-650
"Gooseberries," MPII:SS II-911
"Gusev," MPII:SS III-962
"Kiss, The," MPII:SS III-1270
"Lady with the Dog, The," CLCII II-846; MPII:SS III-1288
"Man in a Case, The," MPII:SS IV-1434
"Rothschild's Fiddle," MPII:SS V-1994
Seagull, The, CLC II-1015; MP X-5868
"Steppe, The," CLCII IV-1474; MPII:SS V-2224
Three Sisters, The, CLC II-1129; MP XI-6518
"Trifling Occurrence, A," MPII:SS VI-2411
Uncle Vanya, CLC II-1179; MP XII-6818
"Ward No. 6," MPII:SS VI-2548
CHESNUTT, CHARLES WADDELL, CWA I-364
Conjure Woman, The, CLC I-197; MP II-1080; MP:AF I-211
House Behind the Cedars, The, CLCII II-705; MPII:AF II-748
"Sheriff's Children, The," MPII:SS V-2072
CHESTERFIELD, PHILIP DORMER STANHOPE, LORD, CWA I-365
Letters to His Son, MP VI-3374
CHESTERTON, G. K., CWA I-366
Autobiography, MPII:NF I-109
Essays of G. K. Chesterton, The, MP IV-1859
Everlasting Man, The, MPII:NF II-471
"Invisible Man, The," MPII:SS III-1191
Man Who Was Thursday, The, CLC I-661; MP VII-3676; MP:BF II-859

Napoleon of Notting Hill, The, CLC II-757; MP VII-4140; MP:BF II-1026
CHIKAMATSU MONZAEMON, CWA I-368
Sonezaki Shinjû, CLC II-1059; MP XI-6141
CHILDRESS, ALICE
Trouble in Mind, CLCII IV-1616; MPII:D IV-1654
CHIN, FRANK, CWAII I-335
Chickencoop Chinaman, The, CLCII I-270; MPII:D I-323
Year of the Dragon, The, CLCII IV-1761; MPII:D IV-1783
CHODERLOS DE LACLOS, PIERRE. See LACLOS, PIERRE CHODERLOS DE
CHOMSKY, NOAM, CWAII I-337
Knowledge of Language, MPII:NF II-786
CHOPIN, KATE, CWAII I-340
"Désirée's Baby," MPII:SS II-572
"Storm, The," MPII:SS V-2235
"Story of an Hour, The," MPII:SS V-2241
CHOU SHU-JÊN. See LU HSÜN
CHRÉTIEN DE TROYES, CWA I-370
Cligés, CLC I-187; MP II-989
Erec and Enide, CLC I-331; MP III-1816
Yvain, CLC II-1277; MP XII-7309
CHRISTIE, AGATHA, CWAII I-342
Mousetrap, The, CLCII III-1052; MPII:D III-1116
Murder of Roger Ackroyd, The, CLCII III-1056; MPII:BCF III-1148
CHURCHILL, CARYL
Cloud Nine, CLCII I-297; MPII:D I-365
Serious Money, CLCII III-1374; MPII:D IV-1438
Top Girls, CLCII IV-1591; MPII:D IV-1613
CHURCHILL, WINSTON, CWA I-371
Crisis, The, CLC I-223; MP II-1207; MP:AF I-235

CHURCHILL, WINSTON, SIR, CWA I-373
Second World War, The, MP X-5890
CIBBER, COLLEY, CWA I-376
Apology for the Life of Colley Cibber, Comedian, An, MP I-266
CICERO, CWA I-378
Cicero's Orations, MP II-959
Treatises of Cicero, The, MP XI-6669
CLARE, JOHN, CWA I-380
Poetry of Clare, The, MP VIII-4863
CLARENDON, EARL OF. See HYDE, EDWARD
CLARÍN. See ALAS, LEOPOLDO
CLARK, JOHN PEPPER, CWAII I-345
Song of a Goat, CLCII IV-1444; MPII:D IV-1483
CLARK, WALTER VAN TILBURG, CWA I-382; CWAII I-347
Ox-Bow Incident, The, CLC II-831; MP VIII-4457; MP:AF II-892
Track of the Cat, The, CLC II-1151; MP XI-6633; MP:AF III-1313
"Wind and the Snow of Winter, The," MPII:SS VI-2642
CLARK, WILLIAM, and MERIWETHER LEWIS, CWA II-1065
Journals of Lewis and Clark, The, MP VI-3065
CLARKE, ARTHUR C., CWAII I-349
Childhood's End, CLCII I-272; MPII:AF I-290
2001: A Space Odyssey, CLCII IV-1627; MPII:AF IV-1707
CLARKE, AUSTIN
As the Crow Flies, CLCII I-74; MPII:D I-94
Twice Round the Black Church, MPII:NF IV-1592
CLARKE, MARTHA
Garden of Earthly Delights, The, CLCII II-565; MPII:D II-654
Vienna: Lusthaus, CLCII IV-1655; MPII:D IV-1682

CLAUDEL, PAUL, CWA I-384
  Break of Noon, CLCII I-199; MPII:D I-237
  Poetry of Claudel, The, MP VIII-4866
  Satin Slipper, The, CLCII III-1338; MPII:D IV-1401
  Tidings Brought to Mary, The, CLCII IV-1563; MPII:D IV-1574
CLEMENS, SAMUEL LANGHORNE.
  See TWAIN, MARK
CLUTHA, JANET PATERSON FRAME.
  See FRAME, JANET
COCTEAU, JEAN, CWA I-386; CWAII I-352
  Holy Terrors, The, CLC I-479; MP V-2675; MP:EF II-648
  Infernal Machine, The, CLCII II-761; MPII:D II-846
  Orpheus, CLCII III-1159; MPII:D III-1185
  Plays of Cocteau, The, MP VIII-4758
COETZEE, J. M., CWAII I-355
  Life & Times of Michael K, CLCII II-884; MPII:BCF II-954
  Waiting for the Barbarians, CLCII IV-1671; MPII:BCF IV-1830
COLERIDGE, SAMUEL TAYLOR, CWA I-388
  Biographia Literaria, MP I-544
  Poetry of Coleridge, The, MP VIII-4869
  Rime of the Ancient Mariner, The, MP X-5600
COLES, ROBERT, CWAII I-357
  Children of Crisis, MPII:NF I-237
COLETTE, CWA I-391; CWAII I-359
  Cat, The, CLCII I-243; MPII:WF I-229
  Chéri, CLC I-172; CLCII I-264; MP II-905; MP:EF I-219; MPII:WF I-243
  Gigi, CLCII II-582; MPII:WF II-539
  "Kepi The," MPII:SS III-1252
  Last of Chéri, The, CLCII I-264; MPII:WF I-243
  Other One, The, CLC II-826; MP VIII-4436; MP:EF II-961

"Rainy Moon, The," MPII:SS V-1887
Ripening Seed, The, CLCII III-1297; MPII:WF III-1282
"Sick Child, The," MPII:SS V-2104
"Tender Shoot, The," MPII:SS V-2316
Vagabond, The, CLCII IV-1649; MPII:WF IV-1705
COLLIER, JOHN, CWAII I-361
  "Wet Saturday," MPII:SS VI-2562
  "Witch's Money," MPII:SS VI-2668
COLLINS, WILKIE, CWA I-393
  Moonstone, The, CLC II-740; MP VII-4059; MP:BF II-1001
  No Name, CLC II-780; MP VII-4227; MP:BF II-1061
  Woman in White, The, CLC II-1256; MP XII-7211; MP:BF III-1753
COLLINS, WILLIAM, CWA I-396
  Poetry of Collins, The, MP VIII-4873
COLUM, PADRAIC, CWAII I-363
  Fiddler's House, The, CLCII II-501; MPII:D II-605
COMPTON-BURNETT, IVY, CWA I-398
  Bullivant and the Lambs, MP VII-3952; MP:BF I-147;
  Heritage and Its History, A, MP V-2594; MP:BF I-570
  Mighty and Their Fall, The, MP VII-3890; MP:BF II-942
  Mother and Son, MP VII-4076; MP:BF II-1012
  Mr. Bullivant and His Lambs, MP VII-3952; MP:BF I-147
  Pastors and Masters, MP VIII-4516; MP:BF II-1167
CONFUCIUS
  Shih Ching, The, MP X-5976
CONGREVE, WILLIAM, CWA I-400
  Double-Dealer, The, CLC I-298; MP III-1624
  Love for Love, CLC I-633;; MP VI-3527
  Old Bachelor, The, CLC II-798; MP VIII-4309
  Way of the World, The, CLC II-1230; MP XII-7066

CONNELL, EVAN S., JR., CWA I-403;
CWAII I-366
Mrs. Bridge, CLCII III-1023; MPII:AF
III-1022
Notes from a Bottle Found on the Beach
at Carmel, MP VII-4258
Points for a Compass Rose, MPII:NF
III-1173
"Saint Augustine's Pigeon," MPII:SS V-
2008
CONNELL, RICHARD
"Most Dangerous Game, The," MPII:SS
IV-1535
CONNELLY, MARC, CWAII I-368
Beggar on Horseback, CLCII I-136;
MPII:D I-153
Green Pastures, The, CLCII II-634;
MPII:D II-717
CONNOLLY, CYRIL, CWAII I-370
Unquiet Grave, The, MPII:NF IV-1617
CONRAD, JOSEPH, CWA I-405; CWAII
I-372
Almayer's Folly, CLC I-30; MP I-149;
MP:BF I-40
Heart of Darkness, CLC I-448; MP V-
2505; MP:BF I-539
"Lagoon, The," MPII:SS III-1292
Lord Jim, CLC I-627; MP VI-3500;
MP:BF II-820
Nigger of the "Narcissus," The, CLC
II-776; MP VII-4209; MP:BF II-
1049
Nostromo, CLC II-783; MP VII-4250;
MP:BF II-1074
"Outpost of Progress, An," MPII:SS
IV-1732
Secret Agent, The, CLC II-1018; MP
X-5893; MP:BF III-1407
"Secret Sharer, The," CLCII III-1368;
MPII:SS V-2061
"Typhoon," CLCII IV-1629; MPII:SS
VI-2448
Under Western Eyes, CLC II-1184; MP
XII-6844; MP:BF III-1647

Victory, CLC II-1200; MP XII-6914;
MP:BF III-1678
"Youth," MPII:SS VI-2741
CONROY, FRANK
Stop-Time, MPII:NF IV-1432
CONSCIENCE, HENDRIK, CWA I-411
Lion of Flanders, The, CLC I-616; MP
VI-3438; MP:EF II-787
CONSTANT, BENJAMIN, CWA I-412
Adolphe, CLC I-10; MP I-39; MP:EF
I-5
COOKE, JOHN ESTEN, CWA I-413
Surry of Eagle's-Nest, CLC II-1097;
MP XI-6355; MP:AF III-1244
Virginia Comedians, The, CLC II-1208;
MP XII-6949; MP:AF III-1388
COOPER, JAMES FENIMORE, CWA I-
415
Chainbearer, The, CLC I-166; MP II-
880; MP:AF I-191
Deerslayer, The, CLC I-260; MP III-
1413; MP:AF I-286
Last of the Mohicans, The, CLC I-596;
MP VI-3261; MP:AF II-639
Pathfinder, The, CLC II-840; MP VIII-
4524; MP:AF II-906
Pilot, The, CLC II-884; MP VIII-4714;
MP:AF II-938
Pioneers, The, CLC II-886; MP VIII-
4722; MP:AF II-944
Prairie, The, CLC II-912; MP IX-5290;
MP:AF II-982
Red Rover, The, CLC II-950; MP IX-
5477; MP:AF III-1013
Redskins, The, CLC II-951; MP IX-
5484; MP:AF III-1021
Satanstoe, CLC II-1007; MP X-5804;
MP:AF III-1090
Spy, The, CLC II-1079; MP XI-6236;
MP:AF III-1208
COOVER, ROBERT, CWAII I-374
"Pedestrian Accident, A," MPII:SS IV-
1796

Universal Baseball Association, Inc., J. Henry Waugh, Prop., The, CLCII IV-1642; MPII:AF IV-1723

COPPARD, A. E., CWA I-418
"Field of Mustard, The," MPII:SS II-771
"Higgler, The," MPII:SS III-1014
Short Stories of A. E. Coppard, The, MP X-5993; MP:BF III-1431
"Third Prize, The," MPII:SS VI-2344

CORBIÈRE, TRISTAN, CWA I-420
Poetry of Corbière, The, MP VIII-4876

CORNEILLE, PIERRE, CWA I-422
Cid, The, CLC I-180; MP II-961
Cinna, CLC I-180; MP II-966
Horace, CLC I-482; MP V-2695
Menteur, Le, CLC I-695; MP VII-3852
Polyeucte, CLC II-899; MP IX-5231

CORNWELL, DAVID JOHN MOORE. See LE CARRÉ, JOHN

CORTÁZAR, JULIO, CWAII I-377
"Apocalypse at Solentiname," MPII:SS I-99
"Blow-Up," MPII:SS I-262
"End of the Game," MPII:SS II-689
Hopscotch, CLCII II-695; MPII:AF II-739
"Instructions for John Howell," MPII:SS III-1180
Manual for Manuel, A, CLCII III-969; MPII:AF III-981
62: A Model Kit, CLCII IV-1420; MPII:AF IV-1433
"Southern Thruway, The," MPII:SS V-2198
Winners, The, CLCII IV-1726; MPII:AF IV-1795

CORVO, BARON, CWA I-424

COSTER, CHARLES DE, CWA I-426
Legend of Tyl Ulenspiegel, The, CLC I-607; MP VI-3321; MP:EF II-768

COUPERUS, LOUIS, CWA I-427
Small Souls, CLC II-1052; MP X-6101; MP:EF III-1170

COWARD, NOËL, CWA 1-429; CWAII I-380

Blithe Spirit, CLCII I-169; MPII:D I-195 Design for Living, CLCII I-394; MPII:D II-486
Private Lives, CLC II-919; CLCII III-1239; MP IX-5347; MPII:D III-1288

COWLEY, ABRAHAM, CWA I-431
Miscellanies, MP VII-3926

COWLEY, MALCOLM, CWAII I-383
Dream of the Golden Mountains, The, MPII:NF I-414
Exile's Return, MPII:NF II-481

COWPER, WILLIAM, CWA I-432
Letters of William Cowper, The, MP VI-3371
Poetry of Cowper, The, MP VIII-4880
Task, The, MP XI-6425

COX, WILLIAM TREVOR. See TREVOR, WILLIAM

COZZENS, JAMES GOULD, CWA I-434; CWAII I-386
By Love Possessed, CLCII I-223; MPII:AF I-226
Guard of Honor, CLC I-431; MP IV-2412; MP:AF II-520
Morning, Noon, and Night, CLCII III-1037; MPII:AF III-1042

CRABBE, GEORGE, CWA I-436
Borough: A Poem in Twenty-Four Letters, The, MP I-602
Village, The, MP XII-6927

CRAIK, DINAH MARIA MULOCK. See MULOCK, DINAH MARIA

CRAMPTON, MARY. See PYM, BARBARA

CRANE, HART, CWA I-437
Bridge, The, MP II-649

CRANE, STEPHEN, CWA I-439
"Blue Hotel, The," MPII:SS I-266
"Bride Comes to Yellow Sky, The," MPII:SS I-300
"Death and the Child," MPII:SS II-520
"Experiment in Misery, An," MPII:SS II-739
Maggie: A Girl of the Streets, CLC I-649; MP VI-3614; MP:AF II-722
"Monster, The," MPII:SS IV-1523

"Open Boat, The," MPII:SS IV-1709
Red Badge of Courage, The, CLC II-
948; MP IX-5468; MP:AF III-1008
CRASHAW, RICHARD, CWA I-442
Poetry of Crashaw, The, MP VIII-4883
CRAYENCOUR, MARGUERITE DE.
See YOURCENAR, MARGUERITE
CRÉBILLON, PROSPER JOLYOT DE,
CWA I-444
Rhadamistus and Zenobia, CLC II-964;
MP X-5570
CREVECŒUR, MICHEL-GUILLAUME
JEAN DE, CWA I-445
Letters from an American Farmer, MP
VI-3333
CRICHTON, MICHAEL, CWAII I-388
Andromeda Strain, The, CLCII I-44;
MPII:AF I-34
CROCE, BENEDETTO, CWA I-446
Aesthetic, MP I-53
CROCKETT, DAVID, CWA I-448
Narrative of the Life of David Crockett,
A, MP VII-4146
CRONIN, A. J.
Citadel, The, CLCII I-287; MPII:BCF
I-262

Keys of the Kingdom, The, CLCII II-
824; MPII:BCF II-904
CROWLEY, MART, CWAII I-390
Boys in the Band, The, CLCII I-197;
MPII:D I-230
CRUZ, SOR JUANA INÉS DE LA,
CWA I-449
Poetry of Sor Juana Inés de la Cruz,
The, MP IX-5149
CUDDIHY, JOHN MURRAY
Ordeal of Civility, The MPII:NF III-
1092
CULLEN, COUNTÉE, CWAII I-392
One Way to Heaven, CLCII III-1155;
MPII:AF III-1217
CUMMINGS, E. E., CWA I-451
Enormous Room, The, CLC I-328; MP
III-1789; MP:AF I-342
Poetry of Cummings, The, MP VIII-
4887
CUNHA, EUCLIDES DA, CWAII I-395
Rebellion in the Backlands, CLCII III-
1276; MPII:AF III-1317
CZACZKES, SHMUEL YOSEF. See
AGNON, SHMUEL YOSEF

D

DAHL, ROALD
"Lamb to the Slaughter," MPII:SS III-1295
DAICHES, DAVID, CWAII I-398
Two Worlds, MPII:NF IV-1597
DANA, RICHARD HENRY, JR., CWA I-453
Two Years Before the Mast, MP XII-6785
DANIEL, SAMUEL, CWA I-454
Poetry of Daniel, The, MP VIII-4889
D'ANNUNZIO, GABRIELE, CWA I-456
Triumph of Death, The, CLC II-1161; MP XI-6717; MP:EF III-1307
DANTE ALIGHIERI, CWA I-458
Divine Comedy, The, CLC I-272; MP III-1529
Vita Nuova, The, MP XII-6968
D'ARBLAY, MADAME. See BURNEY, FANNY
DARÍO, RUBÉN, CWA I-462
DARWIN, CHARLES, CWA I-464
Descent of Man, and Selection in Relation to Sex, The, MP III-1455
On the Origin of Species, MP VIII-4376
Voyage of the Beagle, The, MP XII-6987
DAUDET, ALPHONSE, CWA I-466
Kings in Exile, CLC I-578; MP VI-3176; MP:EF II-733
"Last Class, The," MPII:SS III-1298
Sappho, CLC II-1005; MP X-5790; MP:EF III-1127
Tartarin of Tarascon, CLC II-1110; MP XI-6417; MP:EF III-1264
DAVENANT, SIR WILLIAM, CWA I-468
Siege of Rhodes, The, CLC II-1036; MP X-6035
DAVENPORT, GUY, CWAII I-401
"Aeroplanes at Brescia, The," MPII:SS I-34
"Bowmen of Shu, The," MPII:SS I-293
"Herakleitos," MPII:SS III-1003

DAVIE, DONALD, CWAII I-403
These the Companions, MPII:NF IV-1495
DAVIES, ROBERTSON, CWAII I-406
Deptford Trilogy, The, CLCII I-390; MPII:BCF I-375
Rebel Angels, The, CLCII III-1275; MPII:BCF III-1399
What's Bred in the Bone, CLCII IV-1708; MPII:BCF IV-1890
DA VINCI, LEONARDO. See LEONARDO DA VINCI
DAVIS, H. L., CWA I-469
Harp of a Thousand Strings, CLC I-445; MP V-2484; MP:AF II-529
Honey in the Horn, CLC I-480; MP V-2688; MP:AF II-555
DAY, CLARENCE, JR., CWA I-471
Life with Father, CLC I-612; MP VI-3415; MP:AF II-670
DAY, DOROTHY, CWAII II-409
Long Loneliness, The, MPII:NF II-861
DAY, THOMAS, CWA I-473
Sandford and Merton, CLC II-1004; MP X-5784; MP:BF III-1398
DAZAI, OSAMU, CWAII II-411
"Eight Views of Tokyo," MPII:SS II-672
No Longer Human, CLCII III-1107; MPII:WF III-1103
Setting Sun, The, CLCII IV-1379; MPII:WF IV-1388
"Villon's Wife," MPII:SS VI-2504
DE AMICIS, EDMONDO. See AMICIS, EDMONDO DE
DE BEAUVOIR, SIMONE. See BEAUVOIR, SIMONE DE
DE COSTER, CHARLES. See COSTER, CHARLES DE
DE CRAYENCOUR, MARGUERITE. See YOURCENAR, MARGUERITE
DEFOE, DANIEL, CWA I-475
Captain Singleton, CLC I-149; MP II-783; MP:BF I-168

History of Colonel Jacque, The, CLC I-475; MP V-2627; MP:BF I-586

Journal of the Plague Year, A, MP V-3047; MP:BF II-717;

Memoirs of a Cavalier, The, CLC I-691; MP VII-3826; MP:BF II-912

Moll Flanders, CLC II-732; MP VII-4020; MP:BF II-988

Robinson Crusoe, CLC II-979; MP X-5647; MP:BF III-1341

Roxana, CLC II-996; MP X-5725; MP:BF III-1384

DE FOREST, JOHN WILLIAM, CWA I-478

Miss Ravenel's Conversion from Secession to Loyalty, CLC II-717; MP VII-3945; MP:AF II-792

DEKKER, EDUARD DOUWES. See MULTATULI

DEKKER, THOMAS, CWA I-480

Gull's Hornbook, The, MP IV-2426

Honest Whore, Part Two, The, MP V-2684

Honest Whore, The, CLC I-479

Old Fortunatus, CLC II-802; MP VIII-4319

Satiromastix, CLC II-1008; MP X-5817

Shoemaker's Holiday, The, CLC II-1035; MP X-5988

DEKKER, THOMAS, and THOMAS MIDDLETON

Honest Whore, Part One, The, CLC I-479; MP V-2680

DE LA MARE, WALTER, CWA I-482

Collected Poems, MP II-1022

Memoirs of a Midget, CLC I-692; MP VII-3833; MP:BF II-920

"Recluse, A," MPII:SS V-1913

Return, The, CLC II-958; MP X-5536; MP:BF III-1307

"Revenant, A," MPII:SS V-1948

"Seaton's Aunt," MPII:SS V-2049

"Trumpet, The," MPII:SS VI-2421

DELANEY, SHELAGH, CWAII II-414

Taste of Honey, A, CLCII IV-1517; MPII:D IV-1538

DELANY, SAMUEL R., CWAII II-416

Babel-17, CLCII I-99; MPII:AF I-102

Triton, CLCII IV-1614; MPII:AF IV-1692

DE LA RAMÉE, MARIE LOUISE. See OUIDA

DE LA ROCHE, MAZO, CWA I-484

Jalna, CLC I-539; MP V-2973; MP:AF II-611

DELBLANC, SVEN

Speranza, CLCII IV-1461; MPII:WF IV-1510

DELEDDA, GRAZIA, CWA I-485

Mother, The, CLC II-744; MP VII-4068; MP:EF II-894

DeLILLO, DON, CWAII II-418

End Zone, CLCII II-457; MPII:AF II-472

DELONEY, THOMAS, CWA I-487

Jack of Newberry, CLC I-538; MP V-2964; MP:BF II-671

DEMBY, WILLIAM, CWAII II-420

Beetlecreek, CLCII I-133; MPII:AF I-126

DE MORGAN, WILLIAM, CWA I-488

Joseph Vance, CLC I-554; MP V-3041; MP:BF II-713

DEMOSTHENES, CWA I-490

Philippics, The, MP VIII-4644

DENNISON, GEORGE

"Smiles of Konarak, The," MPII:SS V-2146

DE QUINCEY, THOMAS, CWA I-492

Confessions of an English Opium Eater, MP II-1063

DERRIDA, JACQUES, CWAII II-422

Of Grammatology, MPII:NF III-1057

Writing and Difference, MPII:NF IV-1730

DESAI, ANITA, CWAII II-425

Clear Light of Day, CLCII I-294; MPII:BCF I-267

Fire on the Mountain, CLCII II-509; MPII:BCF II-504

DESCARTES, RENÉ, CWA I-494
  Passions of the Soul, The, MP VIII-4510
DE STAËL, MADAME. *See* STAËL, MADAME DE
DE STAËL-HOLSTEIN, BARONNE. *See* STAËL, MADAME DE
DESTOUCHES, LOUIS FUCH. *See* CÉLINE, LOUIS-FERDINAND
DESTOUCHES, LOUIS-FERDINAND. *See* CÉLINE, LOUIS-FERDINAND
DE VRIES, PETER, CWAII II-427
  Blood of the Lamb, The, CLCII I-170; MPII:AF I-181
  Tents of Wickedness, The, CLCII IV-1528; MPII:AF IV-1583
D'EXILES, ANTOINE-FRANÇOIS PRÉVOST. *See* PRÉVOST, ABBÉ
DICKENS, CHARLES, CWA I-496
  Barnaby Rudge, CLC I-81; MP I-431; MP:BF I-85
  Bleak House, CLC I-107; MP I-566; MP:BF I-118
  Christmas Carol, A, CLC I-179; MP II-947; MP:BF I-207
  David Copperfield, CLC I-242; MP III-1324; MP:BF I-283
  Dombey and Son, CLC I-286; MP III-1574; MP:BF I-341
  Great Expectations, CLC I-418; MP IV-2349; MP:BF I-491
  Hard Times, CLC I-443; MP V-2477; MP:BF I-532
  Little Dorrit, CLC I-617; MP VI-3448; MP:BF II-803
  Martin Chuzzlewit, CLC I-675; MP VII-3751; MP:BF II-877
  Mystery of Edwin Drood, The, CLC II-755; MP VII-4125; MP:BF II-1022
  Nicholas Nickleby, CLC II-771; MP VII-4195; MP:BF II-1044
  Old Curiosity Shop, The, CLC II-799; MP VIII-4316; MP:BF II-1087
  Oliver Twist, CLC II-812; MP VIII-4358; MP:BF II-1105
  Our Mutual Friend, CLC II-827; MP VIII-4440; MP:BF II-1141
  Pickwick Papers, The, CLC II-874; MP VIII-4680; MP:BF III-1212
  Tale of Two Cities, A, CLC II-1100; MP XI-6373; MP:BF III-1485
DICKEY, JAMES, CWA 1-499
  Poetry of Dickey, The, MP VIII-4896
DICKINSON, EMILY, CWA I-501
  Letters of Emily Dickinson, The, MP VI-3344
  Poetry of Emily Dickinson, The, MP IX-4935
DIDEROT, DENIS, CWA I-504
  Jacques the Fatalist and His Master, CLCII II-785; MPII:WF II-748
  Rameau's Nephew, CLC II-939; MP IX-5429; MP:EF III-1054
DIDION, JOAN, CWAII II-429
  Democracy, CLCII I-387; MPII:AF I-389
  Play It As It Lays, CLCII III-1212; MPII:AF III-1266
  Salvador, MPII:NF III-1280
  Slouching Towards Bethlehem, MPII:NF IV-1366
DILLARD, ANNIE, CWAII II-431
  American Childhood, An, MPII:NF I-39
  Pilgrim at Tinker Creek, MPII:NF III-1163
DINESEN, ISAK, CWA I-506; CWAII II-433
  "Blank Page, The," MPII:SS I-246
  "Deluge at Norderney, The," MPII:SS II-561
  "Monkey, The," MPII:SS IV-1519
  Seven Gothic Tales, MP X-5926; MP:EF III-1147
  "Sorrow-Acre," MPII:SS V-2190
  "Supper at Elsinore, The," MPII:SS V-2281
DISRAELI, BENJAMIN, CWA I-508
  Coningsby, CLC I-196; MP II-1077; MP:BF I-238
  Vivian Grey, CLC II-1212; MP XII-6971; MP:BF III-1698

DÖBLIN, ALFRED, CWAII II-435
Berlin Alexanderplatz, CLCII I-143;
MPII:WF I-146
November 1918, CLCII III-1117;
MPII:WF III-1118
DOCTOROW, E. L., CWAII II-438
Ragtime, CLCII III-1259; MPII:AF III-1310
DODERER, HEIMITO VON, CWAII II-440
Demons, The, CLCII I-389; MPII:WF I-369
Waterfalls of Slunj, The, CLCII IV-1689; MPII:WF IV-1729
DODGSON, CHARLES LUTWIDGE.
See CARROLL, LEWIS
DONLEAVY, J. P., CWAII II-442
Ginger Man, The, CLCII II-585;
MPII:AF II-618; MPII:BCF II-586
DONNADIEU, MARGUERITE. See
DURAS, MARGUERITE
DONN-BYRNE, BRIAN OSWALD. See
BYRNE, DONN
DONNE, JOHN, CWA I-510
Death's Duell, MP III-1391
Ignatius His Conclave, MP V-2834
Poetry of Donne, The, MP VIII-4900
DONOSO, JOSÉ, CWAII II-445
Coronation, CLCII I-337; MPII:AF I-341
Obscene Bird of Night, The, CLCII III-1125; MPII:AF III-1160
Sacred Families, CLCII III-1325;
MPII:AF III-1357
This Sunday, CLCII IV-1552; MPII:AF IV-1640
DOOLITTLE, HILDA. See H. D.
DOS PASSOS, JOHN, CWA I-514
Manhattan Transfer, CLC I-663; MP VII-3693; MP:AF II-748
Three Soldiers, CLC II-1130; MP XI-6522; MP:AF III-1285
U.S.A., CLC II-1187; MP XII-6863;
MP:AF III-1358

DOSTOEVSKI, FYODOR
MIKHAILOVICH, CWA I-516;
CWAII II-447
"Bobok," MPII:SS I-273
Brothers Karamazov, The, CLC I-129;
MP II-688; MP:EF I-144
Crime and Punishment, CLC I-221; MP II-1197; MP:EF I-299
Diary of a Writer, MP III-1506
Double, The, CLCII II-419; MPII:WF I-390
"Dream of a Ridiculous Man, The,"
MPII:SS II-628
Gambler, The, CLC I-390; MP IV-2195; MP:EF II-547
House of the Dead, The, CLCII II-711;
MPII:WF II-623
Idiot, The, CLC I-510; MP V-2817;
MP:EF II-682
Insulted and the Injured, The, CLCII II-767; MPII:WF II-706
Letters from the Underworld, CLC I-608; MP VI-3336; MP:EF II-776
"Nasty Story, A," MPII:SS IV-1586
Netochka Nezvanova, CLCII III-1084;
MPII:WF III-1089
"Peasant Marey, The," MPII:SS IV-1789
Poor People, CLC II-900; MP IX-5237;
MP:EF III-1020
Possessed, The, CLC II-905; MP IX-5264; MP:EF III-1024
Raw Youth, A, CLCII III-1271;
MPII:WF III-1262
"White Nights," MPII:SS VI-2589
DOUGHTY, CHARLES M., CWA I-520
Travels in Arabia Deserta, MP XI-6647
DOUGLAS, ELLEN, CWAII II-450
Rock Cried Out, The, CLCII III-1309;
MPII:AF III-1344
DOUGLAS, GEORGE, CWA I-522
House With the Green Shutters, The,
CLC I-492; MP V-2739; MP:BF II-608

DOUGLAS, LLOYD C., CWA I-523
Magnificent Obsession, The, CLC I-652; MP VI-3626; MP:AF II-726
DOUGLAS, MARY
Natural Symbols, MPII:NF III-1003
DOUGLAS, NORMAN, CWA I-524
Old Calabria, MP VIII-4313
South Wind, CLC II-1072; MP XI-6202; MP:BF III-1473
DOVLATOV, SERGEI, CWAII II-452
Compromise, The, CLCII I-317; MPII:WF I-295
Zone, The, CLCII IV-1770; MPII:WF IV-1808
DOWSON, ERNEST CHRISTOPHER, CWA I-526
Poetry of Dowson, The, MP VIII-4903
DOYLE, SIR ARTHUR CONAN, CWA I-528
"Adventure of the Dancing Men, The," MPII:SS I-23
"Adventure of the Speckled Band, The," MPII:SS I-31
"Greek Interpreter, The," MPII:SS III-936
Micah Clarke, CLC II-699; MP VII-3869; MP:BF II-931
"Red-Headed League, The," MPII:SS V-1922
"Scandal in Bohemia, A," MPII:SS V-2029
Sign of Four, The, CLC II-1037; MP X-6037; MP:BF III-1449
Study in Scarlet, A, CLC II-1092; MP XI-6322; MP:BF III-1477
White Company, The, CLC II-1237; MP XII-7111; MP:BF III-1735
DRABBLE, MARGARET, CWAII II-455
Ice Age, The, CLCII II-731; MPII:BCF II-787
Middle Ground, The, CLCII III-1005; MPII:BCF III-1091
Needle's Eye, The, CLCII III-1083; MPII:BCF III-1188
Waterfall, The, CLCII IV-1688; MPII:BCF IV-1859

DRAYTON, MICHAEL, CWA I-530
Poetry of Drayton, The, MP VIII-4906
DREISER, THEODORE, CWA I-531
American Tragedy, An, CLC I-35; MP I-175; MP:AF I-53
Bulwark, The, CLC I-135; MP II-707; MP:AF I-154
Financier, The, CLC I-367; MP IV-2067; MP:AF I-391
"Genius," The, CLC I-395; MP IV-2221; MP:AF I-428
Jennie Gerhardt, CLC I-544; MP V-2996; MP:AF II-619
Sister Carrie, CLC II-1045; MP X-6070; MP:AF III-1171
Stoic, The, CLC II-1081; MP XI-6255; MP:AF III-1219
Titan, The, CLC II-1135; MP XI-6560; MP:AF III-1293
DRYDEN, JOHN, CWA I-534
Absalom and Achitophel, CLC I-4; MP I-19
All for Love, CLC I-24; MP I-117
Essay of Dramatic Poesy, An, MP III-1831
Marriage à la Mode, CLC I-673; MP VII-3742
Poetry of Dryden, The, MP IX-4909
Spanish Friar, The, CLC II-1073; The, MP XI-6205
DUDEVANT, AMANDINE-AURORE-LUCILE DUPIN, BARONNE. See SAND, GEORGE
DU GARD, ROGER MARTIN. See MARTIN DU GARD, ROGER
DUGGAN, ALFRED, CWA I-537
Lady for Ransom, The, MP VI-3203; MP:BF II-761
Leopards and Lilies, MP VI-3327; MP:BF II-792
DUMAS, ALEXANDRE (fils), CWA I-542
Camille, CLC I-142; MPII II-751
DUMAS, ALEXANDRE (père), CWA I-539

Chevalier of the Maison Rouge, The, CLC I-174; MP II-912; MP:EF I-223

Corsican Brothers, The, CLC I-202; MP II-1124; MP:EF I-260

Count of Monte-Cristo, The, CLC I-204; MP II-1136; MP:EF I-269

Countess de Charny, The, CLC I-207; MP II-1146; MP:EF I-281

Memoirs of a Physician, CLC I-692; MP VII-3836; MP:EF II-854

Queen's Necklace, The, CLC II-930; MP IX-5394; MP:EF III-1046

Three Musketeers, The, CLC II-1127; MP XI-6511; MP:EF III-1279

Twenty Years After, CLC II-1169; MP XII-6762; MP:EF III-1319

Vicomte de Bragelonne, The, CLC II-1199; MP XII-6904; MP:EF III-1341

DUMAS, HENRY, CWAII II-457
"Ark of Bones," MPII:SS I-110

DU MAURIER, DAPHNE, CWA I-543
Rebecca, CLC II-943; MP IX-5452; MP:BF III-1302

DU MAURIER, GEORGE, CWA I-544
Peter Ibbetson, CLC II-864; MP VIII-4618; MP:BF II-1194
Trilby, CLC II-1158; MP XI-6701; MP:BF III-1600

DUMITRIU, PETRU, CWA I-546
Incognito, MP V-2868; MP:EF II-696

DUNBAR, PAUL LAURENCE, CWAII II-459
"Scapegoat, The," MPII:SS V-2037
Sport of the Gods, The, CLCII IV-1465; MPII:AF IV-1516

DUNCAN, ROBERT, CWAII II-461
Truth and Life of Myth, The, MPII:NF IV-1574

DUNN, ELSIE. See SCOTT, EVELYN

DUNSANY, LORD, CWAII II-464
"Idle Days on the Yann," MPII:SS III-1112

DUPIN, AMANDINE LUCILE AURORE. See SAND, GEORGE

DURANG, CHRISTOPHER, CWAII II-466
Sister Mary Ignatius Explains It All for You, CLCII IV-1419; MPII:D IV-1471

DURAS, MARGUERITE, CWAII II-468
Lover, The, CLCII III-931; MPII:WF II-901
Ravishing of Lol Stein, The, CLCII III-1270; MPII:WF III-1257
Sea Wall, The, CLCII III-1355; MPII:WF III-1367

DURKHEIM, ÉMILE, CWAII II-471
Elementary Forms of the Religious Life, The, MPII:NF II-443

DURKHEIM, ÉMILE, and MARCEL MAUSS
Primitive Classification, MPII:NF III-1190

DURRELL, LAWRENCE, CWA I-548; CWAII II-473
Alexandria Quartet, The, MP I-96; MP:BF I-20
Prospero's Cell, MPII:NF III-1210

DÜRRENMATT, FRIEDRICH, CWAII II-475
Physicists, The, CLCII III-1206; MPII:D III-1246
Romulus the Great, CLCII III-1310; MPII:D IV-1367
Visit, The, CLCII IV-1659; MPII:D IV-1688

DUUN, OLAV, CWA I-551
People of Juvik, The, CLC II-857; MP VIII-4587; MP:EF III-999

E

EBERHART, RICHARD, CWA I-552
Poetry of Eberhart, The, MP IX-4918
EÇA DE QUEIRÓS, JOSÉ MARIA,
CWAII IV-1235
Cousin Bazilio, CLCII I-348; MPII:WF
I-337
ECHEGARAY, JOSÉ, CWA I-554
Great Galeoto, The, CLC I-420; MP
IV-2355
ECHENOZ, JEAN
Cherokee, CLCII I-265; MPII:WF I-248
ECKERMANN, JOHANN PETER, CWA
I-556
Conversations of Goethe with
Eckermann and Soret, MP II-1109
ECO, UMBERTO, CWAII II-478
Name of the Rose, The, CLCII III-
1072; MPII:WF III-1065
EDGEWORTH, MARIA, CWA I-558
Absentee, The, CLC I-5; MP I-21;
MP:BF I-1
Castle Rackrent, CLC I-157; MP II-
834; MP:BF I-183
EDMONDS, HELEN WOODS. See
KAVAN, ANNA
EDMONDS, WALTER D., CWA I-560
Drums Along the Mohawk, CLC I-307;
MP III-1659; MP:AF I-317
Rome Haul, CLC II-989; MP X-5697;
MP:AF III-1072
EDWARDS, JONATHAN, CWA I-562
Works of Jonathan Edwards, MP XII-
7256
EGAN, PIERCE, CWA I-564
Life in London, CLC I-610; MP VI-
3394; MP:BF II-799
EGGLESTON, EDWARD, CWA I-566
Hoosier Schoolmaster, The, CLC I-481;
MP V-2691; MP:AF II-559
EHRENBURG, ILYA, CWAII II-481
Thaw, The, CLCII IV-1533; MPII:WF
IV-1575
EICHENDORFF, JOSEF VON, CWA I-
568

Poetry of Eichendorff, The, MP IX-
4922
EISELEY, LOREN
Immense Journey, The, MPII:NF II-699
EKWENSI, CYPRIAN, CWAII II-483
People of the City, CLCII III-1192;
MPII:BCF III-1302
ELIADE, MIRCEA, CWAII II-485
Forbidden Forest, The, CLCII II-532;
MPII:WF II-491
ELIOT, GEORGE, CWA I-570
Adam Bede, CLC I-7; MP I-29; MP:BF
I-7
Daniel Deronda, CLC I-237; MP III-
1304; MP:BF I-278
Felix Holt, The Radical, CLC I-365;
MP IV-2029; MP:BF I-410
Middlemarch, CLC II-700; MP VII-
3879; MP:BF II-935
Mill on the Floss, The, CLC II-705;
MP:BF II-945
Romola, CLC II-992; MP X-5705;
MP:BF III-1369
Silas Marner, CLC II-1038; MP X-
6043; MP:BF III-1455
ELIOT, T. S., CWA I-573; CWAII II-488
After Strange Gods, MP I-60
Ash Wednesday, MP I-339
Cocktail Party, The, CLC I-190; MP II-
1010
Confidential Clerk, The, MP II-1074
Dante, MP III-1308
Elder Statesman, The, MP III-1728
Family Reunion, The, CLC I-355; MP
IV-1983
Four Quartets, MP IV-2148
John Dryden: The Poet, The Dramatist,
The Critic, MP V-3020
Murder in the Cathedral, CLC II-748;
MP VII-4094
Notes Towards the Definition of
Culture, MPII:NF III-1034
Sacred Wood: Essays on Poetry and
Criticism, The, MP X-5748
Waste Land, The, MP XII-7047

ELKIN, STANLEY, CWAII II-490
Franchiser, The, CLCII II-543;
MPII:AF II-576
"I Look Out for Ed Wolfe," MPII:SS
III-1088
ELLIOTT, GEORGE P.
"Among the Dangs," MPII:SS I-85
ELLISON, RALPH, CWA I-576;
CWAII II-492
"Flying Home," MPII:SS II-803
Invisible Man, MP V-2915; MP:AF II-
599
ELLUL, JACQUES, CWAII II-494
Technological Society, The, MPII:NF
IV-1473
EMERSON, RALPH WALDO, CWA I-
578
Essays: First and Second Series, MP
IV-1845
Poetry of Emerson, The, MP IX-4928
Representative Men, MP IX-5518
Society and Solitude, MP X-6122
EMPSON, WILLIAM, CWAII II-496
Seven Types of Ambiguity, MPII:NF
IV-1335
ENCHI, FUMIKO, CWAII II-499
"Boxcar of Chrysanthemums," MPII:SS
I-297
Masks, CLCII III-983; MPII:WF III-
970
ENDŌ, SHUSAKU, CWAII II-501
Samurai, The, CLCII III-1332;
MPII:WF III-1345
Silence, CLCII IV-1405; MPII:WF IV-
1425
When I Whistle, CLCII IV-1709;
MPII:WF IV-1745
Wonderful Fool, CLCII IV-1740;
MPII:WF IV-1789
ERASMUS, DESIDERIUS, CWA I-582
Praise of Folly, The, MP IX-5294

ERDRICH, LOUISE, CWAII II-504
"Beet Queen, The," MPII:SS I-177
Love Medicine, CLCII III-927;
MPII:AF III-938
"Saint Marie," MPII:SS V-2012
ESCHENBACH, WOLFRAM VON. See
WOLFRAM VON ESCHENBACH
ESENIN, SERGEI, CWA I-584
Poetry of Esenin, The, MP IX-4938
ETHEREGE, SIR GEORGE, CWA I-586
Man of Mode, The, CLC I-660; MP
VII-3672
EURIPIDES, CWA I-588
Alcestis, CLC I-18; MP I-84
Andromache, CLC I-40; MP I-216
Bacchae, The, CLC I-74; MP I-405
Children of Heracles, The, CLC I-176;
MP II-930
Cyclops, The, CLC I-230; MP III-1252
Electra, CLC I-320; MP III-1735
Helen, CLC I-458; MP V-2544
Herakles Mad, CLC I-468; MP V-2584
Hippolytus, CLC I-474; MP V-2620
Ion, CLC I-529; MP V-2925
Iphigenia in Aulis, CLC I-530; MP V-
2928
Iphigenia in Tauris, CLC I-532; MP V-
2931
Medea, CLC I-686; MP VII-3798
Phoenician Women, The, CLC II-872;
MP VIII-4670
Suppliants, The, CLC II-1096; MP XI-
6349
Trojan Women, The, CLC II-1164; MP
XI-6729
EVANS, MARIAN. See ELIOT,
GEORGE
EVANS, MARY ANN. See ELIOT,
GEORGE
EVELYN, JOHN, CWA I-591
Diary, MP III-1494

F

FAIRFIELD, CICILY ISABEL. *See*
WEST, REBECCA
FANON, FRANTZ, CWAII II-506
Wretched of the Earth, The, MPII:NF
IV-1725
FANU, JOSEPH SHERIDAN LE. *See*
LE FANU, JOSEPH SHERIDAN
FARQUHAR, GEORGE, CWA I-593
Beaux' Stratagem, The, CLC I-91; MP
I-464
Recruiting Officer, The, CLC II-945;
MP IX-5459
FARRELL, J. G., CWAII II-508
Siege of Krishnapur, The, CLCII IV-
1401; MPII:BCF IV-1543
Singapore Grip, The, CLCII IV-1416;
MPII:BCF IV-1558
Troubles, CLCII IV-1617; MPII:BCF
IV-1747
FARRELL, JAMES T., CWA I-595;
CWAII II-510
"Saturday Night," MPII:SS V-2025
Studs Lonigan: A Trilogy, CLC II-
1091; MP XI-6320; MP:AF III-1235
FAULKNER, WILLIAM, CWA I-597;
CWAII II-512
Absalom, Absalom! CLC I-3; MP I-14;
MP:AF I-1
As I Lay Dying, CLC I-64; MP I-330;
MP:AF I-80
"Barn Burning," MPII:SS I-158
"Delta Autumn," MPII:SS II-557
"Dry September," MPII:SS II-646
Fable, A, CLC I-346; MP IV-1942;
MP:AF I-354
Go Down, Moses, MP IV-2272;
MP:AF I-453
Hamlet, The, CLC I-436; MP V-2454;
MP:AF II-525
Intruder in the Dust, CLC I-527; MP V-
2911; MP:AF II-595
Light in August, CLC I-613; MP VI-
3423; MP:AF II-679
Mansion, The, MP VII-3707; MP:AF
II-752

Mosquitoes, CLCII III-1042; MPII:AF
III-1066
Pylon, CLCII III-1239; MPII:AF III-
1291
"Red Leaves," MPII:SS V-1918
Reivers, The, MP IX-5489; MP:AF III-
1027
Requiem for a Nun, MP X-5525;
MP:AF III-1040
"Rose for Emily, A," MPII:SS V-1986
Sanctuary, CLC II-1003; MP X-5780;
MP:AF III-1082
Sartoris, MP X-5801; MP:AF III-1086
Soldiers' Pay, CLCII IV-1437;
MPII:AF IV-1459
Sound and the Fury, The, CLC II-1070;
MP XI-6194; MP:AF III-1193
"Spotted Horses," MPII:SS V-2210
"That Evening Sun," MPII:SS VI-2325
Town, The, CLC II-1149; MP XI-6623;
MP:AF III-1302
Unvanquished, The, MP XII-6860;
MP:AF III-1354
"Wash," MPII:SS VI-2552
Wild Palms, The, MP XII-7142;
MP:AF III-1437
FAUSET, JESSIE REDMON, CWAII II-
514
Plum Bun, CLCII III-1215; MPII:AF
III-1271
FÊNG MÊNG-LUNG
Lieh-kuo Chih, MP VI-3385; MP:EF II-
782
FERBER, EDNA, CWA I-601; CWAII II-
516
So Big, MP X-6115; MP:AF III-1176
FERMOR, PATRICK LEIGH
Violins of Saint-Jacques, The, CLCII
IV-1656; MPII:BCF IV-1790
FERNÁNDEZ DE LIZARDI, JOSÉ
JOAQUÍN, CWA I-603
Itching Parrot, The, CLC I-536; MP V-
2955; MP:AF II-607
FERREIRA, ANTÓNIO, CWA I-604
Inês de Castro, CLC I-524; MP V-2883

FEUCHTWANGER, LION, CWA I-605
Power, CLC II-909; MP IX-5277;
MP:EF III-1030
Ugly Duchess, The, CLC II-1174; MP
XII-6796; MP:EF III-1326
FIELDING, GABRIEL
Birthday King, The, CLCII I-158;
MPII:BCF I-134
In the Time of Greenbloom, CLCII II-
751; MPII:BCF II-814
FIELDING, HENRY, CWA I-607
Amelia, CLC I-33; MP I-161; MP:BF
I-44
Jonathan Wild, CLC I-551; MP V-3030;
MP:BF II-699
Joseph Andrews, CLC I-552; MP V-
3036; MP:BF II-707
Temple Beau, The, CLC II-1113; MP
XI-6435
Tom Jones, CLC II-1143; MP XI-6598;
MP:BF III-1571
Tom Thumb the Great, CLC II-1146;
MP XI-6609
FIERSTEIN, HARVEY, CWAII II-518
Torch Song Trilogy, CLCII IV-1592;
MPII:D IV-1618
FIGES, EVA
Light, CLCII II-890; MPII:BCF II-965
Seven Ages, The, CLCII IV-1381;
MPII:BCF IV-1510
FINDLEY, TIMOTHY, CWAII II-520
Wars, The, CLCII IV-1683; MPII:BCF
IV-1848
FISHER, DOROTHY CANFIELD
Home-maker, The, CLCII II-686;
MPII:AF II-728
FISHER, VARDIS, CWA I-610
Children of God, CLC I-175; MP II-
927; MP:AF I-196
FITZGERALD, EDWARD, CWA I-612
Rubáiyát of Omar Khayyám, The,
MP X-5730
FITZGERALD, F. SCOTT, CWA I-613;
CWAII II-522
"Absolution," MPII:SS I-5
"Babylon Revisited," MPII:SS I-140

Beautiful and Damned, The, CLCII I-
127; MPII:AF I-122
Crack-Up, The, MPII:NF I-293
"Crazy Sunday," MPII:SS I-452
"Diamond as Big as the Ritz, The,"
MPII:SS II-582
"Freshest Boy, The," MPII:SS II-813
Great Gatsby, The, CLC I-421; MP IV-
2358; MP:AF I-496
Last Tycoon, The, CLC I-599; MP VI-
3277; MP:AF II-649
Letters of F. Scott Fitzgerald, The, MP
VI-3347
"May Day," MPII:SS IV-1485
"Rich Boy, The," MPII:SS V-1952
Tender Is the Night, CLC II-1117; MP
XI-6448; MP:AF III-1266
This Side of Paradise, CLCII IV-1550;
MPII:AF IV-1635
"Winter Dreams," MPII:SS VI-2645
FITZGERALD, ZELDA
Save Me the Waltz, CLCII III-1340;
MPII:AF III-1370
FLACCUS, QUINTUS HORATIUS. See
HORACE
FLAUBERT, GUSTAVE, CWA I-615
Bouvard and Pécuchet, CLC I-117; MP
II-615; MP:EF I-127
"Herodias," MPII:SS III-1007
"Legend of St. Julian, Hospitaler, The,"
MPII:SS III-1328
Madame Bovary, CLC I-645; MP VI-
3599; MP:EF II-806
Salammbô, CLC II-1001; MP X-5769;
MP:EF III-1118
Sentimental Education, A, CLC II-1023;
MP X-5909; MP:EF III-1141
"Simple Heart, A," MPII:SS V-2120
Temptation of Saint Anthony, The, CLC
II-1114; MP XI-6438; MP:EF III-
1268
FLECKER, JAMES ELROY, CWA I-618
Poetry of Flecker, The, MP IX-4941
FLETCHER, JOHN
Faithful Shepherdess, The, CLC I-352;
MP IV-1962

Rule a Wife and Have a Wife, MP X-5732; CLC II-996

Woman's Prize, The, CLC II-1260; MP XII-7229

FLETCHER, JOHN, *and* FRANCIS BEAUMONT, CWA I-137

Coxcomb, The, CLC I-218; MP II-1185

King and No King, A, CLC I-569; MP VI-3133

Maid's Tragedy, The, CLC I-654; MP VI-3638

Philaster, CLC II-868; MP VIII-4639

Scornful Lady, The, CLC II-1012; MP X-5848

Woman Hater, The, CLC II-1255; MP XII-7207

FLETCHER, JOHN, *and* PHILIP MASSINGER

Beggars' Bush, The, CLC I-92; MP I-472

Sir John van Olden Barnavelt, CLC II-1042; MP X-6063

FLETCHER, JOHN, *and* WILLIAM SHAKESPEARE

Two Noble Kinsmen, The, CLC II-1172; MP XII-6775

FO, DARIO, CWAII II-525

Accidental Death of an Anarchist, CLCII I-8; MPII:D I-6

FOGAZZARO, ANTONIO, CWA I-620

Patriot, The, CLC II-843; MP VIII-4534; MP:EF III-973

Saint, The, CLC II-998; MP X-5751; MP:EF III-1109

FONTAINE, JEAN DE LA. *See* LA FONTAINE, JEAN DE

FONTANE, THEODOR, CWA I-622

Effi Briest, CLC I-317; MP III-1716; MP:EF I-464

FOQUÉ, FRIEDRICH DE LA MOTTE-. *See* LA MOTTE-FOUQUÉ, FRIEDRICH DE

FORBES, ESTHER, CWA I-623

Mirror for Witches, A, CLC II-710; MP VII-3917; MP:AF II-782

FORD, FORD MADOX, CWA I-624

Fifth Queen, The, MP IV-2055; MP:BF I-420

Good Soldier, The, CLCII II-613; MPII:BCF II-637

Parade's End, CLC II-833; MP VIII-4477; MP:BF II-1155

FORD, JOHN, CWA I-626

'Tis Pity She's a Whore, CLC II-1134; MP XI-6556

FORD, JOHN, THOMAS MIDDLETON, *and* WILLIAM ROWLEY

Spanish Gipsy, The, MP XI-6208

FORESTER, C. S., CWA I-627

Captain Horatio Hornblower, CLC I-148; MP II-779; MP:BF I-163

FORREST, LEON, CWAII II-528

There Is a Tree More Ancient Than Eden, CLCII IV-1538; MPII:AF IV-1615

FORSTER, E. M., CWA I-628; CWAII II-530

"Celestial Omnibus, The," MPII:SS I-348

Howards End, CLC I-493; MP V-2745; MP:BF II-616

Longest Journey, The, CLC I-625; MP VI-3487; MP:BF II-816

Maurice, CLCII III-989; MPII:BCF III-1076

Passage to India, A, CLC II-838; MP VIII-4500; MP:BF II-1161

Room with a View, A, CLC II-994; MP X-5712; MP:BF III-1376

Short Stories of E. M. Forster, The, MP X-5998; MP:BF III-1434

Where Angels Fear to Tread, CLC II-1236; MP XII-7104; MP:BF III-1731

FOUCAULT, MICHEL, CWAII II-533

Madness and Civilization, MPII:NF II-866

Order of Things, The, MPII:NF III-1098

FOUQUÉ, FRIEDRICH DE LA MOTTE. *See* LA MOTTE-FOUQUÉ, FRIEDRICH DE

FOURNIER, HENRI-ALAIN. *See* ALAIN-FOURNIER

FOWLES, JOHN, CWAII II-535
Collector, The, CLCII I-307; MPII:BCF I-281
Daniel Martin, CLCII I-364; MPII:BCF I-354
Ebony Tower, The, CLCII II-440; MPII:BCF I-422
French Lieutenant's Woman, The, CLCII II-546; MPII:BCF II-549
Magus, The, CLCII III-945; MPII:BCF III-1044

FRAME, JANET, CWAII II-537
Intensive Care, CLCII II-769; MPII:BCF II-831

FRANCE, ANATOLE, CWA I-630
At the Sign of the Reine Pédauque, CLC I-68; MP I-345; MP:EF I-77
Crime of Sylvestre Bonnard, The, CLC I-222; MP II-1202; MP:EF I-304
Gods Are Athirst, The, CLC I-405; MP IV-2282; MP:EF II-571
Penguin Island, CLC II-855; MP VIII-4579; MP:EF III-994
Revolt of the Angels, The, CLC II-963; MP X-5558; MP:EF III-1088

FRANCIS, DICK, CWAII II-540
Bonecrack, CLCII I-186; MPII:BCF I-172

FRANKL, VIKTOR
Man's Search for Meaning, MPII:NF III-896

FRANKLIN, BENJAMIN, CWA I-633
Autobiography of Benjamin Franklin, The, MP I-362

FRANKLIN, MILES
My Brilliant Career, CLCII III-1060; MPII:BCF III-1161

FRAYN, MICHAEL, CWAII II-542
Benefactors, CLCII I-142; MPII:D I-158

FRAZER, SIR JAMES GEORGE, CWA I-638
Golden Bough, The, MP IV-2296

FREDERIC, HAROLD, CWA I-640
Copperhead, The, CLC I-200; MP II-1113; MP:AF I-220
Damnation of Theron Ware, The, CLC I-235; MP III-1279; MP:AF I-251

FREEMAN, DOUGLAS SOUTHALL, CWA I-642
R. E. Lee, MP IX-5497

FREEMAN, MARY E. WILKINS
"Old Woman Magoun," MPII:SS IV-1684

FRENCH, MARILYN, CWAII II-544
Women's Room, The, CLCII IV-1737; MPII:AF IV-1810

FRENEAU, PHILIP, CWA I-643
Poetry of Freneau, The, MP IX-4943

FREUD, SIGMUND, CWA I-645; CWAII II-546
General Introduction to Psychoanalysis, A, MP IV-2218
Interpretation of Dreams, The, MP V-2908
Moses and Monotheism, MPII:NF III-982
Totem and Taboo, MPII:NF IV-1553
Wit and Its Relation to the Unconscious, MPII:NF IV-1704

FREUD, SIGMUND, *and* JOSEF BREUER
Studies on Hysteria, MP XI-6317

FREYTAG, GUSTAV, CWA I-648
Debit and Credit, CLC I-258; MP III-1393; MP:EF I-367

FRIEDAN, BETTY
Feminine Mystique, The, MPII:NF II-507

FRIEL, BRIAN, CWAII II-548
Freedom of the City, The, CLCII II-545; MPII:D II-633
Philadelphia, Here I Come! CLCII III-1202; MPII:D III-1230
Translations, CLCII IV-1600; MPII:D IV-1634
Volunteers, CLCII IV-1665; MPII:D IV-1695

FRISCH, MAX, CWAII II-550
Andorra, CLCII I-43; MPII:D I-60
Bluebeard, CLCII I-178; MPII:WF I-169
Chinese Wall, The, CLCII I-280; MPII:D I-347
Firebugs, The, CLCII II-510; MPII:D II-610
Homo Faber, CLCII II-692; MPII:WF II-608
I'm Not Stiller, CLCII II-740; MPII:WF II-669
Man in the Holocene, CLCII III-954; MPII:WF III-920
Sketchbook, 1946-1949, *and* Sketchbook, 1966-1971, MPII:NF IV-1361
FROISSART, JEAN, CWA I-649
Chronicles of Froissart, MP II-953
FROMENTIN, EUGÈNE, CWA I-650
Dominique, CLC I-288; MP III-1579; MP:EF I-422
FROST, ROBERT, CWA I-651
Letters of Robert Frost, The, MP VI-3358
Poetry of Frost, The, MP IX-4946
FRY, CHRISTOPHER, CWA I-656
Lady's Not for Burning, The, CLC I-589; MP VI-3219
FRYE, NORTHROP, CWAII II-552
Anatomy of Criticism, MPII:NF I-61
FUENTES, CARLOS, CWA I-658; CWAII II-555
Aura, CLCII I-90; MPII:AF I-76
Change of Skin, A, CLCII I-259; MPII:AF I-279

Death of Artemio Cruz, The, MP III-1369; MP:AF I-273
Distant Relations, CLCII I-406; MPII:AF I-418
Good Conscience, The, CLCII II-610; MPII:AF II-650
Holy Place, CLCII II-684; MPII:AF II-717
Terra Nostra, CLCII IV-1530; MPII:AF IV-1593
"Two Elenas, The," MPII:SS VI-2436
Where the Air Is Clear, MP XII-7107; MP:AF III-1420
FUGARD, ATHOL, CWAII II-558
Blood Knot, The, CLCII I-169; MPII:D I-200
Boesman and Lena, CLCII I-183; MPII:D I-225
Lesson from Aloes, A, CLCII II-875; MPII:D III-959
"MASTER HAROLD" . . . and the boys, CLCII III-986; MPII:D III-1059
Notebooks, 1960-1977, MPII:NF III-1019
Road to Mecca, The, CLCII III-1303; MPII:D IV-1362
FULLER, R. BUCKMINSTER
Critical Path, MPII:NF I-299
FULLER, THOMAS, CWA I-662
Holy State and the Profane State, The, MP V-2672
FUTRELLE, JACQUES, CWAII II-560
"Problem of Cell 13, The," MPII:SS IV-1856

G

GABORIAU, ÉMILE, CWA I-664
File No. 113, CLC I-366; MP IV-2058;
MP:EF II-515
Monsieur Lecoq, CLC II-736; MP VII-
4040; MP:EF II-883
GADAMER, HANS-GEORG, CWAII II-
562
Truth and Method, MPII:NF IV-1580
GADDA, CARLO EMILIO, CWAII II-
565
Acquainted with Grief, CLCII I-10;
MPII:WF I-16
That Awful Mess on Via Merulana,
CLCII IV-1532; MPII:WF IV-1565
GADDIS, WILLIAM, CWAII II-567
Recognitions, The, CLCII III-1277;
MPII:AF III-1324
GAINES, ERNEST J., CWAII II-569
Autobiography of Miss Jane Pittman,
The, CLCII I-93; MPII:AF I-87
"Sky Is Gray, The," MPII:SS V-2128
GALDÓS, BENITO PÉREZ. See
PÉREZ GALDÓS, BENITO
GALEANO, EDUARDO, CWAII II-571
Memory of Fire, MPII:NF III-937
GALIANO, JUAN VALERA Y
ALCALÁ. See VALERA Y
ALCALÁ GALIANO, JUAN
GALLANT, MAVIS
"Ice Wagon Going Down the Street,
The," MPII:SS III-1103
"Jorinda and Jorindel," MPII:SS III-
1237
"Other Paris, The," MPII:SS IV-1719
GALLEGOS, RÓMULO, CWA II-665
Doña Bárbara, CLC I-296; MP III-
1614; MP:AF I-304
GALLICO, PAUL
"Enchanted Doll, The," MPII:SS II-683
GALSWORTHY, JOHN, CWA II-666
Country House, The, CLC I-210; MP
II-1155; MP:BF I-246
Forsyte Saga, The, CLC I-376; MP IV-
2119; MP:BF I-438

Fraternity, CLC I-386; MP IV-2159;
MP:BF I-470
"Japanese Quince, The," MPII:SS III-
1211
Justice, CLC I-564; MP VI-3108
Loyalties, CLC I-638; MP VI-3544
Modern Comedy, A, CLC II-729; MP
VII-4005; MP:BF II-983
Patrician, The, CLC II-842; MP VIII-
4531; MP:BF II-1171
Strife, CLC II-1091; MP XI-6311
GALT, JOHN, CWA II-669
Annals of the Parish, CLC I-47; MP I-
240; MP:BF I-54
GARCÍA LORCA, FEDERICO, CWA
II-671
Blood Wedding, CLC I-112; MP I-574
GARCÍA MÁRQUEZ, GABRIEL,
CWAII II-574
Autumn of the Patriarch, The, CLCII I-
95; MPII:AF I-92
"Blacamán the Good, Vendor of
Miracles," MPII:SS I-227
Chronicle of a Death Foretold, CLCII I-
284; MPII:AF I-300
"Handsomest Drowned Man in the
World, The," MPII:SS III-977
Leaf Storm, CLCII II-864; MPII:AF II-
868
No One Writes to the Colonel, CLCII
III-1108; MPII:AF III-1151
One Hundred Years of Solitude, CLCII
III-1150; MPII:AF III-1207
GARDAM, JANE
Crusoe's Daughter, CLCII I-352;
MPII:BCF I-333
God on the Rocks, CLCII II-600;
MPII:BCF II-617
GARDNER, JOHN, CWAII II-577
"Art of Living, The," MPII:SS I-114
Grendel, CLCII II-637; MPII:AF II-677
"John Napper Sailing Through the
Universe," MPII:SS III-1226
"King's Indian, The," CLCII II-835;
MPII:SS III-1265

Mickelsson's Ghosts, CLCII III-1001; MPII:AF III-1002

Nickel Mountain, CLCII III-1091; MPII:AF III-1134

October Light, CLCII III-1127; MPII:AF III-1165

On Moral Fiction, MPII:NF III-1077

Sunlight Dialogues, The, CLCII IV-1495; MPII:AF IV-1555

Wreckage of Agathon, The, CLCII IV-1758; MPII:AF IV-1830

GARLAND, HAMLIN, CWA II-673

Main-Travelled Roads, MP VI-3650; MP:AF II-735

"Return of a Private, The," MPII:SS V-1937

Son of the Middle Border, A, MP X-6138

GARNER, HELEN

Monkey Grip, CLCII III-1030; MPII:BCF III-1137

GARNETT, DAVID, CWA II-675

Lady into Fox, CLC I-587; MP VI-3210; MP:BF II-765

GARRETT, GEORGE, CWA II-677; CWAII II-580

Death of the Fox, CLCII I-379; MPII:AF I-384

"Evening Performance, An," MPII:SS II-727

Poetry of Garrett, The, MP IX-4952

GASCOIGNE, GEORGE, CWA II-679

Poetry of Gascoigne, The, MP IX-4955

GASKELL, MRS. ELIZABETH, CWA II-682

Cranford, CLC I-219; MP II-1191; MP:BF I-250

Mary Barton, MP VII-3756; MP:BF II-883

GASS, WILLIAM H., CWA II-684; CWAII II-582

"In the Heart of the Heart of the Country," MPII:SS III-1150

Omensetter's Luck, CLCII III-1140; MPII:AF III-1184

"Pedersen Kid, The," MPII:SS IV-1793

GASSET, JOSÉ ORTEGA Y. See ORTEGA Y GASSET, JOSÉ

GAUTIER, THÉOPHILE, CWA II-685

Mademoiselle de Maupin, CLC I-647; MP VI-3604; MP:EF II-812

Poetry of Gautier, The, MP IX-4961

GAY, JOHN, CWA II-687

Beggar's Opera, The, CLC I-94; MP I-476

GEERTZ, CLIFFORD, CWAII II-584

Interpretation of Cultures, The, MPII:NF II-747

GELBER, JACK

Connection, The, CLCII I-330; MPII:D I-391

GENET, JEAN, CWAII II-586

Balcony, The, CLCII I-103; MPII:D I-109

Blacks, The, CLCII I-167; MPII:D I-190

Deathwatch, CLCII I-382; MPII:D II-471

Maids, The, CLCII III-946; MPII:D III-1031

Miracle of the Rose, CLCII III-1013; MPII:WF III-1011

Our Lady of the Flowers, CLCII III-1164; MPII:WF III-1163

Screens, The, CLCII III-1352; MPII:D IV-1416

GEORGE, STEFAN, CWA II-689

Poetry of Stefan George, The, MP IX-5155

GIBBON, EDWARD, CWA II-691

History of the Decline and Fall of the Roman Empire, The, MP V-2649

GIBBON, LEWIS GRASSIC

Scots Quair, A, CLCII III-1349; MPII:BCF III-1465

GIBBONS, STELLA, CWA II-693

Cold Comfort Farm, MP II-1016; MP:BF I-230

GIBRAN, KAHLIL

Prophet, The, MP IX-5372

GIBSON, WILLIAM
  Miracle Worker, The, CLCII III-1015;
    MPII:D III-1089
  Two for the Seesaw, CLCII IV-1625;
    MPII:D IV-1670
GIDE, ANDRÉ, CWA II-695
  Counterfeiters, The, CLC I-206; MP II-
    1140; MP:EF I-274
  Immoralist, The, CLCII II-743;
    MPII:WF II-673
  Journals of André Gide, The, MP VI-
    3059
  Lafcadio's Adventures, CLCII II-847;
    MPII:WF II-806
  Strait Is the Gate, CLCII IV-1477;
    MPII:WF IV-1529
GIEDION, SIGFRIED
  Eternal Present, The, MPII:NF II-460
  Space, Time, and Architecture,
    MPII:NF IV-1408
GILBERT, SANDRA M., and SUSAN
  GUBAR, CWAII II-588
  Madwoman in the Attic, The, MPII:NF
    II-872
GILBERT, W. S., CWA II-698
  Gondoliers, The, CLC I-409; MP IV-
    2310
  H. M. S. Pinafore, CLC I-478; MP V-
    2669
  Iolanthe, CLC I-528; MP V-2922
  Mikado, The, CLC II-704; MP VII-
    3893
  Patience, CLC II-842; MP VIII-4528
  Pirates of Penzance, The, CLC II-888;
    MP VIII-4726
  Trial by Jury, CLC II-1156; MP XI-
    6692
GILLPARZER, FRANZ
  Jewess of Toledo, The, CLC I-547
  Sappho, CLC II-1006
GILMAN, CHARLOTTE PERKINS,
  CWAII II-590
  Herland, CLCII II-676; MPII:AF II-706
GILMAN, RICHARD
  Faith, Sex, Mystery, MPII:NF II-497

GILROY, FRANK D.
  Subject Was Roses, The, CLCII IV-
    1486; MPII:D IV-1503
GINZBURG, NATALIA, CWAII II-592
  All Our Yesterdays, CLCII I-31;
    MPII:WF I-34
  City and the House, The, CLCII I-289;
    MPII:WF I-262
GIONO, JEAN, CWA II-700; CWAII II-
  594
  Blue Boy, CLCII I-175; MPII:WF I-158
  Horseman on the Roof, The, CLCII II-
    699; MPII:WF II-618
  Joy of Man's Desiring, CLCII II-802;
    MPII:WF II-786
  Song of the World, The, CLC II-1067;
    MP XI-6163; MP:EF III-1201
GIOVANNI, NIKKI, CWAII II-596
  Gemini, MPII:NF II-549
GIRARD, RENÉ, CWAII II-599
  Scapegoat, The, MPII:NF III-1293
GIRAUDOUX, JEAN, CWA II-702
  Amphitryon 38, CLC I-37; MP I-189
  Madwoman of Chaillot, The, CLC I-
    649; MP VI-3611
  Tiger at the Gates, MP XI-6539
GIRONELLA, JOSÉ MARÍA, CWA II-
  704
  Cypresses Believe in God, The, MP III-
    1259; MP:EF I-319
GISSING, GEORGE, CWA II-706
  New Grub Street, The, CLC II-763; MP
    VII-4174; The, MP:BF II-1034
  Private Papers of Henry Ryecroft, The,
    CLC II-920; MP IX-5350; MP:BF
    III-1270
GLASGOW, ELLEN, CWA II-708
  Barren Ground, CLC I-84; MP I-438;
    MP:AF I-96
  "Difference, The," MPII:SS II-595
  "Jordan's End," MPII:SS III-1234
  Romantic Comedians, The, CLC II-986;
    MP X-5684; MP:AF III-1067
  Sheltered Life, The, CLC II-1033; MP
    X-5969; MP:AF III-1130

Vein of Iron, CLCII IV-1651; MPII:AF IV-1738

GLASS, PHILIP, *and* ROBERT WILSON
Einstein on the Beach, CLCII II-449; MPII:D II-551

GLASSER, RONALD
365 Days, MPII:NF IV-1518

GODDEN, RUMER, CWAII II-601
Time to Dance, No Time to Weep, A, MPII:NF IV-1527

GODWIN, GAIL, CWAII II-604
Mother and Two Daughters, A, CLCII III-1043; MPII:AF III-1072
Odd Woman, The, CLCII III-1131; MPII:AF III-1176

GODWIN, WILLIAM, CWA II-712
Caleb Williams, CLC I-141; MP II-740; MP:BF I-158
Inquiry Concerning Political Justice, An, MP V-2901

GOETHE, JOHANN WOLFGANG VON, CWA II-714
Egmont, CLC I-317; MP III-1719
Elective Affinities, CLC I-319; MP III-1731; MP:EF I-468
Faust, CLC I-362; MP IV-2020
Poetry and Truth from My Own Life, MP VIII-4792
Sorrows of Young Werther, The, CLC II-1069; MP XI-6182; MP:EF III-1206
Wilhelm Meister's Apprenticeship, CLC II-1243; MP XII-7148; MP:EF III-1390
Wilhelm Meister's Travels, CLC II-1245; MP XII-7152; MP:EF III-1395

GOFFMAN, ERVING
Relations in Public, MPII:NF III-1236

GOGGAN, JOHN PATRICK. *See* PATRICK, JOHN

GOGOL, NIKOLAI VASILYEVICH, CWA II-718
Dead Souls, CLC I-248; MP III-1342; MP:EF I-345
"Diary of a Madman, The," MPII:SS II-591

Inspector General, The, CLC I-526; MP V-2904
"Nose, The," MPII:SS IV-1633
"Old-World Landowners," MPII:SS IV-1688
"Overcoat, The," CLC II-830; MP VIII-4452; MP:EF III-965; MPII:SS IV-1745
Taras Bulba, CLC II-1108; MP XI-6408; MP:EF III-1260
"Viy," MPII:SS VI-2513

GÖKÇELI, YAŞAR KEMAL. *See* KEMAL, YASHAR

GOLDEMBERG, ISAAC
Fragmented Life of Don Jacobo Lerner, The, CLCII II-542; MPII:AF II-572

GOLDING, WILLIAM, CWA II-721; CWAII II-606
Darkness Visible, CLCII I-367; MPII:BCF I-360
Free Fall, MP IV-2163; MP:BF I-475
Inheritors, The, MP V-2894; MP:BF II-645
Lord of the Flies, MP VI-3505; MP:BF II-825
Paper Men, The, CLCII III-1175; MPII:BCF III-1277
Pincher Martin, CLCII III-1208; MPII:BCF III-1325
Rites of Passage, CLCII III-1299; MPII:BCF III-1422
Spire, The, CLCII IV-1462; MPII:BCF IV-1593

GOLDONI, CARLO, CWA II-724
Mistress of the Inn, The, CLC II-724; MP VII-3982

GOLDSMITH, OLIVER, CWA II-725
Poetry of Goldsmith, The, MP IX-4964
She Stoops to Conquer, CLC II-1030; MP X-5957
Vicar of Wakefield, The, CLC II-1198; MP XII-6901; MP:BF III-1674

GOMBRICH, ERNST HANS JOSEF, CWAII II-608
Art and Illusion, MPII:NF I-90

GOMBROWICZ, WITOLD, CWAII II-610

Cosmos, CLCII I-340; MPII:WF I-328

Diary, MPII:NF I-367

Ferdydurke, CLCII II-499; MPII:WF II-451

Ivona, Princess of Burgundia, CLCII II-782; MPII:D II-857

Marriage, The, CLCII III-977; MPII:D III-1054

Operetta, CLCII III-1156; MPII:D III-1180

Pornografia, CLCII III-1221; MPII:WF III-1221

GONCHAROV, IVAN ALEXANDROVICH, CWA II-729

Oblomov, CLC II-787; MP:EF II-949; MP VII-4270

GONCOURT, EDMOND DE, and JULES DE GONCOURT, CWA II-731

Charles Demailly, CLC I-168; MP II-888; MP:EF I-210

Germinie Lacerteux, CLC I-398; MP IV-2242; MP:EF II-563

Goncourt Journals, The, MP IV-2307

Manette Salomon, CLC I-662; MP VII-3686; MP:EF II-821

Renée Mauperin, CLC II-957; MP IX-5514; MP:EF III-1078

Sister Philoméne, CLC II-1046; MP X-6075; MP:EF III-1159

GORDIMER, NADINE, CWAII II-612

Burger's Daughter, CLCII I-212; MPII:BCF I-201

Conservationist, The, CLCII I-331; MPII:BCF I-318

July's People, CLCII II-807; MPII:BCF II-872

"Livingstone's Companions," MPII:SS III-1383

Occasion for Loving, CLCII III-1126; MPII:BCF III-1248

"Open House," MPII:SS IV-1712

"Smell of Death and Flowers, The," MPII:SS V-2142

"Soldier's Embrace, A," MPII:SS V-2166

"Something Out There," MPII:SS V-2182

"Town and Country Lovers," MPII:SS VI-2397

World of Strangers, A, CLCII IV-1754; MPII:BCF IV-1940

GORDON, CAROLINE, CWA II-733; CWAII II-614

Aleck Maury, Sportsman, CLC I-20; MP I-93; MP:AF I-28

"Ice House, The," MPII:SS III-1099

"Old Red," MPII:SS IV-1676

GORDON, MARY, CWAII II-616

Company of Women, The, CLCII I-316; MPII:AF I-315;

Final Payments, CLCII II-504; MPII:AF II-542

GORKY, MAXIM, CWA II-734

Artamonov Business, The, CLC I-64; MP I-326; MP:EF I-68

Foma Gordeyev, CLC I-373; MP IV-2100; MP:EF II-526

Lower Depths, The, CLC I-636; MP VI-3540

Mother, CLC II-744; MP VII-4072; MP:EF II-899

"Twenty-six Men and a Girl," MPII:SS VI-2429

GOTTFRIED VON STRASSBURG, CWA II-737

Tristan and Isolde, CLC II-1159; MP XI-6705

GOURMONT, REMY DE, CWA II-738

Night in the Luxembourg, A, CLC II-778; MP VII-4215; MP:EF II-946

GOYEN, WILLIAM

"Faces of Blood Kindred, The," MPII:SS II-743

"Ghost and Flesh, Water and Dirt," MPII:SS II-839

"Shape of Light, A," MPII:SS V-2068

GOYTISOLO, JUAN, CWAII II-618

Count Julian, CLCII III-974; MPII:WF III-958

Juan the Landless, CLCII III-974;
MPII:WF III-958
Marks of Identity, CLCII III-974;
MPII:WF III-958
GRAHAME, KENNETH, CWA II-740
Wind in the Willows, The, CLC II-
1247; MP XII-7159; MP:BF III-1739
GRAMSCI, ANTONIO, CWAII II-621
Prison Notebooks, MPII:NF III-1200
GRANVILLE-BARKER, HARLEY, CWA
II-742
Madras House, The, CLC I-648; MP
VI-3607
GRASS, GÜNTER, CWA II-743; CWAII
II-623
Cat and Mouse, MP II-842; MP:EF I-
195
Dog Years, CLCII II-412; MPII:WF I-
386
Flounder, The, CLCII II-525; MPII:WF
II-481
Headbirths, CLCII II-665; MPII:WF II-
578
Local Anaesthetic, CLCII III-902;
MPII:WF II-872
Meeting at Telgte, The, CLCII III-991;
MPII:WF III-994
Rat, The, CLCII III-1266; MPII:WF
III-1252
Tin Drum, The, MP XI-6553; MP:EF
III-1290
GRAU, SHIRLEY ANN, CWAII II-626
"Black Prince, The," MPII:SS I-235
Keepers of the House, The, CLCII II-
822; MPII:AF II-835
GRAVES, ROBERT, CWA II-745;
CWAII II-628
Claudius the God and His Wife
Messalina, CLC I-184; MP II-981;
MP:BF I-216
Good-bye to All That, MPII:NF II-567
I, Claudius, CLC I-507; MP V-2803;
MP:BF II-632
King Jesus, CLCII II-830; MPII:BCF
II-915

Poetry of Graves, The, MP IX-4968
White Goddess, The, MPII:NF IV-1692
GRAY, ALASDAIR
Lanark, CLCII II-850; MPII:BCF II-
934
GRAY, SIMON, CWAII II-631
Butley, CLCII I-222; MPII:D I-273
Otherwise Engaged, CLCII III-1161;
MPII:D III-1191
GRAY, THOMAS, CWA II-747
Letters of Thomas Gray, The, MP VI-
3361
Poetry of Gray, The, MP IX-4971
GREEN, HANNAH, CWAII II-635. *See
also* GREENBERG, JOANNE
I Never Promised You a Rose Garden,
CLCII II-728; MPII:AF II-769
GREEN, HENRY, CWA II-749; CWAII
II-633
Caught, CLCII I-248; MPII:BCF I-230
Concluding, CLCII I-318; MPII:BCF I-
307
Living, CLCII III-899; MPII:BCF II-
984
Loving, CLC I-636; MP VI-3537;
MP:BF II-839
Nothing, CLCII III-1114; MPII:BCF
III-1224
Pack My Bag, MPII:NF III-1118
Party Going, CLCII III-1179;
MPII:BCF III-1288
GREEN, JULIAN, CWA II-751
Closed Garden, The, CLC I-189; MP
II-998; MP:EF I-240
Dark Journey, The, CLC I-240; MP III-
1313; MP:EF I-338
GREENBERG, JOANNE, CWAII II-635.
See also GREEN, HANNAH
"Hunting Season," MPII:SS III-1085
"Supremacy of the Hunza, The,"
MPII:SS V-2285
GREENE, GRAHAM, CWA II-753;
CWAII II-638
"Basement Room, The," MPII:SS I-166
Brighton Rock, CLCII I-206; MPII:BCF
I-191

Burnt-Out Case, A, MP II-711; MP:BF I-150

"Cheap in August," MPII:SS I-361

Comedians, The, CLCII I-311; MPII:BCF I-288

"Drive in the Country, A," MPII:SS II-636

End of the Affair, The, CLCII II-454; MPII:BCF I-442

Heart of the Matter, The, CLC I-450; MP V-2515; MP:BF I-550

Honorary Consul, The, CLCII II-693; MPII:BCF II-732

Ministry of Fear, The, CLC II-708; MP VII-3909; MP:BF II-951

Potting Shed, The, CLCII III-1228; MPII:D III-1274

Power and the Glory, The, CLC II-910; MP IX-5280; MP:BF III-1250

Quiet American, The, CLCII III-1252; MPII:BCF III-1364

Sort of Life, A, MPII:NF IV-1393

Ways of Escape, MPII:NF IV-1665

GREENE, ROBERT, CWA II-756

Friar Bacon and Friar Bungay, CLC I-386; MP IV-2172

Greene's Groatsworth of Wit Bought with a Million of Repentance, MP IV-2394

GREGORY, ANDRÉ, and WALLACE SHAWN

My Dinner with André, CLCII III-1061; MPII:D III-1121

GREGORY, LADY AUGUSTA, CWA II-758

Grania, CLCII II-622; MPII:D II-696

Seven Short Plays, MP X-5932

Workhouse Ward, The, CLCII IV-1748; MPII:D IV-1778

GREKOVA, I.

Ladies' Hairdresser, CLCII II-841; MPII:WF II-802

GREVE, FELIX PAUL. See GROVE, FREDERICK PHILIP

GRIFFIN, GERALD, CWA II-760

Collegians, The, CLC I-191; MP II-1028; MP:BF I-234

GRILLPARZER, FRANZ, CWA II-761

Jewess of Toledo, The, MP V-3008

Sappho, MP X-5793

GRIMMELSHAUSEN, H. J. C. VON, CWA II-763

Simplicissimus the Vagabond, CLC II-1040; MP X-6053; MP:EF III-1155

GROTIUS, HUGO, CWA II-765

On the Law of War and Peace, MP VIII-4373

GROVE, FREDERICK PHILIP

Fruits of the Earth, CLCII II-554; MPII:BCF II-553

Master of the Mill, The, CLCII III-987; MPII:BCF III-1072

Search for America, A, CLCII III-1356; MPII:BCF III-1472

Settlers of the Marsh, CLCII IV-1380; MPII:BCF IV-1506

GRUŠA, JIŘÍ

Questionnaire, The, CLCII III-1249; MPII:WF III-1240

GUARE, JOHN, CWAII II-641

House of Blue Leaves, The, CLCII II-710; MPII:D II-789

Lydie Breeze, CLCII III-938; MPII:D III-1007

GUBAR, SUSAN, and SANDRA M. GILBERT, CWAII II-588

Madwoman in the Attic, The, MPII:NF II-872

GUÐJÓNSSON, HALLDÓR KILJAN. See LAXNESS, HALLDÓR

GUILLAUME DE LORRIS, and JEAN DE MEUNG, CWA II-767

GUIMARÁES ROSA, JOÁO, CWAII II-643

"Third Bank of the River, The," MPII:SS VI-2341

GÜIRALDES, RICARDO, CWA II-768

Don Segundo Sombra, CLC I-296; MP III-1609; MP:AF I-299

GUNNARSSON, GUNNAR, CWA II-769
Guest the One-Eyed, CLC I-432; MP
IV-2416; MP:EF II-607
GURNEY, A. R., JR., CWAII II-646
Dining Room, The, CLCII I-402;
MPII:D II-497
Scenes from American Life, CLCII III-
1345; MPII:D IV-1411
GUSTAFSSON, LARS
Death of a Beekeeper, The, CLCII I-
378; MPII:WF I-349
Sigismund, CLCII IV-1403; MPII:WF
IV-1419
Tennis Players, The, CLCII IV-1525;
MPII:WF IV-1560

GUTHRIE, A. B., JR., CWA II-771;
CWAII II-648
Big Sky, The, CLC I-102; MP I-531;
MP:AF I-116
These Thousand Hills, CLCII IV-1541;
MPII:AF IV-1620
Way West, The, CLCII IV-1698;
MPII:AF IV-1773
GUZMÁN, MARTÍN LUIS, CWA II-
772
Eagle and the Serpent, The, MP III-
1679; MP:AF I-322

H

HĀFIZ, CWA II-775
Divan, The, MP III-1527
HAGGARD, H. RIDER, CWA II-776
King Solomon's Mines, CLC I-576; MP
VI-3163; MP:BF II-751
She, CLC II-1029; MP X-5952; MP:BF
III-1421
HAKIM, TAWFIQ AL-, CWAII II-653
Tree Climber, The, CLCII IV-1607;
MPII:D IV-1648
Voyage to Tomorrow, CLCII IV-1669;
MPII:D IV-1706
HAKLUYT, RICHARD, CWA II-778
Hakluyt's Voyages, MP V-2450
HALE, EDWARD EVERETT, CWA II-
779
Man Without a Country, The, CLC I-
662; MP VII-3683; MP:AF II-744
HALE, NANCY, CWAII II-656
"Empress's Ring, The," MPII:SS II-680
HALÉVY, LUDOVIC, CWA II-780
Abbé Constantin, The, CLC I-1; MP I-
1; MP:EF I-1
HALEY, ALEX, CWAII II-658
Roots, MPII:NF III-1251
HALL, DONALD, CWA II-781
Poetry of Hall, The, MP IX-4973
HALL, JAMES NORMAN, and
CHARLES NORDOFF, CWA II-
1314
Mutiny on the Bounty, CLC II-749; MP
VII-4099; MP:AF II-819
HALL, RADCLYFFE, CWAII II-660
"Miss Ogilvy Finds Herself," MPII:SS
IV-1509
HAMILTON, ALEXANDER, CWA II-
782
HAMILTON, ALEXANDER, JAMES
MADISON, and JOHN JAY
Federalist, The, MP IV-2025
HAMMETT, DASHIELL, CWA II-787;
CWAII II-662
Glass Key, The, CLC I-403; MP IV-
2267; MP:AF I-449

"House in Turk Street, The," MPII:SS
III-1045
Maltese Falcon, The, CLC I-658; MP
VI-3661; MP:AF II-740
Thin Man, The, CLC II-1123; MP XI-
6489; MP:AF III-1275
HAMSUN, KNUT, CWA II-788; CWAII
II-664
Growth of the Soil, CLC I-429; MP IV-
2404; MP:EF II-599
Hunger, CLC I-502; MP V-2780;
MP:EF II-670
Mysteries, CLCII III-1068; MPII:WF
III-1059
On Overgrown Paths, MPII:NF III-1082
Pan, CLCII III-1172; MPII:WF III-1168
Victoria, CLCII IV-1655; MPII:WF IV-
1709
Women at the Pump, The, CLCII IV-
1733; MPII:WF IV-1779
HANDKE, PETER, CWAII II-667
Across, CLCII I-11; MPII:WF I-20
Goalie's Anxiety at the Penalty Kick,
The, CLCII II-598; MPII:WF II-549
Kaspar, CLCII II-816; MPII:D III-890
Left-Handed Woman, The, CLCII II-
870; MPII:WF II-830
Moment of True Feeling, A, CLCII III-
1029; MPII:WF III-1026
Offending the Audience, CLCII III-
1132; MPII:D III-1164
Ride Across Lake Constance, The,
CLCII III-1292; MPII:D III-1330
Short Letter, Long Farewell, CLCII IV-
1395; MPII:WF IV-1398
Slow Homecoming, CLCII IV-1425;
MPII:WF IV-1462
Sorrow Beyond Dreams, A, CLCII IV-
1448; MPII:WF IV-1496
Weight of the World, The, MPII:NF
IV-1675
HANLEY, JAMES
Dream Journey, A, CLCII II-423;
MPII:BCF I-403

HANSBERRY, LORRAINE, CWAII II-669
Raisin in the Sun, A, CLCII III-1262; MPII:D III-1300
Sign in Sidney Brustein's Window, The, CLCII IV-1404; MPII:D IV-1458
HARDWICK, ELIZABETH
Seduction and Betrayal, MPII:NF III-1324
HARDY, THOMAS, CWA II-791
Dynasts, The, CLC I-310; MP III-1675
Far from the Madding Crowd, CLC I-356; MP IV-1990; MP:BF I-405
Jude the Obscure, CLC I-557; MP VI-3079; MP:BF II-721
Mayor of Casterbridge, The, CLC I-683; MP VII-3784; MP:BF II-896
Poetry of Hardy, The, MP IX-4976
Return of the Native, The, CLC II-959; MP X-5545; MP:BF III-1317
Tess of the D'Urbervilles, CLC II-1118; MP XI-6457; MP:BF III-1509
Under the Greenwood Tree, CLC II-1181; MP XII-6829; MP:BF III-1634
Woodlanders, The, CLC II-1263; MP XII-7247; MP:BF III-1764
HARE, DAVID, CWAII II-671
Plenty, CLCII III-1213; MPII:D III-1258
HARE, DAVID, and HOWARD BRENTON
Pravda, CLCII III-1232; MPII:D III-1278
HARRIS, JOEL CHANDLER, CWA II-794
"Sad Fate of Mr. Fox, The," MPII:SS V-2002
Tales of Uncle Remus, MP XI-6384; MP:AF III-1256
"Wonderful Tar-Baby Story, The," MPII:SS VI-2684
HARRIS, MARK, CWAII II-673
Bang the Drum Slowly, CLCII I-112; MPII:AF I-111
Southpaw, The, CLCII IV-1455; MPII:AF IV-1505

HARRIS, WILSON, CWAII II-675
Guyana Quartet, The, CLCII II-646; MPII:BCF II-679
HART, LORENZ, CWAII II-678
HART, MOSS, CWAII II-680
HART, MOSS, and GEORGE S. KAUFMAN
Man Who Came to Dinner, The, CLCII III-954; MPII:D III-1043
Once in a Lifetime, CLCII III-1145; MPII:D III-1174
You Can't Take It with You, CLCII IV-1764; MPII:D IV-1788
HARTE, BRET, CWA II-796
Luck of Roaring Camp and Other Sketches, The, MP VI-3551; MP:AF II-713
"Luck of Roaring Camp, The," MPII:SS IV-1412
"Outcasts of Poker Flat, The," MPII:SS IV-1727
HARTLEY, L. P., CWAII II-682
Go-Between, The, CLCII II-597; MPII:BCF II-612
HARTMANN VON AUE, CWA II-798
Arme Heinrich, Der, CLC I-60; MP I-307
HAŠEK, JAROSLAV, CWA II-799
Good Soldier: Schweik, The, MP IV-2324; MP:EF II-580
HAUPTMANN, GERHART, CWA II-801
Beaver Coat, The, CLC I-92;; MP I-469
Sunken Bell, The, CLC II-1094; MP XI-6341
Weavers, The, CLC II-1231; MP XII-7073
HAVEL, VÁCLAV, CWAII II-684
Garden Party, The, CLCII II-567; MPII:D II-660
Increased Difficulty of Concentration, The, CLCII II-757; MPII:D II-835
Largo Desolato, CLCII II-851; MPII:D III-926
Letters to Olga, MPII:NF II-825

Memorandum, The, CLCII III-995; MPII:D III-1077

Temptation, CLCII IV-1523; MPII:D IV-1554

HAWKES, JOHN, CWA II-803

Cannibal, The, MP II-763; MP:AF I-171

Lime Twig, The, MP VI-3431; MP:AF II-684

HAWKINS, SIR ANTHONY HOPE. See HOPE, ANTHONY

HAWTHORNE, NATHANIEL, CWA II-806

"Ambitious Guest, The," MPII:SS I-78

American Notebooks, The, MP I-172

"Artist of the Beautiful, The," MPII:SS I-122

"Birthmark, The," MPII:SS I-210

Blithedale Romance, The, CLC I-110; MP I-571; MP:AF I-131

"Dr. Heidegger's Experiment," MPII:SS II-617

English Notebooks, The, MP III-1784

"Ethan Brand," MPII:SS II-720

House of the Seven Gables, The, CLC I-491; MP V-2734; MP:AF II-572

Marble Faun, The, CLC I-667; MP VII-3710; MP:AF II-756

"Minister's Black Veil, The," MPII:SS IV-1501

"My Kinsman, Major Molineux," MPII:SS IV-1556

"Rappaccini's Daughter," MPII:SS V-1897

Scarlet Letter, The, CLC II-1009; MP X-5826; MP:AF III-1096

"Wakefield," MPII:SS VI-2521

"Young Goodman Brown," MPII:SS VI-2737

HAXTON, JOSEPHINE. See DOUGLAS, ELLEN

HAYDON, BENJAMIN ROBERT, CWA II-810

Autobiography of Benjamin Robert Haydon, The, MP I-365

HAZLITT, WILLIAM, CWA II-812

Critical Essays of William Hazlitt, The, MP II-1217

Familiar Essays of William Hazlitt, The, MP IV-1974

Liber Amoris, CLC I-609; MP VI-3379

H. D., CWA II-814; CWAII II-650

End to Torment, MPII:NF II-454

Tribute to Freud, MPII:NF IV-1558

Poetry of H. D., The, MP IX-4979

HEAD, BESSIE, CWAII II-687

"Collector of Treasures, The," MPII:SS I-413

Maru, CLCII III-980; MPII:BCF III-1062

Question of Power, A, CLCII III-1247; MPII:BCF III-1360

HEARN, LAFCADIO, CWA II-815

Chita, CLC I-178; MP II-940; MP:AF I-200

Youma, CLC II-1277; MP XII-7306; MP:AF III-1476

HEATH, ROY A. K.

Murderer, The, CLCII III-1057; MPII:BCF III-1153

HEAT-MOON, WILLIAM LEAST

Blue Highways, MPII:NF I-184

HEBBEL, FRIEDRICH, CWA II-817

Maria Magdalena, CLC I-670; MP VII-3725

HEGGEN, THOMAS, CWA II-819

Mister Roberts, CLC II-720; MP VII-3964; MP:AF II-796

HEIDENSTAM, VERNER VON, CWA II-820

Tree of the Folkungs, The, CLC II-1153; MP XI-6679; MP:EF III-1297

HEINE, HEINRICH, CWA II-821

Book of Songs, MP I-593

HEINLEIN, ROBERT A., CWAII II-690

"All You Zombies--", MPII:SS I-63

Moon is a Harsh Mistress, The, CLCII III-1036; MPII:AF III-1037

Stranger in a Strange Land, CLCII IV-1478; MPII:AF IV-1536

HELLER, ERICH, CWAII II-692
Disinherited Mind, The, MPII:NF I-393
HELLER, JOSEPH, CWA II-824; CWAII
II-694
Catch-22, MP II-848; MP:AF I-181
Something Happened, CLCII IV-1440;
MPII:AF IV-1465
HELLMAN, LILLIAN, CWA II-826;
CWAII II-696
Children's Hour, The, CLCII I-279;
MPII:D I-341
Little Foxes, The, CLC I-620; MP VI-
3451
Pentimento, MPII:NF III-1135
Unfinished Woman, An, MPII:NF IV-
1607
Watch on the Rhine, CLCII IV-1684;
MPII:D IV-1712
HELPRIN, MARK, CWAII II-698
"Schreuderspitze, The," MPII:SS V-
2041
HEMINGWAY, ERNEST, CWA II-827;
CWAII II-701
Across the River and into the Trees,
CLCII I-11; MPII:AF I-1
"After the Storm," MPII:SS I-46
"Alpine Idyll, An," MPII:SS I-66
"Big Two-Hearted River," MPII:SS I-
206
"Canary for One, A," MPII:SS I-323
"Clean, Well-Lighted Place, A,"
MPII:SS I-406
Death in the Afternoon, MPII:NF I-337
Farewell to Arms, A, CLC I-357; MP
IV-1995; MP:AF I-366
For Whom the Bell Tolls, CLC I-374;
MP IV-2114; MP:AF I-413
Green Hills of Africa, MPII:NF II-595
"Hills Like White Elephants," MPII:SS
III-1018
"In Another Country," MPII:SS III-
1130
"Indian Camp," MPII:SS III-1162
Islands in the Stream, CLCII II-780;
MPII:AF II-803
"Killers, The," MPII:SS III-1259

Moveable Feast, A, MP VII-4087
Old Man and the Sea, The, CLC II-804;
MP VIII-4325; MP:AF II-874
"Short Happy Life of Francis
Macomber, The," MPII:SS V-2088
Short Stories of Ernest Hemingway,
The, MP X-6002; MP:AF III-1145
"Soldier's Home," MPII:SS V-2170
Sun Also Rises, The, CLC II-1093; MP
XI-6335; MP:AF III-1238
"Three-Day Blow, The," MPII:SS VI-
2358
To Have and Have Not, CLCII IV-
1577; MPII:AF IV-1668
Torrents of Spring, The, CLCII IV-
1593; MPII:AF IV-1682
HÉMON, LOUIS, CWA II-830
Maria Chapdelaine, CLC I-669; MP
VII-3721; MP:AF II-769
HENLEY, BETH, CWAII II-704
Crimes of the Heart, CLCII I-350;
MPII:D I-407
HENLEY, WILLIAM ERNEST, CWA II-
831
Poetry of Henley, The, MP IX-4982
HENRY, O., CWA II-833
"Gift of the Magi, The," MPII:SS II-
847
"Ransom of Red Chief, The," MPII:SS
V-1894
Short Stories of O. Henry, The, MP X-
6021; The, MP: AF III-1149
HERBERT, FRANK, CWAII II-706
Dune trilogy, The, CLCII II-430;
MPII:AF I-451
HERBERT, GEORGE, CWA II-836
Temple, The, MP XI-6432
HERBERT, XAVIER
Capricornia, CLCII I-234; MPII:BCF I-
220
HERBERT, ZBIGNIEW, CWAII II-708
Barbarian in the Garden, MPII:NF I-138
HEREDIA, JOSÉ MARÍA DE, CWA II-
837
Poetry of Heredia, The, MP IX-4984

HERGESHEIMER, JOSEPH, CWA II-839
Java Head, CLC I-543; MP V-2985;
MP:AF II-615
Three Black Pennys, The, CLC II-1126;
The, MP XI-6500; MP:AF III-1279
HERLIHY, JAMES LEO, CWA II-840
All Fall Down, MP I-112
HERNÁNDEZ, JOSÉ, CWA II-841
Gaucho: Martin Fierro, The, CLC I-394; MP IV-2213
HERODOTUS, CWA II-842
History of the Persian Wars, The, MP V-2655
HERR, MICHAEL
Dispatches, MPII:NF I-398
HERRICK, ROBERT, CWA II-844
Hesperides, MP V-2606
HERRIOT, JAMES, CWAII II-710
All Creatures Great and Small, MPII:NF I-29
HERSEY, JOHN, CWA II-846; CWAII II-712
Bell for Adano, A, CLC I-96; MP I-488; MP:AF I-104
Call, The, CLCII I-227; MPII:AF I-237
Hiroshima, MPII:NF II-641
Wall, The, CLCII IV-1674; MPII:AF IV-1748
HESIOD, CWA II-848
Works and Days, MP XII-7254
HESSE, HERMANN, CWA II-849; CWAII II-714
Demian, CLCII I-386; MPII:WF I-364
Glass Bead Game, The, CLCII II-592; MPII:WF II-543
Klingsor's Last Summer, CLCII II-839; MPII:WF II-797
Narcissus and Goldmund, CLCII III-1077; MPII:WF III-1074
"Poet, The," MPII:SS IV-1828
Rosshalde, CLCII III-1314; MPII:WF III-1300
Siddhartha, CLCII IV-1400; MPII:WF IV-1414
Steppenwolf, CLC II-1081; MP XI-6250; MP:EF III-1221

"Within and Without," MPII:SS VI-2672
HEYWARD, DUBOSE, CWA II-851
Porgy, CLC II-902; MP IX-5247; MP:AF II-968
HEYWOOD, THOMAS, CWA II-853
Woman Killed with Kindness, A, CLC II-1257; MP XII-7217
HIGHWATER, JAMAKE, CWAII II-717
Journey to the Sky, CLCII II-801; MPII:AF II-814
HILDA DOOLITTLE. See H. D.
HILDESHEIMER, WOLFGANG, CWAII II-719
Marbot, CLCII III-973; MPII:WF III-952
"World Ends, A," MPII:SS VI-2701
HILL, SUSAN, CWAII II-721
"Albatross, The," MPII:SS I-49
HILLESUM, ETTY
Interrupted Life, An, MPII:NF II-751
HILTON, JAMES, CWA II-855
Goodbye, Mr. Chips, CLC I-412; MP IV-2328; MP:BF I-487
Lost Horizon, CLC I-629; MP VI-3512; MP:BF II-833
HIMES, CHESTER, CWAII II-723
If He Hollers Let Him Go, CLCII II-734; MPII:AF II-778
HIRAOKA, KIMITAKE. See MISHIMA, YUKIO
HIRAYAMA TŌGO. See IHARA, SAIKAKU
HIROAKA, KIMITAKE. See MISHIMA, YUKIO
HIRSCH, E. D., JR., CWAII II-726
Cultural Literacy, MPII:NF I-316
HOAGLAND, EDWARD, CWAII II-728
Notes from the Century Before, MPII:NF III-1023
HOBBES, THOMAS, CWA II-857
Leviathan, MP VI-3376
HOCHHUTH, ROLF, CWAII II-731
Deputy, The, CLCII I-393; MPII:D II-481

HODGSON, RALPH, CWA II-858
  Poetry of Hodgson, The, MP IX-4986
HOFFMANN, E. T. A., CWA II-860
  Devil's Elixir, The, CLC I-267; MP III-1467; MP:EF I-384
  Life and Opinions of Kater Murr, The, CLCII II-883; MPII:WF II-849
  "New Year's Eve Adventure, A," MPII:SS IV-1616
  "Ritter Gluck," MPII:SS V-1964
  "Sandman, The," MPII:SS V-2020
  "Story of Serapion, The," MPII:SS V-2248
HOFMANNSTHAL, HUGO VON, CWA II-861
  Poetry of Hofmannsthal, The, MP IX-4988
HOFSTADTER, DOUGLAS R., CWAII II-734
  Gödel, Escher, Bach, MPII:NF II-561
HÖLDERLIN, JOHANN CHRISTIAN FRIEDRICH, CWA II-863
  Poetry of Hölderlin, The, MP IX-4991
HOLMES, OLIVER WENDELL, CWA II-865
  Autocrat of the Breakfast-Table, The, MP I-379
HOMER, CWA II-868
  Iliad, The, CLC I-513; MP V-2837
  Odyssey, The, CLC II-788; MP VII-4275
HOPE, ANTHONY, CWA II-870
  Prisoner of Zenda, The, CLC II-917; MP IX-5340; MP:BF III-1266
HOPKINS, GERARD MANLEY, CWA II-872
  Poetry of Hopkins, The, MP IX-4994
HORACE, CWA II-874
  Ars Poetica, MP I-319
  Epistles of Horace, The, MP III-1808
  Poetry of Horace, The, MP IX-4997
HORATIUS FLACCUS, QUINTUS. See HORACE
HORENSTEIN, IRVING. See HOWE, IRVING

HORGAN, PAUL, CWAII II-737
  Great River, MPII:NF II-584
  "National Honeymoon," MPII:SS IV-1590
  "Peach Stone, The," MPII:SS IV-1782
HOSPITAL, JANETTE TURNER
  Borderline, CLCII I-193; MPII:BCF I-177
  Ivory Swing, The, CLCII II-784; MPII:BCF II-843
HOUSMAN, A. E., CWA II-876
  Shropshire Lad, A, MP X-6030
HOWARD, HENRY, EARL OF SURREY, CWA II-878
HOWARD, HENRY, EARL OF SURREY, and SIR THOMAS WYATT
  Poetry of Wyatt and Surrey, The, MP IX-5219
HOWE, EDGAR WATSON, CWA II-880
  Story of a Country Town, The, CLC II-1083; MP XI-6268; MP:AF III-1231
HOWE, IRVING, CWAII II-740
  Margin of Hope, A, MPII:NF III-901
HOWELLS, WILLIAM DEAN, CWA II-881
  Hazard of New Fortunes, A, CLC I-446; MP V-2495; MP:AF II-535
  Indian Summer, CLC I-522; MP V-2877; MP:AF II-591
  Modern Instance, A, CLC II-730; MP VII-4010; MP:AF II-811
  Rise of Silas Lapham, The, CLC II-973; MP X-5618; MP:AF III-1047
HRABAL, BOHUMIL
  Closely Watched Trains, CLCII I-296; MPII:WF I-272
HUDSON, W. H., CWA II-884
  Far Away and Long Ago, MP IV-1986
  Green Mansions, CLC I-425; MP IV-2386; MP:BF I-497
  Hampshire Days, MP V-2462
  Purple Land, The, CLC II-928; MP IX-5382; MP:BF III-1278
HUEFFER, FORD MADOX. See FORD, FORD MADOX

HUGHES, LANGSTON, CWA II-886;
CWAII II-743
Big Sea, The, MPII:NF I-156
"Gospel Singers," MPII:SS II-918
Not Without Laughter, CLCII III-1113;
MPII:AF III-1155
"Thank You, M'am," MPII:SS VI-2323
HUGHES, RICHARD, CWA II-888
Innocent Voyage, The, CLC I-525; MP
V-2897; MP:BF II-649
HUGHES, THOMAS, CWA II-889
Tom Brown's School Days, CLC II-
1141; MP XI-6585; MP:BF III-1556
HUGO, VICTOR, CWA II-890
Hunchback of Notre Dame, The, CLC
I-500; MP V-2774; MP:EF II-663
Misérables, Les, CLC II-713; MP VII-
3931; MP:EF II-866
Poetry of Hugo, The, MP IX-5000
Toilers of the Sea, The, CLC II-1140;
MP XI-6581; MP:EF III-1293
HUIZINGA, JOHAN, CWA II-893
Waning of the Middle Ages, The, MP
XII-7017
HULME, KERI
Bone People, The, CLCII I-185;
MPII:BCF I-168
HUME, DAVID, CWA II-894
Enquiry Concerning Human
Understanding, An, MP III-1793
HUNT, LEIGH, CWA II-896
Autobiography of Leigh Hunt, The, MP
I-373
HURSTON, ZORA NEALE, CWAII II-
745
Moses, CLCII III-1041; MPII:AF III-
1061

"Sweat," MPII:SS V-2293
Their Eyes Were Watching God, CLCII
IV-1534; MPII:AF IV-1598
HUTCHINSON, A. S. M., CWA II-898
If Winter Comes, CLC I-513; MP V-
2831; MP:BF II-636
HUXLEY, ALDOUS, CWA II-899;
CWAII II-747
After Many a Summer Dies the Swan,
CLCII I-17; MPII:BCF I-22
Brave New World, CLC I-121; MP II-
631; MP:BF I-128
Crome Yellow, CLC I-225; MP III-
1226; MP:BF I-258
Essays of Aldous Huxley, The, MP IV-
1851
Eyeless in Gaza, CLCII II-480;
MPII:BCF I-478
Point Counter Point, CLC II-898; MP
IX-5227; MP:BF III-1237
HUXLEY, SIR JULIAN, CWA II-902
Essays of a Biologist, MP IV-1848
HUXLEY, THOMAS HENRY, CWA II-
904
Physical Basis of Life, The, MP VIII-
4677
HUYSMANS, JORIS-KARL, CWA II-906
Against the Grain, CLC I-13; MP I-62;
MP:EF I-13
Down There, CLC I-300; MP III-1627;
MP:EF I-441
HYDE, EDWARD, EARL OF
CLARENDON, CWA II-908
History of the Rebellion and Civil Wars
in England, MP V-2658

I

IBÁÑEZ, VICENTE BLASCO. *See* BLASCO IBÁÑEZ, VICENTE

IBARA, SAIKAKU, CWA II-910
Five Women Who Loved Love, CLC I-372; MP IV-2082; MP:EF II-522

IBSEN, HENRIK, CWA II-912
Brand, CLC I-120; MP II-627
Doll's House, A, CLC I-284; MP III-1570
Enemy of the People, An, CLC I-326; MP III-1777
Ghosts, CLC I-399; MP IV-2250
Hedda Gabler, CLC I-454; MP V-2532
Lady from the Sea, The, CLC I-586; MP VI-3206
Master Builder, The, CLC I-679; MP VII-3759
Peer Gynt, CLC II-848; MP VIII-4559
Pillars of Society, The, CLC II-883; MP VIII-4710
Rosmersholm, CLC II-995; MP X-5718
When We Dead Awaken, CLC II-1236; MP XII-7100
Wild Duck, The, CLC II-1242; MP XII-7137

ICAZA, JORGE, CWA II-916
Huasipungo, CLC I-494; MP V-2750
Villagers, The, MP:AF III-1375

IHARA, SAIKAKU, CWAII II-750
Life of an Amorous Man, The, CLCII II-888; MPII:WF II-860

IKKU, JIPPENSHA. *See* JIPPENSHA IKKU

INFANTE, GUILLERMO CABRERA. *See* CABRERA INFANTE, GUILLERMO

INGALLS, RACHEL, CWAII II-753
Mrs. Caliban, CLCII III-1024; MPII:BCF III-1131

INGE, WILLIAM, CWAII II-755
Bus Stop, CLCII I-221; MPII:D I-267
Come Back, Little Sheba, CLCII I-310; MPII:D I-387

Picnic, CLCII III-1207; MPII:D III-1252

INGOLDSBY, THOMAS, CWA II-917
Ingoldsby Legends, The, MP V-2891

INNAURATO, ALBERT, CWAII II-757
Transfiguration of Benno Blimpie, The, CLCII IV-1599; MPII:D IV-1629

IONESCO, EUGÈNE, CWA II-919; CWAII II-759
Bald Soprano, The, CLCII I-105; MPII:D I-116
Chairs, The, CLCII I-255; MPII:D I-305
Exit the King, CLCII II-475; MPII:D II-585
Killer, The, CLCII II-827; MPII:D III-905
Lesson, The, CLCII II-875; MPII:D III-954
Rhinoceros, MP X-5574

IRON, RALPH. *See* SCHREINER, OLIVE

IRVING, JOHN, CWAII II-762
Hotel New Hampshire, The, CLCII II-703; MPII:AF II-743
Setting Free the Bears, CLCII IV-1378; MPII:AF III-1392
World According to Garp, The, CLCII IV-1749; MPII:AF IV-1825

IRVING, WASHINGTON, CWA II-921
"Adventure of the German Student," MPII:SS I-27
Chronicle of the Conquest of Granada, A, MP II-950
"Devil and Tom Walker, The," MPII:SS II-579
History of New York, A, MP V-2643
"Legend of Sleepy Hollow, The," CLC I-606; MP VI-3314; MP:AF II-659; MPII:SS III-1331
Legend of the Moor's Legacy, CLC I-607; MP VI-3317; MP:AF II-663

J

JACKSON, CHARLES, CWA II-925
Lost Weekend, The, CLC I-632; MP
VI-3524; MP:AF II-710
JACKSON, SHIRLEY, CWAII II-766
"Charles," MPII:SS I-359
"Lottery, The," MPII:SS IV-1406
"One Ordinary Day, with Peanuts,"
MPII:SS IV-1705
JACOBSEN, JENS PETER, CWA II-926
Niels Lyhne, CLC II-776; MP VII-
4205; MP:EF II-938
JACOBSON, DAN, CWAII II-768
"Beggar My Neighbor," MPII:SS I-181
Dance in the Sun, A, CLCII I-361;
MPII:BCF I-350
Wonder-Worker, The, CLCII IV-1738;
MPII:BCF IV-1921
"Zulu and the Zeide, The," MPII:SS
VI-2745
JAMES, C. L. R., CWAII II-770
Minty Alley, CLCII III-1012;
MPII:BCF III-1109
JAMES, HENRY, CWA II-927; CWAII
II-772
"Altar of the Dead, The," MPII:SS I-70
Ambassadors, The, CLC I-32; MP I-
156; MP:AF I-44
American Scene, The, MPII:NF I-44
American, The, CLC I-34; MP I-166;
MP:AF I-49
"Aspern Papers, The," CLCII I-77;
MPII:SS I-125
Awkward Age, The, MP I-387; MP:AF
I-85
"Beast in the Jungle, The," MPII:SS I-
169
Bostonians, The, MP I-605; MP:AF I-
135
Daisy Miller, CLC I-234; MP III-1270;
MP:AF I-248
"Figure in the Carpet, The," MPII:SS
II-777
Golden Bowl, The, CLC I-406; MP IV-
2299; MP:AF I-469

"Great Good Place, The," MPII:SS III-
929
"In the Cage," MPII:SS III-1141
"Jolly Corner, The," MPII:SS III-1230
"Lesson of the Master, The," MPII:SS
III-1339
Portrait of a Lady, The, CLC II-903;
MP IX-5250; MP:AF II-971
Princess Casamassima, The, MP IX-
5327; MP:AF II-990
"Pupil, The," MPII:SS V-1865
"Real Thing, The," MPII:SS V-1905
Roderick Hudson, MP X-5652; MP:AF
III-1062
Sacred Fount, The, MP X-5743;
MP:AF III-1076
Spoils of Poynton, The, CLC II-1078;
MP XI-6228; MP:AF III-1202
Tragic Muse, The, MP XI-6636;
MP:AF III-1317
"Tree of Knowledge, The," MPII:SS
VI-2407
Turn of the Screw, The, CLC II-1167;
MP XI-6748; MP:AF III-1335
Washington Square, CLC II-1224; MP
XII-7041; MP:AF III-1405
What Maisie Knew, CLC II-1235; MP
XII-7094; MP:AF III-1416
Wings of the Dove, The, CLC II-1250;
MP XII-7176; MP:AF III-1445
JAMES, M. R., CWAII II-775
"Oh, Whistle, and I'll Come to You,
My Lad," MPII:SS IV-1660
JAMES, WILLIAM, CWA II-931
Pragmatism, MP IX-5287
JARRELL, RANDALL, CWA II-933
Poetry of Jarrell, The, MP IX-5003
JARRY, ALFRED, CWAII II-777
Ubu Roi, CLCII IV-1631; MPII:D IV-
1676
JAY, JOHN, CWA II-935
JAY, JOHN, ALEXANDER
HAMILTON, and JAMES
MADISON
Federalist, The, MP IV-2025

JEAN DE MEUNG and GUILLAUME DE LORRIS, CWA II-767
JEAN PAUL, CWAII II-779
Titan, CLCII IV-1574; MPII:WF IV-1610
JEFFERS, ROBINSON, CWA II-937
Cawdor, CLC I-161; MP II-858
Poetry of Jeffers, The, MP IX-5006
Roan Stallion, CLC II-977; MP X-5636
Tamar, CLC II-1103; MP XI-6393
JEFFERSON, THOMAS, CWA II-939
Notes on the State of Virginia, MP VII-4260
JENSEN, JOHANNES V., CWA II-943
Long Journey, The, CLC I-623; MP VI-3477; MP:EF II-791
JEROME, JEROME K., CWA II-945
Three Men in a Boat, CLC II-1127; MP:BF III-1532; MP XI-6508
JEWETT, SARAH ORNE, CWA II-946
Country Doctor, A, CLC I-208; MP II-1149; MP:AF I-224
Country of the Pointed Firs, The, CLC I-211; MP II-1158; MP:AF I-227
Deephaven, CLC I-260; MP III-1409; MP:AF I-282
"Miss Tempy's Watchers," MPII:SS IV-1513
"Native of Winby, A," MPII:SS IV-1594
"Town Poor, The," MPII:SS VI-2401
"White Heron, A," MPII:SS VI-2581
JHABVALA, RUTH PRAWER, CWAII II-782
Esmond in India, CLCII II-468; MPII:BCF I-456
Heat and Dust, CLCII II-671; MPII:BCF II-710
Householder, The, CLCII II-716; The, MPII:BCF II-758
JIMÉNEZ, JUAN RAMÓN, CWA II-949
Platero and I, MP VIII-4752; MP:EF III-1017
Poetry of Jiménez, The, MP IX-5009

JIPPENSHA, IKKU, CWA II-951
Hizakurige, CLC I-478; MP V-2667; MP:EF II-646
JOHNSON, CHARLES RICHARD, CWAII II-784
Faith and the Good Thing, CLCII II-487; MPII:AF II-510
JOHNSON, JAMES WELDON, CWAII II-786
Autobiography of an Ex-Coloured Man, The, CLCII I-92; MPII:AF I-81
JOHNSON, MARGUERITE. See ANGELOU, MAYA
JOHNSON, SAMUEL, CWA II-953
Idler, The, MP V-2822
Life of Richard Savage, MP VI-3406
Lives of the Poets, MP VI-3468
Poetry of Johnson, The, MP IX-5011
Preface to Shakespeare, MP IX-5299
Rambler, The, MP IX-5426
Rasselas, CLC II-941; MP IX-5441; MP:BF III-1293
JOHNSON, UWE, CWA II-957; CWAII II-788
Anniversaries, CLCII I-53; MPII:WF I-55
Speculations About Jakob, MP XI-6219; MP:EF III-1218
JOHNSTON, MARY, CWA II-959
Great Valley, The, CLC I-423; MP IV-2372; MP:AF I-505
To Have and to Hold, CLCII IV-1578; MPII:AF IV-1673
JÓKAI, MAURUS, CWA II-961
Modern Midas, A, CLC II-731; MP VII-4015; MP:EF II-872
JOLLEY, ELIZABETH, CWAII II-790
Miss Peabody's Inheritance, CLCII III-1016; MPII:BCF III-1116
Well, The, CLCII IV-1703; MPII:BCF IV-1885
JOLYOT, PROSPER. See CRÉBILLON, PROSPER JOLYOT DE
JONES, EVERETT LEROI. See BARAKA, AMIRI

JONES, GAYL
  Corregidora, CLCII I-339; MPII:AF I-346
  Eva's Man, CLCII II-471; MPII:AF II-481
JONES, HENRY ARTHUR, CWA II-962
  Michael and His Lost Angel, CLC II-699; MP VII-3873
  Mrs. Dane's Defence, CLC II-724; MP VII-3978
JONES, JAMES, CWA II-963; CWAII II-792
  From Here to Eternity, CLCII II-551; MPII:AF II-586
  Thin Red Line, The, CLCII IV-1542; MPII:AF IV-1624
JONES, LEROI. *See* BARAKA, AMIRI
JONES, PRESTON
  Last Meeting of the Knights of the White Magnolia, The, CLCII II-854; MPII:D III-932
  Lu Ann Hampton Laverty Oberlander, CLCII III-932; MPII:D III-997
  Oldest Living Graduate, The, CLCII III-1139; MPII:D III-1169
JONSON, BEN, CWA II-965
  Alchemist, The, CLC I-19; MP I-88
  Bartholomew Fair, CLC I-86; MP I-446
  Catiline, CLC I-159; MP II-852
  Every Man in His Humour, CLC I-343; MP IV-1918
  Every Man out of His Humour, CLC I-344; MP IV-1924
  Poetry of Jonson, The, MP IX-5014
  Sejanus, CLC II-1019; MP X-5896
  Silent Woman, The, CLC II-1039; MP X-6046
  Volpone, CLC II-1213; MP XII-6978

JONSON, BEN, GEORGE CHAPMAN, *and* JOHN MARSTON
  Eastward Ho! CLC I-313; MP III-1693
JOYCE, JAMES, CWA II-968; CWAII II-794
  "Araby," MPII:SS I-106
  "Boarding House, The," MPII:SS I-270
  "Clay," MPII:SS I-403
  "Counterparts," MPII:SS I-433
  "Dead, The," CLCII I-372; MPII:SS II-510
  "Eveline," MPII:SS II-724
  Exiles, CLC I-345; MP IV-1939
  Finnegans Wake, CLC I-370; MP IV-2076; MP:BF I-430
  "Ivy Day in the Committee Room," MPII:SS III-1197
  "Little Cloud, A," MPII:SS III-1371
  Portrait of the Artist as a Young Man, A, CLC II-904; MP IX-5259; MP:BF III-1245
  "Sisters, The," MPII:SS V-2124
  "Two Gallants," MPII:SS VI-2439
  Ulysses, CLC II-1175; MP XII-6799; MP:BF III-1616
JUGO, MIGUEL DE UNAMUNO Y. *See* UNAMUNO Y JUGO, MIGUEL DE
JUNG, CARL GUSTAV, CWA II-972; CWAII II-796
  Two Essays on Analytical Psychology, MP XII-6769
  Memories, Dreams, Reflections, MPII:NF III-928
JUVENAL, CWA II-974
  Satires, MP X-5812

K

KABAPHES, KONSTANTINOS P. *See* CAVAFY, CONSTANTINE P.

KAFKA, FRANZ, CWA II-975; CWAII II-799
Amerika, CLCII I-40; MPII:WF I-45
"Burrow, The," MPII:SS I-312
Castle, The, CLC I-154; MP II-820; MP:EF I-185
"Country Doctor, A," MPII:SS I-437
Diaries of Kafka: 1910-1923, The, MP III-1491
"Great Wall of China, The," MPII:SS III-932
"Hunger Artist, A," MPII:SS III-1077
"Hunter Gracchus, The," MPII:SS III-1081
"In the Penal Colony," MPII:SS III-1154
"Jackals and Arabs," MPII:SS III-1205
"Josephine the Singer," MPII:SS III-1241
Letters to Felice, MPII:NF II-819
"Metamorphosis, The," CLCII III-999; MPII:SS IV-1493
"Report to an Academy, A," MPII:SS V-1929
Trial, The, CLC II-1155; MP XI-6687; MP:EF III-1302

KAHN, ROGER
Boys of Summer, The, MPII:NF I-206

KALIDASA, CWA II-977
Sakuntala, CLC II-1001; MP X-5765

KANE, CHEIKH HAMIDOU, CWAII II-802
Ambiguous Adventure, CLCII I-34; MPII:WF I-39

KANT, IMMANUEL, CWA II-978
Critique of Pure Reason, MP II-1220

KANTOR, TADEUSZ, CWAII II-804
Dead Class, The, CLCII I-373; MPII:D II-456
Wielopole, Wielopole, CLCII IV-1717; MPII:D IV-1745

KAO MING. *See* KAO TSE-CH'ENG

KAO TSE-CH'ENG, CWA II-980
Story of the Guitar, CLC II-1088; MP XI-6288

KAPUŚCIŃSKI, RYSZARD, CWAII II-806
Emperor, The, MPII:NF II-449
Shah of Shahs, MPII:NF IV-1341

KAUFMAN, GEORGE S., CWAII II-809

KAUFMAN, GEORGE S., *and* MOSS HART
Man Who Came to Dinner, The, CLCII III-954; MPII:D III-1043
Once in a Lifetime, CLCII III-1145; MPII:D III-1174
You Can't Take It with You, CLCII IV-1764; MPII:D IV-1788

KAVAN, ANNA
Ice, CLCII II-730; MPII:BCF II-782
"Julia and the Bazooka," MPII:SS III-1245

KAVANAGH, PATRICK, CWAII II-811
Green Fool, The, MPII:NF II-589

KAWABATA, YASUNARI, CWA II-981; CWAII II-813
Beauty and Sadness, CLCII I-128; MPII:WF I-136
House of the Sleeping Beauties, The, CLCII II-712; MPII:WF II-629
Master of Go, The, CLCII III-986; MPII:WF III-983
Snow Country, CLCII IV-1433; MPII:WF IV-1475
Sound of the Mountain, The, CLCII IV-1450; MPII:WF IV-1501
Thousand Cranes, CLCII IV-1554; MPII:WF IV-1589

KAYE-SMITH, SHEILA, CWA II-982
Joanna Godden, CLC I-548; MP V-3012; MP:BF II-687

KAZANTZAKIS, NIKOS, CWA II-984; CWAII II-816
Freedom or Death, MP IV-2166; MP:EF II-543
Greek Passion, The, MP IV-2375; MP:EF II-589

Last Temptation of Christ, The, CLCII
II-859; MPII:WF II-820
Zorba the Greek, MP XII-7331; MP:EF
III-1435
KAZIN, ALFRED
Starting Out in the Thirties, MPII:NF
IV-1427
Walker in the City, A, MPII:NF IV-
1651
KEATS, JOHN, CWA II-986
Eve of St. Agnes, The, CLC I-340; MP
IV-1909
Letters of John Keats, The, MP VI-3350
KELLER, GOTTFRIED, CWA II-989
Grüne Heinrich, Der, CLC I-430; MP
IV-2408; MP:EF II-603
KELLEY, EDITH SUMMERS
Weeds, CLCII IV-1702; MPII:AF IV-
1777
KELLEY, WILLIAM MELVIN, CWAII
II-819
Different Drummer, A, CLCII I-400;
MPII:AF I-404
"Visit to Grandmother, A," MPII:SS
VI-2510
KELLOGG, MARJORIE
Tell Me That You Love Me, Junie
Moon, CLCII IV-1520; MPII:AF IV-
1568
KEMAL, YASHAR, CWAII III-821
Iron Earth, Copper Sky, CLCII IV-
1718; MPII:WF IV-1754
Memed, My Hawk, CLCII III-993;
MPII:WF III-999
Undying Grass, The, CLCII IV-1718;
MPII:WF IV-1754
Wind from the Plain, The, CLCII IV-
1718; MPII:WF IV-1754
KEMPIS, THOMAS À. See THOMAS À
KEMPIS
KENEALLY, THOMAS, CWAII III-824
Chant of Jimmie Blacksmith, The,
CLCII I-262; MPII:BCF I-247
Confederates, CLCII I-322; MPII:BCF
I-312

Gossip from the Forest, CLCII II-621;
MPII:BCF II-655
Survivor, The, CLCII IV-1499;
MPII:BCF IV-1649
KENNEDY, ADRIENNE, CWAII III-827
Funnyhouse of a Negro, CLCII II-558;
MPII:D II-645
Rat's Mass, A, CLCII III-1269; MPII:D
III-1305
KENNEDY, JOHN PENDLETON, CWA
II-990
Horseshoe Robinson, CLC I-483; MP
V-2702; MP:AF II-563
Swallow Barn, CLC II-1098; MP XI-
6359; MP:AF III-1248
KENNEDY, WILLIAM, CWAII III-829
Albany Cycle, The, MPII:AF I-18
Billy Phelan's Greatest Game, CLCII I-
154
Ironweed, CLCII II-776
Legs, CLCII II-871
KENNER, HUGH, CWAII III-831
Counterfeiters, The, MPII:NF I-275
KENZABURŌ ŌE. See ŌE,
KENZABURŌ
KEROUAC, JACK, CWAII III-834
Dharma Bums, The, CLCII I-397;
MPII:AF I-394
On the Road, CLCII III-1145; MPII:AF
III-1193
KESEY, KEN, CWAII III-837
One Flew over the Cuckoo's Nest,
CLCII III-1149; MPII:AF III-1203
Sometimes a Great Notion, CLCII IV-
1442; MPII:AF IV-1476
KIELY, BENEDICT, CWAII III-839
Captain with the Whiskers, The, CLCII
I-237; MPII:BCF I-225
"Heroes in the Dark House, The,"
MPII:SS III-1011
Nothing Happens in Carmincross,
CLCII III-1115; MPII:BCF III-1228
KIERKEGAARD, SÖREN, CWA II-992
Sickness unto Death, The, MP X-6032
KIMITAKE HIRAOKA. See MISHIMA,
YUKIO

KINCAID, JAMAICA, CWAII III-841
"At the Bottom of the River," MPII:SS
I-135
KING, FRANCIS
Custom House, The, CLCII I-357;
MPII:BCF I-344
KING, STEPHEN, CWAII III-843
Danse Macabre, MPII:NF I-327
Shining, The, CLCII III-1393; MPII:AF
IV-1407
Stand, The, CLCII IV-1470; MPII:AF
IV-1532
KINGSLEY, CHARLES, CWA II-994
Hereward the Wake, CLC I-470; MP
V-2591; MP:BF I-566
Hypatia, CLC I-504; MP V-2794;
MP:BF II-627
Westward Ho! CLC II-1233; MP XII-
7084; MP:BF III-1726
KINGSLEY, HENRY, CWA II-996
Ravenshoe, CLC II-942; MP IX-5446;
MP:BF III-1298
KINGSTON, MAXINE HONG, CWAII
III-846
China Men, MPII:NF I-244
Woman Warrior, The, MPII:NF IV-
1709
KIPLING, RUDYARD, CWA II-998
Brushwood Boy, The, CLC I-130; MP
II-696; MP:BF I-143
Captains Courageous, CLC I-150; MP
II-787; MP:BF I-173
"Gardener, The," MPII:SS II-828
Jungle Books, The, CLC I-561; MP VI-
3097; MP:BF II-731
Kim, CLC I-568; MP VI-3130; MP:BF
II-743
"Lispeth," MPII:SS III-1367
"Man Who Would Be King, The,"
CLCII III-960; MPII:SS IV-1447
Poetry of Kipling, The, MP IX-5019
"Strange Ride of Morrowbie Jukes,
The," MPII:SS V-2252
"They," MPII:SS VI-2337
"Thrown Away," MPII:SS VI-2362

"Wireless," MPII:SS VI-2656
"Wish House, The," MPII:SS VI-2660
KIRKLAND, JACK
Tobacco Road, CLCII IV-1582; MPII:D
IV-1596
KIŠ, DANILO, CWAII III-849
Garden, Ashes, CLCII II-564;
MPII:WF II-507
Peščanik, CLCII III-1197; MPII:WF
III-1199
Tomb for Boris Davidovich, A, CLCII
IV-1586; MPII:WF IV-1629
KLEE, PAUL, CWAII III-851
Diaries of Paul Klee, The, MPII:NF I-
361
KLEIST, HEINRICH VON, CWA II-
1001; CWAII III-853
"Beggarwoman of Locarno, The,"
MPII:SS I-184
Broken Jug, The, CLC I-127; MP II-
671
"Earthquake in Chile, The," MPII:SS
II-661
"Engagement in Santo Domingo, The,"
MPII:SS II-698
"Marquise of O--, The," CLCII III-976;
MPII:SS IV-1466
Prince of Homburg, The, CLC II-916;
MP IX-5321
KLIMENTOV, ANDREI
PLATONOVICH. See PLATONOV,
ANDREI
KNIGHT, ERIC, CWA II-1003
This Above All, CLC II-1124; MP XI-
6497; MP:BF III-1528
KNOWLES, JOHN, CWAII III-855
Separate Peace, A, CLCII III-1373;
MPII:AF III-1387
KOCH, C. J.
Year of Living Dangerously, The,
CLCII IV-1760; MPII:BCF IV-1955
KOESTLER, ARTHUR, CWA II-1004
Darkness at Noon, CLC I-242; MP III-
1321; MP:EF I-342
KONIGSBERG, ALLEN STEWART. See
ALLEN, WOODY

MASTERPLOTS

KONRÁD, GEORGE, CWAII III-857
City Builder, The, CLCII I-292;
MPII:WF I-267
Loser, The, CLCII III-915; MPII:WF
II-884
KONWICKI, TADEUSZ, CWAII III-859
Dreambook for Our Time, A, CLCII II-
426; MPII:WF I-395
Minor Apocalypse, A, CLCII III-1011;
MPII:WF III-1006
Moonrise, Moonset, CLCII III-1037;
MPII:WF III-1041
Polish Complex, The, CLCII III-1218;
MPII:WF III-1207
KOPIT, ARTHUR, CWAII III-862
Indians, CLCII II-759; MPII:D II-840
Wings, CLCII IV-1725; MPII:D IV-
1751
KOPS, BERNARD
Ezra, CLCII II-481; MPII:D II-590
Hamlet of Stepney Green, The, CLCII
II-653; MPII:D II-732
KORZENIOWSKI, JÓSEF TEODOR
KONRAD NALECZ. See
CONRAD, JOSEPH
KOSINSKI, JERZY, CWAII III-864
Painted Bird, The, CLCII III-1170;
MPII:AF III-1243

KOSTROWITSKY, WILHELM
APOLLINARIS DE. See
APOLLINAIRE, GUILLAUME
KUHN, THOMAS S., CWAII III-867
Structure of Scientific Revolutions, The,
MPII:NF IV-1452
KUNDERA, MILAN, CWAII III-870
Book of Laughter and Forgetting, The,
CLCII I-190; MPII:WF I-174
"Edward and God," MPII:SS II-664
Farewell Party, The, CLCII II-494;
MPII:WF I-446
"Hitchhiking Game, The," MPII:SS III-
1026
Joke, The, CLCII II-795; MPII:WF II-
766
Life Is Elsewhere, CLCII II-886;
MPII:WF II-855
Unbearable Lightness of Being, The,
CLCII IV-1633; MPII:WF IV-1689
KYD, THOMAS, CWA II-1006
Spanish Tragedy, The, CLC II-1076;
MP XI-6211
KYŌDEN, SANTŌ. See SANTŌ
KYŌDEN

L

LABRUNIE, GÉRARD. *See* NERVAL, GÉRARD DE
LACAN, JACQUES, CWAII III-873
Écrits, MPII:NF I-425
LACLOS, PIERRE CHODERLOS DE, CWA II-1008
Dangerous Acquaintances, CLC I-236; MP III-1299; MP:EF I-330
LA FARGE, OLIVER, CWAII III-876
Laughing Boy, CLCII II-860; MPII:AF II-860
LA FAYETTE, MADAME MARIE DE, CWA II-1009
Princess of Clèves, The, CLC II-917; MP IX-5330; MP:EF III-1034
LA FONTAINE, JEAN DE, CWA II-1010
Fables, MP IV-1951
LAFORGUE, JULES, CWA II-1012
Poetry of Laforgue, The, MP IX-5022
LAGERKVIST, PÄR, CWA II-1014; CWAII III-878
Barabbas, CLC I-78; MP I-419; MP:EF I-96
"Children's Campaign, The," MPII:SS I-380
Dwarf, The, CLCII II-435; MPII:WF I-399
Sibyl, The, CLCII IV-1399; MPII:WF IV-1409
Tobias Trilogy, The, CLCII IV-1583; MPII:WF IV-1623
LAGERLÖF, SELMA, CWA II-1016
Diary of Selma Lagerlöf, The, MPII:NF I-380
"Silver Mine, The," MPII:SS V-2116
Story of Gösta Berling, The, CLC II-1087; MP XI-6281; MP:EF III-1236
LA GUMA, ALEX
Walk in the Night, A, CLCII IV-1672; MPII:BCF IV-1837
LAMARTINE, ALPHONSE DE, CWA II-1018
Poetry of Lamartine, The, MP IX-5025

LAMB, CHARLES, CWA II-1020
Essays of Elia and Last Essays of Elia, MP IV-1857
Letters of Charles Lamb, The, MP VI-3341
LAMBERT, GAVIN
"Slide Area, The," MPII:SS V-2132
LAMMING, GEORGE, CWAII III-881
In the Castle of My Skin, CLCII II-747; MPII:BCF II-809
Natives of My Person, CLCII III-1078; MPII:BCF III-1176
Season of Adventure, CLCII III-1360; MPII:BCF III-1476
LA MOTTE-FOUQUÉ, FRIEDRICH DE, CWA II-1023
Undine, CLC II-1186; MP XII-6852; MP:EF III-1338
LAMPEDUSA, GIUSEPPE TOMASI DI. *See* TOMASI DI LAMPEDUSA, GIUSEPPE
LANDOLFI, TOMMASO
"Gogol's Wife," MPII:SS II-871
LANDOR, WALTER SAVAGE, CWA II-1025
Imaginary Conversations, MP V-2842
Poetry of Landor, The, MP IX-5028
LANGLAND, WILLIAM, CWA II-1027
Vision of William, Concerning Piers the Plowman, The, CLC II-1212; MP XII-6965
LANIER, SIDNEY, CWA II-1028
Poetry of Lanier, The, MP IX-5032
LAO SHE, CWAII III-883
Rickshaw, CLCII III-1291; MPII:WF III-1278;
LARDNER, RING, CWA II-1030
"Golden Honeymoon, The," MPII:SS II-893
"Haircut," MPII:SS II-970
"Harmony," MPII:SS II-989
"Some Like Them Cold," MPII:SS V-2173
You Know Me Al, CLC II-1276; MP XII-7303; MP:AF III-1472

LARKIN, PHILIP, CWA II-1032; CWAII
  III-886
  Girl in Winter, A, CLCII II-589;
    MPII:BCF II-597
  Jill, CLCII II-790; MPII:BCF II-857
  Poetry of Larkin, The, MP IX-5035
LA ROCHEFOUCAULD, FRANÇOIS,
  CWA II-1033
  Maxims, The, MP VII-3782
LARSEN, NELLA, CWAII III-888
  Passing, CLCII III-1182; MPII:AF III-
    1253
  Quicksand, CLCII III-1250; MPII:AF
    III-1296
LAURENCE, MARGARET, CWAII III-
  890
  Diviners, The, CLCII I-407; MPII:BCF
    I-383
  Fire-Dwellers, The, CLCII II-506;
    MPII:BCF II-509
  Loons, The," MPII:SS IV-1399
  Stone Angel, The, CLCII IV-1475;
    MPII:BCF IV-1614
LAVIN, MARY
  "Nun's Mother, The," MPII:SS IV-1640
  "Widow's Son, The," MPII:SS VI-2616
  "Will, The," MPII:SS VI-2623
LAWLER, RAY
  Summer of the Seventeenth Doll, CLCII
    IV-1493; MPII:D IV-1520
LAWRENCE, D. H., CWA II-1035;
  CWAII III-892
  Aaron's Rod, CLCII I-1; MPII:BCF I-1
  Apocalypse, MPII:NF I-85
  Collected Letters of D. H. Lawrence,
    The, MP II-1019
  Fox, The, CLCII II-541; MPII:BCF II-
    538
  "Horse Dealer's Daughter, The,"
    MPII:SS III-1041
  Kangaroo, CLCII II-812; MPII:BCF II-
    877
  Lady Chatterley's Lover, CLCII II-842;
    MPII:BCF II-927
  Mornings in Mexico, MPII:NF III-976

"Odour of Chrysanthemums," MPII:SS
    IV-1648
  Plumed Serpent, The, CLC II-895; MP
    VIII-4765; MP:BF III-1232
  Poetry of Lawrence, The, MP IX-5037
  "Prussian Officer, The," MPII:SS V-
    1859
  Rainbow, The, CLC II-935; MP IX-
    5410; MP:BF III-1288
  "Rocking-Horse Winner, The," MPII:SS
    V-1971
  Sea and Sardinia, MPII:NF III-1303
  Short Stories of D. H. Lawrence, The,
    MP X-5995; MP:BF III-1439
  Sons and Lovers, CLC II-1067; MP XI-
    6177; MP:BF III-1468
  Studies in Classic American Literature,
    MP XI-6314
  "Sun," MPII:SS V-2278
  "Tickets, Please," MPII:SS VI-2365
  Twilight in Italy, MP XII-6766
  Virgin and the Gipsy, The, CLCII IV-
    1658; MPII:BCF IV-1797
  "White Stocking, The," MPII:SS VI-
    2593
  "Woman Who Rode Away, The,"
    MPII:SS VI-2680
  Women in Love, MP XII-7239; MP:BF
    III-1760
LAWRENCE, T. E., CWA II-1039
  Seven Pillars of Wisdom, MP X-5929
LAWSON, HENRY, CWAII III-895
  "Drover's Wife, The," MPII:SS II-639
LAXNESS, HALLDÓR, CWA II-1041
  Independent People, CLC I-521; MP V-
    2872; MP:EF II-701
LAYAMON, CWA II-1043
  Brut, The, CLC I-131; MP II-699
LAYE, CAMARA, CWAII III-898
  Dark Child, The, CLCII I-366;
    MPII:WF I-345
  Guardian of the Word, The, CLCII II-
    643; MPII:WF II-567
  Radiance of the King, The, CLCII III-
    1258; MPII:WF III-1245

LEAVIS, F. R., CWAII III-900
Living Principle, The, MPII:NF II-850
LEAVITT, DAVID, CWAII III-903
"Territory," MPII:SS V-2320
LE CARRÉ, JOHN, CWAII III-905
Honourable Schoolboy, The, CLCII II-694; MPII:BCF II-737
Perfect Spy, A, CLCII III-1194; MPII:BCF III-1306
Smiley's People, CLCII II-694; MPII:BCF IV-1710
Spy Who Came in from the Cold, The, CLCII IV-1469; MPII:BCF IV-1599
Tinker, Tailor, Soldier, Spy, CLCII II-694; MPII:BCF IV-1710
LEE, HARPER, CWAII III-907
To Kill a Mockingbird, CLCII IV-1580; MPII:AF IV-1677
LEE, WILLIAM. See BURROUGHS, WILLIAM S.
LE FANU, JOSEPH SHERIDAN, CWA II-1045
"Green Tea," MPII:SS III-940
House by the Churchyard, The, CLC I-484; MP V-2705; MP:BF II-597
Uncle Silas, CLC II-1177; MP XII-6808; MP:BF III-1627
LÉGER, ALEXIS ST.-LÉGER. See PERSE, ST.-JOHN
LE GUIN, URSULA K., CWAII III-909
Dispossessed, The, CLCII I-405; MPII:AF I-413
Left Hand of Darkness, The, CLCII II-869; MPII:AF III-878
"Sur," MPII:SS V-2288
LEHMANN, ROSAMOND, CWAII III-911
Dusty Answer, CLCII II-433; MPII:BCF I-408
Echoing Grove, The, CLCII II-442; MPII:BCF I-427
Weather in the Streets, The, CLCII IV-1701; MPII:BCF IV-1880
LEM, STANISŁAW, CWAII III-913
Chain of Chance, The, CLCII I-253; MPII:WF I-234

Fiasco, CLCII II-500; MPII:WF II-456
His Master's Voice, CLCII II-678; MPII:WF II-588
Investigation, The, CLCII II-773; MPII:WF II-717
Invincible, The, CLCII II-774; MPII:WF II-722
Solaris, CLCII IV-1435; MPII:WF IV-1486
LEONARD, HUGH
Da, CLCII I-360; MPII:D II-431
Life, A, CLCII II-880; MPII:D III-970
LEONARDO DA VINCI, CWA II-1046
Notebooks of Leonardo da Vinci, The, MP VII-4255
LEOPARDI, GIACOMO, CWA II-1049
Poetry of Leopardi, The, MP IX-5040
LERMONTOV, MIKHAIL YURIEVICH, CWA II-1051
Demon: An Eastern Tale, The, MP III-1449
Hero of Our Time, A, CLC I-471; MP V-2597; MP:EF II-636
Novice, The, MP VII-4263
LE SAGE, ALAIN RENÉ, CWA II-1053
Diable boiteux, Le, CLC I-268; MP III-1474; MP:EF I-388
Gil Blas, CLC I-401; MP IV-2260; MP:EF II-567
Turcaret, CLC II-1166; MP XI-6744
LESKOV, NIKOLAI, CWAII III-916
"Lady Macbeth of the Mtsensk District," CLCII II-844; MPII:SS III-1280
"Lefty," MPII:SS III-1320
LESSING, DORIS, CWAII III-919
Children of Violence, CLCII I-275; MPII:BCF I-252
"Day Stalin Died, The," MPII:SS II-502
Golden Notebook, The, CLCII II-605; MPII:BCF II-621
Good Terrorist, The, CLCII II-614; MPII:BCF II-643
"How I Finally Lost My Heart," MPII:SS III-1064
"Mrs. Fortescue," MPII:SS IV-1515

Shikasta, CLCII IV-1391; MPII:BCF IV-1533

LESSING, GOTTHOLD EPHRAIM, CWA II-1055

Emilia Galotti, CLC I-323; MP III-1758

Minna von Barnhelm, CLC II-709; MP VII-3912

Nathan the Wise, CLC II-759; MP VII-4149

LEVER, CHARLES JAMES, CWA II-1057

Charles O'Malley, CLC I-169; MP II-892; MP:BF I-198

Tom Burke of Ours, CLC II-1141; MP XI-6588; MP:BF III-1560

LEVI, CARLO, CWAII III-922

Christ Stopped at Eboli, CLCII I-283; MPII:WF I-257

LEVI, PRIMO, CWAII III-924

Drowned and the Saved, The, MPII:NF I-420

If Not Now, When? CLCII II-735; MPII:WF II-653

If This Is a Man, MPII:NF II-678

Monkey's Wrench, The, CLCII III-1032; MPII:WF III-1031

Periodic Table, The, MPII:NF III-1141

LÉVI-STRAUSS, CLAUDE, CWAII III-927

Tristes Tropiques, MPII:NF IV-1563

LEWARS, MRS. E. S. See SINGMASTER, ELSIE

LEWIS, ALUN, CWAII III-930

"Wanderers, The," MPII:SS VI-2541

LEWIS, CECIL DAY, CWA II-1059

Poetry of Lewis, The, MP IX-5043

LEWIS, C. S., CWA II-1061; CWAII III-932

Allegory of Love, The, MP I-138

Grief Observed, A, MPII:NF II-601

Space trilogy, The, CLCII IV-1456; MPII:BCF IV-1588

Surprised by Joy, MPII:NF IV-1462

Till We Have Faces, CLCII IV-1565; MPII:BCF IV-1700

LEWIS, MATTHEW GREGORY, CWA II-1064

Monk, The, CLC II-733; MP VII-4027; MP:BF II-993

LEWIS, MERIWETHER, and WILLIAM CLARK, CWA II-1065

Journals of Lewis and Clark, The, MP VI-3065

LEWIS, SINCLAIR, CWA II-1067

Arrowsmith, CLC I-61; MP I-313; MP:AF I-75

Babbitt, CLC I-72; MP I-400; MP:AF I-90

Cass Timberlane, CLC I-153; MP II-813; MP:AF I-178

Dodsworth, CLC I-283; MP III-1565; MP:AF I-294

Elmer Gantry, MP III-1742; MP:AF I-335

Main Street, CLC I-655; MP VI-3645; MP:AF II-730

LEWIS, WYNDHAM, CWA II-1070; CWAII III-935

Apes of God, The, CLCII I-59; MPII:BCF I-58

Blasting and Bombardiering, MPII:NF I-168

Human Age, The, CLCII II-718; MPII:BCF II-764

Revenge for Love, The, CLCII III-1290; MPII:BCF III-1410

Self Condemned, CLCII III-1371; MPII:BCF IV-1496

Snooty Baronet, CLCII IV-1432; MPII:BCF IV-1567

Tarr, CLC II-1109; MP XI-6413; MP:BF III-1500

Time and Western Man, MPII:NF IV-1523

"Time the Tiger," MPII:SS VI-2369

LEZAMA LIMA, JOSÉ

Paradiso, CLCII III-1176; MPII:AF III-1248

LIE, JONAS, CWA II-1072

Family at Gilje, The, CLC I-354; MP IV-1977; MP:EF II-497

LINCOLN, ABRAHAM, CWA II-1074
Addresses, MP I-32
LINDSAY, VACHEL, CWA II-1078
Poetry of Lindsay, The, MP IX-5046
LINNEY, ROMULUS, CWAII III-938
Childe Byron, CLCII I-271; MPII:D I-329
Holy Ghosts, CLCII II-683; MPII:D II-769
Sand Mountain, CLCII III-1333; MPII:D IV-1396
LINS, OSMAN, CWAII III-940
Avalovara, CLCII I-97; MPII:AF I-97
LINS DO RÊGO, JOSÉ, CWA II-1080
Dead Fires, CLC I-247; MP III-1339
Fogo morto, MP:AF I-400
Plantation Boy, MP VIII-4748; MP:AF II-954
LISPECTOR, CLARICE, CWAII III-942
Apple in the Dark, The, CLCII I-62; MPII:AF I-48
"Smallest Woman in the World, The," MPII:SS V-2138
LIU E, CWAII III-945
Travels of Lao Ts'an, The, CLCII IV-1604; MPII:WF IV-1646
LIU T'IEH-YUN. See LIU E
LIVIUS, TITUS. See LIVY
LIVY, CWA II-1082
Annals of the Roman People, MP I-243
LIZARDI, JOSÉ JOAQUÍN FERNÁNDEZ DE. See FERNÁNDEZ DE LIZARDI, JOSÉ JOAQUÍN
LLEWELLYN, RICHARD, CWA II-1083
How Green Was My Valley, CLC I-493; MP V-2742; MP:BF II-612
LLOYD, D. V. LLEWELLYN. See LLEWELLYN, RICHARD
LLOYD, RICHARD DAVID VIVIAN LLEWELLYN. See LLEWELLYN, RICHARD
LOBEIRA, VASCO DE, CWA II-1086
Amadís de Gaul, CLC I-31; MP I-152; MP:EF I-26

LOCKE, JOHN, CWA II-1087
Essay Concerning Human Understanding, An, MP III-1828
LOCKRIDGE, ROSS, JR., CWA II-1089
Raintree County, CLC II-936; MP IX-5415; MP:AF II-1001
LODGE, DAVID, CWAII III-947
Changing Places, CLCII I-260; MPII:BCF I-241
Small World, CLCII IV-1429; MPII:BCF IV-1563
Souls and Bodies, CLCII IV-1448; MPII:BCF IV-1577
LO KUAN-CHUNG, CWA II-1085
Romance of the Three Kingdoms, CLC II-985; MP X-5681; MP:EF III-1105
LONDON, JACK, CWA II-1090
Call of the Wild, The, CLC I-142; MP II-748; MP:AF I-167
"Piece of Steak, A," MPII:SS IV-1807
Sea Wolf, The, CLC II-1015; MP X-5865; MP:AF III-1106
"To Build a Fire," MPII:SS VI-2377
LONGFELLOW, HENRY WADSWORTH, CWA II-1092
Courtship of Miles Standish, The, CLC I-213; MP II-1172
Evangeline, CLC I-340; MP IV-1906
Song of Hiawatha, The, CLC II-1060; MP XI-6147
LONGINUS, CASSIUS, CWA II-1094
LONGSTREET, AUGUSTUS BALDWIN, CWA II-1095
Georgia Scenes, MP IV-2233; MP:AF I-433
LONGUS, CWA II-1096
Daphnis and Chloë, CLC I-239; MP III-1310; MP:EF I-335
LÖNNROT, ELIAS, CWA II-1097
Kalevala, The, CLC I-565; MP VI-3111
LOPE DE VEGA. See VEGA, LOPE DE
LORCA, FEDERICO GARCÍA. See GARCÍA LORCA, FEDERICO
LORD, ALBERT B.
Singer of Tales, The, MPII:NF IV-1356

LORRIS, GUILLAUME DE. *See* GUILLAUME DE LORRIS *and* JEAN DE MEUNG

LOTI, PIERRE, CWA II-1098
Iceland Fisherman, An, CLC I-508; MP V-2810; MP:EF II-678

LOVECRAFT, H. P., CWAII III-949
"Dunwich Horror, The," MPII:SS II-657

LOVELACE, EARL, CWAII III-951
Dragon Can't Dance, The, CLCII II-421; MPII:BCF I-398
"Shoemaker Arnold," MPII:SS V-2080
Wine of Astonishment, The, CLCII IV-1723; MPII:BCF IV-1909

LOVELACE, RICHARD, CWA II-1099
Poetry of Lovelace, The, MP IX-5048

LOVER, SAMUEL, CWA II-1100
Handy Andy, CLC I-441; MP V-2470; MP:BF I-524
Rory O'More, CLC II-995; MP X-5715; MP:BF III-1380

LOWELL, JAMES RUSSELL, CWA II-1101
Biglow Papers, The, MP I-535
Fable for Critics, A, MP IV-1948
Lyric Poetry of Lowell, The, MP VI-3565

LOWELL, ROBERT, JR., CWA II-1104
Poetry of Robert Lowell, The, MP IX-5121

LOWRY, MALCOLM, CWA II-1105; CWAII III-953
Under the Volcano, MP XII-6833; MP:BF III-1639
Ultramarine, CLCII IV-1632; MPII:BCF IV-1766

LOYOLA BRANDÃO, IGNÁCIO DE, CWAII I-238
Zero, CLCII IV-1769; MPII:AF IV-1852

LUCIAN, CWA II-1106
Satires, MP X-5814
True History, The, MP XI-6737; MP:EF III-1311

LUCRETIUS, CWA II-1107
De rerum natura, MP III-1337

LU HSÜN, CWAII III-955
True Story of Ah Q, The, CLCII IV-1620; MPII:WF IV-1671

LURIA, A. R.
Making of Mind, The, MPII:NF II-884

LURIE, ALISON, CWAII III-958
War Between the Tates, The, CLCII IV-1681; MPII:AF IV-1759

LYLY, JOHN, CWA II-1108
Campaspe, CLC I-143; MP II-754
Endymion, CLC I-325; MP III-1774
Euphues and His England, CLC I-338; MP IV-1894; MP:BF I-382
Euphues, the Anatomy of Wit, CLC I-338; MP IV-1898; MP:BF I-387

LYTLE, ANDREW, CWA II-1110
Long Night, The, CLC I-624; MP VI-3483; MP:AF II-694
Velvet Horn, The, MP XII-6884; MP:AF III-1363

LYTTON, EDWARD LYTTON BULWER-. *See* BULWER-LYTTON, EDWARD GEORGE EARLE

M

MACAULAY, ROSE, CWAII III-961
Told by an Idiot, CLCII IV-1585;
MPII:BCF IV-1721
Towers of Trebizond, The, CLCII IV-1596; MPII:BCF IV-1726
World My Wilderness, The, CLCII IV-1752; MPII:BCF IV-1930
MACAULAY, THOMAS BABINGTON,
CWA II-1111
History of England, The, MP V-2631
McCARTHY, CORMAC, CWAII III-964
Outer Dark, CLCII III-1166; MPII:AF
III-1227
Suttree, CLCII IV-1501; MPII:AF IV-1559
McCARTHY, MARY, CWAII III-966
"Cruel and Barbarous Treatment,"
MPII:SS II-467
Group, The, CLCII II-638; MPII:AF II-682
Memories of a Catholic Girlhood,
MPII:NF III-933
McCOY, HORACE, CWA II-1113
They Shoot Horses, Don't They? MP
XI-6486; MP:AF III-1271
McCULLERS, CARSON, CWA II-1115;
CWAII III-968
"Ballad of the Sad Café, The," CLCII
I-109; MPII:SS I-147
Heart Is a Lonely Hunter, The, CLC I-447; MP V-2501; MP:AF II-539
"Madame Zilensky and the King of
Finland," MPII:SS IV-1427
Member of the Wedding, The, CLC I-690; CLCII III-992; MP VII-3815;
MP:AF II-776; MPII:D III-1071
"Tree. A Rock. A Cloud., A," MPII:SS
VI-2404
"Wunderkind," MPII:SS VI-2719
MACDONALD, ROSS, CWAII III-970
Goodbye Look, The, CLCII II-616;
MPII:AF II-655
Underground Man, The, CLCII IV-1636; MPII:AF IV-1711

McELROY, JOSEPH, CWAII III-972
Lookout Cartridge, CLCII III-914;
MPII:AF II-916
McFEE, WILLIAM, CWA II-1118
Casuals of the Sea, CLC I-158; MP II-839; MP:BF I-189
McGAHERN, JOHN, CWAII III-975
Barracks, The, CLCII I-121; MPII:BCF
I-108
Pornographer, The, CLCII III-1222;
MPII:BCF III-1330
McGINLEY, PATRICK, CWAII III-977
Bogmail, CLCII I-184; MPII:BCF I-163
Trick of the Ga Bolga, The, CLCII IV-1612; MPII:BCF IV-1737
McGUANE, THOMAS, CWAII III-979
Ninety-two in the Shade, CLCII III-1102; MPII:AF III-1145
Sporting Club, The, CLCII IV-1466;
MPII:AF IV-1521
MACHADO, ANTONIO, CWA II-1120
Poetry of Machado, The, MP IX-5051
MACHADO DE ASSÍS, JOAQUIM
MARIA, CWA II-1122
Epitaph of a Small Winner, CLC I-330;
MP III-1811; MP:AF I-346
Philosopher or Dog? MP VIII-4650;
MP:AF II-927
"Psychiatrist, The," MPII:SS V-1862
MACHEN, ARTHUR, CWA II-1124
Hill of Dreams, The, CLC I-473; MP
V-2613; MP:BF I-578
MACHIAVELLI, NICCOLÒ, CWA II-1126
Prince, The, MP IX-5314
MacINTYRE, ALASDAIR
After Virtue, MPII:NF I-12
McKAY, CLAUDE, CWAII III-981
Banana Bottom, CLCII I-110; MPII:AF
I-106
Banjo, CLCII I-113; MPII:AF I-116
Home to Harlem, CLCII II-687;
MPII:AF II-722

MACKENZIE, HENRY, CWA II-1128
Man of Feeling, The, CLC I-660; MP
VII-3669; MP:BF II-855
MACLAREN-ROSS, JULIAN
"Bit of a Smash in Madras, A,"
MPII:SS I-218
Memoirs of the Forties, MPII:NF III-
923
MacLEISH, ARCHIBALD, CWA II-1129,
CWAII III-983
Conquistador, MP II-1088
J. B., CLCII II-788; MPII:D III-861
Poetry of MacLeish, The, MP IX-5054
MacLENNAN, HUGH, CWAII III-986
Barometer Rising, CLCII I-118;
MPII:BCF I-103
Two Solitudes, CLCII IV-1625;
MPII:BCF IV-1756
Voices in Time, CLCII IV-1663;
MPII:BCF IV-1812
Watch That Ends the Night, The, CLCII
IV-1685; MPII:BCF IV-1854
McLUHAN, MARSHALL, CWAII III-988
Gutenberg Galaxy, The, MPII:NF II-
624
Understanding Media, MPII:NF IV-
1601
McMURTRY, LARRY, CWAII III-990
Last Picture Show, The, CLCII II-858;
MPII:AF II-854
Terms of Endearment, CLCII IV-1529;
MPII:AF IV-1587
McNALLY, TERRENCE
Where Has Tommy Flowers Gone?
CLCII IV-1711; MPII:D IV-1739
MacNEICE, LOUIS, CWA II-1131
Poetry of MacNeice, The, MP IX-5057
McPHEE, JOHN, CWAII III-992
Coming into the Country, MPII:NF I-
260
Pine Barrens, The, MPII:NF III-1168
McPHERSON, JAMES ALAN, CWAII
III-994
"Gold Coast," MPII:SS II-885
"Private Domain," MPII:SS IV-1852

MADDEN, DAVID, CWAII III-996
"Day the Flowers Came, The," MPII:SS
II-507
Suicide's Wife, The, CLCII IV-1489;
MPII:AF IV-1545
"Willis Carr at Bleak House," MPII:SS
VI-2634
MADISON, JAMES, CWA II-1133
MADISON, JAMES, ALEXANDER
HAMILTON, and JOHN JAY
Federalist, The, MP IV-2025
MAETERLINCK, MAURICE, CWA II-
1137
Blue Bird, The, CLCII I-173; MPII:D I-
213
Pélléas and Mélisande, CLC II-852;
MP VIII-4569
MAILER, NORMAN, CWA II-1139;
CWAII III-998
American Dream, An, CLCII I-38;
MPII:AF I-29
Armies of the Night, The, CLCII I-65;
MPII:AF I-51
Executioner's Song, The, CLCII II-474;
MPII:AF II-486
Marilyn, MPII:NF III-907
Naked and the Dead, The, CLCII III-
1070; MPII:AF III-1110
Of a Fire on the Moon, MPII:NF III-
1052
MALAMUD, BERNARD, CWA II-1141;
CWAII III-1000
"Angel Levine," MPII:SS I-92
Assistant, The, CLCII I-78; MPII:AF I-
61
Fixer, The, CLCII II-519; MPII:AF II-
548
"Idiots First," MPII:SS III-1109
"Jewbird, The," MPII:SS III-1218
"Last Mohican, The," MPII:SS III-1302
"Magic Barrel, The," MPII:SS IV-1431
Natural, The, CLCII III-1080; MPII:AF
III-1119
New Life, A, CLCII III-1088; MPII:AF
III-1129
"Rembrandt's Hat," MPII:SS VI-1926

MALCOLM X, CWAII III-1002
Autobiography of Malcolm X, The,
MPII:NF I-121
MALLARMÉ, STÉPHANE, CWA II-
1143
Poetry of Mallarmé, The, MP IX-5059
MALLEA, EDUARDO, CWA II-1145
All Green Shall Perish, CLCII I-26;
MPII:AF I-25
Bay of Silence, The, CLC I-89; MP I-
454; MP:AF I-101
Fiesta in November, MP IV-2050;
MP:AF I-386
MALLOWAN, AGATHA MARY
CLARISSA. See CHRISTIE,
AGATHA
MALORY, SIR THOMAS, CWA II-1147
Morte d'Arthur, Le, CLC II-742; MP
VII-4063; MP:BF II-1006
MALOUF, DAVID
Harland's Half Acre, CLCII II-658;
MPII:BCF II-695
Imaginary Life, An, CLCII II-742;
MPII:BCF II-799
MALRAUX, ANDRÉ, CWA II-1149;
CWAII III-1004
Anti-Memoirs, MPII:NF I-68
Man's Fate, CLC I-665; MP VII-3700;
MP:EF II-830
Man's Hope, CLCII III-967; MPII:WF
III-945
Royal Way, The, CLCII III-1317;
MPII:WF III-1305
Voices of Silence, The, MP XII-6975
MAMET, DAVID, CWAII III-1006
American Buffalo, CLCII I-37; MPII:D
I-49
Glengarry Glen Ross, CLCII II-595;
MPII:D II-684
Sexual Perversity in Chicago, CLCII
IV-1386; MPII:D IV-1449
Speed-the-Plow, CLCII IV-1458;
MPII:D IV-1486
Woods, The, CLCII IV-1743; MPII:D
IV-1762

MANDELSTAM, NADEZHDA, CWAII
III-1008
Hope Abandoned, MPII:NF II-656
Hope Against Hope, MPII:NF II-662
MANDELSTAM, OSIP, CWAII III-1011
Conversation About Dante, MPII:NF I-
270
Journey to Armenia, MPII:NF II-779
Noise of Time, The, MPII:NF III-1013
MANN, THOMAS, CWA II-1151
Black Swan, The, MP I-559; MP:EF I-
119
Buddenbrooks, CLC I-133; MP II-702;
MP:EF I-150
Confessions of Felix Krull, Confidence
Man, CLC I-195; MP II-1067;
MP:EF I-249
"Death in Venice," CLC I-253; MP III-
1357; MP:EF I-349; MPII:SS II-532
"Disorder and Early Sorrow," MPII:SS
II-604
Doctor Faustus, CLC I-276; MP III-
1539; MP:EF I-406
"Gladius Dei," MPII:SS II-857
Holy Sinner, The, CLCII II-685;
MPII:WF II-599
"Infant Prodigy, The," MPII:SS III-
1173
Joseph and His Brothers, CLCII II-797;
MPII:WF II-772
"Little Herr Friedemann," MPII:SS III-
1375
Magic Mountain, The, CLC I-650; MP
VI-3618; MP:EF II-816
"Mario and the Magician," MPII:SS IV-
1458
"Tonio Kröger," MPII:SS VI-2393
Transposed Heads, The, CLCII IV-
1602; MPII:WF IV-1639
"Tristan," MPII:SS VI-2417
MANNING, FREDERIC
Her Privates, We, CLCII II-675;
MPII:BCF II-717
MANNING, OLIVIA, CWAII III-1014
Balkan Trilogy, The, CLCII I-106;
MPII:BCF I-86

MANSFIELD, KATHERINE, CWA II-1154; CWAII III-1016
"At the Bay," MPII:SS I-132
"Bliss," MPII:SS I-250
"Daughters of the Late Colonel, The," MPII:SS II-495
"Fly, The," MPII:SS II-799
"Her First Ball," MPII:SS III-997
"Miss Brill," MPII:SS IV-1505
"Prelude," MPII:SS IV-1843
Short Stories of Katherine Mansfield, MP X-6018; MP:BF III-1442
"Woman at the Store, The," MPII:SS VI-2676
MANZONI, ALESSANDRO, CWA II-1157
Betrothed, The, CLC I-100; MP I-507; MP:EF I-113
MAQUET, AUGUSTE. See DUMAS, ALEXANDRE, père
MARAN, RENÉ, CWA II-1159
Batouala, CLC I-88; MP I-451; MP:EF I-105
MARCUS AURELIUS, CWA II-1160
Meditations, MP VII-3802
MARIE DE FRANCE, CWA II-1161
Lais of Marie de France, The, MP VI-3230
MARIVAUX, PIERRE CARLET DE CHAMBLAIN, CWA II-1162
Marianne, CLC I-671; MP VII-3728; MP:EF II-834
MARKANDAYA, KAMALA
Nectar in a Sieve, CLCII III-1082; MPII:BCF III-1182
MARKHAM, BERYL, CWAII III-1018
West with the Night, MPII:NF IV-1681
MARLOWE, CHRISTOPHER, CWA II-1163
Doctor Faustus, CLC I-278; MP III-1543
Edward the Second, CLC I-315; MP III-1711
Jew of Malta, The, CLC I-546; MP V-3004

Tamburlaine the Great, CLC II-1104; MP XI-6396
MAROT, CLEMÉNT, CWA II-1166
Poetry of Marot, The, MP IX-5064
MARQUAND, JOHN PHILLIPS, CWA II-1168
Late George Apley, The, CLC I-599; MP VI-3280; MP:AF II-653
Wickford Point, CLC II-1240; MP XII-7126; MP:AF III-1429
MÁRQUEZ, GABRIEL GARCÍA. See GARCÍA MÁRQUEZ, GABRIEL
MARRYAT, FREDERICK, CWA II-1171
Mr. Midshipman Easy, CLC II-719; MP VII-3960; MP:BF II-966
Peter Simple, CLC II-866; MP VIII-4626; MP:BF II-1199
MARSHALL, PAULE, CWAII III-1020
"Barbados," MPII:SS I-154
Praisesong for the Widow, CLCII III-1230; MPII:AF III-1286
MARSTON, JOHN, CWA II-1173
Malcontent, The, CLC I-657; MP VI-3658
MARSTON, JOHN, GEORGE CHAPMAN, and BEN JONSON
Eastward Ho! CLC I-313; MP III-1693
MARTIAL, CWA II-1175
Epigrams of Martial, MP III-1800
MARTIN DU GARD, ROGER, CWA II-1176
World of the Thibaults, The, CLC II-1267; MP XII-7266; MP:EF III-1419
MARTÍNEZ SIERRA, GREGORIO, CWA II-1178
Cradle Song, The, CLC I-218; MP II-1188
Kingdom of God, The, CLC I-578; MP VI-3173
MARVELL, ANDREW, CWA II-1180
Poetry of Marvell, The, MP IX-5067
MARX, KARL, CWA II-1182
Kapital, Das, MP VI-3117
MASEFIELD, JOHN, CWA II-1185

MASSINGER, PHILIP, CWA II-1187
Bondman, The, CLC I-113; MP I-585
Maid of Honour, The, CLC I-653; MP VI-3634
New Way to Pay Old Debts, A, CLC II-765; MP VII-4180
Roman Actor, The, CLC II-982; MP X-5665
MASSINGER, PHILIP, and JOHN FLETCHER
Beggars' Bush, The, CLC I-92; MP I-472
Sir John van Olden Barnavelt, MP X-6063
MASTERS, EDGAR LEE, CWA II-1189
Spoon River Anthology, MP XI-6233
MATHER, COTTON, CWA II-1191
Magnalia Christi Americana, MP VI-3623
MATHESON, RICHARD, CWAII III-1022
"Duel," MPII:SS II-653
MATTHIESSEN, PETER, CWA II-1193; CWAII III-1024
At Play in the Fields of the Lord, CLCII I-81; MPII:AF I-65
Cloud Forest, The, MP II-1003
Far Tortuga, CLCII II-491; MPII:AF II-521
Snow Leopard, The, MPII:NF IV-1378
MATURIN, CHARLES ROBERT, CWA II-1195
Melmoth the Wanderer, CLC I-689; MP VII-3809; MP:BF II-901
MAUGHAM, W. SOMERSET, CWA II-1196; CWAII III-1026
"Alien Corn, The," MPII:SS I-56
Cakes and Ale, CLC I-140; MP II-737; MP:BF I-154
Circle, The, CLCII I-286; MPII:D I-353
Liza of Lambeth, CLC I-622; MP VI-3471; MP:BF II-812
Moon and Sixpence, The, CLC II-739; MP VII-4056; MP:BF II-997

Of Human Bondage, CLC II-794; MP VII-4288; MP:BF II-1080
"Official Position, An," MPII:SS IV-1656
"Outstation, The," MPII:SS IV-1741
"Rain," MPII:SS V-1883
Razor's Edge, The, CLCII III-1273; MPII:BCF III-1394
Summing Up, The, MP XI-6332
MAUPASSANT, GUY DE, CWA II-1199
Bel-Ami, CLC I-95; MP I-481; MP:EF I-108
"Boule de Suif," MPII:SS I-289
"Family Affair, A," MPII:SS II-755
"Madame Tellier's Establishment," MPII:SS IV-1424
Mont-Oriol, CLC II-737; MP VII-4045; MP:EF II-889
"Necklace, The," MPII:SS IV-1597
"Piece of String, The," MPII:SS IV-1810
"Two Little Soldiers," MPII:SS VI-2442
Woman's Life, A, CLC II-1259; MP XII-7224; MP:EF III-1413
MAURIAC, CLAUDE
Dinner Party, The, MP III-1516; MP:EF I-398
MAURIAC, FRANÇOIS, CWA II-1202; CWAII III-1029
Lamb, The, CLCII II-848; MPII:WF II-811
Thérèse, CLC II-1121; MP XI-6477; MP:EF III-1273
Vipers' Tangle, CLCII IV-1657; MPII:WF IV-1715
Woman of the Pharisees, A, CLCII IV-1730; MPII:WF IV-1774
MAURIER, DAPHNE DU. See DU MAURIER, DAPHNE
MAURIER, GEORGE DU. See DU MAURIER, GEORGE
MAUSS, MARCEL, and ÉMILE DURKHEIM
Primitive Classification, MPII:NF III-1190

MAXIMOV, VLADIMIR
Farewell from Nowhere, CLCII II-492; MPII:WF I-440
Seven Days of Creation, The, CLCII IV-1383; MPII:WF IV-1393
MAYAKOVSKY, VLADIMIR, CWA II-1204
Bathhouse, The, CLCII I-124; MPII:D I-133
Bedbug, The, CLCII I-132; MPII:D I-146
Poetry of Mayakovsky, The, MP IX-5070
MEDOFF, MARK, CWAII III-1032
Children of a Lesser God, CLCII I-274; MPII:D I-335
When You Comin' Back, Red Ryder? CLCII IV-1710; MPII:D IV-1733
MEHTA, VED, CWAII III-1034
Sound-Shadows of the New World, MPII:NF IV-1398
Vedi, MPII:NF IV-1635
MELEAGER, CWA II-1206
Epigrams of Meleager, The, MP III-1802
MELVILLE, HERMAN, CWA II-1208
"Bartleby the Scrivener," MPII:SS I-162
"Benito Cereno," CLC I-97; MP I-495; MP:AF I-111; MPII:SS I-188
Billy Budd, Foretopman, CLC I-104; MP I-538; MP:AF I-121
Confidence Man, The, CLC I-196; MP II-1071; MP:AF I-207
Israel Potter, CLC I-533; MP V-2938; MP:AF II-603
Mardi, and a Voyage Thither, CLC I-669; MP VII-3717; MP:AF II-765
Moby Dick, CLC II-725; MP VII-3992; MP:AF II-800
Omoo, CLC II-813; MP VIII-4364; MP:AF II-888
Pierre, CLC II-879; MP VIII-4690; MP:AF II-930
Poetry of Melville, The, MP IX-5073
Redburn, CLC II-951; MP IX-5481; MP:AF III-1017

Typee, CLC II-1173; MP XII-6791; MP:AF III-1340
White-Jacket, CLC II-1239; MP XII-7118; MP:AF III-1425
MENANDER, CWA II-1211
Arbitration, The, CLC I-56; MP I-288
MENCKEN, H. L., CWA II-1212
Prejudices: Six Series, MP IX-5302
MENDOZA, JUAN RUIZ DE ALARCÓN Y. See RUIZ DE ALARCÓN, JUAN
MEREDITH, GEORGE, CWA II-1215
Beauchamp's Career, CLC I-90; MP I-460; MP:BF I-99
Diana of the Crossways, CLC I-269; MP III-1486; MP:BF I-318
Egoist, The, CLC I-318; MP III-1723; MP:BF I-355
Evan Harrington, CLC I-339; MP IV-1902; MP:BF I-391
Ordeal of Richard Feverel, The, CLC II-814; MP VIII-4390; MP:BF II-1121
Poetry of Meredith, The, MP IX-5077
MEREZHKOWSKY, DMITRY, CWA II-1218
Death of the Gods, The, CLC I-256; MP III-1377; MP:EF I-359
Romance of Leonardo da Vinci, The, CLC II-984; MP X-5672; MP:EF III-1101
MÉRIMÉE, PROSPER, CWA II-1220
Carmen, CLC I-152; MP II-803; MP:EF I-178
Colomba, CLC I-192; MP II-1031; MP:EF I-245
MERTON, THOMAS, CWAII III-1037
Conjectures of a Guilty Bystander, MPII:NF I-265
Seven Storey Mountain, The, MPII:NF IV-1330
MERWIN, W. S., CWAII III-1039
Unframed Originals, MPII:NF IV-1612
METCALF, PAUL, CWAII III-1042
Apalache, MPII:NF I-79
Patagoni, MPII:NF III-1129

MEUNG, JEAN DE, and GUILLAUME DE LORRIS, CWA II-767
MICHELANGELO BUONARROTI, CWA I-277
Poetry of Michelangelo, The, MP IX-5080
MICHENER, JAMES A., CWAII III-1044
Hawaii, CLCII II-661; MPII:AF II-688
Source, The, CLCII IV-1452; MPII:AF IV-1498
MIDDLETON, THOMAS, CWA II-1222
Chaste Maid in Cheapside, A, CLC I-171; MP II-900
Trick to Catch the Old One, A, CLC II-1156; MP XI-6695
Women Beware Women, CLC II-1261; MP XII-7235
MIDDLETON, THOMAS, and THOMAS DEKKER
Honest Whore, Part One, The, MP V-2680
MIDDLETON, THOMAS, JOHN FORD, and WILLIAM ROWLEY
Spanish Gipsy, The, CLC II-1074; MP XI-6208
MIDDLETON, THOMAS, and WILLIAM ROWLEY
Changeling, The, CLC I-167; MP II-885
MIKSZÁTH, KÁLMÁN, CWA II-1224
St. Peter's Umbrella, CLC II-999; MP X-5757; MP:EF III-1113
MILL, JOHN STUART, CWA II-1225
On Liberty, MP VIII-4370
Principles of Political Economy, MP IX-5337
MILLAR, KENNETH. See MACDONALD, ROSS
MILLAY, EDNA ST. VINCENT, CWA II-1227
Harp-Weaver and Other Poems, The, MP V-2489
MILLER, ARTHUR, CWA II-1229; CWAII III-1046
After the Fall, CLCII I-20; MPII:D I-17
All My Sons, CLCII I-29; MPII:D I-27

Crucible, The, CLCII I-351; MPII:D I-414
Death of a Salesman, CLC I-255; MP III-1365
Incident at Vichy, CLCII II-756; MPII:D II-831
Price, The, CLCII III-1233; MPII:D III-1283
Timebends, MPII:NF IV-1533
MILLER, HENRY, CWA II-1231; CWAII III-1048
Tropic of Cancer, CLCII IV-1615; MPII:AF IV-1697
Tropic of Capricorn, MP XI-6733; MP:AF III-1330
MILLER, WALTER M., JR.
Canticle for Leibowitz, A, CLCII I-233; MPII:AF I-247
MIŁOSZ, CZESŁAW, CWAII III-1051
Captive Mind, The, MPII:NF I-232
Issa Valley, The, CLCII II-781; MPII:WF II-743
Land of Ulro, The, MPII:NF II-792
Native Realm, MPII:NF III-997
Seizure of Power, The, CLCII III-1370; MPII:WF IV-1377
MILTON, JOHN, CWA II-1233
Areopagitica, MP I-299
Comus, CLC I-194; MP II-1051
Lyric Poetry of Milton, The, MP VI-3569
Paradise Lost, CLC II-835; MP VIII-4482
Paradise Regained, CLC II-887; MP VIII-4487
Samson Agonistes, CLC II-1002; MP X-5776
MING, KAO. See KAO TSE-CH'ENG
MINSKY, MARVIN
Society of Mind, The, MPII:NF IV-1383
MIRANDOLA, GIOVANNI PICO DELLA. See PICO DELLA MIRANDOLA, GIOVANNI
MISHIMA, YUKIO, CWA II-1238; CWAII III-1054

After the Banquet, CLCII I-19; MPII:WF I-24

Confessions of a Mask, CLCII I-325; MPII:WF I-310

"Death in Midsummer," MPII:SS II-524

"Patriotism," MPII:SS IV-1775

Sailor Who Fell from Grace with the Sea, The, CLCII III-1328; MPII:WF III-1332

Sea of Fertility, The, CLCII III-1354; MPII:WF III-1361

Sound of Waves, The, MP XI-6199; MP:EF III-1215

Sun and Steel, MPII:NF IV-1457

Temple of the Golden Pavilion, The, CLCII IV-1522; MPII:WF IV-1554

MISTRAL, GABRIELA, CWA II-1240

Poetry of Gabriela Mistral, The, MP IX-4949

MITCHELL, JAMES LESLIE. *See* GIBBON, LEWIS GRASSIC

MITCHELL, MARGARET, CWA II-1242

Gone with the Wind, CLC I-410; MP IV-2313; MP:AF I-474

MITCHELL, SILAS WEIR, CWA II-1243

Hugh Wynne, Free Quaker, CLC I-497; MP V-2763; MP:AF II-577

MITCHELL, W. O.

Who Has Seen the Wind, CLCII IV-1712; MPII:BCF IV-1895

MITFORD, MARY RUSSELL, CWA II-1245

Our Village, CLC II-830; MP VIII-4446; MP:BF II-1145

MITTELHOLZER, EDGAR, CWAII III-1056

Kaywana Trilogy, The, CLCII II-817; The, MPII:BCF II-887

MO, TIMOTHY, CWAII III-1059

Insular Possession, An, CLCII II-766; MPII:BCF II-825

Sour Sweet, CLCII IV-1451; MPII:BCF IV-1581

MOLIÈRE, CWA II-1247

Bourgeois Gentleman, The, CLC I-116; MP II-611

Doctor in Spite of Himself, The, CLC I-279; MP III-1546

Don Juan, CLC I-293; MP III-1595

Hypochondriac, The, CLC I-505; MP V-2798

Misanthrope, The, CLC II-711; MP VII-3921

Miser, The, CLC II-712; MP VII-3928

Romantic Ladies, The, CLC II-988; MP X-5689

School for Husbands, The, CLC II-1010; MP X-5834

School for Wives, The, CLC II-1012; MP X-5843

Tartuffe, CLC II-1111; MP XI-6421

MOLNAR, FERENC, CWA II-1250

Liliom, CLC I-615; MP VI-3428

MOMADAY, N. SCOTT, CWAII III-1061

House Made of Dawn, CLCII II-707; MPII:AF II-754

Names, The, MPII:NF III-991

Way to Rainy Mountain, The, MPII:NF IV-1660

MONTAIGNE, MICHEL EYQUEM DE, CWA II-1252

Essais, MP III-1825

MONTESQUIEU, CHARLES DE, CWA II-1255

Persian Letters, MP VIII-4607

Spirit of the Laws, The, MP XI-6222

MOORE, BRIAN, CWAII III-1064

Black Robe, CLCII I-163; MPII:BCF I-150

Lonely Passion of Judith Hearne, The, CLCII III-907; MPII:BCF III-998

Luck of Ginger Coffey, The, CLCII III-935; MPII:BCF III-1039

MOORE, GEORGE, CWA II-1257

Esther Waters, CLC I-332; MP IV-1870; MP:BF I-374

MOORE, MARIANNE, CWA II-1259

Poetry of Marianne Moore, The, MP IX-5062

MOORE, THOMAS, CWA II-1261
Irish Melodies, MP V-2935
Lalla Rookh, CLC I-590; MP VI-3237
MORAL, JOSÉ ZORRILLA Y. See
ZORRILLA, JOSÉ
MORANTE, ELSA
Arturo's Island, CLCII I-70; MPII:WF
I-71
History, CLCII II-679; MPII:WF II-593
MORAVIA, ALBERTO, CWA II-1263;
CWAII III-1066
"Bitter Honeymoon," MPII:SS I-222
Conformist, The, CLCII I-329;
MPII:WF I-319
Ghost at Noon, A, CLCII II-578;
MPII:WF II-529
1934, CLCII III-1101; MPII:WF III-
1098
Time of Indifference, The, CLCII IV-
1568; MPII:WF IV-1605
Two Women, MP XII-6782; MP:EF
III-1323
Woman of Rome, The, CLC II-1259;
MP XII-7221; MP:EF III-1409
MORE, PAUL ELMER, CWA II-1265
Shelburne Essays, MP X-5966
MORE, SIR THOMAS, CWA II-1267
History of King Richard III, MP V-
2637
Utopia, CLC II-1189; MP XII-6868
MORGAN, WILLIAM DE. See DE
MORGAN, WILLIAM
MORIER, JAMES JUSTINIAN, CWA II-
1269
Hajji Baba of Ispahan, CLC I-436; MP
V-2446; MP:BF I-511
MÖRIKE, EDUARD, CWA II-1270
Poetry of Mörike, The, MP IX-5084
MORRIS, WILLIAM, CWA II-1272
Defence of Guenevere and Other
Poems, The, MP III-1417
Earthly Paradise, The, MP III-1687
MORRIS, WRIGHT, CWA II-1274;
CWAII III-1068
Ceremony in Lone Tree, MP II-872;
MP:AF I-186

Cloak of Light, A, MPII:NF IV-1696
Field of Vision, The, MP IV-2042;
MP:AF I-378
Fork River Space Project, The, CLCII
II-534; MPII:AF II-561
"Glimpse into Another Country,"
MPII:SS II-863
Inhabitants, The, MPII:NF II-736
Plains Song, for Female Voices, CLCII
III-1210; MPII:AF III-1262
"Ram in the Thicket, The," MPII:SS V-
1890
"Victrola," MPII:SS VI-2497
Will's Boy, Solo, MPII:NF IV-1696
Works of Love, The, CLCII IV-1749;
MPII:AF IV-1820
MORRISON, TONI, CWAII III-1071
Bluest Eye, The, CLCII I-180;
MPII:AF I-191
Song of Solomon, CLCII IV-1445;
MPII:AF IV-1485
Sula, CLCII IV-1490; MPII:AF IV-
1550
MORTIMER, JOHN, CWAII III-1074
Clinging to the Wreckage, MPII:NF I-
249
Voyage Round My Father, A, CLCII
IV-1668; MPII:D IV-1701
MOSCHUS
Poetry of Moschus, The, MP IX-5087
MOTTE-FOUQUÉ, FRIEDRICH DE LA.
See LA MOTTE-FOUQUÉ,
FRIEDRICH DE
MPHAHLELE, EZEKIEL
Wanderers, The, CLCII IV-1677;
MPII:BCF IV-1843
MROŻEK, SŁAWOMIR
Police, The, CLCII III-1217; MPII:D
III-1264
Tango, CLCII IV-1515; MPII:D IV-
1534
MUIR, JOHN, CWA II-1276
Story of My Boyhood and Youth, The,
MP XI-6286
MUKHERJEE, BHARATI, CWAII III-
1077

"World According to Hsü, The,"
MPII:SS VI-2696
MULOCK, DINAH MARIA, CWA II-1278
John Halifax, Gentleman, CLC I-550;
MP V-3023; MP:BF II-691
MULTATULI, CWA II-1280
Max Havelaar, CLC I-682; MP VII-3778; MP:EF II-844
MUMFORD, LEWIS, CWA II-1281
Brown Decades, The, MP II-693
MUNIF, ABDELRAHMAN, CWAII III-1079
Cities of Salt, CLCII I-287
Mudun al-milh, MPII:WF III-1049
MUNRO, ALICE, CWAII III-1081
Lives of Girls and Women, CLCII III-898; MPII:BCF II-980
"Wild Swans," MPII:SS VI-2619
MUNRO, HECTOR HUGH. See SAKI
MURASAKI SHIKIBU, LADY, CWA II-1283
Tale of Genji, The, CLC II-1100; MP XI-6369; MP:EF III-1252
MURDOCH, IRIS, CWA II-1284; CWAII III-1083
Bell, The, MP I-485; MP:BF I-104
Black Prince, The, CLCII I-162; MPII:BCF I-145
Bruno's Dream, CLCII I-208; MPII:BCF I-196

Fairly Honourable Defeat, A, CLCII II-485; MPII:BCF I-483
Good Apprentice, The, CLCII II-608; MPII:BCF II-627
Nuns and Soldiers, CLCII III-1120; MPII:BCF III-1238
Sandcastle, The, CLCII III-1334; MPII:BCF III-1444
Severed Head, A, CLCII IV-1385; MPII:BCF IV-1516
Sovereignty of Good, The, MPII:NF IV-1402
Unicorn, The, CLCII IV-1639; MPII:BCF IV-1771
Word Child, A, CLCII IV-1744; MPII:BCF IV-1926
MURGER, HENRI, CWA II-1286
Bohemians of the Latin Quarter, The, CLC I-113; MP I-581; MP:EF I-122
MUSIL, ROBERT, CWAII III-1085
Man Without Qualities, The, CLCII III-962; MPII:WF III-930
Young Törless, CLCII IV-1766; MPII:WF IV-1797
MUSSET, ALFRED DE, CWA II-1287
No Trifling with Love, CLC II-781; MP VII-4231
Poetry of Musset, The, MP IX-5089

N

NABOKOV, VLADIMIR, CWA II-1289; CWAII III-1087

Ada or Ardor, CLCII I-12; MPII:AF I-6

Bend Sinister, CLCII I-141; MPII:AF I-142

"Cloud, Castle, Lake," MPII:SS I-409

Defense, The, CLCII I-384; MPII:WF I-359

Gift, The, CLCII II-581; MPII:WF II-534

Invitation to a Beheading, CLCII II-775; MPII:WF II-732

Laughter in the Dark, CLCII II-861; MPII:WF II-825

Lolita, CLCII III-904; MPII:AF II-901

Mary, CLCII III-981; MPII:WF III-965

Pale Fire, MP VIII-4462; MP:AF II-897

Pnin, CLCII III-1216; MPII:AF III-1277

Real Life of Sebastian Knight, The, MP IX-5450; MP:AF III-1005

"Return of Chorb, The," MPII:SS V-1941

Speak, Memory, MPII:NF IV-1414

NAIPAUL, SHIVA, CWAII III-1090

Fireflies, CLCII II-511; MPII:BCF II-514

NAIPAUL, V. S., CWAII III-1092

Among the Believers, MPII:NF I-50

Bend in the River, A, CLCII I-139; MPII:BCF I-124

Guerrillas, CLCII II-644; MPII:BCF II-675

House for Mr. Biswas, A, CLCII II-706; MPII:BCF II-748

In a Free State, CLCII II-744; MPII:BCF II-804

Middle Passage, The, MPII:NF III-950

Miguel Street, CLCII III-1008; MPII:BCF III-1102

Mimic Men, The, CLCII III-1010; MPII:BCF III-1106

Mr. Stone and the Knights Companion, CLCII III-1022; MPII:BCF III-1126

Prologue to an Autobiography, MPII:NF III-1204

NARAYAN, R. K., CWA II-1291, CWAII III-1094

"Astrologer's Day, An," MPII:SS I-129

Financial Expert, The, CLCII II-505; MPII:BCF II-493

Grateful to Life and Death, CLCII II-623; MPII:BCF II-660

Guide, The, MP IV-2418; MP:EF II-610

"Horse and Two Goats, A," MPII:SS III-1037

Printer of Malgudi, The, CLCII III-1236; MPII:BCF III-1346

"Uncle," MPII:SS VI-2452

Vendor of Sweets, The, CLCII IV-1653; MPII:BCF IV-1780

NARIHIRA, ARIHARA NO. See ARIHARA NO NARIHIRA

NASH, THOMAS, CWA II-1293

Unfortunate Traveller, The, CLC II-1186; MP XII-6855; MP:BF III-1650

NATSUME, SŌSEKI, CWAII III-1096

Botchan, CLCII I-196; MPII:WF I-188

I Am a Cat, CLCII II-724; MPII:WF II-648

Three-Cornered World, The, CLCII IV-1555; MPII:WF IV-1595

NAYLOR, GLORIA, CWAII III-1098

Women of Brewster Place, The, CLCII IV-1734; MPII:AF IV-1805

NEEDHAM, RODNEY

Counterpoints, MPII:NF I-281

NEKRASOV, NIKOLAI, CWA II-1294

Poetry of Nekrasov, The, MP IX-5092

NEMEROV, HOWARD, CWAII III-1100

Journal of the Fictive Life, MPII:NF II-762

NERUDA, PABLO, CWA II-1296; CWAII III-1102

Poetry of Neruda, The, MP IX-5095

Memoirs, MPII:NF III-912

NERVAL, GÉRARD DE, CWA II-1298
Poetry of Nerval, The, MP IX-5098
NEWMAN, JOHN HENRY, CWA II-1300
Apologia pro Vita Sua, MP I-263
NEWTON, SIR ISAAC, CWA II-1303
Philosophiae Naturalis Principia
Mathematica, MP VIII-4653
NEXÖ, MARTIN ANDERSEN, CWA II-1305
Pelle the Conqueror, CLC II-851; MP VIII-4566; MP:EF III-987
NGUGI WA THIONG'O, CWAII III-1105
Black Hermit, The, CLCII I-160; MPII:D I-185
Detained, MPII:NF I-348
Petals of Blood, CLCII III-1198; MPII:BCF III-1320
River Between, The, CLCII III-1300; MPII:BCF III-1428
NGUGI WA THIONG'O and NGUGI WA MIRII
I Will Marry When I Want, CLCII II-729; MPII:D II-804
NICHOLS, PETER, CWAII III-1108
Day in the Death of Joe Egg, A, CLCII I-370; MPII:D II-443
Passion Play, CLCII III-1185; MPII:D III-1209
NICOLSON, SIR HAROLD GEORGE, CWA II-1307
Some People, MP X-6132
NIETZSCHE, FRIEDRICH WILHELM, CWA II-1309
Beyond Good and Evil, MP I-520
Thus Spake Zarathustra, MP XI-6532
NIEVO, IPPOLITO, CWA II-1312
Castle of Fratta, The, CLC I-155; MP II-823; MP:EF I-189

NIIHARA, RYŪNOSUKE. See AKUTAGAWA, RYŪNOSUKE
NIN, ANAÏS, CWAII III-1110
Diary of Anaïs Nin, The, MPII:NF I-373
Spy in the House of Love, A, CLCII IV-1468; MPII:AF IV-1527
"Under a Glass Bell," MPII:SS VI-2461
NORDHOFF, CHARLES, and JAMES NORMAN HALL, CWA II-1314
Mutiny on the Bounty, CLC II-749; MP VII-4099; MP:AF II-819
NORMAN, MARSHA, CWAII III-1112
Getting Out, CLCII II-577; MPII:D II-672
'night, Mother, CLCII III-1095; MPII:D III-1133
Third and Oak: The Laundromat, CLCII IV-1546; MPII:D IV-1562
NORRIS, FRANK, CWA II-1316
"Deal in Wheat, A," MPII:SS II-516
McTeague, CLC I-644; MP VI-3594; MP:AF II-717
Octopus, The, CLCII III-1129; MPII:AF III-1171
Pit, The, CLC II-889; MP VIII-4729; MP:AF II-949
Responsibilities of the Novelist, The, MP X-5528
NORTON, THOMAS, and THOMAS SACKVILLE, CWA II-1319
Gorboduc, CLC I-412; MP IV-2332
NOVAK, JOSEPH. See KOSINSKI, JERZY
NOZICK, ROBERT
Philosophical Explanations, MPII:NF III-1153

O

O. HENRY. *See* HENRY, O.

OAKESHOTT, MICHAEL, CWAII III-1114

On Human Conduct, MPII:NF III-1071

OATES, JOYCE CAROL, CWA II-1321, CWAII III-1116

Bellefleur, CLCII I-138; MPII:AF I-136

Bloodsmoor Romance, A, CLCII I-171; MPII:AF I-186

"How I contemplated the world from the Detroit House of Correction and began my life over again," MPII:SS III-1060

"My Warszawa," MPII:SS IV-1571

"Nairobi," MPII:SS IV-1582

them, CLCII IV-1535; MPII:AF IV-1604

Unholy Loves, CLCII IV-1637; MPII:AF IV-1717

"Unmailed, Unwritten Letters," MPII:SS VI-2471

"Upon the Sweeping Flood," MPII:SS VI-2478

"Waiting," MPII:SS VI-2517

"What Is the Connection Between Men and Women?" MPII:SS VI-2565

"Where Are You Going, Where Have You Been?" MPII:SS VI-2577

Wonderland, CLCII IV-1741; MPII:AF IV-1815

O'BRIEN, EDNA, CWAII III-1118

Country Girls trilogy, The, CLCII I-341; MPII:BCF I-327

Mother Ireland, MPII:NF III-987

Night, CLCII III-1092; MPII:BCF III-1198

Pagan Place, A, CLCII III-1169; MPII:BCF III-1267

"Paradise," MPII:SS IV-1759

"Rose in the Heart of New York, A," MPII:SS V-1990

"Scandalous Woman, A," MPII:SS V-2033

O'BRIEN, FITZ-JAMES

"Diamond Lens, The," MPII:SS II-587

"Wondersmith, The," MPII:SS VI-2687

O'BRIEN, FLANN, CWAII III-1120

At Swim-Two-Birds, CLCII I-82; MPII:BCF I-77

Third Policeman, The, CLCII IV-1548; MPII:BCF IV-1686

O'BRIEN, KATE, CWA II-1323

Last of Summer, The, CLC I-595; MP VI-3253; MP:BF II-776

O'CASEY, SEAN, CWA II-1324; CWAII III-1122

Cock-a-Doodle Dandy, CLCII I-301; MPII:D I-370

Juno and the Paycock, CLC I-562; MP VI-3100

Mirror in My House, MPII:NF III-971

Plough and the Stars, The, CLC II-894; MP VIII-4761

Purple Dust, CLC II-927; MP IX-5378

Red Roses for Me, CLCII III-1282; MPII:D III-1315

Shadow of a Gunman, The, CLCII IV-1387; MPII:D IV-1454

Silver Tassie, The, CLCII IV-1413; MPII:D IV-1465

Within the Gates, CLC II-1254; MP XII-7199

O'CONNOR, FLANNERY, CWA II-1326; CWAII III-1124

"Artificial Nigger, The," MPII:SS I-118

"Displaced Person, The," MPII:SS II-607

"Enduring Chill, The," MPII:SS II-692

"Everything That Rises Must Converge," MPII:SS II-735

"Good Country People," MPII:SS II-900

"Good Man Is Hard to Find, A," MPII:SS II-903

"Greenleaf," MPII:SS III-944

Habit of Being, The, MPII:NF II-630

"Parker's Back," MPII:SS IV-1768

"Revelation," MPII:SS V-1945

Short Stories of Flannery O'Connor, The, MP X-6008; MP:AF III-1152

Violent Bear It Away, The, MP XII-6937; MP:AF III-1380

Wise Blood, MP XII-7192; MP:AF III-1450

O'CONNOR, FRANK, CWAII III-1127

"Christmas Morning," MPII:SS I-388

"Drunkard, The," MPII:SS II-643

"Guests of the Nation," MPII:SS III-956

"Legal Aid," MPII:SS III-1325

"My Oedipus Complex," MPII:SS IV-1564

"Story by Maupassant, A," MPII:SS V-2238

ODETS, CLIFFORD, CWA III-1327; CWAII III-1129

Awake and Sing! CLCII I-98; MPII:D I-104

Big Knife, The, CLCII I-150; The MPII:D I-169

Flowering Peach, The, CLCII II-527; MPII:D II-616

Golden Boy, CLC I-409; MP IV-2304

O'DONOVAN, MICHAEL FRANCIS. See O'CONNOR, FRANK

ŌE, KENZABURŌ, CWAII III-1131

"Catch, The," MPII:SS I-340

Personal Matter, A, CLCII III-1197; MPII:WF III-1195

Silent Cry, The, CLCII IV-1407; MPII:WF IV-1431

O'FAOLÁIN, SEÁN, CWA III-1328; CWAII III-1133

"Innocence," MPII:SS III-1176

"Man Who Invented Sin, The," MPII:SS IV-1440

"Midsummer Night Madness," MPII:SS IV-1497

Nest of Simple Folk, A, CLC II-762; MP VII-4165; MP:BF II-1030

"Up the Bare Stairs," MPII:SS VI-2474

O'FLAHERTY, LIAM, CWA III-1330; CWAII III-1135

Informer, The, CLC I-524; MP V-2886; MP:BF II-640

"Mountain Tavern, The," MPII:SS IV-1541

"Post Office, The," MPII:SS IV-1835

"Sniper, The," MPII:SS V-2158

"Two Lovely Beasts," MPII:SS VI-2445

O'HARA, JOHN, CWA III-1332; CWAII III-1137

Appointment in Samarra, CLC I-55; MP I-276; MP:AF I-70

"Doctor's Son, The," MPII:SS II-621

From the Terrace, CLCII II-552; MPII:AF II-591

Ten North Frederick, CLCII IV-1524; MPII:AF IV-1573

OLDENBOURG, ZOÉ, CWA III-1334

Cornerstone, The, MP II-1121; MP:EF I-257

OLESHA, YURY, CWAII III-1139

Envy, CLCII II-463; MPII:WF I-421

OLIVER, DIANE, CWAII III-1141

"Neighbors," MPII:SS IV-1605

OLIVER, GEORGE. See ONIONS, OLIVER

OLSEN, TILLIE, CWAII III-1143

"I Stand Here Ironing," MPII:SS III-1091

Silences, MPII:NF IV-1346

"Tell Me a Riddle," MPII:SS V-2308

Yonnondio, CLCII IV-1763; MPII:AF IV-1841

O'NEILL, EUGENE, CWA III-1336

All God's Chillun Got Wings, CLCII I-26; MPII:D I-22

Anna Christie, CLC I-43; MP I-226

Desire Under the Elms, CLC I-265; MP III-1458

Emperor Jones, The, CLC I-325; MP III-1769

Great God Brown, The, CLCII II-628; MPII:D II-701

Hairy Ape, The, CLCII II-651; MPII:D II-723

Iceman Cometh, The, CLCII II-732; MPII:D II-809

Lazarus Laughed, CLCII II-863; MPII:D III-944

Long Day's Journey into Night, CLCII III-908; MPII:D III-986

Moon for the Misbegotten, A, CLCII III-1035; MPII:D III-1100

Mourning Becomes Electra, CLC II-745; MP VII-4081

Strange Interlude, CLC II-1089; MP XI-6294

ONETTI, JUAN CARLOS

Brief Life, A, CLCII I-201; MPII:AF I-212

Shipyard, The, CLCII IV-1394; MPII:AF IV-1411

ONG, WALTER J., CWAII III-1145

Presence of the Word, The, MPII:NF III-1179

ONIONS, OLIVER

"Beckoning Fair One, The," MPII:SS I-173

O'NOLAN, BRIAN. See O'BRIEN, FLANN

ORIGO, IRIS

Images and Shadows, MPII:NF II-694

ORTEGA Y GASSET, JOSÉ, CWA III-1339

Revolt of the Masses, The, MP X-5562

ORTON, JOE, CWAII III-1148

Entertaining Mr. Sloane, CLCII II-462; MPII:D II-574

Loot, CLCII III-915; MPII:D III-992

What the Butler Saw, CLCII IV-1707; MPII:D IV-1728

ORWELL, GEORGE, CWA III-1341; CWAII III-1150

Animal Farm, CLCII I-51; MPII:BCF I-53

Burmese Days, CLCII I-214; MPII:BCF I-206

Coming Up for Air, CLCII I-314; MPII:BCF I-297

Down and Out in Paris and London, MPII:NF I-409

Homage to Catalonia, MPII:NF II-645

Keep the Aspidistra Flying, CLCII II-820; MPII:BCF II-894

Nineteen Eighty-Four, CLC II-779; MP VII-4224; MP:BF II-1057

Road to Wigan Pier, The, MPII:NF III-1247

OSBORNE, JOHN, CWA III-1344; CWAII III-1153

Better Class of Person, A, MPII:NF I-144

Entertainer, The, CLCII II-461; MPII:D II-569

Inadmissible Evidence, CLCII II-755; MPII:D II-826

Look Back in Anger, MP VI-3490

Luther, CLCII III-937; MPII:D III-1002

OTWAY, THOMAS, CWA III-1346

Orphan, The, CLC II-823; MP VIII-4425

Soldier's Fortune, The, CLC II-1057; MP X-6128

Venice Preserved, CLC II-1195; MP XII-6890

OUIDA, CWA III-1347

Under Two Flags, CLC II-1183; MP XII-6840; MP:BF III-1643

OUSMANE, SEMBÈNE. See SEMBÈNE, OUSMANE

OVID, CWA III-1349

Amores, MP I-183

Ars Amatoria, MP I-317

Heroides, MP V-2601

Metamorphoses, The, MP VII-3866

OWEN, WILFRED, CWA III-1351

Poetry of Owen, The, MP IX-5105

OWENS, ROCHELLE

Karl Marx Play, The, CLCII II-815; MPII:D III-883

OZ, AMOS, CWAII III-1155

Elsewhere, Perhaps, CLCII II-450; MPII:WF I-403

My Michael, CLCII III-1065; MPII:WF III-1054

Perfect Peace, A, CLCII III-1193; MPII:WF III-1190

OZICK, CYNTHIA, CWAII III-1157

"Envy," MPII:SS II-712

"Rosa," MPII:SS V-1982

P

PAGE, THOMAS NELSON, CWA III-1353
  Marse Chan, CLC I-674; MP VII-3748; MP:AF II-773
PAINE, THOMAS, CWA III-1355
  Age of Reason, The, MP I-70
  Crisis, The, MP II-1211
PALEY, GRACE, CWAII III-1159
  "Dreamers in a Dead Language," MPII:SS II-632
  "Faith in a Tree," MPII:SS II-747
  "Interest in Life, An," MPII:SS III-1184
PALMER, VANCE
  Passage, The, CLCII III-1180; MPII:BCF III-1293
PARK, MUNGO
  Travels to the Interior Districts of Africa, MP XI-6656
PARKER, DOROTHY, CWAII III-1161
  "Big Blonde," MPII:SS I-203
PARKMAN, FRANCIS, CWA III-1357
  Count Frontenac and New France Under Louis XIV, MP II-1133
  Old Regime in Canada, The, MP VIII-4338
  Oregon Trail, The, MP VIII-4394
PARRINGTON, VERNON LOUIS, CWA III-1359
  Main Currents in American Thought, MP VI-3642
PASCAL, BLAISE, CWA III-1361
  Pensées, MP VIII-4584
PASSOS, JOHN DOS. See DOS PASSOS, JOHN
PASTERNAK, BORIS LEONIDOVICH, CWA III-1362, CWAII III-1163
  "Childhood of Luvers, The," MPII:SS I-372
  Doctor Zhivago, MP III-1561; MP:EF I-417
  Poetry of Pasternak, The, MP IX-5107
  Safe-Conduct, A, MPII:NF III-1274
PASTON FAMILY
  Paston Letters A.D. 1422-1509, The, MP VIII-4513

PATER, WALTER, CWA III-1364
  Marius the Epicurean, CLC I-671; MP VII-3732; MP:BF II-868
  Renaissance, The, MP IX-5511
PATON, ALAN, CWA III-1365
  Cry, the Beloved Country, CLC I-227; MP III-1235; MP:EF I-310
PATRICK, JOHN
  Hasty Heart, The, CLCII II-660; MPII:D II-747
  Teahouse of the August Moon, The, CLCII IV-1519; MPII:D IV-1548
PAUSTOVSKY, KONSTANTIN, CWAII III-1166
  Story of a Life, The, MPII:NF IV-1437
PAVESE, CESARE, CWAII III-1168
  Among Women Only, CLCII I-41; MPII:WF I-50
  Burning Brand, The, MPII:NF I-218
  House on the Hill, The, CLCII II-715; MPII:WF II-639
  Moon and the Bonfires, The, CLCII III-1034; MPII:WF III-1036
PAZ, OCTAVIO, CWA III-1366; CWAII III-1170
  Bow and the Lyre, The, MPII:NF I-196
  Labyrinth of Solitude, The, MP VI-3200
  Poetry of Paz, The, MP IX-5109
PEACOCK, THOMAS LOVE, CWA III-1369
  Crotchet Castle, CLC I-226; MP III-1229; MP:BF I-261
  Headlong Hall, CLC I-447; MP V-2498; MP:BF I-536
  Nightmare Abbey, CLC II-778; MP VII-4221; MP:BF II-1053
PEAKE, MERVYN, CWAII III-1172
  Gormenghast trilogy, The, CLCII II-618; MPII:BCF II-648
PEATTIE, DONALD CULROSS, CWA III-1371
  Almanac for Moderns, An, MP I-146
PEDERSEN, KNUT. See HAMSUN, KNUT

PEELE, GEORGE, CWA III-1373
  Old Wives' Tale, The, CLC II-809; MP
    VIII-4349
PÉGUY, CHARLES-PIERRE, CWA III-
    1375
  Poetry of Péguy, The, MP IX-5112
PEPYS, SAMUEL, CWA III-1377
  Diary, MP III-1497
PERCY, WALKER, CWAII III-1174
  Last Gentleman, The, CLCII II-853;
    MPII:AF II-850
  Love in the Ruins, CLCII III-925;
    MPII:AF III-933
  Message in the Bottle, The, MPII:NF
    III-944
  Moviegoer, The, CLCII III-1053;
    MPII:AF III-1083
  Second Coming, The, CLCII III-1363;
    MPII:AF III-1376
PEREDA, JOSÉ MARÍA DE, CWA III-
    1380
  Pedro Sánchez, CLC II-847; MP VIII-
    4556; MP:EF III-983
  Peñas arriba, CLC II-852; MP VIII-
    4572; MP:EF III-991
  Sotileza, CLC II-1070; MP XI-6186;
    MP:EF III-1211
PERELMAN, S. J., CWAII III-1177
  "Critical Introduction to The Best of S.
    J. Perelman by Sidney Namlerep,"
    MPII:SS I-456
  "Love Decoy, The," MPII:SS IV-1409
PERETZ, ISAAC LEIB
  "Bontsha the Silent," MPII:SS I-277
PÉREZ GALDÓS, BENITO, CWA III-
    1382
  Ángel Guerra, CLC I-42; MP I-223;
    MP:EF I-43
  Doña Perfecta, CLC I-298; MP III-
    1618; MP:EF I-438
  Fortunata and Jacinta, CLC I-379; MP
    IV-2132; MP:EF II-534
  Our Friend Manso, CLCII III-1163;
    MPII:WF III-1157
  Saragossa, CLC II-1006; MP X-5796;
    MP:EF III-1131

PERSE, ST.-JOHN, CWA III-1384
  Anabasis, MP I-196
  Chronique, MP II-956
  Èloges and Other Poems, MP III-1746
  Seamarks, MP X-5874
PERSONS, TRUMAN STRECKFUS. See
  CAPOTE, TRUMAN
PESHKOV, ALEKSEI MAKSIMOVICH.
  See GORKY, MAXIM
PETRARCH, FRANCESCO, CWA III-
    1386
  Rime of Petrarch, Le, MP X-5597
PETRONIUS, CWA III-1388
  Satyricon, The, CLC II-1008; MP X-
    5820; MP:EF III-1135
PHILLIPS, JAYNE ANNE, CWAII III-
    1180
  "Black Tickets," MPII:SS I-239
  "Home," MPII:SS III-1033
PICA, PETER. See ALDISS, BRIAN W.
PICO DELLA MIRANDOLA,
    GIOVANNI, CWA II-1236
  Oration on the Dignity of Man, MP
    VIII-4385
PIERCY, MARGE, CWAII III-1182
  Small Changes, CLCII IV-1426;
    MPII:AF IV-1448
  Woman on the Edge of Time, CLCII
    IV-1732; MPII:AF IV-1800
PILNYAK, BORIS, CWA III-1390
  Naked Year, The, CLC II-755; MP VII-
    4131; MP:EF II-913
PINCHERLE, ALBERTO. See
  MORAVIA, ALBERTO
PINDAR, CWA III-1392
  Epinicia, The, MP III-1805
PINERO, ARTHUR WING, CWA III-
    1393
  Mid-Channel, CLC II-700; MP VII-
    3877
  Second Mrs. Tanqueray, The, CLC II-
    1017; MP X-5882
PINGET, ROBERT, CWAII III-1184
  Baga, CLCII I-102; MPII:WF I-107
  Inquisitory, The, CLCII II-764;
    MPII:WF II-701

That Voice, CLCII IV-1532; MPII:WF IV-1570

PINTER, HAROLD, CWA III-1395; CWAII III-1186

Betrayal, CLCII I-145; MPII:D I-163

Birthday Party, The, CLCII I-159; MPII:D I-180

Caretaker, The, MP II-800

Dumb Waiter, The, CLCII II-429; MPII:D II-524

Family Voices, CLCII II-490; MPII:D II-595

Homecoming, The, CLCII II-688; MPII:D II-774

Kind of Alaska, A, CLCII II-829; MPII:D III-910

PIRANDELLO, LUIGI, CWA III-1397

Each in His Own Way, CLCII II-436; MPII:D II-534

Henry IV, CLCII II-674; MPII:D II-764

Late Mattia Pascal, The, CLC I-600; MP VI-3285; MP:EF II-759

Old and the Young, The, CLC II-797; MP VIII-4305; MP:EF II-953

Right You Are--If You Think So, CLC II-970; MP X-5593

Six Characters in Search of an Author, CLC II-1047; MP X-6079

Tonight We Improvise, CLCII IV-1588; MPII:D IV-1601

"War," MPII:SS VI-2544

PIRSIG, ROBERT M., CWAII III-1189

Zen and the Art of Motorcycle Maintenance, MPII:NF IV-1741

PLANTE, DAVID, CWAII III-1191

"Work," MPII:SS VI-2692

PLATH, SYLVIA, CWAII III-1193

Bell Jar, The, CLCII I-137; MPII:AF I-163

PLATO, CWA III-1400

Dialogues of Plato, The, MP III-1482

Republic, The, MP IX-5522

PLATONOV, ANDREI, CWAII III-1195

Chevengur, CLCII I-266; MPII:WF I-248

Foundation Pit, The, CLCII II-534; MPII:WF II-497

PLAUTUS, CWA III-1403

Amphitryon, CLC I-37; MP I-185

Braggart Soldier, The, CLC I-119; MP II-623

Captives, The, CLC I-151; MP II-797

Menaechmi, The, CLC I-694; MP VII-3849

Pot of Gold, The, CLC II-908; MP IX-5273

Slipknot, The, CLC II-1050; MP X-6094

Trickster, The, CLC II-1157; MP XI-6698

PLINY THE YOUNGER, CWA III-1405

Letters of Pliny the Younger, The, MP VI-3355

PLUNKETT, EDWARD JOHN MORETON DRAX. See DUNSANY, LORD

PLUTARCH, CWA III-1407

Parallel Lives, MP VIII-4490

PODHORETZ, NORMAN, CWAII III-1197

Making It, MPII:NF II-878

POE, EDGAR ALLAN, CWA III-1409

"Black Cat, The," MPII:SS I-231

"Cask of Amontillado, The," MPII:SS I-334

"Descent into the Maelström, A," MPII:SS II-568

Essays of Edgar Allan Poe, The, MP IV-1854

"Fall of the House of Usher, The," CLC I-353; MP IV-1968;; MP:AF I-360; MPII:SS II-751

"Gold Bug, The," CLC I-406; MP IV-2286; MP:AF I-462; MPII:SS II-889

"Ligeia," CLC I-613; MP VI-3418; MP:AF II-674;" MPII:SS III-1352

"Masque of the Red Death, The," MPII:SS IV-1471

"Ms. Found in a Bottle," MPII:SS IV-1451

"Murders in the Rue Morgue, The,"
MPII:SS IV-1544
Narrative of Arthur Gordon Pym, CLC
II-758; MP VII-4143; The, MP:AF
II-828
"Pit and the Pendulum, The," MPII:SS
IV-1821
"Purloined Letter, The," MPII:SS V-
1868
"Tell-Tale Heart, The," MPII:SS V-
2312
"William Wilson," MPII:SS VI-2630
POHL, FREDERIK, CWAII III-1199
Way the Future Was, The, MPII:NF
IV-1656
POLANYI, MICHAEL, CWAII III-1202
Personal Knowledge, MPII:NF III-1146
POLITIAN, CWA III-1412
Orfeo, CLC II-814; MP VIII-4398
POLO, MARCO, CWA III-1413
Travels of Marco Polo, The, MP XI-
6650
PONTOPPIDAN, HENRIK, CWA III-
1415
Promised Land, The, CLC II-926; MP
IX-5368; MP:EF III-1038
POPE, ALEXANDER, CWA III-1417
Dunciad, The, MP III-1672
Essay on Criticism, MP III-1834
Essay on Man, MP IV-1837
Rape of the Lock, The, CLC II-940;
MP IX-5436
POQUELIN, JEAN BAPTISTE. See
MOLIÈRE
PORTER, COUNTÉE. See CULLEN,
COUNTÉE
PORTER, HAL
Tilted Cross, The, CLCII IV-1566;
MPII:BCF IV-1705
PORTER, JANE, CWA III-1419
Scottish Chiefs, The, CLC II-1013; MP
X-5851; MP:BF III-1402
Thaddeus of Warsaw, CLC II-1120; MP
XI-6462; MP:BF III-1514
PORTER, KATHERINE ANNE, CWA
III-1420; CWAII III-1205

"Flowering Judas," MPII:SS II-795
"Leaning Tower, The," MPII:SS III-
1309
"Noon Wine," MPII:SS IV-1628
"Old Mortality," CLC II-804; MP VIII-
4330; MP:AF II-879; MPII:SS IV-
1672
Pale Horse, Pale Rider, MP VIII-4465;
MP:AF II-901
"Pale Horse, Pale Rider," MPII:SS IV-
1756
"Rope," MPII:SS V-1978
Ship of Fools, MP X-5979; MP:AF III-
1134
PORTER, WILLIAM SYDNEY. See
HENRY, O.
POTOK, CHAIM, CWAII III-1207
Book of Lights, The, CLCII I-192;
MPII:AF I-202
Chosen, The, CLCII I-281; MPII:AF I-
295
In the Beginning, CLCII II-746;
MPII:AF II-782
My Name Is Asher Lev, CLCII III-
1067; MPII:AF III-1105
Promise, The, CLCII I-281; MPII:AF I-
295
POUND, EZRA, CWA III-1423; CWAII
III-1210
ABC of Reading, MPII:NF I-1
Cantos, MP II-776
Gaudier-Brzeska, MPII:NF II-544
Guide to Kulchur, MPII:NF II-611
Personae, MP VIII-4612
Women of Trachis, (trans.) CLCII IV-
1736; MPII:D IV-1757
POWELL, ANTHONY, CWA III-1426;
CWAII III-1213
Afternoon Men, CLCII I-21; MPII:BCF
I-27
Agents and Patients, CLCII I-23;
MPII:BCF I-32
Dance to the Music of Time, A, MP III-
1288; MP:BF I-269; MP III-1293
Fisher King, The, CLCII II-518;
MPII:BCF II-520

O, How the Wheel Becomes It! CLCII
III-1123; MPII:BCF III-1243
To Keep the Ball Rolling, MPII:NF IV-
1538
Venusberg, CLCII IV-1654; MPII:BCF
IV-1785
POWERS, J. F., CWAII III-1215
"Lions, Harts, Leaping Does," MPII:SS
III-1363
Morte d'Urban, CLCII III-1040;
MPII:AF III-1055
"Old Bird," MPII:SS IV-1664
"Prince of Darkness," MPII:SS IV-1848
POWYS, JOHN COWPER, CWA III-1428
Wolf Solent, CLC II-1255; MP XII-
7203; MP:BF III-1749
POWYS, LLEWELYN, CWA III-1430
Ebony and Ivory, MP III-1697; MP:BF
I-352
POWYS, T. F., CWA III-1432
Mr. Weston's Good Wine, CLC II-721;
MP VII-3970; MP:BF II-974
PRESCOTT, WILLIAM HICKLING,
CWA III-1434
History of the Conquest of Mexico, MP
V-2646
PRÉVOST, ABBÉ, CWA III-1435
Manon Lescaut, CLC I-664; MP VII-
3696; MP:EF II-826
PRICE, REYNOLDS, CWA III-1437;
CWAII III-1217
"Chain of Love, A," MPII:SS I-351
Generous Man, A, CLCII II-574;
MPII:AF II-607
Long and Happy Life, A, MP VI-3474;
MP:AF II-691
"Truth and Lies," MPII:SS VI-2425
PRICHARD, KATHARINE SUSANNAH
Coonardoo, CLCII I-335; MPII:BCF I-
322
PRIESTLEY, J. B., CWA III-1438;
CWAII III-1219
Angel Pavement, CLCII I-45;
MPII:BCF I-43
Eden End, CLCII II-444; MPII:D II-
546

Good Companions, The, CLC I-410;
MP IV-2316; MP:BF I-483
Inspector Calls, An, CLCII II-765;
MPII:D II-852
Time and the Conways, CLCII IV-1567;
MPII:D IV-1579
PRIOR, MATTHEW, CWA III-1440
Poetry of Prior, The, MP IX-5115
PRITCHETT, V. S., CWAII III-1222
Cab at the Door, A, MPII:NF I-223
"Camberwell Beauty, The," MPII:SS I-
320
Dead Man Leading, CLCII I-374;
MPII:BCF I-364
"It May Never Happen," MPII:SS III-
1194
"Many Are Disappointed," MPII:SS IV-
1455
Midnight Oil, MPII:NF III-955
Mr. Beluncle, CLCII III-1018;
MPII:BCF III-1121
PROKOSCH, FREDERIC, CWA III-1442;
CWAII III-1224
Asiatics, The, CLCII I-76; MPII:AF I-
56
Missolonghi Manuscript, The, CLCII
III-1018; MPII:AF III-1012
Seven Who Fled, The, CLC II-1026;
MP X-5934; MP:AF III-1117
PROPERTIUS, SEXTUS, CWA III-1444
Elegies of Propertius, The, MP III-1739
PROUST, MARCEL, CWA III-1446
Remembrance of Things Past, CLC II-
953; MP IX-5500; MP:EF III-1072
PUIG, MANUEL, CWAII III-1227
Betrayed by Rita Hayworth, CLCII I-
146; MPII:AF I-146
Heartbreak Tango, CLCII II-670;
MPII:AF II-701
Kiss of the Spider Woman, CLCII II-
837; MPII:AF II-845
PURDY, JAMES, CWA III-1449; CWAII
III-1229
Color of Darkness, MP II-1034; MP:AF
I-203
"Color of Darkness," MPII:SS I-418

"Daddy Wolf," MPII:SS II-474
Malcolm, MP VI-3655; MP:AF II-737
PUSHKIN, ALEXANDER, CWA III-1453
"Blizzard, The," MPII:SS I-254
Boris Godunov, CLC I-115; MP I-599
Bronze Horseman: A Petersburg Tale,
    The, MP II-674
Captain's Daughter, The, CLC I-150;
    MP II-792; MP:EF I-172
Eugene Onegin, CLC I-334; MP IV-
    1883
"Queen of Spades, The," CLCII III-
    1244; MPII:SS V-1872
Ruslan and Lyudmila, MP X-5740
"Shot, The," MPII:SS V-2093
"Station-master, The," MPII:SS V-2220
P'U SUNG-LING, CWA III-1451
Strange Stories from a Chinese Studio,
    MP XI-6299; MP:EF III-1241
PYM, BARBARA, CWAII III-1231
Excellent Women, CLCII II-473;
    MPII:BCF I-466

Glass of Blessings, A, CLCII II-594;
    MPII:BCF II-607
Less than Angels, CLCII II-873;
    MPII:BCF II-949
Quartet in Autumn, CLCII III-1243;
    MPII:BCF III-1355
Sweet Dove Died, The, CLCII IV-1507;
    MPII:BCF IV-1659
Very Private Eye, A, MPII:NF IV-1641
PYNCHON, THOMAS, CWAII III-1233
Crying of Lot 49, The, CLCII I-354;
    MPII:AF I-361
"Entropy," MPII:SS II-709
Gravity's Rainbow, CLCII II-624;
    MPII:AF II-661
"Secret Integration, The," MPII:SS V-
    2053
"Under the Rose," MPII:SS VI-2464
V., CLCII IV-1646; MPII:AF IV-1727

Q

QUEIRÓS, JOSÉ MARIA EÇA DE. *See* EÇA DE QUEIRÓS, JOSÉ MARIA

QUEIROZ, RACHEL DE, CWAII IV-1237

Dôra, Doralina, CLCII II-418; MPII:AF I-445

Three Marias, The, CLCII IV-1557; MPII:AF IV-1648

QUENEAU, RAYMOND, CWAII IV-1239

Bark Tree, The, CLCII I-116; MPII:WF I-111

Sunday of Life, The, CLCII IV-1494; MPII:WF IV-1533

Zazie in the Metro, CLCII IV-1767; MPII:WF IV-1803

R

RAABE, WILHELM, CWAII IV-1241
Horacker, CLCII II-697; MPII:WF II-612
Tubby Schaumann, CLCII IV-1622; MPII:WF IV-1676
RABE, DAVID, CWAII IV-1243
Basic Training of Pavlo Hummel, The, CLCII I-122; MPII:D I-127
Hurlyburly, CLCII II-723; MPII:D II-794
Streamers, CLCII IV-1483; MPII:D IV-1496
RABELAIS, FRANÇOIS, CWA III-1455
Gargantua and Pantagruel, CLC I-393; MP IV-2208; MP:EF II-553
RABINOWITZ, SHOLOM. See ALEICHEM, SHOLOM
RACINE, JEAN BAPTISTE, CWA III-1458
Andromache, CLC I-41; MP I-219
Bérénice, CLC I-99; MP I-504
Britannicus, CLC I-125; MP II-662
Mithridate, CLC II-725; MP VII-3987
Phèdra, CLC II-867; MP VIII-4632
Plaideurs, Les, CLC II-891; MP VIII-4740
RADCLIFFE, MRS. ANN, CWA III-1460
Italian, The, CLC I-535; MP V-2948; MP:BF II-657
Mysteries of Udolpho, The, CLC II-753; MP VII-4115; MP:BF II-1015
Romance of the Forest, The, CLC II-984; MP X-5675; MP:BF III-1358
RALEIGH, SIR WALTER, CWA III-1462
Poetry of Raleigh, The, MP IX-5118
RAMÉE, MARIE LOUISE DE LA. See OUIDA
RAMUZ, CHARLES-FERDINAND, CWA III-1464
When the Mountain Fell, CLC II-1235; MP XII-7097; MP:EF III-1383
RANSOM, JOHN CROWE, CWA III-1465
New Criticism, The, MP VII-4171
Selected Poems, MP X-5899

RAO, RAJA, CWAII IV-1245
Kanthapura, CLCII II-813; MPII:BCF II-882
Serpent and the Rope, The, CLCII IV-1377; MPII:BCF IV-1501
RASPE, RUDOLF ERICH, CWA III-1467
Baron Münchausen's Narrative, CLC I-84; MP I-435; MP:EF I-101
RATTIGAN, TERENCE, CWAII IV-1247
Browning Version, The, CLCII I-207; MPII:D I-250
French Without Tears, CLCII II-547; MPII:D II-639
RAWLINGS, MARJORIE KINNAN, CWA III-1469
Yearling, The, CLC II-1272; MP XII-7286; MP:AF III-1459
READE, CHARLES, CWA III-1470
Cloister and the Hearth, The, CLC I-188; MP II-993; MP:BF I-225
Peg Woffington, CLC II-850; MP VIII-4562; MP:BF II-1175
REANEY, JAMES
Colours in the Dark, CLCII I-309; MPII:D I-382
Killdeer, The, CLCII II-825; MPII:D II-900
REED, ISHMAEL, CWAII IV-1249
Flight to Canada, CLCII II-522; MPII:AF II-551
Mumbo Jumbo, CLCII III-1055; MPII:AF III-1094
Yellow Back Radio Broke-Down, CLCII IV-1762; MPII:AF IV-1835
RÊGO, JOSÉ LINS DO. See LINS DO RÊGO, JOSÉ
REID, FORREST, CWA III-1472
Bracknels, The, CLC I-119; MP II-619; MP:BF I-124
REID, VICTOR STAFFORD
New Day, CLCII III-1087; MPII:BCF III-1193
REIZENSTEIN, ELMER LEOPOLD. See RICE, ELMER

REMARK, ERICH PAUL. *See*
REMARQUE, ERICH MARIA
REMARQUE, ERICH MARIA, CWA III-
1474
All Quiet on the Western Front, CLC I-
27; MP I-130; MP:EF I-23
RENAULT, MARY, CWA III-1476;
CWAII IV-1251
Bull from the Sea, The, CLCII II-831;
MPII:BCF II-920
Fire from Heaven, CLCII II-508;
MPII:BCF II-498
Funeral Games, CLCII II-557;
MPII:BCF II-561
King Must Die, The, CLCII II-831;
MPII:BCF II-920
Last of the Wine, The, MP VI-3271;
MP:BF II-784
Persian Boy, The, CLCII III-1195;
MPII:BCF III-1313
REXROTH, KENNETH, CWAII IV-1253
Autobiographical Novel, An, MPII:NF
I-104
REYES, ALFONSO, CWA III-1477
Visión de Anáhuac, MP XII-6961
REYES, NEFTALÍ RICARDO. *See*
NERUDA, PABLO
REYMONT, WŁADYSŁAW, CWA III-
1480
Peasants, The, CLC II-845; MP VIII-
4544; MP:EF III-977
RHYS, JEAN, CWAII IV-1256
Good Morning, Midnight, CLCII II-
612; MPII:BCF II-632
"Outside the Machine," MPII:SS IV-
1737
Wide Sargasso Sea, CLCII IV-1714;
MPII:BCF IV-1899
RIBMAN, RONALD, CWAII IV-1258
Ceremony of Innocence, The, CLCII I-
252; MPII:D I-299
Cold Storage, CLCII I-306; MPII:D I-
377
RICE, ELMER, CWA III-1482; CWAII
IV-1261

Adding Machine, The, CLCII I-14;
MPII:D I-11
Street Scene, CLC II-1090; MP XI-6304
RICHARDS, I. A., CWA III-1484
Principles of Literary Criticism, MP IX-
5334
RICHARDSON, DOROTHY M., CWA
III-1486
Pilgrimage, CLC II-880; MP VIII-4696;
MP:BF III-1222
RICHARDSON, HENRY HANDEL,
CWA III-1487
Fortunes of Richard Mahony, The, CLC
I-382; MP IV-2142; MP:BF I-458
RICHARDSON, SAMUEL, CWA III-
1488
Clarissa, CLC I-183; MP II-976;
MP:BF I-211
Pamela, CLC II-832; MP VIII-4472;
MP:BF II-1149
Sir Charles Grandison, CLC II-1041;
MP X-6056; MP:BF III-1459
RICHLER, MORDECAI, CWAII IV-1264
Apprenticeship of Duddy Kravitz, The,
CLCII I-63; MPII:BCF I-63
St. Urbain's Horseman, CLCII III-1330;
MPII:BCF III-1440
RICHTER, CONRAD, CWA III-1491
Fields, The, CLC I-366; MP IV-2046;
MP:AF I-382
Sea of Grass, The, CLC II-1014; MP
X-5861; MP:AF III-1102
Simple Honorable Man, A, MP X-6050;
MP:AF III-1168
Town, The, CLC II-1150; MP XI-6628;
MP:AF III-1308
Trees, The, CLC II-1154; MP XI-6683;
MP:AF III-1326
Waters of Kronos, The, MP XII-7049;
MP:AF III-1409
RICHTER, JOHANN PAUL
FRIEDRICH. *See* JEAN PAUL
RICKETTS, EDWARD F., *and* JOHN
STEINBECK
Sea of Cortez, MPII:NF III-1309

RIESMAN, DAVID
Lonely Crowd, The, MPII:NF II-856
RIGGS, LYNN, CWA III-1494
Green Grow the Lilacs, CLC I-425; MP
IV-2382
RILKE, RAINER MARIA, CWA III-
1495; CWAII IV-1266
Duino Elegies, MP III-1669
Letters on Cézanne, MPII:NF II-812
Sonnets to Orpheus, MP XI-6175
RIMBAUD, ARTHUR, CWA III-1498
Season in Hell, A, MP X-5876
RIVERA, TOMÁS, CWAII IV-1269
". . . and the earth did not part,"
MPII:SS I-89
ROA BASTOS, AUGUSTO
Son of Man, CLCII IV-1444; MPII:AF
IV-1481
ROBBE-GRILLET, ALAIN, CWAII IV-
1271
Erasers, The, CLCII II-467; MPII:WF
I-430
In the Labyrinth, CLCII II-750;
MPII:WF II-686
Jealousy, CLCII II-790; MPII:WF II-
755
ROBERTS, ELIZABETH MADOX, CWA
III-1500
Great Meadow, The, CLC I-422; MP
IV-2363; MP:AF I-501
My Heart and My Flesh, CLCII III-
1062; MPII:AF III-1100
Time of Man, The, CLC II-1132; MP
XI-6545; MP:AF III-1289
ROBERTS, KENNETH, CWA III-1503
Northwest Passage, MP VII-4247;
MP:AF II-852
ROBERTSON, ETHEL FLORENCE
RICHARDSON. See
RICHARDSON, HENRY HANDEL
ROBERTSON, THOMAS WILLIAM,
CWA III-1505
Caste, CLC I-154; MP II-816
ROBINSON, EDWIN ARLINGTON,
CWA III-1506

Man Against the Sky, The, MP VI-3664
Tristram, MP XI-6709
ROBINSON, HENRY CRABB, CWA III-
1509
Diary of Henry Crabb Robinson, MP
III-1509
ROCHEFOUCAULD, FRANÇOIS LA.
See LA ROCHEFOUCAULD,
FRANÇOIS
RODRIGUEZ, RICHARD
Hunger of Memory, MPII:NF II-668
ROETHKE, THEODORE, CWA III-1511
Poetry of Roethke, The, MP IX-5126
ROGERS, SAMUEL SHEPARD. See
SHEPARD, SAM
ROJAS, FERNANDO DE, CWA III-1512
Celestina, CLC I-163; MP II-865;
MP:EF I-201
ROLFE, FREDERICK WILLIAM. See
CORVO, BARON
ROLLAND, ROMAIN, CWA III-1513
Jean-Christophe, CLC I-543; MP V-
2988; MP:EF II-714
RÖLVAAG, O. E., CWA III-1516
Giants in the Earth, CLC I-400; MP IV-
2255; MP:AF I-440
Peder Victorious, CLC II-847; MP
VIII-4549; MP:AF II-914
ROMERO, JOSÉ RUBÉN
Futile Life of Pito Perez, The, CLCII
II-559; MPII:AF II-597
RONSARD, PIERRE DE, CWA III-1518
Poetry of Ronsard, The, MP IX-5131
ROOKE, LEON
Shakespeare's Dog, CLCII IV-1388;
MPII:BCF IV-1523
ROREM, NED, CWAII IV-1273
Paris and New York Diaries of Ned
Rorem, The, MPII:NF III-1124
RORTY, RICHARD, CWAII IV-1275
Philosophy and the Mirror of Nature,
MPII:NF III-1158
ROSENFELD, ISAAC, CWAII IV-1277
"King Solomon," MPII:SS III-1262
ROSS, ALAN
Blindfold Games, MPII:NF I-172

ROSS, SINCLAIR
As for Me and My House, CLCII I-72;
MPII:BCF I-72
Sawbones Memorial, CLCII III-1342;
MPII:BCF III-1455
ROSSETTI, CHRISTINA, CWA III-1519
Poetry of Christina Rossetti, The, MP
VIII-4860
ROSSETTI, DANTE GABRIEL, CWA
III-1521
Poetry of Dante Gabriel Rossetti, The,
MP VIII-4893
ROSTAND, EDMOND, CWA III-1523
Cyrano de Bergerac, CLC I-233; MP
III-1262
L'Aiglon, CLC I-590; MP VI-3222
ROTH, HENRY, CWA III-1525
Call It Sleep, MP II-744; MP:AF I-162
ROTH, JOSEPH, CWAII IV-1279
Job, CLCII II-792; MPII:WF II-760
ROTH, PHILIP, CWAII IV-1282
Anatomy Lesson, The, CLCII I-42
"Conversion of the Jews, The,"
MPII:SS I-429
"Defender of the Faith," MPII:SS II-550
Facts, The, MPII:NF II-492
Ghost Writer, The, CLCII II-580
Great American Novel, The, CLCII II-
626; MPII:AF II-666
Letting Go, CLCII II-878; MPII:AF III-
883
Portnoy's Complaint, CLCII III-1224;
MPII:AF III-1281
Prague Orgy, The, CLCII III-1229
Zuckerman Bound, MPII:AF IV-1856
Zuckerman Unbound, CLCII IV-1774
ROUSSEAU, JEAN-JACQUES, CWA III-
1527
Confessions, MP II-1060
Discourse on the Origin of Inequality,
MP III-1522
Émile, CLC I-322; MP III-1755;
MP:EF I-476
New Héloïse, The, CLC II-764; MP
VII-4177; MP:EF II-928

ROWLEY, WILLIAM, and THOMAS
MIDDLETON
Changeling, The, CLC I-167; MP II-
885
ROWLEY, WILLIAM, JOHN FORD, and
THOMAS MIDDLETON
Spanish Gipsy, The, MP XI-6208
RUIZ DE ALARCÓN, JUAN, CWA III-
1530
Truth Suspected, CLC II-1166; MP XI-
6740
RULFO, JUAN, CWA III-1531
Pedro Páramo, MP VIII-4552; MP:AF
II-918
RUSHDIE, SALMAN, CWAII IV-1284
Midnight's Children, CLCII III-1007;
MPII:BCF III-1097
Shame, CLCII IV-1389; MPII:BCF IV-
1528
RUSHFORTH, PETER
Kindergarten, CLCII II-829; MPII:BCF
II-909
RUSKIN, JOHN, CWA III-1533
King of the Golden River, The, CLC I-
574; MP VI-3153; MP:BF II-747
Stones of Venice, The, MP XI-6262
RUSS, JOANNA, CWAII IV-1287
Female Man, The, CLCII II-496;
MPII:AF II-532
RUSSELL, GEORGE WILLIAM. See Æ
RUSSELL, W. CLARK, CWA III-1535
Wreck of the Grosvenor, The, CLC II-
1269; MP XII-7278; MP:BF III-1772
RYBCZYNSKI, WITOLD, CWAII IV-
1289
Home, MPII:NF II-651
RYDBERG, VIKTOR, CWA III-1536
Last Athenian, The, CLC I-592; MP
VI-3243; MP:EF II-750
RYGA, GEORGE
Ecstasy of Rita Joe, The, CLCII II-443;
MPII:D II-540

S

SÁBATO, ERNESTO, CWAII IV-1291
On Heroes and Tombs, CLCII III-1142;
MPII:AF III-1188
Outsider, The, CLCII III-1167;
MPII:AF III-1232
SACHS, HANS, CWA III-1537
Wandering Scholar from Paradise, The,
CLC II-1219; MP XII-7014
SACKLER, HOWARD
Great White Hope, The, CLCII II-630;
MPII:D II-706
SACKS, OLIVER, CWAII IV-1293
Awakenings, MPII:NF I-132
SACKVILLE, THOMAS, and THOMAS
NORTON, CWA II-1319
Gorboduc, CLC I-412; MP IV-2332
SADE, THE MARQUIS DE, CWA III-
1538
SAGE, ALAIN RENÉ LE. See
LE SAGE, ALAIN RENÉ
SAID, EDWARD W., CWAII IV-1295
Orientalism, MPII:NF III-1102
SAIKAKU. See IHARA, SAIKAKU
ST. AUGUSTINE. See AUGUSTINE, ST.
ST. OMER, GARTH
Room on the Hill, A, CLCII III-1312;
MPII:BCF II1435
ST. VINCENT MILLAY, EDNA. See
MILLAY, EDNA ST. VINCENT
SAINTE-BEAUVE, CHARLES
AUGUSTIN, CWA III-1540
Monday Conversations, MP VII-4025
Volupté, CLC II-1215; MP XII-6983;
MP:EF III-1360
SAINT-EXUPÉRY, ANTOINE DE,
CWA III-1542
Night Flight, CLC II-777; MP VII-
4212; MP:EF II-942
Wind, Sand and Stars, MP XII-7163;
MP:EF III-1400
Wisdom of the Sands, The, MP XII-
7189
SAINZ, GUSTAVO
Gazapo, CLCII II-572; MPII:AF II-602

SAKI, CWA III-1544
"Interlopers, The," MPII:SS III-1187
"Laura," MPII:SS III-1305
"Open Window, The," MPII:SS IV-
1716
Short Stories of Saki, The, MP X-6027;
MP:BF III-1445
"Sredni Vashtar," MPII:SS V-2217
Unbearable Bassington, The, CLC II-
1177; MP XII-6804; MP:BF III-1622
SALINGER, J. D., CWA III-1546;
CWAII IV-1297
Catcher in the Rye, The, CLCII I-244;
MPII:AF I-259
"De Daumier-Smith's Blue Period,"
MPII:SS II-546
"For Esmé--with Love and Squalor,"
MPII:SS II-809
Franny and Zooey, MP IV-2157;
MP:AF I-418
"Perfect Day for Bananafish, A,"
MPII:SS IV-1800
"Uncle Wiggily in Connecticut,"
MPII:SS VI-2457
SALTEN, FELIX, CWA III-1548
Bambi, CLC I-78; MP I-415; MP:EF I-
92
SALZMANN, SIEGMUND. See
SALTEN, FELIX
SAMSONOV, LEV. See MAXIMOV,
VLADIMIR
SÁNCHEZ, FLORENCIO, CWA III-1549
Gringa, La, CLC I-429; MP IV-2401
SANCHEZ, SONIA, CWAII IV-1299
"After Saturday Nite Comes Sunday,"
MPII:SS I-38
SAND, GEORGE, CWA III-1551
Consuelo, CLC I-199; MP II-1106;
MP:EF I-253
Indiana, CLC I-523; MP V-2880;
MP:EF II-707
SANDBURG, CARL, CWA III-1553
Abraham Lincoln, MP I-11
Chicago Poems, MP II-918

People, Yes, The, MP VIII-4593
Remembrance Rock, CLC II-955; MP
IX-5505; MP:AF III-1032
SANDOZ, MARI, CWAII IV-1302
Cheyenne Autumn, CLCII I-267;
MPII:AF I-285
SANSOM, WILLIAM, CWAII IV-1304
"How Claeys Died," MPII:SS III-1056
"Vertical Ladder, The," MPII:SS VI-
2493
"Wall, The," MPII:SS VI-2530
SANTAYANA, GEORGE, CWA III-1556
Last Puritan, The, CLC I-598; MP VI-
3274; MP:AF II-645
Skepticism and Animal Faith, MP X-
5831
SANTŌ KYŌDEN, CWA III-1559
Inazuma-byōshi, CLC I-520; MP V-
2864; MP:EF II-691
SAPPHO, CWA III-1561
Ode to Aphrodite, MP VII-4273
SARDUY, SEVERO
From Cuba with a Song, CLCII II-550;
MPII:AF II-581
SARGESON, FRANK, CWAII IV-1306
I for One . . ., CLCII II-726;
MPII:BCF II-772
Joy of the Worm, CLCII II-803;
MPII:BCF II-866
SAROYAN, WILLIAM, CWA III-1562;
CWAII IV-1308
"Daring Young Man on the Flying
Trapeze, The," MPII:SS II-484
Human Comedy, The, CLC I-498; MP
V-2766; MP:AF II-581
"Parsley Garden, The," MPII:SS IV-
1771
"Summer of the Beautiful White Horse,
The," MPII:SS V-2275
Time of Your Life, The, CLCII IV-
1571; MPII:D IV-1585
SARRAUTE, NATHALIE, CWAII IV-
1311
"Fools Say," CLCII II-530; MPII:WF
II-486

Planetarium, The, CLCII III-1211;
MPII:WF III-1203
Portrait of a Man Unknown, CLCII III-
1226; MPII:WF III-1225
SARTON, MAY, CWAII IV-1313
Journal of a Solitude, MPII:NF II-756
Mrs. Stevens Hears the Mermaids
Singing, CLCII III-1025; MPII:AF
III-1028
Small Room, The, CLCII IV-1427;
MPII:AF IV-1454
SARTRE, JEAN-PAUL, CWA III-1564;
CWAII IV-1315
Flies, The, MP IV-2089
Nausea, CLC II-761; MP VII-4157;
MP:EF II-924
No Exit, CLCII III-1103; MPII:D III-
1148
Roads to Freedom, The, CLCII III-
1303; MPII:WF III-1288
"Wall, The," MPII:SS VI-2534
Words, The, MPII:NF IV-1714
SASSOON, SIEGFRIED, CWA III-1566
Memoirs of a Fox-Hunting Man, CLC
I-691; MP VII-3830; MP:BF II-916
Memoirs of an Infantry Officer, CLC I-
693; MP VII-3842; MP:BF II-924
SAUSER, FRÉDÉRIC LOUIS. See
CENDRARS, BLAISE
SAUSSURE, FERDINAND DE, CWAII
IV-1318
Course in General Linguistics, MPII:NF
I-288
SAYERS, DOROTHY L., CWAII IV-
1320
Gaudy Night, CLCII II-571; MPII:BCF
I-577
Nine Tailors, The, CLCII III-1100;
MPII:BCF III-1208
SCHELL, JONATHAN
Fate of the Earth, The, MPII:NF II-502
SCHILLER, FRIEDRICH VON, CWA
III-1568
Don Carlos, CLC I-289; MP III-1582
Wallenstein, CLC II-1216; MP XII-
7001

William Tell, CLC II-1246; MP XII-7156

SCHMITZ, ETTORE. *See* SVEVO, ITALO

SCHNEIDER, PETER
Wall Jumper, The, CLCII IV-1676; MPII:WF IV-1720

SCHNITZLER, ARTHUR, CWAII IV-1323
Ronde, La, CLCII III-1312; MPII:D IV-1372

SCHOLEM, GERSHOM
From Berlin to Jerusalem, MPII:NF II-534

SCHOPENHAUER, ARTHUR, CWA III-1571
World as Will and Idea, The, MP XII-7259

SCHREINER, OLIVE, CWA III-1573
Story of an African Farm, The, CLC II-1084; MP XI-6272; MP:EF III-1227

SCHULZ, BRUNO, CWAII IV-1326
"Cinnamon Shops," MPII:SS I-396
"Sanatorium Under the Sign of the Hourglass," MPII:SS V-2016
"Street of Crocodiles, The," MPII:SS V-2256

SCHUMACHER, E. F., CWAII IV-1328
Small Is Beautiful, MPII:NF IV-1372

SCHWARTZ, DELMORE, CWAII IV-1331
"America! America!" MPII:SS I-81
"In Dreams Begin Responsibilities," MPII:SS III-1134

SCHWARZ-BART, ANDRÉ, CWAII IV-1333
Last of the Just, The, CLCII II-856; MPII:WF II-816

SCHWEITZER, ALBERT
Out of My Life and Thought, MP VIII-4449

SCIASCIA, LEONARDO, CWAII IV-1335
Equal Danger, CLCII II-464; MPII:WF I-425

Man's Blessing, A, CLCII III-966; MPII:WF III-939

SCOTT, EVELYN
Wave, The, CLCII IV-1695; MPII:AF IV-1769

SCOTT, MICHAEL, CWA III-1574
Tom Cringle's Log, CLC II-1142; MP XI-6594; MP:BF III-1567

SCOTT, PAUL
Raj Quartet, The, CLCII III-1263; MPII:BCF III-1376

SCOTT, CAPTAIN ROBERT FALCON, CWA III-1575
Scott's Last Expedition, MP X-5855

SCOTT, SIR WALTER, CWA III-1577
Antiquary, The, CLC I-49; MP I-254; MP:BF I-58
Bride of Lammermoor, The, CLC I-122; MP II-640; MP:BF I-134
Fair Maid of Perth, The, CLC I-351; MP IV-1958; MP:BF I-400
Fortunes of Nigel, The, CLC I-380; MP IV-2137; MP:BF I-452
Guy Mannering, CLC I-433; MP IV-2429; MP:BF I-507
Heart of Midlothian, The, CLC I-449; MP V-2510; MP:BF I-544
Ivanhoe, CLC I-536; MP V-2959; MP:BF II-665
Kenilworth, CLC I-566; MP VI-3123; MP:BF II-735
Lady of the Lake, The, CLC I-588; MP VI-3213
Lay of the Last Minstrel, The, CLC I-603; MP VI-3299
Marmion, CLC I-672; MP VII-3739
Old Mortality, CLC II-805; MP VIII-4334; MP:BF II-1091
Quentin Durward, CLC II-931; MP IX-5398; MP:BF III-1282
Rob Roy, CLC II-977; MP X-5638; MP:BF III-1331
St. Ronan's Well, CLC II-1000; MP X-5761; MP:BF III-1389
Talisman, The, CLC II-1102; MP XI-6387; MP:BF III-1490

MASTERPLOTS

"Two Drovers, The," MPII:SS VI-2432
Waverley, CLC II-1226; MP XII-7052;
MP:BF III-1710
Woodstock, CLC II-1265; MP XII-
7251; MP:BF III-1768
SCUDÉRY, MADELEINE DE, CWA III-
1580
Artamène, CLC I-63; MP I-322;
MP:EF I-64
SEARLE, JOHN
Minds, Brains, and Science, MPII:NF
III-965
SELVON, SAMUEL
Brighter Sun, A, CLCII I-203;
MPII:BCF I-185
Lonely Londoners, The, CLCII III-905;
MPII:BCF III-993
SEMBÈNE, OUSMANE, CWAII IV-1337
God's Bits of Wood, CLCII II-601;
MPII:WF II-553
Xala, CLCII IV-1759; MPII:WF IV-
1793
SEMPRUN, JORGE
Long Voyage, The, CLCII III-911;
MPII:WF II-878
What a Beautiful Sunday! CLCII IV-
1704; MPII:WF IV-1739
SENECA, LUCIUS ANNAEUS, CWA
III-1581
Philosophical Treatises and Moral
Reflections of Seneca, MP VIII-4656
Thyestes, CLC II-1131; MP XI-6535
SETTLE, MARY LEE, CWAII IV-1339
Beulah Quintet, The, MPII:AF I-151
Killing Ground, The, CLCII II-827
Know Nothing, CLCII II-839
O Beulah Land, CLCII III-1122
Prisons, CLCII III-1237
Scapegoat, The, CLCII III-1343
SÉVIGNÉ, MADAME MARIE DE,
CWA III-1583
Letters of Madame de Sévigné, The,
MP VI-3353
SEXTUS PROPERTIUS. See
PROPERTIUS, SEXTUS

SHAFFER, ANTHONY
Sleuth, CLCII IV-1424; MPII:D IV-
1477
SHAFFER, PETER, CWAII IV-1342
Amadeus, CLCII I-33; MPII:D I-37
Equus, CLCII II-466; MPII:D II-579
Royal Hunt of the Sun, The, CLCII III-
1316; MPII:D IV-1384
SHAKESPEARE, WILLIAM, CWA III-
1585
All's Well That Ends Well, CLC I-29;
MP I-143
Antony and Cleopatra, CLC I-50; MP I-
258
As You Like It, CLC I-66; MP I-334
Comedy of Errors, CLC I-192; MP II-
1037
Coriolanus, CLC I-201; MP II-1116
Cymbeline, CLC I-231; MP III-1255
Hamlet, Prince of Denmark, CLC I-
437; MP V-2457
Henry the Eighth, CLC I-460; MP V-
2555
Henry the Fifth, CLC I-462; MP V-
2558
Henry the Fourth, CLC I-464; MP V-
2562; MP V-2567
Henry the Fourth, Part One, CLC I-
464; MP V-2562
Henry the Fourth, Part Two, CLC I-
464; MP V-2567
Henry the Sixth, CLC I-466, MP V-
2572; MP V-2576; MP V-2580
Henry the Sixth, Part One, CLC I-466;
MP V-2572
Henry the Sixth, Part Two, CLC I-466;
MP V-2576
Henry the Sixth, Part Three, CLC I-
466; MP V-2580
Julius Caesar, CLC I-559; MP VI-3089
King John, CLC I-570; MP VI-3144
King Lear, CLC I-572; MP VI-3148
Love's Labour's Lost, CLC I-634; MP
VI-3534
Macbeth, CLC I-642; MP VI-3589

232

Measure for Measure, CLC I-685; MP VII-3793

Merchant of Venice, The, CLC I-695; MP VII-3855

Merry Wives of Windsor, The, CLC I-697; MP VII-3860

Midsummer Night's Dream, A, CLC II-703; MP VII-3885

Much Ado about Nothing, CLC II-746; MP VII-4090

Othello, CLC II-825; MP VIII-4431

Pericles, Prince of Tyre, CLC II-861; MP VIII-4603

Rape of Lucrece, The, CLC II-940; MP IX-5432

Richard the Second, CLC II-965; MP X-5580

Richard the Third, CLC II-967; MP X-5585

Romeo and Juliet, CLC II-990; MP X-5700

Sonnets of Shakespeare, The, MP XI-6170

Taming of the Shrew, The, CLC II-1106; MP XI-6401

Tempest, The, CLC II-1112; MP XI-6427

Timon of Athens, CLC II-1133; MP XI-6549

Titus Andronicus, CLC II-1135; MP XI-6565

Troilus and Cressida, CLC II-1162; MP XI-6720

Twelfth Night, CLC II-1168; MP XII-6753

Two Gentlemen of Verona, CLC II-1170; MP XII-6772

Venus and Adonis, CLC II-1196; MP XII-6893

Winter's Tale, The, CLC II-1251; MP XII-7181

SHAKESPEARE, WILLIAM, and JOHN FLETCHER

Two Noble Kinsmen, The, CLC II-1172; MP XII-6775

SHALAMOV, VARLAM, CWAII IV-1345

"Child's Drawings, A," MPII:SS I-384

"Snake Charmer, The," MPII:SS V-2150

SHAMS UD-DIN MOHAMMED. See HĀFIZ

SHANGE, NTOZAKE, CWAII IV-1347

for colored girls who have considered suicide/when the rainbow is enuf, CLCII II-531; MPII:D II-627

Photograph: Lovers in Motion, A, CLCII III-1204; MPII:D III-1241

SHAPIRO, KARL, CWA III-1589

Poetry of Shapiro, The, MP IX-5133

SHAW, GEORGE BERNARD, CWA III-1591; CWAII IV-1349

Arms and the Man, CLCII I-67; MPII:D I-88

Back to Methuselah, CLC I-75; MP I-412

Caesar and Cleopatra, CLC I-138; MP II-728

Candida, CLC I-143; MP II-757

Heartbreak House, CLC I-451; CLCII II-669; MP V-2520; MPII:D II-752

John Bull's Other Island, CLCII II-794; MPII:D III-871

Major Barbara, CLC I-656; MP VI-3652

Man and Superman, CLC I-658; MP VI-3667

Mrs. Warren's Profession, CLCII III-1026; MPII:D III-1095

Pygmalion, CLC II-928; MP IX-5385

Saint Joan, CLC II-998; MP X-5755

SHAW, IRWIN, CWAII IV-1352

"Eighty-Yard Run, The," MPII:SS II-677

"Girls in Their Summer Dresses, The," MPII:SS II-853

"Sailor Off the Bremen," MPII:SS V-2005

Young Lions, The, CLCII IV-1765; MPII:AF IV-1846

SHAWN, WALLACE
Aunt Dan and Lemon, CLCII I-86;
MPII:D I-99
SHAWN, WALLACE, and ANDRÉ
GREGORY
My Dinner with André, CLCII III-
1061; MPII:D III-1121
SHELLEY, MARY WOLLSTONECRAFT
GODWIN, CWA III-1596
Frankenstein, CLC I-385; MP IV-2154;
MP:BF I-466
SHELLEY, PERCY BYSSHE, CWA III-
1598
Cenci, The, CLC I-164; MP II-869
Defence of Poetry, A, MP III-1423
Prometheus Unbound, CLC II-925; MP
IX-5365
SHEPARD, SAM, CWAII IV-1354
Buried Child, CLCII I-213; MPII:D I-
260
Curse of the Starving Class, CLCII I-
356; MPII:D I-420
Fool for Love, CLCII II-529; MPII:D
II-622
Geography of a Horse Dreamer, CLCII
II-577; MPII:D II-666
Lie of the Mind, A, CLCII II-879;
MPII:D III-964
Tooth of Crime, The, CLCII IV-1589;
MPII:D IV-1607
True West, CLCII IV-1621; MPII:D
IV-1660
SHERIDAN, RICHARD BRINSLEY,
CWA III-1601
Critic, The, CLC I-224; MP II-1214
Rivals, The, CLC II-974; MP X-5624
School for Scandal, The, CLC II-1011;
MP X-5838
SHERRIFF, ROBERT C., CWA III-1604
Journey's End, CLC I-556; MP VI-
3071
SHERWOOD, ROBERT E., CWA III-
1605
Abe Lincoln in Illinois, CLC I-1; MP I-
4

Petrified Forest, The, CLCII III-1200;
MPII:D III-1225
SHIH NAI-AN, CWA III-1607
All Men Are Brothers, CLC I-26; MP
I-125; MP:EF I-17
SHIRLEY, JAMES, CWA III-1608
Hyde Park, CLC I-503; MP V-2787
Traitor, The, CLC II-1151; MP XI-
6643
SHKLOVSKY, VIKTOR, CWAII IV-1357
Sentimental Journey, A, CLCII III-
1372; MPII:WF IV-1382
Third Factory, CLCII IV-1546;
MPII:WF IV-1584
Zoo, CLCII IV-1771; MPII:WF IV-
1814
SHOLOKHOV, MIKHAIL, CWA III-1609
And Quiet Flows the Don, CLC I-38;
MP I-202; MP:EF I-31
Don Flows Home to the Sea, The, CLC
I-290; MP III-1585; MP:EF I-426
SHORTHOUSE, JOSEPH HENRY, CWA
III-1611
John Inglesant, CLC I-551; MP V-3026;
MP:BF II-695
SHOSTAKOVICH, DMITRI
Testimony, MPII:NF IV-1485
SHU CH'ING-CH'UN. See LAO SHE
SHUDRAKA, CWA III-1612
Little Clay Cart, The, CLC I-617; MP
VI-3444
SHŪJI', TSUSHIMA. See DAZAI,
OSAMU
SIDNEY, SIR PHILIP, CWA III-1613
Arcadia, CLC I-57; MP I-293; MP:BF
I-62
Defence of Poesie, MP III-1420
Poetry of Sidney, The, MP IX-5136
SIENKIEWICZ, HENRYK, CWA III-
1615
Quo Vadis? CLC II-933; MP IX-5404;
MP:EF III-1050
With Fire and Sword, CLC II-1253; MP
XII-7195; MP:EF III-1404
SIERRA, GREGORIO MARTÍNEZ. See
MARTÍNEZ SIERRA, GREGORIO

SILKO, LESLIE MARMON, CWAII IV-1361
"Lullaby," MPII:SS IV-1416
Storyteller, MPII:NF IV-1442
"Yellow Woman," MPII:SS VI-2724
SILLANPÄÄ, FRANS EEMIL, CWA III-1617
Meek Heritage, CLC I-687; MP VII-3804; MP:EF II-849
SILLITOE, ALAN, CWAII IV-1363
Down from the Hill, CLCII II-420; MPII:BCF I-393
"Loneliness of the Long-Distance Runner, The," MPII:SS IV-1391
Lost Flying Boat, The, CLCII III-918; MPII:BCF III-1008
"Ragman's Daughter, The," MPII:SS V-1876
Saturday Night and Sunday Morning, CLCII III-1339; MPII:BCF III-1449
"Sniper, The," MPII:SS V-2158
Widower's Son, The, CLCII IV-1715; MPII:BCF IV-1695
SILONE, IGNAZIO, CWA III-1618
Bread and Wine, CLC I-122; MP II-636; MP:EF I-131
Fontamara, MP IV-2104; MP:EF II-530
SIMENON, GEORGES, CWAII IV-1366
Blue Room, The, CLCII I-177; MPII:WF I-164
Man Who Watched the Trains Go By, The, CLCII III-959; MPII:WF III-925
Snow Was Black, The, CLCII IV-1434; MPII:WF IV-1481
Watchmaker of Everton, The, CLCII IV-1686; MPII:WF IV-1725
SIMMS, WILLIAM GILMORE, CWA III-1620
Yemassee, The, CLC II-1274; MP XII-7295; MP:AF III-1463
SIMON, CLAUDE, CWAII IV-1370
Battle of Pharsalus, The, CLCII I-125; MPII:WF I-131
Flanders Road, The, CLCII II-520; MPII:WF II-475

Triptych, CLCII IV-1613; MPII:WF IV-1666
Wind, The, CLCII IV-1717; MPII:WF IV-1750
SIMON, NEIL, CWAII IV-1373
Barefoot in the Park, CLCII I-115; MPII:D I-122
Biloxi Blues, CLCII I-155; MPII:D I-175
Brighton Beach Memoirs, CLCII I-205; MPII:D I-243
Last of the Red-Hot Lovers, CLCII II-857; MPII:D III-938
Odd Couple, The, CLCII III-1130; MPII:D III-1158
SINCLAIR, MAY, CWA III-1622
"Bambino, The," MPII:SS I-151
Divine Fire, The, CLC I-275; MP III-1534; MP:BF I-329
Mary Olivier, CLCII III-982
Three Sisters, The, CLCII IV-1558
SINCLAIR, UPTON, CWA III-1624
Jungle, The, CLC I-560; MP VI-3094; MP:AF II-623
SINGER, ISAAC BASHEVIS, CWAII IV-1375
"Admirer, The," MPII:SS I-16
Enemies, CLCII II-458; MPII:AF II-476; MPII:WF I-409
"Friend of Kafka, A," MPII:SS II-817
"Gentleman from Cracow, The," MPII:SS II-831
"Gimpel the Fool," MPII:SS II-850
In My Father's Court, MPII:NF II-719
Little Boy in Search of God, A, MPII:NF II-835
Lost in America, MPII:NF II-835
Magician of Lublin, The, CLCII III-944; MPII:AF III-954; MPII:WF III-905
"Moon and Madness," MPII:SS IV-1528
"Short Friday," MPII:SS V-2084
Shosha, CLCII IV-1396; MPII:AF IV-1417; MPII:WF IV-1404

Slave, The, CLCII IV-1422; MPII:AF
IV-1443; MPII:WF IV-1453
"Spinoza of Market Street, The,"
MPII:SS V-2202
"Yentl the Yeshiva Boy," MPII:SS VI-
2729
Young Man in Search of Love, A,
MPII:NF II-835
SINGER, ISRAEL JOSHUA, CWA III-
1627
Brothers Ashkenazi, The, CLC I-128;
MP II-684; MP:EF I-140
SINGMASTER, ELSIE, CWA III-1628
Gettysburg, MP IV-2246; MP:AF I-436
High Wind Rising, A, CLC I-472; MP
V-2609; MP:AF II-551
I Speak for Thaddeus Stevens, MP V-
2806
SINYAVSKY, ANDREI, CWAII IV-1378
Goodnight! CLCII-617
"Graphomaniacs," MPII:SS II-922
"Icicle, The," MPII:SS III-1106
Makepeace Experiment, The, CLCII III-
947; MPII:WF III-909
"Pkhentz," MPII:SS IV-1824
Spokoinoi nochi, MPII:WF IV-1524
Trial Begins, The, CLCII IV-1610;
MPII:WF IV-1656
Voice from the Chorus, A, MPII:NF
IV-1646
SITWELL, EDITH, CWA III-1631
Poetry of Edith Sitwell, The, MP IX-
4920
SKELTON, JOHN, CWA III-1633
Poetry of Skelton, The, MP IX-5141
ŠKVORECKÝ, JOSEF, CWAII IV-1381
Bass Saxophone, The, CLCII I-123;
MPII:WF I-126
Cowards, The, CLCII I-349; MPII:WF
I-341
Engineer of Human Souls, The, CLCII
II-460; MPII:WF I-414
SMART, CHRISTOPHER, CWA III-1635
Poetry of Smart, The, MP IX-5146

SMEDLEY, AGNES, CWAII IV-1383
Daughter of Earth, CLCII I-368;
MPII:AF I-373
SMITH, ADAM, CWA III-1637
Wealth of Nations, The, MP XII-7070
SMITH, BETTY, CWA III-1639
Tree Grows in Brooklyn, A, CLC II-
1152; MP XI-6672; MP:AF III-1322
SMITH, HOMER W., CWA III-1640
Kamongo, MP VI-3115; MP:AF II-630
SMITH, LULA CARSON. See
McCULLERS, CARSON
SMOLLETT, TOBIAS, CWA III-1642
Humphry Clinker, CLC I-499; MP V-
2769; MP:BF II-621
Peregrine Pickle, CLC II-859; MP VIII-
4599; MP:BF II-1185
Roderick Random, CLC II-979; MP X-
5656; MP:BF III-1347
SNORRI STURLUSON, CWA III-1644
Heimskringla, The, CLC I-456; MP V-
2537; MP:EF II-623
SNOW, C. P., CWA III-1646; CWAII IV-
1385
Affair, The, MP I-56; MP:BF I-11
Conscience of the Rich, The, MP II-
1091; MP:BF I-242
Masters, The, MP VII-3768; MP:BF II-
892
Strangers and Brothers, CLCII IV-1480;
MPII:BCF IV-1619
SOCRATES, CWA III-1648
SOKOLOV, SASHA, CWAII IV-1388
School for Fools, A, CLCII III-1347;
MPII:WF III-1356
SOLZHENITSYN, ALEKSANDR, CWA
III-1651; CWAII IV-1391
August 1914, CLCII I-84; MPII:WF I-
90
Cancer Ward, CLCII I-228; MPII:WF
I-205
First Circle, The, CLCII II-512;
MPII:WF II-465
Gulag Archipelago, 1918-1956, The,
MPII:NF II-617

"Matryona's House," MPII:SS IV-1480

Oak and the Calf, The, MPII:NF III-1046

Oktiabr shestnadtsatogo, CLCII III-1135; MPII:WF III-1134

One Day in the Life of Ivan Denisovich, CLCII III-1147; MPII:WF III-1152

SONTAG, SUSAN, CWAII IV-1394

Against Interpretation and Other Essays, MPII:NF I-19

Illness as Metaphor, MPII:NF II-689

SOPHOCLES, CWA III-1653

Ajax, CLC I-16; MP I-77

Antigone, CLC I-48; MP I-250

Oedipus at Colonus, CLC II-792; MP VII-4280

Oedipus Tyrannus, CLC II-793; MP VII-4284

Philoctetes, CLC II-870; MP VIII-4647

Women of Trachis, CLC II-1262; CLCII IV-1736; MP XII-7242; MPII:D IV-1757

SŌSEKI. See NATSUME, SŌSEKI

SOUTHEY, ROBERT, CWA III-1656

Life of Nelson, MP VI-3403

SOYINKA, WOLE, CWAII IV-1396

Aké, MPII:NF I-24

Dance of the Forests, A, CLCII I-362; MPII:D II-437

Death and the King's Horseman, CLCII I-377; MPII:D II-463

Interpreters, The, CLCII II-770; MPII:BCF II-836

Lion and the Jewel, The, CLCII III-893; MPII:D III-981

Madmen and Specialists, CLCII III-942; MPII:D III-1023

Man Died, The, MPII:NF III-889

Road, The, CLCII III-1302; MPII:D IV-1356

Season of Anomy, CLCII III-1362; MPII:BCF III-1482

SPARK, MURIEL, CWA III-1658; CWAII IV-1398

Abbess of Crewe, The, CLCII I-1; MPII:BCF I-6

Bachelors, The, MP I-409; MP:BF I-75

Ballad of Peckham Rye, The, CLCII I-108; MPII:BCF I-91

Comforters, The, CLCII I-312; MPII:BCF I-293

"Father's Daughters, The," MPII:SS II-767

Loitering with Intent, CLCII III-903; MPII:BCF III-989

Mandelbaum Gate, The, CLCII III-964; MPII:BCF III-1057

Memento Mori, MP VII-3820; MP:BF II-908

"Portobello Road, The," MPII:SS IV-1831

Prime of Miss Jean Brodie, The, CLCII III-1235; MPII:BCF III-1340

Takeover, The, CLCII IV-1513; MPII:BCF IV-1677

SPENDER, STEPHEN, CWA III-1660; CWAII IV-1400

Poetry of Spender, The, MP IX-5152

Journals, 1939-1983, MPII:NF II-767

SPENSER, EDMUND, CWA III-1662

Faerie Queene, The, CLC I-347; MP IV-1953

Lyric Poetry of Spenser, The, MP VI-3573

Mother Hubberd's Tale, MP VII-4078

Shepheardes Calendar, The, MP X-5972

SPINOZA, BENEDICTUS DE, CWA III-1665

Ethics, MP IV-1876

STAËL, MADAME DE, CWA III-1667

Considerations on the Principal Events of the French Revolution, MP II-1100

Delphine, CLC I-263; MP III-1436; MP:EF I-380

STAFFORD, JEAN, CWAII IV-1403

"Bad Characters," MPII:SS I-144

"Country Love Story, A," MPII:SS I-444

"Reasonable Facsimile, A," MPII:SS V-1908

STALLINGS, LAURENCE, *and* MAXWELL ANDERSON
What Price Glory? CLCII IV-1706; MPII:D IV-1723
STANHOPE, PHILIP DORMER. *See* CHESTERFIELD, PHILIP DORMER STANHOPE, LORD
STAPLEDON, OLAF
Last and First Men, MPII:BCF II-939
STATIUS, CWA III-1668
Thebais, The, MP XI-6469
STEAD, CHRISTINA, CWAII IV-1406
House of All Nations, CLCII II-708; MPII:BCF II-753
Little Hotel, The, CLCII III-896; MPII:BCF II-975
Man Who Loved Children, The, CLCII III-958; MPII:BCF III-1050
STEELE, SIR RICHARD, CWA III-1669
Conscious Lovers, The, CLC I-198; MP II-1094
Funeral, The, CLC I-390; MP IV-2188
STEELE, SIR RICHARD, JOSEPH ADDISON, *and* EUSTACE BUDGELL
Sir Roger de Coverley Papers, The, CLC II-1044; MP X-6067
STEFFENS, LINCOLN, CWAII IV-1409
Autobiography of Lincoln Steffens, The, MPII:NF I-115
STEGNER, WALLACE, CWAII IV-1411
Angle of Repose, CLCII I-48; MPII:AF I-38
"Beyond the Glass Mountain," MPII:SS I-196
STEIN, GERTRUDE, CWAII IV-1414
Making of Americans, The, CLCII III-948; MPII:AF III-958
Three Lives, CLCII IV-1555; MPII:AF IV-1643
STEINBECK, JOHN, CWA III-1672; CWAII IV-1416
Cannery Row, CLCII I-231; MPII:AF I-242
"Chrysanthemums, The," MPII:SS I-392

East of Eden, CLC I-313; MP III-1689; MP:AF I-326
"Flight," MPII:SS II-792
"Gift, The," MPII:SS II-843
Grapes of Wrath, The, CLC I-417; MP IV-2344; MP:AF I-491
In Dubious Battle, CLC I-518; MP V-2850; MP:AF II-588
Of Mice and Men, CLC II-795; MP VII-4294; MP:AF II-861
"Pearl, The," CLCII III-1188; MPII:SS IV-1785
Red Pony, The, CLCII III-1281; MPII:AF III-1334
Tortilla Flat, CLCII IV-1595; MPII:AF IV-1688
STEINBECK, JOHN, *and* EDWARD F. RICKETTS
Sea of Cortez, MPII:NF III-1309
STEINER, GEORGE, CWAII IV-1418
After Babel, MPII:NF I-7
Portage to San Cristóbal of A. H., The, CLCII III-1223; MPII:BCF III-1335
STENDHAL, CWA III-1675
Charterhouse of Parma, The, CLC I-169; MP II-895; MP:EF I-214
Lucien Leuwen, CLC I-639; MP VI-3547; MP:EF II-802
Red and the Black, The, CLC II-947; MP IX-5463; MP:EF III-1062
STEPHENS, JAMES, CWA III-1677
Crock of Gold, The, CLC I-224; MP III-1223; MP:BF I-254
Deirdre, CLC I-262; MP III-1428; MP:BF I-305
STERN, RICHARD, CWAII IV-1421
"Wissler Remembers," MPII:SS VI-2664
STERNE, LAURENCE, CWA III-1679
Journal to Eliza, MP V-3053
Sentimental Journey, A, CLC II-1024; MP X-5914; MP:BF III-1415
Tristram Shandy, CLC II-1159; MP XI-6712; MP:BF III-1605

STEVENS, JAMES, CWA III-1683
  Paul Bunyan, CLC II-843; MP VIII-
  4537; MP:AF II-910
STEVENS, WALLACE, CWA III-1684
  Harmonium, MP V-2480
  Poetry of Stevens, The, MP IX-5161
STEVENSON, ROBERT LOUIS, CWA
  III-1687
  Beach of Falesá, The, CLC I-89; MP
  I-456; MP:BF I-95
  Black Arrow, The, CLC I-106; MP I-
  552; MP:BF I-113
  "Bottle Imp, The," MPII:SS I-281
  Dr. Jekyll and Mr. Hyde, CLC I-280;
  MP III-1550; MP:BF I-333
  Kidnapped, CLC I-568; MP VI-3127;
  MP:BF II-739
  "Lodging for the Night, A," MPII:SS
  IV-1387
  Master of Ballantrae, The, CLC I-680;
  MP VII-3764; MP:BF II-887
  "Suicide Club, The," MPII:SS V-2262
  Travels with a Donkey, MP XI-6659
  Treasure Island, CLC II-1152; MP XI-
  6662; MP:BF III-1589
STIFTER, ADALBERT, CWAII IV-1423
  Indian Summer, CLCII II-757;
  MPII:WF II-691
STILL, JAMES, CWA III-1690
  River of Earth, CLC II-975; MP X-
  5629; MP:AF III-1054
STOCKTON, FRANK R., CWAII IV-
  1425
  "Lady or the Tiger?, The," MPII:SS III-
  1284
STOKER, BRAM, CWA III-1692
  Dracula, CLC I-301; MP III-1633;
  MP:BF I-347
STONE, IRVING
  Agony and the Ecstasy, The, CLCII I-
  24; MPII:AF I-12
STONE, ROBERT, CWAII IV-1430
  Dog Soldiers, CLCII II-411; MPII:AF
  I-423

STONG, PHIL, CWA III-1693
  State Fair, CLC II-1080; MP XI-6246;
  MP:AF III-1215
STOPPARD, TOM, CWAII IV-1432
  Dirty Linen, CLCII I-404; MPII:D
  II502
  Hapgood, CLCII II-656; MPII:D II-737
  Jumpers, CLCII II-808; MPII:D III-877
  New-Found-Land, CLCII I-404;
  MPII:D II-502
  Night and Day, CLCII III-1093;
  MPII:D III-1128
  Real Thing, The, CLCII III-1274;
  MPII:D III-1310
  Rosencrantz and Guildenstern Are Dead,
  CLCII III-1314; MPII:D IV-1378
  Travesties, CLCII IV-1606; MPII:D IV-
  1643
STOREY, DAVID, CWAII IV-1435
  Changing Room, The, CLCII I-261;
  MPII:D I-312
  Contractor, The, CLCII I-333; MPII:D
  I-397
  Radcliffe, CLCII III-1257; MPII:BCF
  III-1370
  This Sporting Life, CLCII IV-1551;
  MPII:BCF IV-1690
STOW, RANDOLPH, CWAII IV-1437
  Girl Green as Elderflower, The, CLCII
  II-587; MPII:BCF II-590
  Merry-Go-Round in the Sea, The,
  CLCII III-998; MPII:BCF III-1081
  Visitants, CLCII IV-1661; MPII:BCF
  IV-1802
STOWE, HARRIET BEECHER, CWA
  III-1695
  Oldtown Folks, CLC II-810; MP VIII-
  4353; MP:AF II-883
  Uncle Tom's Cabin, CLC II-1178; MP
  XII-6814; MP:AF III-1345
STRACHEY, LYTTON, CWA III-1697
  Eminent Victorians, MP III-1760
  Queen Victoria, MP IX-5390
STRASSBURG, GOTTFRIED VON. See
  GOTTFRIED VON STRASSBURG

STRAUSS, BOTHO, CWAII IV-1439
Devotion, CLCII I-396; MPII:WF I-376
STRAUSSLER, TOMAS. *See*
STOPPARD, TOM
STRINDBERG, AUGUST, CWA III-1699
Comrades, CLC I-194; MP II-1047
Confession of a Fool, The, CLCII I-324; MPII:WF I-304
Dance of Death, The, CLC I-236; MP III-1283
Dream Play, A, CLCII II-425; MPII:D II-518
Father, The, CLC I-358; MP IV-2000
Ghost Sonata, The, CLCII II-579; MPII:D II-678
Inferno, CLCII II-762; MPII:WF II-697
Link, The, CLC I-615; MP VI-3434
Miss Julie, CLC II-715; MP VII-3936
Natives of Hemsö, The, CLCII III-1077; MPII:WF III-1079
Pelican, The, CLCII III-1189; MPII:D III-1214
Red Room, The, CLC II-949; MP IX-5473; MP:EF III-1067
Stormy Weather, CLCII IV-1476; MPII:D IV-1491
There Are Crimes and Crimes, CLC II-1121; MP XI-6473
STRONG, L. A. G., CWA III-1702
Garden, The, CLC I-392; MP IV-2200; MP:BF I-479
STRUGATSKY, ARKADY, *and* BORIS STRUGATSKY, CWAII IV-1441
Roadside Picnic, CLCII III-1306; MPII:WF III-1295
Snail on the Slope, The, CLCII IV-1430; MPII:WF IV-1469
STUART, JESSE, CWA III-1704; CWAII IV-1443
Beyond Dark Hills, MPII:NF I-150
"Dawn of Remembered Spring," MPII:SS II-499
Man with a Bull-Tongue Plow, MP VII-3680
"Split Cherry Tree, The," MPII:SS V-2206

"Spring Victory," MPII:SS V-2214
Taps for Private Tussie, CLC II-1107; MP XI-6405; MP:AF III-1259
Thread That Runs So True, The, MPII:NF IV-1513
STURLUSON, SNORRI. *See* SNORRI STURLUSON
STYRON, WILLIAM, CWA III-1707; CWAII IV-1445
Confessions of Nat Turner, The, CLCII I-326; MPII:AF I-330
Lie Down in Darkness, MP VI-3382; MP:AF II-667
Set This House on Fire, MP X-5919; MP:AF III-1113
Sophie's Choice, CLCII IV-1446; MPII:AF IV-1492
SUCKLING, SIR JOHN, CWA III-1709
Poetry of Suckling, The, MP IX-5164
SUCKOW, RUTH, CWA III-1711
Folks, The, MP IV-2094; MP:AF I-404
SUDERMANN, HERMANN, CWA III-1713
Dame Care, CLC I-234; MP III-1275; MP:EF I-326
Song of Songs, The, CLC II-1063; MP XI-6156; MP:EF III-1197
SUE, EUGÈNE, CWA III-1715
Mysteries of Paris, The, CLC II-752; MP VII-4111; MP:EF II-904
Wandering Jew, The, CLC II-1218; MP XII-7010; MP:EF III-1370
SUETONIUS, CWA III-1717
Concerning Illustrious Men, MP II-1054
Lives of the Caesars, MP VI-3464
SUMNER, WILLIAM GRAHAM, CWA III-1718
Folkways, MP IV-2097
SURREY, EARL OF. *See* HOWARD, HENRY
SURTEES, ROBERT SMITH, CWA III-1720
Handley Cross, CLC I-440; MP V-2467; MP:BF I-520
Hillingdon Hall, CLC I-474; MP V-2616; MP:BF I-582

Jorrocks' Jaunts and Jollities, CLC I-552; MP V-3033; MP:BF II-703

Mr. Facey Romford's Hounds, CLC II-718; MP VII-3954; MP:BF II-959

Mr. Sponge's Sporting Tour, CLC II-721; MP VII-3967; MP:BF II-970

SVEVO, ITALO, CWAII IV-1448

As a Man Grows Older, CLCII I-71; MPII:WF I-75

Confessions of Zeno, CLCII I-328; MPII:WF I-315

SWEDENBORG, EMANUEL, CWA III-1723

Divine Love and Wisdom, MP III-1537

SWIFT, GRAHAM, CWAII IV-1450

Shuttlecock, CLCII IV-1398; MPII:BCF IV-1538

Waterland, CLCII IV-1691; MPII:BCF IV-1865

SWIFT, JONATHAN, CWA III-1725

Gulliver's Travels, CLC I-432; MP IV-2421; MP:BF I-501

Journal to Stella, MP V-3056

Poetry of Swift, The, MP IX-5167

Tale of a Tub, A, MP XI-6366; MP:BF III-1481

SWINBURNE, ALGERNON CHARLES, CWA III-1729

Atalanta in Calydon, CLC I-69; MP I-353

Poems and Ballads, MP VIII-4780

SWINNERTON, FRANK, CWA III-1732

Nocturne, CLC II-781; MP VII-4235; MP:BF II-1065

SYNGE, JOHN MILLINGTON, CWA III-1734

Deirdre of the Sorrows, CLC I-263; MP III-1432

In the Shadow of the Glen, CLCII II-750; MPII:D II-815

Playboy of the Western World, The, CLC II-893; MP VIII-4755

Riders to the Sea, CLCII III-1294; MPII:D III-1337

SZWARCBART, ABRAHAM. See SCHWARZ-BART, ANDRÉ

T

TACITUS, CWA III-1736
Annals of Tacitus, The, MP I-236
TAINE, HIPPOLYTE, CWA III-1737
Philosophy of Art, MP VIII-4659
TANIZAKI, JUN'ICHIRŌ, CWAII IV-1452
"Bridge of Dreams, The," MPII:SS I-304
Diary of a Mad Old Man, CLCII I-398; MPII:WF I-381
In Praise of Shadows, MPII:NF II-731
Makioka Sisters, The, CLCII III-950; MPII:WF III-915
Naomi, CLCII III-1074; MPII:WF III-1070
Secret History of the Lord of Musashi, The, CLCII III-1367; MPII:WF III-1372
Some Prefer Nettles, CLCII IV-1439; MPII:WF IV-1491
TARGAN, BARRY
"Old Vemish," MPII:SS IV-1680
TARKINGTON, BOOTH, CWA III-1739
Alice Adams, CLC I-21; MP I-104
Kate Fennigate, CLC I-565; MP VI-3120; MP:AF II-632
Monsieur Beaucaire, CLC II-735; MP VII-4034; MP:AF II-816
Seventeen, CLC II-1027; MP X-5942; MP:AF III-1122
TARKOVSKY, ANDREY
Sculpting in Time, MPII:NF III-1298
TASSO, TORQUATO, CWA III-1741
Jerusalem Delivered, CLC I-545; MP V-3000
TATE, ALLEN, CWA III-1743
Fathers, The, MP IV-2012; MP:AF I-371
Poetry of Tate, The, MP IX-5172
TAYLOR, EDWARD, CWA III-1745
Poetical Works of Edward Taylor, The, MP VIII-4786
TAYLOR, ELIZABETH
Wreath of Roses, A, CLCII IV-1756; MPII:BCF IV-1950

TAYLOR, KAMALA PURNAIYA. See MARKANDAYA, KAMALA
TAYLOR, PETER, CWAII IV-1455
"Fancy Woman, The," MPII:SS II-759
"Old Forest, The," MPII:SS IV-1668
Short Stories of Peter Taylor, The, MP X-6024; MP:AF III-1156
"Venus, Cupid, Folly, and Time," MPII:SS VI-2489
TEGNÉR, ESAIAS, CWA III-1747
Frithiof's Saga, CLC I-387; MP IV-2175
TEILHARD DE CHARDIN, PIERRE
Phenomenon of Man, The, MP VIII-4636
TENNYSON, LORD ALFRED, CWA III-1748
Enoch Arden, CLC I-328; MP III-1787
Idylls of the King, The, CLC I-511; MP V-2825
In Memoriam, MP V-2853
Poems, MP VIII-4777
Princess, The, MP IX-5324
TERENCE, CWA III-1751
Andria, CLC I-38; MP I-212
Brothers, The, CLC I-127; MP II-681
Eunuch, The, CLC I-336; MP IV-1891
Phormio, CLC II-873; MP VIII-4673
Self-Tormentor, The, CLC II-1021; MP X-5902
TERRY, MEGAN
Keep Tightly Closed in a Cool Dry Place, CLCII II-821; MPII:D III-895
TERTZ, ABRAM. See SINYAVSKY, ANDREI
THACKERAY, WILLIAM MAKEPEACE, CWA III-1753
Barry Lyndon, CLC I-85; MP I-443; MP:BF I-91
Henry Esmond, CLC I-459; MP V-2550; MP:BF I-560
Newcomes, The, CLC II-766; MP VII-4185; MP:BF II-1038
Pendennis, CLC II-853; MP VIII-4575; MP:BF II-1179

Vanity Fair, CLC II-1190; MP XII-6875; MP:BF III-1660
Virginians, The, CLC II-1209; MP XII-6956; MP:BF III-1692
THEOCRITUS, CWA III-1756
Poetry of Theocritus, The, MP IX-5175
THEROUX, PAUL, CWAII IV-1457
Saint Jack, CLCII III-1329; MPII:AF III-1362
THIBAULT, JACQUES-ANATOLE-FRANÇOIS. See FRANCE, ANATOLE
THOMAS, DYLAN, CWA III-1757
"After the Fair," MPII:SS I-43
Collected Poems, 1934-1952, MP II-1025
"Enemies, The," MPII:SS II-695
"Fight, The," MPII:SS II-774
Portrait of the Artist as a Young Dog, MP IX-5256; MP:BF III-1241
Under Milk Wood, MP XII-6825
THOMAS, LEWIS, CWAII IV-1459
Lives of a Cell, The, MPII:NF II-846
THOMAS À KEMPIS, CWA III-1760
Imitation of Christ, The, MP V-2845
THOMAS AQUINAS. See AQUINAS, THOMAS
THOMPSON, DANIEL PIERCE, CWA III-1761
Green Mountain Boys, The, CLC I-426; MP IV-2389; MP:AF II-514
THOMPSON, D'ARCY WENTWORTH
On Growth and Form, MPII:NF III-1063
THOMPSON, FRANCIS, CWA III-1762
Poetry of Thompson, The, MP IX-5177
THOMSON, JAMES, CWA III-1763
Seasons, The, MP X-5879
THOREAU, HENRY DAVID, CWA III-1765
Essays of Henry David Thoreau, The, MP IV-1863
Journal of Thoreau, The, MP V-3050
Poetry of Thoreau, The, MP IX-5179
Walden, MP XII-6996

Week on the Concord and Merrimack Rivers, A, MP XII-7081
THUCYDIDES, CWA III-1768
History of the Peloponnesian War, MP V-2652
THURBER, JAMES, CWA III-1769, CWAII IV-1461
"Catbird Seat, The," MPII:SS I-337
My Life and Hard Times, MP VII-4108
"Secret Life of Walter Mitty, The," MPII:SS V-2057
Years with Ross, The, MPII:NF IV-1736
THURMAN, WALLACE, CWAII IV-1464
Blacker the Berry, The, CLCII I-166; MPII:AF I-175
TOCQUEVILLE, ALEXIS DE, CWA III-1771
Democracy in America, MP III-1443
TOLKIEN, J. R. R., CWA III-1773, CWAII IV-1466
Fellowship of the Ring, The, MP IV-2033; MP:BF I-414
Hobbit, The, CLCII II-681; MPII:BCF II-727
Return of the King, The, MP X-5540; MP:BF III-1611
Silmarillion, The, CLCII IV-1410; MPII:BCF IV-1548
Two Towers, The, MP XII-6778; MP:BF III-1611
TOLSTOY, LEO, CWA III-1775, CWAII IV-1468
"Alyosha the Pot," MPII:SS I-74
Anna Karénina, CLC I-44; MP I-229; MP:EF I-47
Childhood, Boyhood, Youth, MP II-924; MP:EF I-229
Cossacks, The, CLC I-203; MP II-1128; MP:EF I-264
"Death of Ivan Ilyich, The," CLC I-256; MP III-1373; MP:EF I-354; MPII:SS II-542
Family Happiness, CLCII II-489; MPII:WF I-435

Hadji Murad, CLCII II-649; MPII:WF
II-571
"How Much Land Does a Man Need?"
MPII:SS III-1070
Kreutzer Sonata, The, CLC I-583; MP
VI-3192; MP:EF II-736
"Master and Man," MPII:SS IV-1475
Power of Darkness, The, CLC II-911;
MP IX-5283
"Raid, The," CLCII III-1261; MPII:SS
V-1880
Resurrection, CLC II-958; MP X-5531;
MP:EF III-1082
"Snow-Storm, The," MPII:SS V-2163
"Three Deaths," MPII:SS VI-2351
"Three Hermits, The," MPII:SS VI-
2355
War and Peace, CLC II-1220; MP XII-
7028; MP:EF III-1374
TOMASI DI LAMPEDUSA, GIUSEPPE,
CWA III-1024
Leopard, The, MP VI-3324; MP:EF II-
772
TOMLINSON, CHARLES, CWAII IV-
1471
Some Americans, MPII:NF IV-1388
TOMLINSON, H. M., CWA III-1778
Sea and the Jungle, The, MP X-5858
TOOLE, JOHN KENNEDY, CWAII IV-
1473
Confederacy of Dunces, A, CLCII I-
320; MPII:AF I-319
TOOMER, JEAN, CWA III-1780; CWAII
IV-1475
"Blood-Burning Moon," MPII:SS I-258
"Esther," MPII:SS II-716
TORSVAN, BERICK TRAVEN. See
TRAVEN, B.
TORSVAN, TRAVEN. See TRAVEN, B.
TOTH, SUSAN ALLEN, CWAII IV-1477
Blooming, MPII:NF I-178
TOURGÉE, ALBION WINEGAR, CWA
III-1782
Fool's Errand, A, MP IV-2110; MP:AF
I-408

TOURNEUR, CYRIL, CWA III-1784
Revenger's Tragedy, The, CLC II-961;
MP X-5554
TOURNIER, MICHEL, CWAII IV-1479
Friday, CLCII II-548; MPII:WF II-502
Gemini, CLCII II-573; MPII:WF II-542
Ogre, The, CLCII III-1133; MPII:WF
III-1129
TOYNBEE, ARNOLD, CWA III-1786
Study of History, A, MP XI-6326
TRAHERNE, THOMAS, CWA III-1788
Poetry of Traherne, The, MP IX-5181
TRAVEN, B., CWA III-1790
Death Ship, The, MP III-1388; MP:AF
I-278
TRAVERSO, DINO BUZZATI. See
BUZZATI, DINO
TREVELYAN, GEORGE MACAULAY,
CWA III-1793
England Under the Stuarts, MP III-1781
TREVOR, WILLIAM, CWAII IV-1481
Boarding-House, The, CLCII I-182;
MPII:BCF I-158
"Going Home," MPII:SS II-876
Other People's Worlds, CLCII III-1161;
MPII:BCF III-1262
TRIFONOV, YURY, CWAII IV-1483
Another Life, CLCII I-57; MPII:WF I-
60
House on the Embankment, The, CLCII
II-713; MPII:WF II-633
Old Man, The, CLCII III-1138;
MPII:WF III-1141
TRILLING, LIONEL, CWAII IV-1486
Liberal Imagination, The, MPII:NF II-
830
Middle of the Journey, The, CLCII III-
1006; MPII:AF III-1007
"Of This Time, Of That Place,"
MPII:SS IV-1652
TROGDON, WILLIAM. See HEAT-
MOON, WILLIAM LEAST
TROLLOPE, ANTHONY, CWA III-1795
Autobiography, An, MP I-359
Barchester Towers, CLC I-80; MP I-
426; MP:BF I-79

Doctor Thorne, CLC I-281; MP III-1558; MP:BF I-337

Framley Parsonage, CLC I-383; MP IV-2151; MP:BF I-462

Last Chronicle of Barset, The, CLC I-592; MP VI-3246; MP:BF II-768

Orley Farm, CLC II-821; MP VIII-4415; MP:BF II-1130

Phineas Finn, CLC II-871; MP VIII-4662; MP:BF III-1203

Phineas Redux, CLC II-871; MP VIII-4666; MP:BF III-1207

Small House at Allington, The, CLC II-1050; MP X-6097; MP:BF III-1463

Vicar of Bullhampton, The, CLC II-1197; MP XII-6897; MP:BF III-1670

Warden, The, CLC II-1222; MP XII-7038; MP:BF III-1706

TROWBRIDGE, JOHN TOWNSEND, CWA III-1798

Cudjo's Cave, CLC I-228; MP III-1238; MP:AF I-239

TROYES, CHRÉTIEN DE. See CHRÉTIEN DE TROYES

TS'AO HSUËH-CH'IN

Dream of the Red Chamber, CLC I-302; MP III-1648; MP:EF I-448

TSUSHIMA SHŪJI'. See DAZAI, OSAMU

TUOHY, FRANK, CWAII IV-1488

"Admiral and the Nuns, The," MPII:SS I-12

TURGENEV, IVAN, CWA III-1799

Asya, CLCII I-80; MPII:WF I-85

"Bezhin Meadow," MPII:SS I-200

"District Doctor, The," MPII:SS II-614

Fathers and Sons, CLC I-361; MP IV-2015; MP:EF II-510

First Love, CLCII II-516; MPII:WF II-470

"Hamlet of the Shchigrovsky District," MPII:SS II-973

House of Gentlefolk, A, CLC I-487; MP V-2725; MP:EF II-657

"Living Relic, A," MPII:SS III-1379

Month in the Country, A, CLC II-738; MP VII-4052

On the Eve, CLCII III-1143; MPII:WF III-1152

Rudin, CLCII III-1319; MPII:WF III-1310

Smoke, CLC II-1053; MP X-6105; MP:EF III-1174

Torrents of Spring, The, CLCII IV-1594; MPII:WF IV-1634

Virgin Soil, CLC II-1206; MP XII-6944; MP:EF III-1354

"Yermolai and the Miller's Wife," MPII:SS VI-2733

TURNER, FREDERICK JACKSON, CWA III-1803

Frontier in American History, The, MP IV-2182

TUTUOLA, AMOS, CWA III-1805, CWAII IV-1490

My Life in the Bush of Ghosts, CLCII III-1063; MPII:BCF III-1167

Palm-Wine Drinkard, The, MP VIII-4469; MP:EF III-970

TWAIN, MARK, CWA III-1807; CWAII IV-1492

Adventures of Huckleberry Finn, CLC I-495; MP V-2755; MP:AF I-11

Adventures of Tom Sawyer, CLC II-1145; MP XI-6604; MP:AF I-17

"Celebrated Jumping Frog of Calaveras County, The," MPII:SS I-344

Connecticut Yankee in King Arthur's Court, A, CLC I-198; MP II-1083; MP:AF I-215

"Jim Baker's Bluejay Yarn," MPII:SS III-1222

Life on the Mississippi, MP VI-3412

"Man That Corrupted Hadleyburg, The," MPII:SS IV-1437

"Mysterious Stranger, The," CLCII III-1069; MPII:SS IV-1578

"£1,000,000 Bank Note, The," MPII:SS IV-1697

Prince and the Pauper, The, CLC II-915; MP IX-5317; MP:AF II-986
Roughing It, MP X-5722
TWAIN, MARK, *and* CHARLES DUDLEY WARNER
Gilded Age, The, CLC I-402; MP IV-2263; MP:AF I-445

TWEEDSMUIR, BARON. *See* BUCHAN, JOHN
TYLER, ANNE, CWAII IV-1495
Dinner at the Homesick Restaurant, CLCII I-403; MPII:AF I-409

U

UDALL, NICHOLAS, CWA III-1811
Ralph Roister Doister, CLC II-937; MP
IX-5418
UNAMUNO Y JUGO, MIGUEL DE,
CWA III-1813; CWAII IV-1497
Abel Sánchez, CLCII I-3; MPII:WF I-
1
Saint Manuel Bueno, Martyr, CLCII III-
1329; MPII:WF III-1338
Tragic Sense of Life in Men and in
Peoples, The, MP XI-6640
UNDSET, SIGRID, CWA III-1814
Axe, The, CLC I-71; MP I-391;
MP:EF I-88
In the Wilderness, CLC I-519; MP V-
2861; MP:EF II-687
Kristin Lavransdatter, CLC I-584; MP
VI-3195; MP:EF II-740
Snake Pit, The, CLC II-1055; MP X-
6109; MP:EF III-1178
Son Avenger, The, CLC II-1058; MP
X-6134; MP:EF III-1182
UNKNOWN
Abraham and Isaac, CLC I-2; MP I-8
Arabian Nights' Entertainments, The,
CLC I-55; MP I-281; MP:EF I-52
Aucassin and Nicolette, CLC I-70; MP
I-356; MP:EF I-85
Beowulf, MP I-500
Bevis of Hampton, CLC I-101; MP I-
516
Cadmus, MP II-725; MP:EF I-160
Circle of Chalk, The, CLC I-182; MP
II-973
Cupid and Psyche, MP III-1245;
MP:EF I-314
Epic of Gilgamesh, The, CLC I-329;
MP III-1796
Everyman, CLC I-345; MP IV-1928
Finn Cycle, The, CLC I-369; MP IV-
2071; MP:BF I-424
Grettir the Strong, CLC I-427; MP IV-
2396; MP:EF II-593
Guy of Warwick, CLC I-434; MP IV-
2433

Havelock the Dane, CLC I-445; MP V-
2492
Hercules and His Twelve Labors, MP
V-2587; MP:EF II-631
Huon de Bordeaux, CLC I-502; MP V-
2784; MP:EF II-674
Jason and the Golden Fleece, MP V-
2981; MP:EF II-710
King Horn, MP VI-3137
Lay of Igor's Campaign, The, MP VI-
3296
Lazarillo de Tormes, CLC I-604; MP
VI-3302; MP:EF II-763
Mabinogion, The, CLC I-641; MP VI-
3582; MP:BF II-847
Mahabharata, The, CLC I-652; MP VI-
3629
Nibelungenlied, The, CLC II-770; MP
VII-4190; MP:EF II-932
On the Sublime, MP VIII-4378
Orpheus and Eurydice, MP VIII-4428;
MP:EF II-957
Pilgrimage of Charlemagne, The, CLC
II-881; MP VIII-4700
Poem of the Cid, CLC II-897; MP VIII-
4773
Proserpine and Ceres, MP IX-5374;
MP:EF III-1042
Reynard the Fox, CLC II-963; MP X-
5565; MP:EF III-1092
Robin Hood's Adventures, CLC II-978;
MP X-5642; MP:BF III-1336
Second Shepherd's Play, The, CLC II-
1017; MP X-5886
Sir Gawain and the Green Knight, CLC
II-1042; MP X-6060
Song of Roland, CLC II-1061; MP XI-
6150; MP:EF III-1190
Star of Seville, The, CLC II-1079; MP
XI-6242
Story of Burnt Njal, The, CLC II-1085;
MP XI-6276; MP:EF III-1231
UPDIKE, JOHN, CWA III-1816; CWAII
IV-1500
"A & P," MPII:SS I-1

"Ace in the Hole," MPII:SS I-9

Buchanan Dying, CLCII I-209; MPII:D I-255

Centaur, The, CLCII I-250; MPII:AF I-269

Coup, The, CLCII I-342; MPII:AF I-351

Couples, CLCII I-345; MPII:AF I-356

"Gun Shop, The," MPII:SS III-959

"Leaves," MPII:SS III-1313

"Lifeguard," MPII:SS III-1345

Month of Sundays, A, CLCII III-1033; MPII:AF III-1032

"Pigeon Feathers," MPII:SS IV-1817

Poorhouse Fair, The, MP IX-5244; MP:AF II-965

Rabbit Angstrom Novels, The, CLCII III-1253, 1254, 1257; MP IX-5407; MP:AF II-998; MPII:AF III-1300

Rabbit Is Rich, CLCII III-1253; MPII:AF III-1300

Rabbit Redux, CLCII III-1254; MPII:AF III-1300

Rabbit, Run, CLCII III-1257; MP IX-5407; MP:AF II-998; MPII:AF III-1300

Short Stories of John Updike, The, MP X-6014; MP:AF III-1160

"Tomorrow and Tomorrow and So Forth," MPII:SS VI-2389

"Walter Briggs," MPII:SS VI-2537

URIS, LEON, CWAII IV-1503

Exodus, CLCII II-475; MPII:AF II-491

V

VALDEZ, LUIS MIGUEL, CWAII IV-1505
"I Don't Have to Show You No Stinking Badges!" CLCII II-726; MPII:D II-799
Zoot Suit, CLCII IV-1773; MPII:D IV-1799
VALENZUELA, LUISA, CWAII IV-1507
He Who Searches, CLCII II-663; MPII:AF II-696
Lizard's Tail, The, CLCII III-900; MPII:AF III-896
VALERA, JUAN, CWA III-1818
Pepita Jiménez, CLC II-858; MP VIII-4595; MP:EF III-1006
VALÉRY, PAUL, CWA III-1820
Poetry of Valéry, The, MP IX-5184
VALMIKI, CWA III-1822
Ramayana, The, CLC II-938; MP IX-5421
VANBRUGH, SIR JOHN, CWA III-1823
Relapse, The, CLC II-952; MP IX-5493
VAN ITALLIE, JEAN-CLAUDE
America Hurrah, CLCII I-36; MPII:D I-44
VAN VECHTEN, CARL, CWA III-1825
Peter Whiffle, CLC II-867; MP VIII-4629; MP:AF II-923
VARGAS LLOSA, MARIO, CWAII IV-1509
Aunt Julia and the Scriptwriter, CLCII I-87; MPII:AF I-71
Conversation in the Cathedral, CLCII I-334; MPII:AF I-335
Green House, The, CLCII II-632; MPII:AF II-672
Time of the Hero, The, CLCII IV-1569; MPII:AF IV-1663
War of the End of the World, The, CLCII IV-1682; MPII:AF IV-1764
VAUGHAN, HENRY, CWA III-1826
Poetry of Vaughan, The, MP IX-5187
VAZOV, IVAN, CWA III-1828
Under the Yoke, CLC II-1182; MP XII-6836; MP:EF III-1334

VEBLEN, THORSTEIN, CWA III-1829
Theory of the Leisure Class, The, MP XI-6471
VEGA, LOPE DE, CWA III-1831
Gardener's Dog, The, CLC I-392; MP IV-2203
King, the Greatest Alcalde, The, CLC I-577; MP VI-3168
Sheep Well, The, CLC II-1031; MP X-5962
VENTSEL, YELENA SERGEYEVNA. See GREKOVA, I.
VERGA, GIOVANNI, CWA III-1834
"Cavalleria Rusticana," CLC I-160; MP II-855; MP:EF I-198
"Consolation," MPII:SS I-425
House by the Medlar Tree, The, CLC I-485; MP V-2709; MP:EF II-652
Mastro-don Gesualdo, CLC I-681; MP VII-3771; MP:EF II-838
"She-Wolf, The," MPII:SS V-2076
VERGIL, CWA III-1836
Aeneid, The, CLC I-11; MP I-46
Eclogues, MP III-1702
Georgics, MP IV-2236
VERGNE, MARIE-MADELEINE PIOCHE DE LA. See LA FAYETTE, MADAME DE
VERLAINE, PAUL, CWA III-1838
Fêtes galantes and Other Poems, MP IV-2038
VERNE, JULES, CWA III-1840
Around the World in Eighty Days, CLCII I-68; MPII:WF I-66
Journey to the Center of the Earth, CLCII II-800; MPII:WF II-781
Mysterious Island, The, CLC II-754; MP VII-4121; MP:EF II-909
Twenty Thousand Leagues Under the Sea, CLC II-1169; MP XII-6758; MP:EF III-1315
VIAUD, JULIEN. See LOTI, PIERRE
VIAUD, LOUIS MARIE JULIEN. See LOTI, PIERRE

VIDAL, GORE, CWAII IV-1512
  Burr, CLCII I-219; MPII:AF I-221
  City and the Pillar, The, CLCII I-291;
    MPII:AF I-306
  1876, CLCII II-446; MPII:AF I-457
  Lincoln, CLCII II-892; MPII:AF III-
    887
VIGNY, ALFRED VICTOR DE, CWA
    III-1842
  Cinq-Mars, CLC I-181; MP II-969;
    MP:EF I-236
  Poetry of Vigny, The, MP IX-5191
VILLON, FRANÇOIS, CWA III-1844
  Great Testament, The, MP IV-2370
  Lais, Le, MP VI-3226
VINCI, LEONARDO DA. See
    LEONARDO DA VINCI
VITTORINI, ELIO, CWAII IV-1514
  In Sicily, CLCII II-745; MPII:WF II-
    681
  Women of Messina, CLCII IV-1736;
    MPII:WF IV-1784
VOEGELIN, ERIC, CWAII IV-1516
  Anamnesis, MPII:NF I-56
VOGAU, BORIS ANDREYEVICH. See
    PILNYAK, BORIS
VOINOVICH, VLADIMIR, CWAII IV-
    1518

Life and Extraordinary Adventures of
    Private Ivan Chonkin, The, CLCII II-
    881; MPII:WF II-841
Pretender to the Throne, CLCII II-881;
    MPII:WF II-841
VOLTAIRE, FRANÇOIS MARIE
    AROUET DE, CWA III-1846
  Candide, CLC I-144; MP II-759;
    MP:EF I-167
  Zadig, CLC II-1278; MP XII-7314;
    MP:EF III-1430
  Zaïre, CLC II-1279; MP XII-7318
VONNEGUT, KURT, JR., CWAII IV-
    1521
  Cat's Cradle, CLCII I-246; MPII:AF I-
    264
  God Bless You, Mr. Rosewater, CLCII
    II-599; MPII:AF II-634
  Jailbird, CLCII II-786; MPII:AF II-809
  Mother Night, CLCII III-1047;
    MPII:AF III-1078
  Sirens of Titan, The, CLCII IV-1418;
    MPII:AF IV-1427
  Slaughterhouse-Five, CLCII IV-1421;
    MPII:AF IV-1438
VYGOTSKY, LEV, CWAII IV-1523
  Thought and Language, MPII:NF IV-
    1507

W

WAGNER, JANE
  Search for Signs of Intelligent Life in the Universe, The, CLCII III-1357; MPII:D IV-1421
WAIN, JOHN, CWAII IV-1525
  Born in Captivity, CLCII I-194; MPII:BCF I-181
  Dear Shadows, MPII:NF I-331
  Pardoner's Tale, The, CLCII III-1178; MPII:BCF III-1282
  Sprightly Running, MPII:NF IV-1421
  Strike the Father Dead, CLCII IV-1484; MPII:BCF IV-1633
WALCOTT, DEREK, CWAII IV-1528
  Dream on Monkey Mountain, CLCII II-424; MPII:D II-513
  Pantomime, CLCII III-1174; MPII:D III-1202
WALKER, ALICE, CWAII IV-1531
  Color Purple, The, CLCII I-308; MPII:AF I-311
  "Everyday Use," MPII:SS II-731
  Meridian, CLCII III-997; MPII:AF III-997
  "Strong Horse Tea," MPII:SS V-2259
  Third Life of Grange Copeland, The, CLCII IV-1547; MPII:AF IV-1629
WALKER, MARGARET
  Jubilee, CLCII II-806; MPII:AF II-825
WALLACE, LEWIS, CWA III-1849
  Ben Hur, CLC I-96; MP I-491; MP:AF I-107
WALLANT, EDWARD LEWIS, CWA III-1850
  Tenants of Moonbloom, The, MP XI-6445; MP:AF III-1263
WALLER, EDMUND, CWA III-1851
  Poetry of Waller, The, MP IX-5194
WALPOLE, HORACE, CWA III-1853
  Castle of Otranto, The, CLC I-156; MP II-829; MP:BF I-178
  Letters of Walpole, The, MP VI-3368
WALPOLE, SIR HUGH, CWA III-1855
  Fortitude, CLC I-377; MP IV-2124; MP:BF I-443

Fortress, The, CLC I-378; MP IV-2128; MP:BF I-447
Judith Paris, CLC I-558; MP VI-3084; MP:BF II-726
Rogue Herries, CLC II-981; MP X-5661; MP:BF III-1353
Vanessa, CLC II-1189; MP XII-6871; MP:BF III-1656
WALSER, MARTIN, CWAII IV-1534
  Letter to Lord Liszt, CLCII II-876; MPII:WF II-836
  Runaway Horse, CLCII III-1323; MPII:WF III-1321
  Swan Villa, The, CLCII IV-1504; MPII:WF IV-1542
WALSER, ROBERT, CWAII IV-1536
  "Kleist in Thun," MPII:SS III-1273
  "Walk, The," MPII:SS VI-2525
WALTON, IZAAK, CWA III-1857
  Compleat Angler, The, MP II-1044
  Lives, MP VI-3461
WARNER, CHARLES DUDLEY, and MARK TWAIN
  Gilded Age, The, CLC I-402; MP IV-2263; MP:AF I-445
WARNER, REX
  Aerodrome, The, CLCII I-16; MPII:BCF I-16
WARNER, SYLVIA TOWNSEND, CWAII IV-1539
  "But at the Stroke of Midnight," MPII:SS I-316
WARREN, ROBERT PENN, CWA III-1859; CWAII IV-1541
  All the King's Men, CLC I-28; MP I-133; MP:AF I-38
  "Blackberry Winter," MPII:SS I-242
  Night Rider, MP VII-4218; MP:AF II-848
  Poetry of Warren, The, MP IX-5197
  "When the Light Gets Green," MPII:SS VI-2573
  World Enough and Time, CLC II-1266; MP XII-7262; MP:AF III-1454

WASSERMANN, JACOB, CWA III-1861
  World's Illusion, The, CLC II-1268;
    MP XII-7271; MP:EF III-1425
WASSERSTEIN, WENDY
  Heidi Chronicles, The, CLCII II-673;
    MPII:D II-758
WAST, HUGO, CWA III-1863
  Black Valley, CLC I-107; MP I-562;
    MP:AF I-127
  Stone Desert, CLC II-1082; MP XI-
    6259; MP:AF III-1223
WATERS, FRANK, CWAII IV-1543
  Man Who Killed the Deer, The, CLCII
    III-957; MPII:AF III-966
WATSON, JAMES D., CWAII IV-1546
  Double Helix, The, MPII:NF I-404
WAUGH, EVELYN, CWA III-1865;
  CWAII IV-1549
  Black Mischief, CLCII I-161;
    MPII:BCF I-139
  Brideshead Revisited, CLC I-123; MP
    II-645; MP:BF I-139
  Decline and Fall, CLC I-259; MP III-
    1404; MP:BF I-299
  Edmund Campion, MP III-1705
  Handful of Dust, A, CLC I-440; MP V-
    2464; MP:BF I-516
  Loved One, The, CLCII III-929;
    MPII:BCF III-1027
  Ordeal of Gilbert Pinfold, The, MP
    VIII-4387; MP:BF II-1117
  Sword of Honour, CLCII IV-1508;
    MPII:BCF IV-1664
  Vile Bodies, CLC II-1202; MP XII-
    6918; MP:BF III-1682
WEBB, MARY, CWA III-1867
  Precious Bane, CLC II-913; MP IX-
    5296; MP:BF III-1254
WEBB, WALTER PRESCOTT, CWA III-
  1869
  Great Plains, The, MP IV-2367
WEBER, MAX, CWAII IV-1552
  Protestant Ethic and the Spirit of
    Capitalism, The, MPII:NF III-1214

WEBSTER, JOHN, CWA III-1871
  Duchess of Malfi, The, CLC I-308; MP
    III-1664
  White Devil, The, CLC II-1238; MP
    XII-7115
WEDEKIND, FRANK, CWA III-1872
  Awakening of Spring, The, CLC I-71;
    MP I-383
  Pandora's Box, CLCII III-1173; MPII:D
    III-1197
WEIL, SIMONE, CWAII IV-1554
  Factory Journal, MPII:NF II-487
  Gravity and Grace, MPII:NF II-578
  Iliad, The, MPII:NF II-684
WEINSTEIN, NATHAN. *See* WEST,
  NATHANAEL
WEISS, PETER, CWAII IV-1556
  Marat/Sade, CLCII III-971; MPII:D III-
    1049
WELCH, DENTON, CWAII IV-1559
  Journals of Denton Welch, The,
    MPII:NF II-773
  "When I Was Thirteen," MPII:SS VI-
    2569
WELDON, FAY, CWAII IV-1562
  Female Friends, CLCII II-495;
    MPII:BCF I-488
WELLS, H. G., CWA III-1873
  History of Mr. Polly, The, CLC I-476;
    MP V-2640; MP:BF I-590
  Invisible Man, The, CLC I-528; MP V-
    2918; MP:BF II-653
  Kipps, CLC I-580; MP VI-3182;
    MP:BF II-757
  Mr. Britling Sees It Through, CLC II-
    717; MP VII-3949; MP:BF II-955
  Time Machine, The, CLC II-1131; MP
    XI-6542; MP:BF III-1543
  Tono-Bungay, CLC II-1146; MP XI-
    6613; MP:BF III-1578
  War of the Worlds, The, CLC II-1222;
    MP XII-7035; MP:BF III-1702
WELTY, EUDORA, CWA III-1877;
  CWAII IV-1565

"Death of a Traveling Salesman,"
MPII:SS II-539

Delta Wedding, CLC I-264; MP III-
1439; MP:AF I-290

Golden Apples, The, MP IV-2289;
MP:AF I-465

"Keela, the Outcast Indian Maiden,"
MPII:SS III-1248

Losing Battles, CLCII III-917; MPII:AF
II-922

One Writer's Beginnings, MPII:NF III-
1087

Optimist's Daughter, The, CLCII III-
1157; MPII:AF III-1222

"Petrified Man," MPII:SS IV-1804

Ponder Heart, The, MP IX-5234;
MP:AF II-958

"Powerhouse," MPII:SS IV-1839

Robber Bridegroom, The, CLCII III-
1307; MPII:AF III-1339

Short Stories of Eudora Welty, The, MP
X-6005; MP:AF III-1164

"Shower of Gold," MPII:SS V-2097

"Visit of Charity, A," MPII:SS VI-2507

"Why I Live at the P.O.," MPII:SS VI-
2608

"Wide Net, The," MPII:SS VI-2612

"Worn Path, A," MPII:SS VI-2713

WERFEL, FRANZ, CWA III-1879

Forty Days of Musa Dagh, The, CLC I-
382; MP IV-2145; MP:EF II-539

Goat Song, CLC I-404; MP IV-2279

Song of Bernadette, The, CLC II-1060;
MP XI-6144; MP:EF III-1186

WESCOTT, GLENWAY, CWA III-1881

Apple of the Eye, The, CLC I-54; MP
I-273; MP:AF I-66

Grandmothers, The, CLC I-416; MP
IV-2341; MP:AF I-487

Pilgrim Hawk, The, MP VIII-4693;
MP:AF II-934

WESKER, ARNOLD, CWA III-1883;
CWAII IV-1568

Chicken Soup with Barley, CLCII I-
269; MPII:D I-317

Chips with Everything, MP II-937

Kitchen, The, CLCII II-837; MPII:D
III-915

WEST, JESSAMYN, CWAII IV-1570

"Pacing Goose, The," MPII:SS IV-1753

"Road to the Isles," MPII:SS V-1968

WEST, NATHANAEL, CWA III-1884

Miss Lonelyhearts, CLC I-716; MP VII-
3941; MP:AF II-787

WEST, PAUL, CWAII IV-1572

Caliban's Filibuster, CLCII I-225;
MPII:BCF I-215

Quality of Mercy, A, CLCII III-1240;
MPII:BCF III-1351

Rat Man of Paris, CLCII III-1267;
MPII:BCF III-1386

WEST, REBECCA, CWA III-1886;
CWAII IV-1574

Birds Fall Down, The, CLCII I-157;
MPII:BCF I-129

Black Lamb and Grey Falcon, MP I-556

Fountain Overflows, The, CLCII II-540;
MPII:BCF II-532

"Indissoluble Matrimony," MPII:SS III-
1169

Return of the Soldier, The, CLCII III-
1288; MPII:BCF III-1404

WESTCOTT, EDWARD NOYES, CWA
III-1888

David Harum, CLC I-247; MP III-
1331; MP:AF I-260

WHARTON, EDITH, CWA III-1889;
CWAII IV-1576

Age of Innocence, The, CLC I-14; MP
I-65

Custom of the Country, The, CLC I-
229; MP III-1249; MP:AF I-244

Ethan Frome, CLC I-333; MP IV-1873;
MP:AF I-351

Fruit of the Tree, The, CLC I-389; MP
IV-2185; MP:AF I-421

House of Mirth, The, CLC I-489; MP
V-2729; MP:AF II-567

Old Maid, The, CLC II-803; MP VIII-
4322; MP:AF II-870

"Other Two, The," MPII:SS IV-1723

"Roman Fever," MPII:SS V-1974

Valley of Decision, The, CLCII IV-1650; MPII:AF IV-1733

WHELAN, JOHN. *See* O'FAOLÁIN, SEÁN

WHITE, PATRICK, CWA III-1892; CWAII IV-1579

Aunt's Story, The, CLCII I-88; MPII:BCF I-81

Eye of the Storm, The, CLCII II-478; MPII:BCF I-472

"Five-Twenty," MPII:SS II-788

Flaws in the Glass, MPII:NF II-517

Ham Funeral, The, CLCII II-652; MPII:D II-727

Riders in the Chariot, MP X-5590; MP:BF III-1327

Solid Mandala, The, CLCII IV-1438; MPII:BCF IV-1572

Tree of Man, The, MP XI-6676; MP:BF III-1597

Vivisector, The, CLCII IV-1662; MPII:BCF IV-1806

Voss, CLCII IV-1666; MPII:BCF IV-1817

WHITE, T. H., CWA III-1894

Once and Future King, The, MP VIII-4381; MP:BF II-1112

WHITING, JOHN, CWAII IV-1581

Devils, The, CLCII I-395; MPII:D II-492

Penny for a Song, A, CLCII III-1190; MPII:D III-1220

WHITMAN, WALT, CWA III-1896

Democratic Vistas, MP III-1446

Leaves of Grass, MP VI-3307

Specimen Days, MP XI-6216

WHITTIER, JOHN GREENLEAF, CWA III-1900

Poetry of Whittier, The, MP IX-5200

Snow-Bound, CLC II-1056; MP X-6113

WHORF, BENJAMIN LEE, CWAII IV-1583

Language, Thought, and Reality, MPII:NF II-798

WHYTE-MELVILLE, GEORGE J., CWA III-1902

Digby Grand, CLC I-270; MP III-1512; MP:BF I-324

Market Harborough, CLC I-672; MP VII-3736; MP:BF II-873

WIDEMAN, JOHN EDGAR, CWAII IV-1585

Brothers and Keepers, MPII:NF I-212

"Damballah," MPII:SS II-476

Glance Away, A, CLCII II-591; MPII:AF II-628

Homewood Trilogy, The, CLCII II-689; MPII:AF II-732

Hurry Home, CLCII II-724; MPII:AF II-764

"Tommy," MPII:SS VI-2385

WIEBE, RUDY, CWAII IV-1587

Blue Mountains of China, The, CLCII I-176; MPII:BCF I-154

Scorched-Wood People, The, CLCII III-1348; MPII:BCF III-1460

WIESEL, ELIE, CWAII IV-1589

Accident, The, CLCII I-7; MPII:WF I-12

Beggar in Jerusalem, A, CLCII I-135; MPII:WF I-141

Fifth Son, The, CLCII II-502; MPII:WF II-461

Gates of the Forest, The, CLCII II-570; MPII:WF II-520

Night, MPII:NF III-1008

Oath, The, CLCII III-1124; MPII:WF III-1125

WIGHT, JAMES ALFRED. *See* HERRIOT, JAMES

WILBUR, RICHARD, CWA III-1904

Poetry of Wilbur, The, MP IX-5203

WILDE, OSCAR, CWA III-1906

De Profundis, MP III-1334

Importance of Being Earnest, The, CLC I-517; MP V-2847

Lady Windermere's Fan, CLC I-588; MP VI-3216

Picture of Dorian Gray, The, CLC II-878; MP VIII-4686; MP:BF III-1218

Poetry of Wilde, The, MP IX-5206

WILDER, THORNTON, CWA III-1909; CWAII IV-1591
Bridge of San Luis Rey, The, CLC I-124; MP II-651; MP:AF I-139
Cabala, The, CLC I-136; MP II-719; MP:AF I-159
Eighth Day, The, CLCII II-447; MPII:AF I-462
Heaven's My Destination, CLC I-453; MP V-2528; MP:AF II-543
Ides of March, The, CLC I-509; MP V-2814; MP:AF II-584
Matchmaker, The, CLCII III-988; MPII:D III-1065
Our Town, CLC II-829; MP VIII-4443
Skin of Our Teeth, The, CLC II-1048; MP X-6084
Theophilus North, CLCII IV-1536; MPII:AF IV-1609
WILLIAMS, CHARLES, CWA III-1912
All Hallows Eve, MP I-122; MP:BF I-36
Descent into Hell, MP III-1452; MP:BF I-310
WILLIAMS, DENIS
Other Leopards, CLCII III-1160; MPII:BCF III-1258
WILLIAMS, ELLA GWENDOLEN REES. See RHYS, JEAN
WILLIAMS, EMLYN
Corn Is Green, The, CLCII I-336; MPII:D I-402
Night Must Fall, CLCII III-1096; MPII:D III-1138
WILLIAMS, JOHN A., CWAII IV-1594
Captain Blackman, CLCII I-236; MPII:AF I-252
Man Who Cried I Am, The, CLCII III-956; MPII:AF III-962
WILLIAMS, PAULETTE. See SHANGE, NTOZAKE
WILLIAMS, TENNESSEE, CWA III-1915; CWAII IV-1596
Cat on a Hot Tin Roof, MP II-845
Glass Menagerie, The, CLC I-403; MP IV-2270

"Happy August the Tenth," MPII:SS III-981
Night of the Iguana, The, CLCII III-1097; MPII:D III-1143
"Resemblance Between a Violin Case and a Coffin," MPII:SS V-1933
Streetcar Named Desire, A, MP XI-6308
Suddenly Last Summer, CLCII IV-1488; MPII:D IV-1508
Summer and Smoke, CLCII IV-1492; MPII:D IV-1514
Sweet Bird of Youth, CLCII IV-1505; MPII:D IV-1524
Twenty-seven Wagons Full of Cotton, CLCII IV-1624; MPII:D IV-1665
WILLIAMS, THOMAS LANIER. See WILLIAMS, TENNESSEE
WILLIAMS, WILLIAM CARLOS, CWA III-1917; CWAII IV-1599
Autobiography of William Carlos Williams, The, MPII:NF I-127
In the American Grain, MP V-2856
Paterson, MP VIII-4519
Poetry of Williams, The, MP IX-5209
"Use of Force, The," MPII:SS VI-2482
WILLIAMSON, DAVID
Removalists, The, CLCII III-1285; MPII:D III-1320
Travelling North, CLCII IV-1603; MPII:D IV-1639
WILLIAMSON, HENRY, CWA III-1920
Salar the Salmon, MP X-5773; MP:BF III-1394
Tarka the Otter, MP XI-6411; MP:BF III-1497
WILSON, A. N., CWAII IV-1602
Gentlemen in England, CLCII II-575; MPII:BCF II-582
Wise Virgin, CLCII IV-1727; MPII:BCF IV-1915
WILSON, ANGUS, CWAII IV-1604
Anglo-Saxon Attitudes, CLCII I-49; MPII:BCF I-48
Middle Age of Mrs. Eliot, The, CLCII III-1004; MPII:BCF III-1086

No Laughing Matter, CLCII III-1104; MPII:BCF III-1213

WILSON, AUGUST, CWAII IV-1606
Fences, CLCII II-498; MPII:D II-600
Joe Turner's Come and Gone, CLCII II-793; MPII:D II-866
Ma Rainey's Black Bottom, CLCII III-939; MPII:D III-1012

WILSON, EDMUND, CWA III-1922; CWAII IV-1608
Axel's Castle, MP I-395
Fifties, The, MPII:NF IV-1500
Forties, The, MPII:NF IV-1500
Thirties, The, MPII:NF IV-1500

WILSON, ETHEL
Equations of Love, The, CLCII II-465; MPII:BCF I-452
Love and Salt Water, CLCII III-923; MPII:BCF III-1013
Swamp Angel, CLCII IV-1503; MPII:BCF IV-1654

WILSON, JOHN ANTHONY BURGESS. See BURGESS, ANTHONY

WILSON, LANFORD, CWAII IV-1611
Angels Fall, CLCII I-47; MPII:D I-66
Hot l Baltimore, The, CLCII II-701; MPII:D II-783
Mound Builders, The, CLCII III-1049; MPII:D III-1110
Rimers of Eldritch, The, CLCII III-1296; MPII:D IV-1343
Talley's Folly, CLCII IV-1514; MPII:D IV-1529

WILSON, ROBERT
CIVIL warS, the, CLCII I-293; MPII:D I-358

WILSON, ROBERT, and PHILIP GLASS
Einstein on the Beach, CLCII II-449; MPII:D II-551

WISTER, OWEN, CWA III-1924
Virginian, The, CLC II-1208; MP XII-6952; MP:AF III-1392

WITHER, GEORGE, CWA III-1926
Poetry of Wither, The, MP IX-5212

WITKIEWICZ, STANISŁAW IGNACY, CWAII IV-1613

Cuttlefish, The, CLCII I-359; MPII:D I-425
Madman and the Nun, The, CLCII III-941; MPII:D III-1017
Metaphysics of a Two-Headed Calf, CLCII III-1000; MPII:D III-1082
Water Hen, The, CLCII IV-1687; MPII:D IV-1718

WITTGENSTEIN, LUDWIG, CWAII IV-1615
Culture and Value, MPII:NF I-321

WODEHOUSE, P. G., CWAII IV-1617
Full Moon, CLCII II-555; MPII:BCF II-557
Inimitable Jeeves, The, CLCII II-763; MPII:BCF II-820
Leave It to Psmith, CLCII II-868; MPII:BCF II-944

WOIWODE, LARRY, CWAII IV-1620
Beyond the Bedroom Wall, CLCII I-147; MPII:AF I-161
"Change," MPII:SS I-355
"Firstborn," CLCII II-517; MPII:SS II-781
What I'm Going to Do, I Think, CLCII IV-1705; MPII:AF IV-1784

WOLF, CHRISTA, CWAII IV-1622
Cassandra, CLCII I-239; MPII:WF I-210
No Place on Earth, CLCII III-1109; MPII:WF III-1108
Patterns of Childhood, CLCII III-1187; MPII:WF III-1183
Quest for Christa T., The, CLCII III-1245; MPII:WF III-1230

WOLFE, THOMAS, CWA III-1928
Letters of Thomas Wolfe, The, MP VI-3364
Look Homeward, Angel, CLC I-625; MP VI-3494; MP:AF II-698
Of Time and the River, CLC II-796; MP VIII-4300; MP:AF II-865
Web and the Rock, The, CLC II-1232; MP XII-7077; MP:AF III-1412
You Can't Go Home Again, CLC II-1275; MP XII-7299; MP:AF III-1467

WOLFE, TOM, CWAII IV-1624
  Electric Kool-Aid Acid Test, The,
    MPII:NF II-437
  From Bauhaus to Our House, MPII:NF
    II-527
  Radical Chic and Mau-Mauing the Flak
    Catchers, MPII:NF III-1225
  Right Stuff, The, MPII:NF III-1241
WOLFF, TOBIAS, CWAII IV-1626
  "In the Garden of the North American
    Martyrs," MPII:SS III-1146
WOLFRAM VON ESCHENBACH, CWA
    III-1932
  Parzival, CLC II-837; MP VIII-4495
WOOLF, VIRGINIA, CWA III-1933;
    CWAII IV-1628
  Between the Acts, CLC I-101; MP I-
    512; MP:BF I-108
  Diary of Virginia Woolf, The, MPII:NF
    I-386
  Jacob's Room, CLCII II-785;
    MPII:BCF II-848
  Literary Essays of Virginia Woolf, The,
    MP VI-3442
  "Mark on the Wall, The," MPII:SS IV-
    1462
  Mrs. Dalloway, CLC II-722; MP VII-
    3973; MP:BF II-978
  Night and Day, CLCII III-1094;
    MPII:BCF III-1203
  Orlando, CLC II-815; MP VIII-4400;
    MP:BF II-1126
  To the Lighthouse, CLC II-1138; MP
    XI-6573; MP:BF III-1551
  "Together and Apart," MPII:SS VI-
    2381
  Voyage Out, The, CLCII IV-1667;
    MPII:BCF IV-1823
  Waves, The, CLC II-1227; MP XII-
    7057; MP:BF III-1716
  Years, The, CLC II-1273; MP XII-
    7299; MP:BF III-1781
WORDSWORTH, DOROTHY, CWA III-
    1937
  Journals of Dorothy Wordsworth, MP
    VI-3062

WORDSWORTH, WILLIAM, CWA III-
    1939
  Poetry of Wordsworth, The, MP IX-
    5215
  Prelude, The, MP IX-5304
WOUK, HERMAN, CWAII IV-1631
  Caine Mutiny, The, CLCII I-224;
    MPII:AF I-231
  War and Remembrance, CLCII IV-
    1678; MPII:AF IV-1754
  Winds of War, The, CLCII IV-1720;
    MPII:AF IV-1790
WRIGHT, RICHARD, CWA III-1942;
    CWAII IV-1634
  Black Boy, MPII:NF I-162
  Lawd Today, CLCII II-862; MPII:AF
    II-864
  Long Dream, The, CLCII III-909;
    MPII:AF III-906
  "Man Who Was Almost a Man, The,"
    MPII:SS IV-1444
  Native Son, CLC II-760; MP VII-4152;
    MP:AF II-832
  Outsider, The, CLCII III-1168;
    MPII:AF III-1238
WU CH'ENG-EN
  Monkey, CLC II-733; MP VII-4030;
    MP:EF II-878
WYATT, SIR THOMAS, CWA III-1943
WYATT, SIR THOMAS, and HENRY
    HOWARD, EARL OF SURREY
  Poetry of Wyatt and Surrey, The, MP
    IX-5219
WYCHERLEY, WILLIAM, CWA III-
    1945
  Country Wife, The, CLC I-211; MP II-
    1162
  Gentleman Dancing Master, The, CLC
    I-396; MP IV-2226
  Love in a Wood, CLC I-634; MP VI-
    3530
  Plain Dealer, The, CLC II-892; MP
    VIII-4743
WYLIE, ELINOR, CWA III-1947
  Poetry of Elinor Wylie, The, MP IX-
    4925

Venetian Glass Nephew, The, CLC II-1194; MP XII-6887; MP:AF III-1367
WYSS, JOHANN RUDOLF, CWA III-1950

WYSS, JOHANN RUDOLF, *and* JOHANN DAVID WYSS
Swiss Family Robinson, The, CLC II-1099; MP XI-6363; MP:EF III-1248

XYZ

XENOPHON, CWA III-1952
Anabasis, The, MP I-192
Cyropaedia, MP III-1267; MP:EF I-322

YÁÑEZ, AUGUSTÍN, CWA III-1954
Al filo del agua, CLC I-17; MP I-81
Edge of the Storm, The, MP:AF I-331
Lean Lands, The, CLCII II-865;
MPII:AF II-873
YASUNARI KAWABATA. See
KAWABATA, YASUNARI
YEATS, WILLIAM BUTLER, CWA III-
1957
Autobiography of William Butler Yeats,
The, MP I-376
Cathleen ni Houlihan, CLCII I-245;
MPII:D I-284
Poetry of Yeats, The, MP IX-5224
"Tables of the Law, The," MPII:SS V-
2300
Words upon the Window-Pane, The,
CLCII IV-1746; MPII:D IV-1772
YEZIERSKA, ANZIA
Bread Givers, CLCII I-198; MPII:AF I-
207
"Fat of the Land, The," MPII:SS II-763
YORK, HENRY VINCENT. See
GREEN, HENRY
YORKE, HENRY VINCENT. See
GREEN, HENRY
YOUNG, EDWARD, CWA III-1961
Complaint: Or, Night Thoughts, The,
MP II-1042
YOUNG, STARK, CWA III-1962
So Red the Rose, CLC II-1056; MP X-
6118; MP:AF III-1180
YOURCENAR, MARGUERITE, CWA
III-1964; CWAII IV-1636
Abyss, The, CLCII I-5; MPII:WF I-6

Coin in Nine Hands, A, CLCII I-304;
MPII:WF I-286
Coup de Grâce, CLCII I-344; MPII:WF
I-332
Hadrian's Memoirs, MP V-2443;
MP:EF II-620

ZAMYATIN, YEVGENY, CWAII IV-
1638
We, CLCII IV-1700; MPII:WF IV-1734
ZANGWILL, ISRAEL, CWA III-1966
Children of the Ghetto, CLC I-177; MP
II-933; MP:BF I-202
ŻEROMSKI, STEFAN, CWA III-1967
Ashes, CLC I-67; MP I-341; MP:EF I-
73
ZOLA, ÉMILE, CWA III-1968
Doctor Pascal, CLC I-280; MP III-
1553; MP:EF I-411
Downfall, The, CLC I-300; MP III-
1629; MP:EF I-444
Drink, CLC I-306; MP III-1653;
MP:EF I-454
Earth, CLC I-311; MP III-1682; MP:EF
I-458
Germinal, CLC I-397; MP IV-2238;
MP:EF II-558
Nana, CLC II-756; MP VII-4135;
MP:EF II-918
Thérèse Raquin, CLCII IV-1539;
MPII:WF IV-1579
ZORRILLA, JOSÉ, CWA III-1971
Don Juan Tenorio, CLC I-294; MP III-
1599
ZUVIRÍA, GUSTAVA ADOLFO
MARTÍNEZ. See WAST, HUGO
ZWEIG, ARNOLD, CWA III-1972
Case of Sergeant Grischa, The, CLC I-
152; MP II-809; MP:EF I-181